TEACHING READING AND WRITING IN THE CONTENT AREAS

TEACHING READING AND WRITING IN THE CONTENT AREAS

MARY M. DUPUIS
JOYCE W. LEE
BERNARD J. BADIALI
EUNICE N. ASKOV
The Pennsylvania State University

Scott, Foresman and Company

Glenview, Illinois   London, England

Photo Credits

All photos by Joseph Bodkin. Used with permission.

Scott, Foresman Series in Education
Theodore W. Hipple, Series Editor

Library of Congress Cataloging-in-Publication Data

Teaching reading and writing in the content areas / Mary M. Dupuis . . .
  [et al.].
        p.   cm. — (Scott, Foresman series in education)
    Includes bibliographies and index.
    ISBN 0-673-18863-9 :
    1. Content area reading—United States.   2. English language-
-Rhetoric—Study and teaching—United States.   I. Dupuis, Mary M.
II. Series.
LB1050.455.T43 1989
428.4'07'1273—dc19   88-28659
                                                                      CIP

1 2 3 4 5 6 KPF 93 92 91 90 89 88

Teaching Reading and Writing in the Content Areas is designed for those preparing to or already teaching in middle and/or secondary schools. It is appropriate both for those who wish to teach in one of the content areas as well as for those seeking reading specialist and/or consultant positions within the middle or secondary school setting. It is designed to be used by inservice teachers as well as preservice teachers in the later stages of their programs.

Reading and writing are integrated strands of the language process that also includes listening and speaking. Throughout the book you will find this philosophical theme expressed within the context of instructional principles and suggested teaching practices. While many recent textbooks in the field of reading have included ideas for integrating writing across the curriculum, this text provides an exceptional focus on this research-based instructional imperative. Writing instruction in this text is not presented as an add-on component to the curriculum. Instead, each chapter addresses the issue of teaching writing as an integral part of any content area.

The text is divided into five parts. Part One, "Setting the Stage for Teaching Reading and Writing in Content Classrooms," helps students understand how the language processes are interrelated. Part Two, "Teaching Essential Reading and Writing Processes in the Content Classroom," focuses on such contemporary concepts as metacognition and schema theory as they relate to teaching for comprehension. This part gives particular attention to vocabulary instruction as concept development and to effective teaching of study skills.

Part Three, "Gathering Information about Students and Materials," emphasizes how critical it is to assess students' skills and attitudes and interests in both reading and writing in order to select appropriate materials for instruction. Part Four, "Organizing for Instruction in Content Area Reading and Writing," helps students apply the information they obtain through various assessment tools described in Part Three to instruction in all content areas. This text provides detailed information on creating units of study that encourage active student learning through both reading and writing activities. Alternative strategies are suggested for students with special academic needs, and one chapter is devoted to planning for students with differing linguistic and cultural characteristics.

Finally, Part Five suggests ways in which a schoolwide reading-writing program might be developed and used in the middle and secondary school. The text concludes with a chapter encouraging teachers' professional growth through the concept of the "change agent."

Each chapter includes an Overview to help the reader establish purposes for the reading and to preview new vocabulary concepts. Each chapter ends with a brief summary which serves as a review for the reader.

An Instructor's Manual has been prepared to accompany this text. This manual includes a structured overview for each chapter which the instructor may wish to use as an overhead transparency as each chapter is considered. The I.M. also includes a detailed summary for each chapter that should be of help to the instructor in preparing lectures and classroom lessons. Sample discussion and/or examination questions for each chapter are contained in the I.M. as well as suggested activities for sample lesson plan materials.

The authors have endeavored to provide a solid research-based emphasis in this text while keeping the focus on practical applications for the classroom. Students using this text should find themselves well prepared to take their place among the well informed in the teaching ranks of our middle and secondary schools. Reading and writing across the curriculum are more than current buzz words; in *Teaching Reading and Writing in the Content Areas* these concepts emerge, not as abstractions, but as concrete and practical realities for today's teachers.

The authors are indebted to many people who helped in the development of this book. First, we wish to thank the following reviewers for their comments: James Worthington, Seattle Pacific University; Michael A. Martin, Eastern Michigan University; Theodore W. Hipple, The University of Tennessee, Knoxville; Margaret Anderson, Rio Grande School, Santa Fe; and Bobbi Hansen, Lucia Mar Unified School District, Arroyo Grande, California.

We also want to thank all of the students of the State College, Pennsylvania, area schools who appear in the book's photographs. We are grateful, too, to all the teachers who contributed ideas and materials, especially those who wrote segments of the book: Joseph Prewitt-Diaz, Sandra L. Snyder, Brenda Townsend, and Barbara Van Horn. A final thanks goes to our photographer, Joe Bodkin, who took all of the photographs that appear in *Teaching Reading and Writing in the Content Areas*.

Mary M. Dupuis
Joyce W. Lee
Bernard J. Badiali
Eunice N. Askov

Before you begin to read this textbook, you should meet a few special characters who will play key roles in helping you understand the concepts in *Teaching Reading and Writing in the Content Areas*. These characters, all on the staff of Middlewood Middle and Secondary School, will appear in the scenario at the beginning of each chapter. Through them you will be introduced to some of the very real situations that confront teachers as they attempt to integrate the teaching of reading and writing into their various content courses.

As our Middlewood staff members meet over morning coffee, at faculty meetings, and in the local supermarket, we hope you will be sensitized to some of the main ideas in this text. These teachers, who represent various teaching and specialist disciplines in our schools today, provide a cohesive element in the text.

Marge Gottfield: Staff reading specialist; former member of the English department; still teaches one English class

John Roberts: Science teacher, new on the Middlewood staff

Don MacArthur: Social studies teacher; veteran on the staff

Beverly Smith: Math teacher; also a veteran on the staff

Janet Parrish: Business education teacher; new on Middlewood staff and a first-year teacher

Robert Diaz: School district staff psychologist

BRIEF CONTENTS

PART I

SETTING THE STAGE FOR TEACHING READING AND WRITING IN THE CONTENT AREAS   1

Chapter 1: Reading and Writing to Learn   3

Chapter 2: Basic Concepts in Reading and Writing   23

PART II

TEACHING ESSENTIAL READING AND WRITING PROCESSES IN THE CONTENT CLASSROOM   45

Chapter 3: Teaching Comprehension as a Thinking Skill   47

Chapter 4: Teaching Vocabulary to Increase Comprehension   63

Chapter 5: Teaching Study Skills to Enhance Comprehension   97

Chapter 6: A Practical Approach to Teaching Content Area Writing   113

PART III

GATHERING INFORMATION ABOUT STUDENTS AND MATERIALS   135

Chapter 7: Selecting and Evaluating Reading Materials   137

Chapter 8: Assessing Students in Content Area Reading and Writing   167

Chapter 9: Assessing Student Attitudes and Interests   197

PART IV

ORGANIZING FOR INSTRUCTION IN CONTENT AREA READING AND WRITING   215

Chapter 10: Organizing for Instruction: Planning and Grouping   217

Chapter 11: Teacher-Directed and Student-Directed Reading and Writing Activities   243

Chapter 12: Cultural and Linguistic Differences in Students' Reading and Writing   273

Chapter 13: Alternative Strategies for Exceptional Learners   293

PART V

CONTENT AREA READING AND WRITING IN THE TOTAL SCHOOL PROGRAM   319

Chapter 14: The Schoolwide Reading and Writing Program   321

Chapter 15: Encouraging Teachers' Professional Growth   333

Appendix 1: Principles of Learning   348
Appendix 2: Taxonomy of Reading Comprehension   352
Appendix 3: Process and Behavior Terms to Use with Instructional Objectives   357
Appendix 4: Evaluation Procedures Chart   360
Appendix 5: That's News to Me   361
Appendix 6: Doing History, A Learning Activity Packet   364

Author Index   395
Subject Index   398

CONTENTS

PART I

SETTING THE STAGE FOR TEACHING READING AND
WRITING IN THE CONTENT AREAS   1

Chapter 1: Reading and Writing to Learn   3

SCENARIO   3
OVERVIEW   4
READING TO LEARN   5
Reading, Writing, and Cognitive Development   7
Affective Components of Reading and Writing   8
Reading and The Psychomotor Domain   10

TEACHING WRITING SKILLS   11
APPLYING PRINCIPLES OF LEARNING TO
    CONTENT TEACHING   12
LEARNING PRINCIPLES IN READING AND
    WRITING   14
Learning as a Language Process   14
Reading and Writing as Comprehension Processes   15
Reading and Writing as Interactive Processes   17
Metacognition   17

SUMMARY   20
REFERENCES   20
SUGGESTIONS FOR FURTHER READING   21

Chapter 2: Basic Concepts in Reading and Writing   23

SCENARIO   23
OVERVIEW   24
BASIC PRINCIPLES AND COMPONENTS OF
    LANGUAGE   25
Linguistic Differences in Students   26
Social Styles in Language   27

DEFINITIONS OF READING   28
A TAXONOMY OF READING
    COMPREHENSION   31
THREE LEVELS OF READERS   33
ASSESSMENT IN THE CONTENT
    CLASSROOM   35
READING AND WRITING AS COMPLEMENTARY
    LANGUAGE PROCESSES   37
The Functions of Writing   38
Teaching Writing as a Language Process   39
The Whole Language Process   42

SUMMARY   42
REFERENCES   43
SUGGESTIONS FOR FURTHER READING   44

PART II

TEACHING ESSENTIAL READING AND WRITING
PROCESSES IN THE CONTENT CLASSROOM   45

Chapter 3: Teaching Comprehension as a Thinking Skill   47

SCENARIO   47
OVERVIEW   48
IMPROVING STUDENT COMPREHENSION:
    PROCESS VS. PRODUCT   48
The Cognitive Theory: Asking the Right Questions   49
The Schema Theory: "Activating" Prior Knowledge   53
Metacognition: Thinking While Reading   54
Other Text Factors That Affect Comprehension   56

WRITING AND COMPREHENSION   57
SUMMARY   58
REFERENCES   60
SUGGESTIONS FOR FURTHER READING   61

Chapter 4: Teaching Vocabulary to Increase Comprehension   63

SCENARIO   63
OVERVIEW   64
DEFINING VOCABULARY SKILLS   64
The Decoding Process   64
Vocabulary and Meaning   67

USING WORD ATTACK SKILLS IN CONTENT AREA
   READING   70
Context Clues   71
Structure Clues   74
Sound Patterns   78
Outside References   80

TEACHING VOCABULARY AS CONCEPT
   DEVELOPMENT   82
Planning for Concept Teaching   84
Linking Vocabulary to Concept Development   88

SUMMARY   94
REFERENCES   94
SUGGESTIONS FOR FURTHER READING   95

Chapter 5: Teaching Study Skills to Enhance Comprehension   97

SCENARIO   97
OVERVIEW   98
GOALS FOR TEACHING STUDY SKILLS   99
STUDY SKILLS AND METACOGNITION   100
INSTRUCTION IN STUDY SKILLS   101
STUDY GUIDES TO TEACH STUDY SKILLS   103
A Guide for Underachieving Readers   104
A Category Guide   105
An Open-Ended Guide   106

INDEPENDENT STUDY TECHNIQUES   107
SUMMARY   110
REFERENCES   111
SUGGESTIONS FOR FURTHER READING   112

Chapter 6: A Practical Approach to Teaching Content
   Area Writing   113

SCENARIO   113
OVERVIEW   114
GETTING STARTED IN CONTENT AREA WRITING   114
A Suggested Five-Stage Model   115
Assigned Versus Self-Selected Topics   116
Asking Writers the Right Questions   116
The Prewriting Stage   118
The Composing Stage   122
The Revising Stage   124
The Editing Stage   126
The Publishing Stage   131

SUMMARY   132
REFERENCES   132
SUGGESTIONS FOR FURTHER READING   133

PART III

GATHERING INFORMATION ABOUT STUDENTS AND
MATERIALS   135

Chapter 7: Selecting and Evaluating Reading
    Materials   137

SCENARIO   137
OVERVIEW   138
THE SELECTION PROCESS   138
Textbook Adoption   139
Principles of Selection   140

WHAT IS READABILITY?   144
Readability Formulas in Wide Use   148
Other Uses for Readability Assessments   153

EVALUATION OF TEXTS AND PRINT
    MATERIALS   154
USING READING AND MEDIA TO TEACH
    CONTENT   155
Sources of Media   162
Selecting Materials for Lessons or Units   162

ANTICIPATING CHALLENGES TO CLASSROOM
    MATERIALS   163
SUMMARY   164
REFERENCES   165
SUGGESTIONS FOR FURTHER READING   166

Chapter 8: Assessing Students in Content Area Reading
    and Writing   167

SCENARIO   167
OVERVIEW   168
DEFINING SOME TERMS   168
FORMAL TESTS   170
INFORMAL TESTS   171
THE CRITERION-REFERENCED GROUP READING
    INVENTORY   171
Developing a Criterion-Referenced GRI   173

Using a Criterion-Referenced Group Reading
    Inventory   180
Stop to Think   182

THE CLOZE PROCEDURE   183
Developing a Cloze   183
Scoring the Cloze   185

LIMITATIONS OF INFORMAL TESTING   186
ASSESSING AND EVALUATING STUDENT
    WRITING SKILLS   187
EVALUATING STUDENT WRITING   189
Holistic Scoring   190
Traditional Grading   190
Focus Correction   191

SELF AND PEER EVALUATION   192
SUMMARY   193
REFERENCES   194
SUGGESTIONS FOR FURTHER READING   195

Chapter 9: Assessing Student Attitudes and Interests   197

SCENARIO   197
OVERVIEW   198
ATTITUDES AND READING   198
Attitude Factors   199
Student Interests   201
Assessment Procedures for Attitude and Interest   202

MOTIVATION THROUGH ATTITUDES AND
    INTERESTS   205
TECHNIQUES FOR MOTIVATING STUDENTS TO
    READ IN CONTENT CLASSES   209
SUMMARY   211
REFERENCES   212
SUGGESTIONS FOR FURTHER READING   213

PART IV

ORGANIZING FOR INSTRUCTION IN CONTENT AREA
READING AND WRITING   215

Chapter 10: Organizing for Instruction: Planning and
    Grouping   217

SCENARIO   217

OVERVIEW   218
WHAT IS AN INSTRUCTIONAL UNIT?   218
Planning and the Instructional Unit   219
Curriculum Guides   220
Components of an Instructional Unit   222

GROUPING STUDENTS FOR THE INSTRUCTIONAL
    UNIT   230
Grouping Patterns at the Secondary Level   231
Grouping by Reading Levels   233
Grouping by Skill Needs   237
Other Types of Grouping   237

SUMMARY   239
REFERENCES   240
SUGGESTIONS FOR FURTHER READING   241

Chapter 11: Teacher-Directed and Student-Directed
    Reading and Writing Activities   243

SCENARIO   243
OVERVIEW   244
THE DIRECTED READING ACTIVITY   244
Step 1: Establishing a Background   245
Step 2: Building Vocabulary   246
Step 3: Establishing a Purpose for Reading Through
    Prequestioning   246
Step 4: Silent Reading   246
Step 5: Post Questions   247
Step 6: Incorporating a Reading Skill   248
Step 7: Enrichment   250

THE DIRECTED READING/THINKING
    ACTIVITY   251
Step 1: Identifying the Purposes for Reading   251
Step 2: Guiding the Reading Rate   252
Step 3: Directing the Silent Reading   252
Step 4: Developing Critical Thinking Through
    Questioning   252
Step 5: Enhancing Reading Skills   253

THE LANGUAGE EXPERIENCE APPROACH IN THE
    CONTENT AREA CLASSROOM   253
Rewriting Materials   256

USING TEACHER-DIRECTED
    STRATEGIES   260
STUDENT-DIRECTED ACTIVITIES   260
CONTRACTS   261
LEARNING ACTIVITY PACKAGES   262

Developing a Learning Activity Package   262

LEARNING CENTERS   265
Reading Centers   266
Writing Centers   267
Listening Centers   268
Speaking Centers   268
Instructional Games   268

SUMMARY   269
REFERENCES   270
SUGGESTIONS FOR FURTHER READING   271

Chapter 12: Cultural and Linguistic Differences in Students' Reading and Writing   273

SCENARIO   273
OVERVIEW   274
WHAT ARE STUDENT DIFFERENCES?   274
CULTURAL COMPONENTS AND STUDENT DIFFERENCES   276
THREE STUDIES IN LANGUAGE AND CULTURE   279
Black Language and the Black Community   279
Rural White Cultures   282
Hispanic Communities   283

THE ROLE OF THE TEACHER   288
Language, Culture, and the Teaching of Reading   288
Some Specific Strategies   289

SUMMARY   290
REFERENCES   290
SUGGESTIONS FOR FURTHER READING   292

Chapter 13: Alternative Strategies for Exceptional Learners   293

SCENARIO   293
OVERVIEW   294
HANDICAPPING CONDITIONS AND CLASSROOM PLACEMENT   295
Definitions of Handicapping Conditions   296

ATTITUDES TOWARD EXCEPTIONAL CHILDREN   298
Teacher Attitudes   298
Classroom Attitudes   299

WHERE DO READING AND WRITING FIT IN?   300

TEACHING INDEPENDENT LEVEL READERS 303

Instructional Strategies for Independent Level Readers 305

Activities for Independent Readers 305

TEACHING FRUSTRATION LEVEL READERS 306

Instructional Strategies for Frustration Level Readers 308

Alternative Reading Materials 309

The Teacher-Rewritten Textbook Version 309

The Morning Letter Technique 310

The Student-Rewritten Textbook Version 312

The Language Experience Approach 312

Tape Recording 313

Special Techniques 313

SUMMARY 315
REFERENCES 316
SUGGESTIONS FOR FURTHER READING 316

PART V

CONTENT AREA READING AND WRITING IN THE TOTAL SCHOOL PROGRAM 319

Chapter 14: The Schoolwide Reading and Writing Program 321

SCENARIO 321

OVERVIEW 322

COMPONENTS OF A COMPLETE READING PROGRAM 323

The Developmental Reading Component 324

The Content Reading Component 324

The Remedial Reading Component 325

THE ORGANIZATION OF THE SCHOOL READING PROGRAM 325

RESOURCE PERSONS IN THE SCHOOLWIDE PROGRAM 327

WHAT ABOUT THE SCHOOLWIDE WRITING PROGRAM? 330

EVALUATING THE SCHOOLWIDE READING/ WRITING PROGRAM 331

SUMMARY 331

REFERENCES 332

SUGGESTIONS FOR FURTHER READING   332

Chapter 15: Encouraging Teachers' Professional Growth   333

SCENARIO   333
OVERVIEW   334
TEACHER REACTION TO CHANGE   334
THE POSITIVE ASPECTS OF CHANGE   338
A MODEL FOR CHANGE   339
Readiness   340
Planning   341
Training   341
Implementation   342
Maintenance   342

CHANGE AGENTS   343
INDIVIDUAL ROLES IN THE CHANGE
   PROCESS   344
ASSESSING THE CHANGE PROCESS   345
SUMMARY   346
REFERENCES   346
SUGGESTIONS FOR FURTHER READING   347

Appendix 1: Principles of Learning   348
Appendix 2: Taxonomy of Reading
   Comprehension   352
Appendix 3: Process and Behavior Terms to Use with
   Instructional Objectives   357
Appendix 4: Evaluation Procedures Chart   360
Appendix 5: That's News to Me   361
Appendix 6: Doing History, A Learning Activity
   Packet   364

Author Index   395
Subject Index   398

PART I

SETTING THE STAGE FOR TEACHING READING AND WRITING IN CONTENT CLASSROOMS

What do content teachers need to know about teaching reading and
   writing?

Why should they have to deal with these skills?

How do reading and writing relate to content area teaching?

What do these skills have to do with learning?

Answers to these questions are fundamental to the view of teaching in this book. Our Middlewood School teachers face these issues every day and so will you in your classroom. We begin Part I with the basics: our answers to these questions. We offer these to you, expecting you to consider the questions in light of your experience and your continually developing view of your own classroom.

CHAPTER ONE

Reading and Writing to Learn

SCENARIO

Another school year is under way. John Roberts, a new science teacher at Middlewood Middle and Senior High School, and Beverly Smith and Don MacArthur, veterans on the staff, are relaxing in the faculty lounge at the end of the first full week back in the classroom.

"Well, how did it go this week, John? Still glad you took this job?" asked Bev as she collapsed in one of the plastic chairs near the soda machine.

"To tell the truth, Bev, I'm exhausted," replied John as he joined Bev. "I feel like I've been teaching for a month, not a week. My biology classes went really well, but my general science classes are a real worry to me. You'd think eighth graders could read the book! What's wrong with these kids that they won't do the reading I assign?"

"Don't despair, John," said Bev in a soothing voice. "A lot of my math students won't take the time to read the textbook either. They seem to expect me to explain everything in class."

"Sounds like my classes! They aren't interested in reading our wonderful new social studies text either," chimed in Don MacArthur from the other side of the lounge, where he was surrounded by stacks of student papers. "If my students had done the assigned reading, these exams might be easier to grade. I'm about to petition the administration to change that policy about including essay questions on tests. This job is ruining my social life."

"I'm glad to hear you say that, Don," said John. "I thought maybe it had something to do with my being a new teacher."

"I couldn't help overhearing some of that conversation," said Marge Gottfield, the staff reading specialist, as she entered the lounge. "Are all your science students having trouble with the book, John?"

"No, some really seem to be trying. And a few of them seem to have done quite a bit of writing in science classes in the lower grades. They seem more willing to do the reading and did a pretty good job on a sample essay question yesterday. Still, most of them don't make much effort to read the book."

"That's true in my classes, too," said Don. "A few do the reading assignments and are able to do fairly well on essay tests. I think most of my students can read the assignments but just won't. Maybe they're just lazy."

"It's probably a good idea to check their reading test scores before you throw in the towel or make any major decisions like dropping essay tests," suggested Marge. "Maybe some of these students really can't read the assignments and/or don't understand the concepts you want them to write about."

"Aw, I don't believe all those scores anyway. What connection do they really have to kids' work in class?" asked Don, as he pushed another test paper across the table.

Marge poured herself a cup of coffee before answering Don's question. "Test scores don't tell the whole story, of course. But they are a good place to start if you suspect that students are having difficulty with their reading assignments. It would also be worthwhile to investigate how much, and what kind of, writing instruction these students have had in the lower grades. We may be assuming too much. How about if I get a printout of the latest reading achievement test scores for some specific students? Will each of you make me a list of those you are most concerned about? While I'm at it, how about if I take a look at a few student records to see what kind of writing they've done?"

OVERVIEW

What are the problems teachers face with students' reading and writing skills? Are Don's, Bev's, and John's experiences typical? Do students read assignments? If not, why don't they? This chapter begins to answer these questions by looking at reading and writing from the perspective of learning theory. The cognitive, affective, and psychomotor domains relate to reading and writing in specific ways. Commonly accepted learning principles, like motivation, reinforcement, and transfer, are important in using reading and writing to learn. Look for the specific applications of these principles in the teaching of reading and writing in your subject area. Look, too, for common learning principles in reading and writing. Important concepts are comprehension, metacognition, and the interaction between reading and writing. The central topic remains using reading and writing to learn.

READING TO LEARN

John, Beverly, and Don are typical of many teachers in our middle and secondary schools today. They find many of their students unable or unwilling to read materials—especially textbooks—for class. They know they should require their students to do more real writing and less "filling in the blanks," but they are overwhelmed by the time and effort demanded by this task.

The Middlewood staff relaxes in the teachers' lounge, while Marge and Bev discuss Bev's concern for students who don't read their textbooks and who show little interest in learning.

Let's first take a close look at the reading situation described in our opening scenario. These teachers are frustrated. They want to teach students, but they don't know how to reach them or what to do about their reading problems. John, Beverly, and Don may not even understand what their students' reading problems are.

In fact, many teachers find these specific problems with their classes:

1. Students don't know how to read well enough to read the textbook by themselves.

2. Students don't know how to use the textbook's resources to find information they need.
3. Students have little interest in reading (maybe in learning, too), and/or little interest in the subject area.
4. Students within a class have a wide range of reading abilities and interests.

These problems, and others like them, are the subject of this book. What can teachers do to encourage students to read, and, more important, how can teachers organize their classes to make it more likely that students will read and succeed in class?

How well *do* middle and secondary students read? Our best answer lies in the most recent National Assessment of Educational Progress (NAEP). The NAEP has studied reading trends since 1971. The most recent report, issued in 1988, concludes that the average reading proficiency of seventh graders is 49 and eleventh graders is 56 out of a possible 100. Applebee et al. (1988) suggest that "the most interesting feature is that the difference in performance levels between the better and poorer readers remains relatively constant at each grade level" (p. 9). These results suggest that secondary students can read fairly well at the literal level. They also can read fairly well at the intermediate level, which requires students to draw limited inferences and paraphrase reading materials. However, the same NAEP test found that few students were capable of using higher-level reading skills, including analysis and synthesis. Perhaps this was because they have not been asked to use these skills. With the current effort to increase student critical thinking skills and higher-level learning, helping students to read at higher levels is a growing concern of content teachers.

Reading experts suggest that these data, like all data that purport to be national in scope, be interpreted cautiously. Cultural differences and special (or exceptional) students are not carefully accounted for. However, the reading achievement level of students remains an open question. Almost certainly, teachers of all content area subjects will face students who are unable to read, even on a basic level, and many students who cannot read with higher-level skills, e.g., those who use inferential comprehension.

This book looks at students in grades 5–12 as they are reading and learning in content subjects. The social studies, science, and mathematics teachers in our scenario are typical of the content teachers with whom we are concerned. However, we also deal with reading in health, art, music, English, literature, foreign language, business, industrial arts, home economics, and vocational subjects. Many principles and practices are appropriate in all content areas, while some are specific to particular subjects. No matter what the subject, however, three important factors have an impact on a student's reading skill development: the cognitive, the affective, and the psychomotor domains.

Reading, Writing, and Cognitive Development

Most content reading and writing concerns fall in the *cognitive* domain. A major goal of content teachers is to encourage their students' cognitive development. Students can develop this cognitive ability through many sources. They can listen to lectures, audiotapes, or records. They can listen to and view videotapes, movies, slide-tapes, and filmstrips. They can view pictures, graphs, diagrams, or three-dimensional objects like globes and models. But reading has traditionally been the most important source of information in the learning situation, and the textbook is frequently the major source of knowledge in content classes. Even when supplementary materials are used, these materials often involve reading as the process necessary to gain information. A history teacher may require students to read the text's treatment of the American Revolution, or s/he may suggest that the students supplement the text with additional sources. These sources may be primary sources—writings by Thomas Paine, Thomas Jefferson, and others—or other sources written about the war at lower reading levels or with other points of view. However the choice is made, these sources of cognitive information require reading.

Cognitive development may be viewed as a hierarchy (Bloom et al., 1956; Gagne & Briggs, 1974). Such a hierarchy moves from lower to higher level processes, all aimed at the students' cognitive processing. Using Bloom's hierarchy as an example, reading can be involved in each level. The student can move from *knowledge* and *comprehension* (the factual levels) through *application* (such as giving examples), *analysis,* and *synthesis,* to *evaluation* of the knowledge, without moving from a single written source. Figure 1.1 gives the Bloom taxonomy. Reading comprehension will be discussed later in terms of levels parallel to Bloom's. It is worth noting that "comprehension" (Level 2 on Bloom's cognitive scale) does not mean the same thing as reading comprehension, although there are similarities. Bloom's "comprehension" means understanding, being able to restate something in one's own words. Reading comprehension has a broader meaning, subsuming all of reading into the process of understanding at many cognitive levels. In this book, "comprehension" will henceforth refer to this broader meaning related to reading. However, the possible confusion in meaning underlines the essentially cognitive nature of much reading: it is a process of gaining understanding from printed material.

Researchers have recently viewed reading as a series of *schemata,* or structures of knowledge. According to schema theory, the most critical element in reading is the reader's ability to fit the new information in a reading selection to his/her existing schemata, or prior knowledge. Readers need to have two types of schemata. First, they need to understand the *structure of texts,* such as language structures, organization of reading selections, and the larger organization of chapters and whole books. This knowledge will allow readers to anticipate where information can be found in a reading and how it will fit together into a coherent whole (Alvermann et al., 1987).

A second schemata is the reader's goal and his/her purposes for reading, that is, the reader's *expectancy* for the content of the reading. Thus the reader's prior knowledge of the subject area provides him/her with the framework, or knowledge structure, to which s/he can attach any new information from the reading (Otto & White, 1982).

Seen in this view, reading becomes the interaction of reader and text (Kintsch & VanDijk, 1978; Rosenblatt, 1976). The reader must be able to comprehend, or understand, the text by making appropriate inferences and finding in his/her memory the appropriate connections to things s/he already knows. This schema theory of reading places heavy emphasis on the cognitive aspects of reading.

Affective Components of Reading and Writing

Reading and writing have an affective component, as well. Krathwohl et al. (1964) define the affective domain of learning as a value structure, a set of attitudes. (Figure 1.1 also includes Krathwohl's affective hierarchy.) Student attitudes toward reading and the specific subject area are always important but never more so than in the upper grade levels. Students develop attitudes toward reading, as well as toward learning and school, early in life, and parents and community play an important role in this development. *Is* reading important? How does time spent reading compare to time spent watching TV?

By junior high school, students are also affected by their peers' attitudes toward reading and learning. Willingness to read, eagerness to learn new things, and enthusiasm for school (and the negative versions of these statements) are affective concerns. The student who can read, but won't, is the reading equivalent of the old saying about leading a horse to water. If a student refuses to read, to learn, or to care about school, a teacher's best plans and organization by a teacher will not cause that student to learn. This problem is sometimes called "motivation." Developing student interest and enthusiasm—or motivation—is a critical responsibility of teachers.

Student interest in reading reportedly declines during junior high school. It may be that student attitude plays a role in this decline. However, student interest and attitude can be improved by teacher concern

DOMAINS OF LEARNING

Cognitive

1.00 Knowledge
    1.10 Knowledge of specifics
    1.20 Knowledge of ways and means of dealing with specifics
    1.30 Knowledge of the universals and abstractions in a field
2.00 Comprehension
    2.10 Translation
    2.20 Interpretation
    2.30 Extrapolation
3.00 Application
4.00 Analysis
    4.10 Analysis of elements
    4.20 Analysis of relationships
    4.30 Analysis of organizational principles
5.00 Synthesis
    5.10 Production of a unique communication
    5.20 Production of a plan or proposed set of operations
    5.30 Derivation of a set of abstract relations
6.00 Evaluation
    6.10 Judgments in terms of internal evidence
    6.20 Judgments in terms of external criteria

Affective

1.00 Receiving (attending)
    1.10 Awareness
    1.20 Willingness to receive
    1.30 Controlled or selected attention
2.00 Responding
    2.10 Acquiescence in responding
    2.20 Willingness to respond
    2.30 Satisfaction in response
3.00 Valuing
    3.10 Acceptance of a value
    3.20 Preference for a value
    3.30 Commitment
4.00 Organization
    4.10 Conceptualization of a value
    4.20 Organization of a value system
5.00 Characterization by a value or value complex
    5.10 Generalized set
    5.20 Characterization

Psychomotor

1.00 Reflex movements
    1.10 Segmental reflexes
    1.20 Intersegmental reflexes
    1.30 Suprasegmental reflexes
2.00 Basic-fundamental movements
    2.10 Locomotor movements
    2.20 Nonlocomotor movements
    2.30 Manipulative movements
3.00 Perceptual abilities
    3.10 Kinesthetic discrimination
    3.20 Visual discrimination
    3.30 Auditory discrimination
    3.40 Tactile discrimination
    3.50 Coordinated abilities
4.00 Physical abilities
    4.10 Endurance
    4.20 Strength
    4.30 Flexibility
    4.40 Agility
5.00 Skilled movements
    5.10 Simple adaptive skills
    5.20 Compound adaptive skills
    5.30 Complex adaptive skills
6.00 Nondiscursive communication
    6.10 Expressive movement
    6.20 Interpretive movement

Figure 1.1

From B. S. Bloom, ed., *Taxonomy of Educational Objectives* (New York: David McKay, 1956); D. R. Krathwohl, B. S. Bloom, and B. B. Masia, *Taxonomy of Educational Objectives* (New York: David McKay, 1964); A. J. Harrow, *A Taxonomy of the Psychomotor Domain* (New York: David McKay, 1972)

and effort. No teacher can afford to ignore student motivation and the entire affective domain. (Specific techniques for increasing motivation will be described in detail in Chapter 9.)

Reading and the Psychomotor Domain

The third domain of learning is the *psychomotor*, involving the interaction of mind and body, coordination, muscular control, and the like. Harrow's psychomotor hierarchy (1972) moves from *reflex movements* to *basic fundamental skills* (basic muscle control) to *perceptual abilities*, including visual acuity and visual discrimination. At a higher level, *skilled movements* occur when a fluent reader reads, integrating all the physical processes necessary to convey the symbols to the brain. Figure 1.1 shows the Harrow psychomotor hierarchy, as well as the cognitive and affective taxonomies.

One analogy to reading and the psychomotor domain is the process of driving a car. Do you remember learning to drive a car with a manual transmission? The hardest thing to learn is the eye-hand, both-feet coordination involved in starting off in first gear. The new driver jerks, starts, stops, and stalls the car as s/he tries to let out the clutch at the same time s/he presses down on the accelerator. After practice, this same driver starts off without conscious thought.

A beginning reader goes through many similar stages, consciously attending to all the details in the process. By the time s/he becomes a fluent reader, this process has become unconscious and feels natural. Laberge and Samuels (1974) call this achieving *automaticity,* when the process has become automatic. However, a reader who has never gone beyond the beginning stages over several years finds reading a tiring and tiresome process, and s/he may well feel that the results aren't worth all the effort.

Reading also requires certain specific physical processes. Visual acuity and discrimination are essential. Acuity, the ability to see clearly, means focusing on the letters. Acuity problems may require larger print or correction with glasses. Teachers may falsely assume that all vision problems are identified in elementary school. However, a significant number of students develop visual acuity problems as adolescents. Therefore all teachers should be aware of warning signs—squinting, rubbing the eyes, watering eyes—as clues to emerging vision problems.

Visual discrimination or perception may also cause problems with reading. Students must discriminate between letters by shape (as in *b* vs. *d*) and by size (*C* vs. *c*). Students with severe problems in perception may be called learning disabled (LD) or dyslexic. Such students need specialized treatment, but they may well remain in the regular classroom for much of their schooling.

Reading requires that the eyes move efficiently across the letters and words. Readers of the English language are required to move their eyes from left to right and from the top to the bottom of a page. Readers of Hebrew read right to left. Chinese writing requires readers to read from top to bottom. However readers read, their eyes move in regular patterns. These visual signals move directly to the brain for processing, using both the linguistic (language) and cognitive (thinking) parts of the brain. Any interruption in the signals or the processing hampers the comprehension of the reader. The coordination of all these physical and mental processes, like driving a car, becomes natural to most people, but this doesn't make the process any less complex or amazing.

The psychomotor domain may seem to be less susceptible to teachers' control than the cognitive and affective. Teachers can't organize lessons to improve students' visual acuity. However, they can be watching for clues to physical problems and alert students and parents to them. They can take physical problems into account in planning activities, and they can work with resource teachers in teaching children with special needs.

TEACHING WRITING SKILLS

Where does writing fit into this text? Traditionally, teaching writing has been relegated largely (if not entirely) to English teachers at the secondary level. Content area teachers have been admonished to take on some of the responsibility for secondary writing skills instruction, but over the years most have resisted any suggestion that writing become an integral part of the social studies, science, math, or other "content" curriculum. Elementary teachers often separate writing or language arts instruction from reading, and both are separated from science, social studies, math, and other areas. Integrating reading and writing into those content areas is not a common teaching strategy.

Middle and secondary teachers can no longer ignore the mounting evidence that writing is in fact a critical component of learning and as such must be integrated into all content areas. While the research of the past decade clearly establishes how important it is for students to write as they learn, rather than just what they have learned, there is considerable evidence that in fact students in the upper grades often do very little "real" writing in their content courses. For example, while students were found in one study to spend about 44 percent of their classroom time in activities labelled "writing," only 3 percent of this time was devoted to actual composition-type writing tasks. What teachers in this study called "writing" consisted largely of what is sometimes called "short bursts," such as taking notes, filling in blanks, performing calculations, writing brief "phrase" answers (Applebee, Lehr, & Auten, 1981). Findings like these are behind the administrative policy that the Middlewood teachers were discussing in the opening scenario. Requiring essay-type questions on tests is one way to ensure that students do some "real writing" in the content areas.

The authors of this text accept the premise that all content area teachers must share the responsibility for helping students develop competency in writing; they further accept the premise that writing instruction is largely ignored by content teachers for two reasons. First, content teachers, like those in this chapter's opening scenario, are frustrated by the weak writing skill levels of their students. Second, they face the reality of too little time to "teach the curriculum," much less add to it with the overwhelming burden of assigning and correcting written assignments.

This text proposes to deal, in realistic terms, with both issues facing the secondary content area teacher. Students do often enter the middle school years with appallingly weak writing skills. And content teachers must, of course, "teach the curriculum." However, only a steady diet of "real writing tasks" *with feedback* will improve writing skills, and such a steady diet of writing can in fact lead to a more effective, and efficient, means for learning content. Once realizing this, content teachers might find it easier to accept that oft-repeated but generally ignored admonition that every teacher not only must be a teacher of reading but also must and can be a teacher of writing.

APPLYING PRINCIPLES OF LEARNING TO CONTENT TEACHING

Before we attack the dual challenge of including both reading and writing instruction in each content area curriculum, we will review and consider several general principles of learning which relate directly to the effective teaching of content, especially for middle and secondary teachers.

1. **Motivation to learn** is increased by success, by student interest in the material to be learned, and by active involvement in the process of learning. Many students at the secondary level have not had much success in their reading and writing experiences and may therefore be accustomed to failure, unwilling to put forth much effort. In general, they may exhibit negative behaviors when asked to read and write in their content area classes. Including both reading and writing activities in which all students can succeed is a viable alternative to a vicious cycle of frustration for both students and teachers.

2. **Positive reinforcement** is a natural outgrowth of any attempt to increase motivation to learn. In both reading and writing, this means that students need to hear from teachers about their successes and their improvements from earlier efforts. Students will change slowly in their efforts to read, write, and learn content material. Overnight changes are unlikely. Therefore, teachers need to be supportive of serious student attempts, looking at how far students have come, not how far they have to go. Frequent, even daily, feedback will increase student positive response.

3. **Comprehension** is important to learning. Students must understand what new materials mean. This usually involves learning the language of the subject—what we call *vocabulary* instruction. Students also learn better when the meaning of today's lesson is built upon yesterday's and last week's lesson. That is, students learn sequentially. Therefore,

teachers must assess and build on a student's prior knowledge in order that this knowledge might be used effectively as a base for new learning. This principle is directly related to the concept of schemata discussed earlier in this chapter and applies to both reading and writing skill development.

4. **Retention** is a critical issue in learning. How can teachers increase their students' retention of learned material? In both reading and writing, retention is best encouraged through practice, both guided and independent, as long as students receive frequent feedback on their performance. In other words, it is not enough to simply present those concepts the content teacher deems important; classroom activities must allow time for students to practice applying these concepts in a variety of ways. Research clearly indicates that including both reading and writing experiences enhances the learning and retention of content. It is, of course, critical to keep in mind that meaning and retention are closely interrelated; material that is meaningful and therefore learned more easily in the first place is likely to be retained better in the long run.

5. **Transfer** is connecting learning in one area to another area. Teachers want students to apply reading and writing skills learned in elementary classes to the highly demanding requirements of content classes, as well as to their daily lives outside school. To increase transfer, the association between the original learning and the new learning must be made clearly and frequently. Teachers need to show students where, when, and in what context they learned the skills that they need to apply in new contexts in science, social studies, and math. It is important for middle and secondary teachers to recognize, for example, that in the early grades most reading experiences have involved the narrative form, primarily because basic reading skills were the instructional focus. Similarly, the majority of writing undertaken in the early grades has likely been narrative. It is a more challenging task than we think for students to move from the logical, sequential, often highly predictable story line format to the rigorous demands of readings in science and social studies. It is little wonder that many students fail to make the essential transfer of their early reading and writing skills to these content tasks.

6. **Individual differences** are a fact of life in a system based on the principle of universal education. And nowhere are differences in reading ability more evident that in content classes at the middle and secondary level, where students are usually grouped by something other than reading levels. We know that students differ widely in knowledge, learning aptitude, interest, motivation, and a host of other variables. The content teacher's task is to deal with thirty or so highly individual students each period. How can teachers take these differences into

account and still teach the required content material? This book will provide some answers to this challenging question.

The six general principles of learning just reviewed are among the most important for teaching reading and writing effectively in the content area classroom. They are not, however, the only learning principles a teacher must keep in mind in planning and delivering course content. To help the reader with a common set of learning principles, we have included a complete listing in Appendix 1. Consult this listing to support your choices of teaching strategies and learning activities.

LEARNING PRINCIPLES IN READING AND WRITING

We have reviewed several basic learning principles and alluded briefly to how they apply in the content areas. Now we need to look at several specific principles that apply to teaching reading and writing as integral parts of the content curriculum in grades 5–12.

1. Learning is a language process.
2. Reading and writing are comprehension processes.
3. Reading and writing are interactive processes.
4. Metacognition, or learning how to learn, is critical to success in both reading and writing.

Learning as a Language Process

Teachers teach and students learn primarily through language. It is useful to conceptualize language in two categories: *receptive* and *expressive*. Receptive language refers to anything we hear or read while expressive language covers what we say or write.

Classroom language includes teacher talk, videotapes, films, all sorts of reading materials, and textbooks. As they learn, students typically listen a lot (at least they are asked to do so), read some, and talk a little. It is important to keep in mind that oral language (speaking and listening) is the first thing that children learn. Written language (reading and writing) skills develop later, and for some, much later.

The critical issue for content teachers to keep in mind is that students learn more easily, with greater meaning attached to that learning and therefore increased retention, if all the language skills are involved in classroom activities. In other words, the content of the science or social studies curriculum must be presented within a context of both oral and written language. Students must have the opportunity to learn through listening and reading (the receptive modes of language) as well as through speaking and writing (the expressive modes).

Two students discuss new concepts before undertaking a writing assignment. This type of pre-writing activity emphasizes speaking and listening before writing.

This emphasis on the integration of language skills should help clarify why the traditional model of the teacher as "sage on the stage" lecturer, the hallowed "dispenser" of facts to be noted and memorized, has come under so much criticism. Research clearly indicates that students must discuss new concepts as well as listen to lectures; they should read about these concepts as well as write about them. The more often all four language skills are used, the more likely that learning will occur.

Reading and Writing as Comprehension Processes

In the language of the elementary teacher, reading is more than simply decoding the printed message; in other words, the student who is really reading is the one who can go beyond the act of "identifying" the words in the text. You may have heard this concept discussed in terms of the progression from "learning to read" to "reading to learn." Such a view is at best an oversimplification of a complex process, but it does help us understand an important distinction between the mechanical act of decoding and the cognitive act that is true reading.

By the time students reach the upper grades it is our hope that they are reading to learn, not having to struggle to decode great numbers of unfamiliar words. Those struggling to decode are not likely to gain much meaning from their content area reading tasks. It is equally important, however, to accept the fact that students may *appear* to have read with adequate comprehension but have not acquired the critical concepts in a reading passage. Consider this finding of the 1986 National Assessment of Educational Progress (Applebee et al., 1988): Students were asked to respond in writing to reading passages. On one narrative passage, 19 percent of third graders, 46 percent of seventh graders, and 64 percent of eleventh graders wrote satisfactory responses. On a social studies passage, only 12 percent of the eleventh graders responded at the minimal level or better. The authors conclude that these findings paralleled earlier NAEP assessments, indicating "that students in American schools can read with surface understanding, but have difficulty when asked to think more deeply about what they have read, to defend or elaborate upon their ideas, and to communicate them in writing" (p. 25).

Durkin's extensive research in the area of comprehension indicates clearly that teachers recognize the importance of teaching students to comprehend but in fact devote very little classroom time to activities that help students develop this skill (1979, 1981). Instead, what passes for *teaching* comprehension is likely to be an activity for *testing* comprehension.

Reading, then, is gaining *meaning* from print. Reading is a highly cognitive activity, especially in content classrooms. As such, the need to attach new information from today's reading to previous learning, or prior knowledge, is an important basis for selecting instructional activities. Of equal importance is making certain that students are provided with reading tasks commensurate with their current skill levels. Otherwise they are unlikely to focus on comprehension through the cognitive act of attaching new meanings to prior knowledge.

Just as reading must be viewed in terms of comprehension, so must writing. Note that in the Durkin studies, the researchers looked at comprehension, not as correct responses to multiple-choice items but as the ability to summarize a passage in written form. This serves to remind us of the importance of integrating language skills if we are to create classrooms in which effective learning takes place.

In order to understand writing as a comprehension process, it is helpful to use the same analogy as that used for reading. In the early grades, we might say that we emphasize "learning to write," or learning *about* writing. Gradually we need to move students into activities which focus on "writing to learn," just as we move from helping them learn to read into reading to learn. Again, looking at writing in this way is an oversimplification of a complex process, but it should help you accept our premise that students are more likely to learn content if they are expected not only to read about new concepts but to write about them as well (Alvermann et al., 1978).

Reading and Writing as Interactive Processes

Looking at reading and writing as comprehension processes leads naturally to an ancillary concept that is much discussed in the current language research. Over the years a great many researchers have demonstrated the close relationships among the four language skills (Flood & Lapp, 1987). In almost every case, the research shows that high correlations exist among these skills. For example, it has been shown that good readers are likely to be good writers, and that poor readers are likely to be poor writers.

More recently, research efforts have shifted away from correlating the language skills to considering the ways they are interactive. In other words, we are learning more and more about how each language skill depends on the others for maximum learning to take place. Of particular importance in this text, of course, is the way in which both reading and writing can have an impact on learning in the content areas.

The interaction of reading and writing reflects the individual nature of both acts. Alan Purves (1968) describes student response to reading as "an iceberg: only a small part will become apparent to the teacher or even to the student" (p. xiii). Prior knowledge is at the root of this interactive principle, too, but it reminds us that all individual differences in a classroom are reflected in the ways different students respond to a reading selection. In one *Peanuts* cartoon, Charles Schulz shows Charlie Brown pondering this quiz question: "When did Mark Twain write *Tom Sawyer*?" We know what the teacher is asking for: the year it was published. But after considerable reflection, Charlie Brown answers, "If I know him, probably in the evening." Charlie Brown responds based on his own experience and his own individual perception. Perhaps one of the best reasons for including writing in the content curriculum is that only through their composing efforts can teachers begin to know the nature of students' interactions with the reading tasks and the information they have acquired from lectures and other materials (Alvermann et al., 1987).

Metacognition

Metacognition, which is critical to both reading and writing, relates to the issue of transfer. Good readers and good writers know how they learn best. They know how to study. They can identify the steps necessary to solve problems. This skill is especially important when a reader is having trouble understanding a passage, when a writer is having difficulty putting ideas into words. For example, the reader needs to ask, "What is the trouble here? What don't I understand? Is it the vocabulary, the new terminology? Is it the train of thought? Is it the connection between the last paragraph and this one? Is it the data, the tables, the charts?" Skillful readers use their metacognitive understanding of the reading process to assess their own problems (Alvermann et al., 1987).

Learning how to learn from reading is important in every content area because different subjects have different ways of writing, and, therefore, of reading. For example, chemists write in equations:

$$HCl + NaOH \rightarrow NaCl + H_2O$$

Mathematicians write in equations, but with different symbols:

$$3x^2 + 2x = 12$$

Social studies writers use complex sentences:

In the thousands of years before the first Europeans arrived in the New World the Indians of the Americas developed many different ways of living, or cultures. The word culture is used here to refer to all the things that describe how a group of people live. Included in culture are language, literature, art, religion, the way people organize their lives, how they govern themselves, and how they make a living . . . .[1]

Poets write in dense forms:

"Fire and Ice" by Robert Frost

Some say the world will end in fire,
Some say in ice.
From what I've tasted of desire
I hold with those who favor fire.
But if it had to perish twice,
I think I know enough of hate
To say that for destruction ice
Is also great
And would suffice.[2]

Sometimes poetry uses archaic language:

O Romeo, Romeo! Wherefore art thou Romeo?
Deny thy father and refuse thy name!
Or, if thou wilt not, be but sworn my love,
And I'll no longer be a Capulet.

Romeo and Juliet by William Shakespeare, Act II, Sc. ii, v. 33–36.

---

[1]Carol Berkin and Leonard Wood, *Land of Promise; A History of the United States: To 1877.* Scott, Foresman and Company, 1983, p. 13.

[2]"Fire and Ice" by Robert Frost. Copyright 1916, 1923 by Holt, Rinehart and Winston, Inc. and renewed 1944, 1951 by Robert Frost. Reprinted from *The Poetry of Robert Frost* edited by Edward Connery Lathem, by permission of Henry Holt and Company, Inc.

Each content teacher must teach students how to read and write the language of the subject, and students must come to understand how to learn that language.

Selections from content textbooks have several things in common. First, they are *expository* writing: that is, writing which explains something. *Narrative* writing, or telling things in chronological order in a time frame, is the form most often used in elementary reading texts. Hence, reading content textbooks requires different reading skills from the typical elementary reading text. In other words, the schema for reading a content area textbook is vastly different from that required for reading a story in a basal reader.

Second, the writers of content textbooks assume that students want to know what is being discussed. The books are not full of enticements to read. They say things in a straightforward, efficient manner. Their goals are clear: cognitive learning. The authors of this text, for example, assume that you want to learn about teaching reading and writing in your content area.

Third, these books assume background knowledge. Even introductory books assume that students already know certain information in the area, especially information related to important background concepts underlying the content field. For example, we assume that for most of you, this is not an introductory teaching text. For this reason, we do not discuss in detail some of the concepts we assume you have encountered in your introductory courses.

Fourth, content textbooks introduce new terminology and use it in context immediately. Readers must be able not only to decode (or pronounce) these words, but also to understand the meanings of the words and related concepts.

These and many other characteristics of content texts will be discussed throughout this book, but the conclusion is inescapable—content reading is *not* the same as reading narrative materials. Teachers and readers alike need to be alert to the differences and to understand the characteristics of content textbook writing.

Most middle and secondary school students have mastered the basic decoding skills of reading. If they haven't, they should be receiving remedial reading instruction. However, content classes will still include low-functioning readers. Even if they have learned to decode, many students have difficulty moving to higher comprehension and cognitive levels.

Content teachers have the responsibility for assessing students' ability to handle the skills necessary for a subject area. They must decide what is most needed to teach those students who are deficient in particular skills. That is, instruction must be based on a student's needs. This is why Marge suggested to Don that they look at some test scores and student records to determine whether or not those having difficulty in his classes have actually been taught the skills he expects them to demonstrate. For example, one of the things social studies teachers need to know is how well their students can read and interpret maps. Biology and math teachers may have no concern for a student's map skills, but they do rely on students being able to read tables and graphs. All teachers are concerned with how well students can learn new vocabulary. However, English teachers often prefer that students identify word meanings through context, while chemistry teachers require precise definitions. So teachers must identify the reading skills necessary to learn their content material and must devise appropriate reading instruction for their students. The chapters that follow will present teaching techniques to assess student reading skills and develop those that are found to be deficient.

SUMMARY

John, Bev, and Don need to look at reading and writing as integral and complementary parts of the learning process. Teachers like them identify common teaching problems with students who don't read the textbook and show little interest in learning. In addition, national tests indicate that many students are not able to use higher-level cognitive skills.

Reading and writing are related in important ways to cognitive development, affective concerns, and psychomotor processes. Comprehension is critical to the reading process, since reading is defined as the process of gaining understanding from printed material. The concept of the reader's prior knowledge, or schemata, is the basis of teaching for improved comprehension: teachers must find ways to connect a reader's current knowledge to the new material to be learned. Writing is an integral skill for students to use in the process of learning. Writing activities and frequent teacher feedback are necessary components of effective teaching.

Learning principles apply to content teaching. The most important for reading and writing are motivation, reinforcement, meaning, retention, transfer, and individual differences. Specific learning principles involving language include: learning as a language process, reading and writing as comprehension processes, reading and writing as interactive processes, and metacognition (or learning how to learn).

Content teachers who understand these basic principles will want to assess their students' ability to deal with the reading and writing skills that are necessary to handle the content material. They will be concerned with their students' attitudes toward the subject area and toward reading and writing. They will, in essence, take responsibility for their students learning within their classroom.

REFERENCES

Alvermann, D., Moore, D. W., & Conley, M. W. (Eds.). (1987). *Research within reach: Secondary school reading*. Newark, DE: International Reading Association.

Applebee, A. N., Lehr, R., & Auten, A. (1981). Learning to write in the secondary school: How and where. *The English Journal, 70*(5), 78–82.

Applebee, A. N., Langer, J. A., & Mullis, I. N. S. (1988). *Who reads best?*. Princeton, NJ: Educational Testing Service.

Bloom, B. S. (Ed.). (1956). *Taxonomy of educational objectives, handbook I: Cognitive domain.* New York: David McKay.

Durkin, D. (1979). What classroom observations reveal about reading comprehension instruction. *Reading Research Quarterly, 14,* 481–533.

Durkin, D. (1981). Reading comprehension instruction in five basal reading series. *Reading Research Quarterly, 16,* 515–544.

Flood, J., & Lapp, D. (1987). Reading and writing relations: Assumptions and directions. In J. R. Squire (Ed.), *The dynamics of language learning* (pp. 9–26). Urbana, IL: ERIC Clearinghouse on Reading and Communication Skills.

Gagne, R. M., & Briggs, L. J. (1974). *Principles of instructional design.* New York: Holt, Rinehart & Winston.

Harrow, A. J. (1972). *A taxonomy of the psychomotor domain.* New York: David McKay.

Kintsch, W., & VanDijk, T. (1978). Toward a model of text comprehension and production. *Psychological Review, 85,* 364–384.

Krathwohl, D. R. et al. (1964). *Taxonomy of educational objectives, handbook II: Affective domain.* New York: David McKay.

Laberge, D., & Samuels, S. (1974). Toward a theory of automatic information processing in memory. *Cognitive Psychology, 6,* 293–323.

National Assessment of Educational Progress. (1985). *Writing objectives: 1983–84 assessment* [#15–W–10]. Princeton, NJ: Educational Testing Service.

Otto, W., & White, S. (Eds.). (1982). *Understanding expository text.* New York: Academic Press, Inc.

Purves, A. (1968). *Elements of writing about a literary work, a study of response to literature.* Urbana, IL: National Council of Teachers of English.

Rosenblatt, L. (1976). *Literature as exploration* (3rd. ed.). New York: Noble & Noble Publishers, Inc.

SUGGESTIONS FOR FURTHER READING

Alvermann, D., Moore, D. W., & Conley, M. W. (Eds.). (1987). *Research within reach: Secondary school reading.* Newark, DE: International Reading Association.

Dupuis, M. W. (Ed.). (1984). *Reading in the content areas: Research for teachers.* Newark, DE: International Reading Association.

Squire, J. R. (Ed.). (1987). *The dynamics of language learning.* Urbana, IL: ERIC Clearinghouse on Reading and Communication Skills.

CHAPTER TWO

Basic Concepts in Reading and Writing

SCENARIO

Middlewood school has been in session for six weeks now and it is time for the science department's bi-monthly planning meeting. Marge, the staff reading specialist, always attends these meetings.

"Say, Marge, you'll be interested in these papers I just collected from my third and fourth period science classes," called out John as the staff gathered for their meeting. "I decided to use that idea you suggested about asking students what they think reading and writing really mean."

"You're right, John. I *am* interested. How did you handle this?" asked Marge, settling into her place at the conference table in the science office.

"I just made up a simple open-ended questionnaire," explained John. "I was afraid multiple choice wouldn't give me honest answers because the choices would become leading questions. Likewise I decided against true-false items. Here's a copy of what I used."

"I see you asked them to define both reading and writing as used in their content area classes, John. Did they have any trouble responding?"

"No, Marge, to my surprise, both the seventh graders in my third period general science class and my tenth-grade biology students had little difficulty coming up with answers."

"Well, John, don't keep us in suspense. What *do* your students think we mean when we talk about reading and writing?" asked Marge.

"Here's a summary of their answers," said John. "You can see that most look at reading in terms of figuring out 'long' or 'hard' words or as trying to find answers to questions on worksheets. You warned me that this is how too many of our students view reading."

"You're right. I'm not surprised," said Marge. "I do note that a few folks said that reading has something to do with understanding or learning. That's encouraging! How about writing? What did they say about that?"

"Most said that writing means 'filling in the blanks' on study guides or tests or 'doing reports.' Only a few said anything about any of the things you've been trying to convince us are important, like writing about new ideas in order to understand them," lamented John as he handed Marge a second summary sheet.

"Don't despair, John," said Marge. "It will take more than just our talking about reading and writing as more than figuring out words and filling in the blanks. When most teachers on the staff begin focusing on reading and writing as language processes, you'll see a difference in the way students respond to a questionnaire like this."

OVERVIEW

We have already seen that both reading and writing are essential to learning. However, there is a distinct difference between learning to read and reading to learn, and between learning to write and writing to learn. Understanding the distinction should clarify the assumption that underlies every chapter of this book: content teachers need to help students learn subject matter through the language used in each specific content area. The goal of the content teacher thus is best defined as teaching and using both reading and writing as vehicles for learning content material.

In Chapter 1, we introduced several basic principles of learning with an emphasis on how these principles relate to the teaching of both reading and writing. In this chapter we first look at some basic concepts about language definitions and characteristics of language, and we will also discuss the kinds of language students bring to school. We define reading more precisely in the context of teaching in the content areas, focusing on reading as a language comprehension process, and we will suggest a taxonomy which should provide a practical way to conceptualize this language comprehension process. Next you will meet three groups of students who represent the typical range of readers content teachers are expected to teach. Our look at reading as a language comprehension process concludes with an introduction to three reading skill assessment problems content teachers need to consider in planning instruction.

Last, we again look at writing as a language function, consider several kinds of writing, and look at why writing is not only a viable option but a critical activity for learning content. We also provide an overview of a model for teaching writing as a language process.

BASIC PRINCIPLES AND COMPONENTS OF LANGUAGE

Language is a system of sounds used by a group of people to communicate and carry on their normal activities. Linguist Nelson Francis defines language as "an arbitrary system of articulated sounds made use of by a group of humans as a means of carrying on the affairs of their society" (1958, p. 13). This definition includes a number of important principles.

The first important principle is that language is *oral*. It is primarily in speech that humans use language. Listening and speaking are the earliest language processes a child learns. Every human society has oral language. A small minority of languages can be written down and read. Many Native American (Indian) languages have no written form, but each language is complete in itself and is passed down from one generation to another.

A second important principle is that language is *arbitrary*. The symbols used are determined by the society using them, and these arbitrary symbols can be changed by the decision of those who speak them. These *symbols* are important, too, because the words which make up a language only represent the things they stand for. That is, the word "chair" is not the real, physical object; it represents the object. Thus all words and other symbols in a language are representations of the real world. These symbols change from language to language. Within a language they change over time from dialect to dialect.

A third principle is that language has *system*. Every language has an organized process for communicating through sound and word patterns. Such features as sound patterns, word endings, and word order are part of the system in English. The term "system" suggests that the patterns which occur are not random or chance. These patterns recur and mean something to the users of the language. For example, sentences in English normally have this order: subject—verb—object/complement.

Another principle is that language is a series of *habits* which children learn and internalize at an early age. Such habits include using the system of one's native language, learning the accepted word order, word endings, and sound patterns. Most of these habits are learned from a child's immediate environment—parents and other family members. Like other habits, language is not easy to change, especially as one grows older.

The final principle implied in the definition of language is that its purpose is communication. Language is useful only if it allows one person to communicate with another. This may mean speaking to someone who listens or writing for someone to read. The listener and reader are communicating as much as the speaker and writer.

The three basic components of language are sound, syntax, and semantics. *Sound* patterns, which are both oral and written, include the way sounds fit together to make meaningful units, or words. Written sound patterns are given a different name—*spelling*. The sound-to-symbol relationships in reading are called *phonics*, and learning to make orally the sound written on a page is called "learning phonics." Secondary teachers generally assume that upper elementary and secondary students can sound out an unfamiliar word when they see one. This assumption may, however, be erroneous, and we will look more closely at this when we discuss vocabulary.

Syntax is actually a familiar topic but it is commonly known by another term—*grammar*. Syntax refers to the way words fit together, usually into sentences. Word order, identity of phrases and clauses, and organization of sentence patterns are concerns in syntax.

Semantics refers to the meanings of words. Words change meaning depending on who is using them and the context in which they are used. Or, as Humpty Dumpty says in *Alice in Wonderland*, "When I use a word—it means just what I choose it to mean—neither more nor less" (Carroll, 1962, p. 247). We will ask, as Alice does, "whether you can make words mean so many different things" (p. 247). In fact, we know that words change in meaning from one social group to another, from one historical period to another, and from one geographical area to another.

Linguistic Differences in Students

When teachers talk about differences in the language students bring to school, they generally are referring to the distinction between *standard* and *nonstandard* English. Standard English is that English spoken by the majority of Americans in formal situations. In its most obvious form, it is the English of the news broadcaster who is trained so that his/her language reveals no geographic or social distinctions. All other varieties of English are then labelled nonstandard.

The nonstandard forms of English which most people speak are often identified as *dialects*. This term is usually applied to a form of language persisting in a locality or among a specific group. Dialects have specific differences from the standard form of English in sound patterns, syntax, and semantics. Dialects have a system which is regular, following all the rules of any language. For example, some black speakers regularly delete any form of the verb "be" and drop the "g" in the "ing" inflection from their speech. Standard English "He is going" becomes black English "He goin'." Speakers who use this form use it at all times, not as a "mistake."

Nearly all content area reading materials are written in standard English. Therefore, the dialects students bring to school are of importance. Students may have more difficulty understanding what they read if their dialect is different from the standard English of the textbook. This is especially true if the text has new and complex terminology. Questions like these are useful:

—Does the student have a single dialect or can s/he speak, read, understand, and write in more than one dialect?

—If s/he reads standard English, does s/he respond to that reading in standard English or in his/her dialect?

—Does s/he do the same thing in speaking and writing?

Social Styles in Language

A different but equally useful method for describing language is to view it as a series of *registers*. Registers, or styles, may be loosely defined as varieties of language that are appropriate to some given social situation. Everyone uses different language styles in different situations. It is part of communicative competence to be able to change the language used for a particular audience. We don't speak the same way to the boss as we do to a four-year-old. Martin Joos (1961) defines five registers: frozen, formal, consultative, casual, and intimate.

Frozen: A style for writing. It is frozen in the sense that it is not subject to change by interaction with the addressee, and so it is permanent. It may become "literature."

Formal: A style of pre-involvement; a style in which, for instance, introductions take place. It has formal phrases ("May I introduce. . .") in which the addresser is not committing himself to more than a distant relationship.

Consultative: The style for coming to terms with strangers. The addresser supplies background information, because s/he assumes that s/he will not be understood without it; and the addressee participates continuously.

Casual: A style for insiders. People within a particular social group—friends, colleagues, acquaintances—use this style because they do not have to supply information to one another in the way they do to strangers. The casual style is marked by omission of words and syllables. It is also marked by slang. "Can I help you?" is consultative. "C'n I help you?" is casual.

Intimate: Used most often between two people who share so much information that they speak in what Joos called "jargon" (words with a special meaning for those two people) and parts of sentences.

Here is an example of these registers:

Frozen: I shall withdraw to seek repose.
Formal: I believe it is time to retire.
Consultative: I think I'll go to bed.
Casual: It's time for me to turn in.
Intimate: I think I'll hit the sack.

The message is the same, but the register conveys the tone, the relationship between the speakers, and their social status.

Within a school situation teachers are likely to find only three registers, and more probably two—the formal register, used for formal presentations and speeches, and the casual, used in the largest percentage of school time. The consultative may appear in written form. To spend a large percentage of time in the casual mode is a fairly recent development. At one time there was a clear distinction between school language in the formal register and street or home language. Recently, street language, usually in the casual register, seems to have moved into the classroom. This means that the formal language of the textbook and standard written English is frequently different from classroom oral language as well as from street and home language.

Teachers need to look at language as an important component of the learning process. Reading and writing are the two major processes used in the classroom and the topics for major consideration in this book. We began in Chapter 1 by discussing student problems with reading and writing. It is time to look back at the fundamental concepts necessary to understand reading and writing instruction.

DEFINITIONS OF READING

In Chapter 1, we defined reading as including cognitive, affective, and psychomotor learning. Other definitions of reading focus on decoding, a lower level process of identifying words or sounds. Decoding is a necessary process, but it is not sufficient. Reading must extend to the higher levels on all three hierarchies (cognitive, affective, and psychomotor) in order for teachers to be satisfied that a reader is *fluent*, the usual term for a mature reader.

Research in reading has identified three stages of performance as the reader works to understand a text:

1. perception of characters, or visual operations
2. perception of syntax, or sensitivity to grammar and
3. direct perception of the meanings of words (Smith, 1983)

Smith defines these stages as mutually exclusive. That is, when readers are in one stage, they cannot be in either of the others. Often, readers move through the stages rapidly. Fluent readers usually read at stage 3—garnering direct meanings of words. They read only enough of the words to get the meaning. Fluent readers *do not* read every word. However, when readers are reading something unfamiliar or difficult, they must move back to stage 2 and read the material word for word. They may even need to move to stage 1 and sound out some of the words or identify them letter for letter.

Whenever readers move to lower stages of reading, they lose speed and efficiency in reading. Reading becomes more time-consuming and burdensome, less satisfying to the reader. For the many students who have never moved beyond stages 1 or 2, reading is a difficult and unrewarding process. Remember John's findings on his student questionnaire? Most of his students reported that reading is "figuring out long or hard words"! Teachers who look at reading as a three-stage language process for gaining understanding of the material should find it easier to identify a particular student's problems.

Smith uses this set of stages to underscore the importance of *prediction* in reading. He defines prediction as "the prior elimination of unlikely alternatives" (1983, p. 28). That is, readers use their schema, their prior knowledge of the topic, to guess about the meaning of the message. This kind of prediction underscores all the reading we do, accounting, in Smith's view, for students' common belief that a book becomes easier to read as they near its end. This view suggests that, on the contrary, readers become better predictors as they go through the book, developing better schema and, usually, reading more efficiently.

As early as 1908, the prophetic reading researcher Edmund B. Huey stated that "it is well to place the emphasis [in reading] strongly where it really belongs, on reading as *thought getting*" (p. 350). Later, William S. Gray (1937) reinforced this position:

> *The reader not only recognizes the essential facts or ideas presented but also reflects on their significance, evaluates them critically, discovers relationships between them, and clarifies his understanding of the ideas apprehended (p. 5).*

The same levels, the same sense of hierarchy in the fluent reader's approach to reading, are present in Gray's work and in Bloom's, as well as that of others who have suggested hierarchical sequences.

More recent writers in the field of reading echo the same definition. Harold Herber sees reading as "a thinking process which includes decoding of symbols, interpreting the meanings of the symbols, and applying the ideas derived from the symbols" (Herber, 1978, p. 9). Herber's view of reading in content learning is that it is essentially a cognitive process with concern for the affective domain as well.

Another dimension to defining reading is that of identifying the reader's purpose: what schema has the reader developed previously that s/he can connect to the current reading? Stauffer (1969) suggests that the reader's first responsibility is knowing his/her purpose in reading. Purposes for reading may be classified as functional, career-based, or recreational.

Functional reading includes most school reading. The reader reads for a practical reason—to answer questions, to find specific information, to identify the steps in a process—which the teacher should define clearly for the student. A typical reading assignment in biology might be: "Read Chapter 3 on one-celled animals and answer the questions at the end of the chapter." While the purpose given here is functional, it is general and emphasizes the wrong goal—answering questions—rather than a more appropriate goal—understanding one-celled animals. A more effective assignment, then, on the same reading and with the same functional purpose might be: "Read Chapter 3 on one-celled animals. List three animals described in the chapter, giving at least two characteristics for each one." Thus the teacher sets the purpose for reading as s/he makes assignments. It is to the reader's advantage if the teacher sets the purpose as specifically as possible, emphasizing what the reader is to learn from the reading.

Functional reading purposes can range from low-level coping skills to high-level evaluations. Coping skills include reading for everyday living; reading the driver's manual to prepare for the driver's license examination; reading the newspaper; reading job applications. Higher-level functional reading purposes include reading to compare the writing style of two different novelists; reading to prepare for a debate over air pollution controls; reading to compare three alternative ways to conduct a chemistry experiment. Thus, functional reading is not a negative term, nor is it limited to the lowest cognitive levels. It involves a necessary purpose for reading which will be useful. Although functional reading is a major purpose of school reading, its use is not restricted to school. Everyone needs to read functionally throughout life.

Career-based reading involves a specific purpose, aimed at preparing the reader for a career. The reading required for specific jobs tends to focus on material specific to that job and to use language with meanings specific to the job. This language or vocabulary is sometimes called *jargon*. As the reader becomes more familiar with the job's jargon, s/he uses it naturally and unconsciously, and s/he can read material which is unintelligible to the uninitiated. A good example of this is the student who wants to be a mechanic and devours car magazines. S/he can discuss carburetors and exhaust systems in great detail. History and English teachers may well be aghast, since this same student's functional reading level in their classes may be quite low. Generally, reading purposes—or motivation—are stronger for career-based reading, because the reader feels the need to learn about new products, new processes, new information.

Recreational reading is the most common general purpose for reading. Recreational reading means reading for the pure fun of it. English and reading teachers often list this as their major purpose, and helping students read for fun is a major instructional goal. The contradiction in this is that by requiring the reading, for example, of *Huckleberry Finn*, an English teacher is providing the student's purpose: the reading is now functional, not recreational.

Recreational reading means *self-selected* reading—that is, reading material selected by the reader because s/he wants to read it. Since reading requires practice, it is important for readers to read regularly in order to improve their skills and increase their fluency. This is the rationale for *self-selected sustained silent reading*, or SSR, a technique which can occur in any class, or anywhere else, for that matter. In its usual form, SSR involves setting aside a few minutes—fifteen or thirty—at a regular time for everyone to read self-selected material. This can be a magazine, book, or newspaper, and it may include everyone in an entire school. This technique can help to develop fluent reading through practice, and it can help students believe that reading can be fun. The fact remains, however, that most school reading is not recreational, despite teachers' best intentions.

It is worth pointing out that functional reading can be interesting rather than boring, lively rather than dull, personal rather than impersonal. When teachers select reading materials, they can consider these affective concerns as a way to increase student interest.

A TAXONOMY OF READING COMPREHENSION

This book presents the definition of reading as a language process for gaining meaning from printed material. In other words, reading for content area purposes is a process of comprehension. Comprehension is the reason teachers read and the reason teachers ask students to read.

In 1972, Barrett developed a method of showing the relationship between reading comprehension and the cognitive and affective taxonomies that remains a useful tool for teachers in all content areas. Barrett's *Taxonomy of Reading Comprehension* identifies four levels of comprehension: literal, inferential, evaluation, and appreciation. Appendix 2 includes Barrett's definition of these levels and some specific tasks that readers perform at various levels. Here we will consider the four basic levels.

Level 1 is *literal recognition* or *recall*. The literal level is the lowest cognitive level, one at which the reader understands just what the words mean. The information that is stated explicitly in the text is retrieved by the reader in the form given there. Such literal information may be the main idea, a set of specific details, or a sequence of events.

Level 2 is *inference*. Drawing inferences is frequently defined as "reading between the lines." This level of comprehension requires that readers understand the literal information from Level 1 and go beyond it to hypothesize about relationships, unstated ideas, and connections between ideas or events. Such inferences are based upon and can be referred to the basic information in the text (the literal material). However, inferential comprehension is necessary for understanding many cause and effect relationships, figurative language, character development, and complex sequences of events.

Level 3 is *evaluation*. Evaluation requires the reader to make judgments about the reading or to demonstrate the value placed upon the information. Barrett lists the types of judgments which can be made about the "accuracy, acceptability, worth, desirability, completeness, suitability, timeliness, quality, and truthfulness" of the selection.

Level 4 is *appreciation*. Appreciation relates to the emotional responses of readers to a text. This level of comprehension refers to the reader's awareness of the literary and stylistic techniques used by an author to encourage a reader's emotional response. Barrett includes here a series of emotional responses, from simple responses to the plot or theme of the reading to sophisticated analyses of imagery and language use characteristic of a particular author's style.

In subsequent chapters, these four levels of comprehension are used to facilitate comprehension in readers, beginning with comprehension skill development and continuing through instructional procedures, assessment, grouping, and evaluation. For now, it is sufficient to understand the general nature of the four levels. You can refer to Barrett's more complete definition with examples (Appendix 2) later.

The first three of Barrett's levels of comprehension are closely related to Bloom's cognitive levels. Figure 2.1 illustrates this relationship. Figure 2.2 illustrates another way of looking at Barrett's comprehension levels. The triangle shape shows that a great deal of reading, like a great deal of learning, is necessary at the literal level. However, literal comprehension is only the base for higher levels of reading and thinking at the inferential and evaluation levels. Somewhere in the inferential level, and at the evaluation level, comprehension ceases to be convergent and becomes divergent. Convergent comprehension includes all questions and discussion in which there is a single correct answer which readers (students) must discover. Divergent comprehension at higher levels encourages multiple answers to questions, usually assuming that readers can justify or support their answers effectively.

Barrett's fourth level of comprehension, appreciation, fits well with Krathwohl's taxonomy of the affective domain. Appreciation deals with a reader's emotional response to the values included in the reading. Read-

THE COGNITIVE TAXONOMY AND COMPREHENSION LEVELS

Bloom's Taxonomy of the Cognitive Domain	Barrett's Taxonomy of Reading Comprehension
6 Evaluation	3 Evaluation
5 Synthesis	
4 Analysis	2 Inferential
3 Application	
2 Comprehension	1 Literal
1 Knowledge	

Figure 2.1

From B. S. Bloom, ed., *Taxonomy of Educational Objectives* (New York: David McKay, 1956); and adapted from "A Taxonomy of Reading Comprehension," a *Reading 360* Monography by Thomas C. Barrett, 1972, Ginn and Company. Used by permission of Silver, Burdett & Ginn, Inc.

COMPREHENSION LEVELS IN CONTEXT

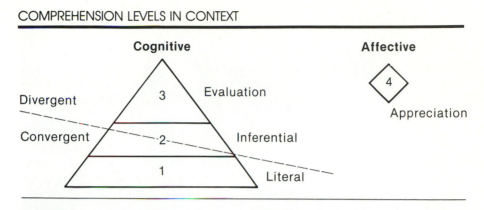

Figure 2.2

ers are asked to consider the value of the material read and to judge whether or not the content is appropriate.

Reading as a language comprehension process remains the most important concern for teachers. Students must comprehend their reading and be able to work with the ideas and concepts gained from reading in the content classroom. Writing concerns are reflected here, too. Any student's writing, indeed any writer's writing, will be comprehended by its readers on these four levels.

THREE LEVELS OF READERS

Teachers know that students are individuals. Each has a different background, interest, and learning ability. Similarly, each student has a different reading ability. Experienced teachers know that an average class includes students with widely varying reading levels. For example, it is possible for a heterogeneously grouped eighth-grade science class to have an eight-year difference in reading ability based on standardized reading test scores (fourth–twelfth grade levels). That is, in a single classroom, one or more students may be reading as much as four years below grade level while a few students are able to read as much as four years above grade level (Burmeister, 1978).

Much of this book describes specific types of students and specific teaching techniques geared to those types. To make the procedures and techniques easy to apply to the "real world," we have identified three groups of students who are typical of students any teacher may have. Throughout the book, these groups will be used as examples of how suggested activities or techniques might work with them and students like them.

The first group consists of *instructional level readers*. These students read at a level appropriate for the grade, and much of the material designed for their subjects and grade will be suitable for them. These

Marge and John discuss student responses to a survey about reading and writing. The results indicate a wide variety of student opinions on what reading and writing are and how students should use them in John's science class.

readers still need instruction in new reading skills and teacher attention and feedback.

The second group is called *frustration level readers*, which suggests that much of the material designed for their grade level is too difficult for them. Frustration readers may enjoy reading if the material is at their level. However, these readers may be discouraged by difficult materials and may be turned off to reading. These are the students most likely to respond to John's question about reading by saying that it just means figuring out hard words.

The third group contains *independent level readers*, those who can read most materials written for their grade level without much difficulty or instruction from the teacher. These are the students who might respond to John's questionnaire in terms of reading meaning "understanding or learning."

These three groups of students representing varying reading skills—instructional, frustration, and independent—will be discussed in detail in Chapter 8. The responses of these three groups to various activities and techniques will be highlighted throughout the book. However they are defined, all teachers can expect to have groups of these three types of students in their classes. Two major questions remain:

—How do teachers know what kinds of students are in their classes?

—How can teachers teach content materials to these different kinds of students?

ASSESSMENT IN THE CONTENT CLASSROOM

Because student reading levels vary, and because the curriculum often suggests that all students should learn the same material, teachers must develop techniques for managing learning at different levels. Careful instruction begins with a clear understanding of the students in the class, what they need to know and how well they currently function. The assessment of current levels is not a concept which is discussed frequently by content teachers. It is usually understood as assessment of a student's cognitive level or his/her mastery of content material. Assessment of reading level may be seen as the responsibility of the reading teacher or, for secondary teachers, the oft-maligned elementary teachers. However, it is important to note:

1. Informal assessment of reading levels is the responsibility of the content teacher.
2. Content teachers can develop, administer, and evaluate informal assessment instruments.
3. Students should be taught with materials and methods which fit their abilities in reading and in content knowledge.
4. Content teachers can use assessment information and teach the necessary reading skills without neglecting their content responsibilities.

You may recall from Chapter 1 that Marge offered to help John, Don, and Bev investigate what skills their students had brought with them to their classes. This process is one of the content area teacher's first steps in assessing a student's reading level. First, teachers must analyze the objectives and materials on which their courses are based to determine which skills students must be able to use in order to be successful in the classes. Then they must determine from previous teachers, curriculum guides, and student records which skills the students have already been taught. Which of these skills have the students mastered? Can students transfer skills learned in reading class (or any other class) to the content material in this class? A great many skills, such as word attack skills using roots and affixes (prefixes and suffixes), are introduced in elementary grade reading classes. The content area teacher's task, then, is to teach for the necessary transfer of these basic vocabulary skills, reinforcing and expanding the skills for particular use in the given content area.

Consider this possibility: students enter the middle or secondary school having some familiarity with roots and with inflectional affixes and some basic derivational affixes. (Inflectional affixes include plurals, verb number and tense markers; derivational affixes change the word's meaning or part of speech.) John, one of our Middlewood science teachers, expects students to begin using specifically scientific affixes and the Greek and Latin roots so common in scientific language. Marge is likely to suggest that he use assessment questions such as these:

1. Can students identify and apply inflectional affixes in nonscientific words, like cars and walked?
2. Can students recognize the component parts of basic scientific terms? Think of *pollution, photosynthesis*, and *sulfate*.
3. Can students build new words from groups of roots and derivational affixes and identify probable meanings? Can they move from microscope, to microscopic, to microscopy?

After the basic skill is transferred and reinforced, John could introduce more elaborate root and affix work, combining basic sound pattern rules (again, these are familiar from elementary school) and the word-building process. The complexity of the process of vocabulary building is important for content teachers to understand.

This set of vocabulary skills, synthesizing several basic known skills in the approach to unfamiliar words, represents the second major assessment problem for content teachers. Once they have determined the students' mastery of skills they were taught earlier, content teachers must assess their mastery of new skills. To learn these skills, students need direct instruction, not merely transfer and reinforcement. These skills must be presented sequentially, planned carefully, and introduced systematically. Examples of developing skills include higher-level problem-solving and searching skills; drawing abstract conclusions, like determining the "theme" of literature; and appreciating figurative language.

A third assessment problem for content teachers at all grade levels is to match the reading level of texts and other pieces of reading to the reading abilities of the students. This match requires that content teachers be able to assess the difficulty of texts. It also requires that they be able to assess the reading levels of their students. With this information, teachers can find reading materials appropriate for the students or, if this is not possible, they can adjust their teaching and the students' uses of the material to account for differences.

Content teachers can develop the skills necessary to incorporate the teaching of reading into their special content. The long-range goal is the synthesis of necessary reading skill instruction with regular content instruction. Selection of content goals is the primary consideration, with the students' mastery of these goals the critical outcome. However, since such mastery will not occur without adequate reading skills, these content goals must be coupled with reading skill instruction. This requires both the application of assessment information and integration of reading objectives with those in the content area.

READING AND WRITING AS COMPLEMENTARY LANGUAGE PROCESSES

The professional literature contains a bulk of information that underscores the need to attend to the teaching of all four language functions: the *receptive*, reading and listening, and the *expressive*, writing and speaking. The receptive language functions are not only closely related to and correlated with each other, but they are related to and correlated with the expressive language functions. Chapter 1 stressed the importance of planning content lessons demanding that students *read* about important concepts and that they view and *listen* to media presentations focusing on these same concepts in order to maximize the learning of content. It also stressed the value of encouraging students in all content classes to *talk* about and *write* about these concepts. Many students fail to learn successfully in content classes because an overemphasis is placed on gaining information through the single language function of reading text. Such dependence on reading alone can, for example, be a major problem for those frustration-level students who are likely to find most content texts far too difficult to read.

Let's look again at why learning is best facilitated when more than one language function is taken into account. You may be aware of the interrelationship between reading and listening if you have ever analyzed your own learning style. While it is true that some of us seem to learn best through visual presentations of new material (primarily reading) and others through auditory presentations (lectures, films, and tapes), many people appear to benefit most from a judicious combination of the visual and auditory.

What teachers in the middle and secondary level often forget is the importance of combining modes in presenting new concepts. Too many content teachers depend upon assigned readings and lectures (the receptive language functions), neglecting the expressive functions of speaking and writing which most teachers in the primary and intermediate grades depend upon heavily. No wonder students flounder when they enter middle and secondary school. In the lower grades they are likely to have had opportunities to *talk* about new concepts; they may have had frequent opportunities to *write* about these concepts. Middle and secondary content teachers are wise to keep in mind that any new material is best learned when presented in a learning environment which includes both the receptive and the expressive language functions.

Some teachers may be quite willing to accept the premise that reading, listening, and talking about new concepts enhance the likelihood of successful learning, but they may not be so willing to accept the premise that writing about these same concepts is of sufficient value to warrant the content teacher's time and energy. Writing as a way of learning may be an unfamiliar idea, perhaps because your own background has not included a strong emphasis on this kind of learning. You may need to look closely at your own learning style and consider whether or not writing activities, along with reading, listening, and speaking activities, might make a significant difference in learning content. A good way to test out the premise would be for you to keep some sort of log or journal as you read this book. Instead of just jotting down "content notes" as many students do, try your hand at writing brief entries summarizing what you've read (or heard in class lectures), analyzing a new idea, or reflecting upon a controversial position.

Writing to learn is not the same as learning to write. In *Writing Across the Curriculum*, John W. Myers (1984) has suggested that writing to learn is based on a growing body of research that tells us that writing can become a powerful strategy for the acquisition of concepts. Students in classrooms where writing is encouraged are likely to learn more content, understand it better, and retain it longer; their writing skills are also likely to improve through use (Myers, 1984). Content writing encourages students to think and to synthesize knowledge. Writing to learn therefore does not, as often argued, take time away from instruction. Instead, writing activities clarify the content, just as listening and oral discussion activities often serve to clarify assigned reading activities.

The Functions of Writing

It might be helpful at this point to consider the various functions or kinds of writing. James Britton's (1975) research suggests these four categories:

1. mechanical uses
2. informational uses
3. personal uses
4. imaginative uses

The first category, *mechanical uses,* includes any task in which the student does not need to compose or create, to organize, or to present information clearly. The second category, *informational uses,* requires the student to record, share, and/or select information as in note-taking and writing essays or reports. *Personal uses* include journal or diary writing, where the emphasis is on the interests and activities of the writer. *Imaginative uses* of writing, the last category, might include tasks in which the writer selects a literary form and creates (or recreates) an experience.

These four writing categories were used for investigating the extent to which secondary students write in content classrooms. Researchers found that a high percentage of content area teachers believed writing to be an important activity across the curriculum. They found that students were in fact engaged in a variety of writing tasks. However, the preponderance of the writing tasks, as we noted earlier, fell into the first category, mechanical uses of writing. Teachers appeared to be performing the tasks of synthesizing information, asking only that students "fill in the blanks" (Applebee, Lehr, & Auten, 1981). In short, writing to learn did not seem to be taking place. Further, writing was not viewed as a *language* process.

Teaching Writing as a Language Process

Having accepted the premise that writing is not only a viable but critical learning activity in the content classroom, you might now well ask, how do you teach writing at the middle and secondary level? Much of what you will read these days about teaching writing focuses on using the *process approach*. The process approach to teaching writing is different from the approach most traditional writing programs have followed. The process approach is, in all likelihood, very different from the approach used when you were learning to write, if in fact you were ever involved in any formalized writing instruction program.

Most experts in the field of writing explain the process approach by saying that traditionally we have emphasized only the final products of writing (graded compositions or reports) instead of helping students work through all the stages real writers go through (the process) before they consider their pieces finished. This "process versus product" illustration is one good way to contrast the two approaches.

Another way to conceptualize the difference between traditional writing instruction and the process approach is to consider the difference between "telling" and "teaching." For years teachers have been telling students the topics and due dates for paragraphs, themes, essays, and term papers; little else occurs, in the way of direct writing instruction, between the telling and the turning in of papers. We might call this the "collect and correct" syndrome.

The alternative of the *telling approach* to writing instruction is, as simple as it sounds, the *teaching approach*. Instead of telling students topics and due dates and sending them off to figure out just how to get from topics to term papers, classrooms can be set up as writing "laboratories" where students are carefully monitored as they move through the various stages of the writing process.

In short, we must not *tell* students to write and wonder why they fail. We must *teach* them that successful writing demands careful attention to the stages of the process approach—prewriting, composing, revising, editing, and publishing. In Chapter 6, we describe in detail how one of our Middlewood teachers orchestrates a sample writing activity which includes each of these five stages of the process approach. For now, let's take a quick look at each stage.

Any writing activity in the content classroom must include careful attention to preparation. The *prewriting* stage of the writing process model fulfills this need. Reading is often one of the activities selected for the prewriting stage. Students might complete a reading assignment, discuss it, and then use new concepts as the basis for a writing activity. Or a listening activity might provide the springboard for writing. A film or filmstrip would serve the same purpose.

The *composing stage* of the writing process can perhaps best be characterized as a period of uninterrupted sustained silent writing. This means that an atmosphere of quiet concentration prevails, at least long enough for students to get their prewriting ideas down in initial draft or sloppy copy form.

The important point is, of course, that students learning to write through the process approach come to see that careful preparation during the prewriting stage can make composing the rough draft a productive and rewarding experience.

John leads a classroom discussion prior to writing. Student discussion is an effective prewriting strategy.

Once students have their first thoughts on paper, they need to share with someone else what they have composed in order to test out the "sound" of their drafts for an audience. The idea of *conferencing for revision* is discussed in some detail in Chapter 6. For now, the important concept to keep in mind is that first thoughts are always subject to change. Students need to *hear* their rough drafts in order to make changes in the *content*; later they need to *look* at each other's work in order to make changes in the mechanics of language such as spelling and punctuation.

Thus, once students believe that they have revised their writings to the best of their ability, an important shift in emphasis takes place in the writing process. Up to this point, the focus has been on *content*. If the teacher has established an environment in which students are willing to take risks, to use words they may not be confident of spelling correctly, to try out various sentence constructions, to experiment with order, then most of their writings should be fairly rich in content.

Commitment to the process approach means freeing students from the pressure to "compose without error." This does not mean, however, that students are never held accountable for spelling, capitalization, and punctuation. It just means that students are encouraged to compose without fear of being wrong; they must understand that the time for "correcting" comes *after* they have all their ideas down on paper and have worked on revisions of *content* with one or more peers, but it does come.

When students reach the editing stage, the time for accountability has arrived. Now the teacher must decide how much s/he can reasonably expect of each student in the mechanics of writing. This stage of the writing process actually allows for the greatest degree of flexibility, in that teachers can tailor editing expectations to individual student differences. What is reasonable for one student is certainly not reasonable for all. Keep in mind the wide variability in reading ability likely in a content area classroom; it is just as likely that a similar variability will exist in writing ability.

Using the process model for writing instruction, students assume more and more responsibility for their own editing and for editing others' papers. Class time is devoted to rereading of drafts, exchanging drafts, and using some sort of checklist for determining whether or not the mechanics of the writing process have been attended to properly. As students correct their errors in capitalization, punctuation, spelling, and sentence structure, they can, of course, continue to make revisions of content. But the focus has definitely changed at this point, and the student's attention is primarily on those "little details" such as commas and sentence fragments.

As the editing stage comes to a close, many writing activities are considered finished, despite the fact that pieces are still in rough draft form, not copied on good paper or otherwise prepared as finished products. It is important to realize that not all writings need to go to the final stage of the process model, publishing. It is, however, just as important that all writings be taken through the editing stage in order that students understand accountability for the mechanics of the writing process.

The Whole Language Process

This chapter has presented a lot of information on basic concepts in language development, with a specific focus on the reading and writing processes. Finding a way to integrate oral language, reading, and writing is one of the teacher's biggest challenges. Above all, teachers must see that language use is pervasive. It is part of all instruction in one form or another. Each language use—speaking, listening, reading, and writing—is complex and requires serious planning in order to provide instruction and practice in its various stages and levels. The three groups of students representing the levels of skill we described here will be referred to throughout the book as we demonstrate techniques for teaching basic language skills in content classes.

SUMMARY

Language, and the four language processes, are the focus of this chapter. Language is a system of sound, syntax, and semantics, and students must come to understand how to use the system. The receptive processes (reading and listening) and the expressive processes (writing and speaking) need to be treated as part of the whole language process.

Students bring language differences to content classes. These differences may be in the form of dialect, geographical differences in language, or in the form of registers or social differences in language. Recognizing and using appropriate levels of language are important skills for students. Teachers must understand these differences and the problems they may create for students.

Stages and types of reading are useful in understanding how students read and how they respond to reading tasks. Barrett's *Taxonomy of Reading Comprehension* is one way of looking at comprehension from a cognitive point of view. This taxonomy helps teachers organize instruction to encourage higher-level comprehension and higher-order thinking. Relating this taxonomy to Bloom's taxonomy helps to put reading tasks into the context of cognitive learning.

Three levels of readers are present in most content classes: instructional, frustration, and independent readers. These three groups need instruction that is aimed at their different reading levels and that is responsive to their needs. Content teachers can learn to assess student reading levels in their classes and prepare appropriate instruction for them.

We have taken a closer look at the interrelationship of reading and writing as language processes. Teachers need to combine language modes in their presentation of content as often as possible in order to facilitate learning. A teacher must understand the mechanical, informational, personal, and imaginative functions of writing before s/he can plan meaningful writing activities for content classes.

Finally, this chapter discussed the difference between traditional product-oriented writing instruction and the use of the process approach with a look at each of the five stages writers need to experience: prewriting, composing, revising, editing, and publishing. These stages serve as a means for implementing process writing instruction in the classroom.

REFERENCES

Applebee, A. N., Lehr, F., & Auten, A. (1981). Learning to write in the secondary school: How and where. *The English Journal, 70* (5), 78–82.

Barrett, T. C. (1972). Taxonomy of reading comprehension. *Reading 360 Monograph*. Lexington, MA: Ginn Press.

Britton, J., Burgess, T., Martin, N., McLeod, A., & Rosen, H. (1975). *The development of writing abilities*. London: Macmillan Education Ltd. for the Schools Council.

Burmeister, L. E. (1978). *Reading strategies for middle and secondary school teachers* (2nd ed.). Reading, MA: Addison-Wesley Publishing Co.

Carroll, L. (1962). *Alice's adventures in Wonderland*. New York: Collier Books.

Francis, W. N. (1958). *The structure of American English*. New York: Ronald Press Co.

Graves, D. H. (1983). *Writing: Teachers and children at work*. Portsmouth, NH: Heinemann Educational Books, Inc.

Gray, W. S. (1937). *The nature and types of reading. The teaching of reading: A second report*. Thirty-sixth Yearbook of the National Society for the Study of Education, Part I. Bloomington, IL: Public Schools.

Herber, H. L. (1978). *Teaching reading in content areas* (2nd ed.). Englewood Cliffs, NJ: Prentice-Hall, Inc.

Huey, E. B. (1968). *The psychology and pedagogy of reading*. Cambridge: MIT Press. (First published in 1908.)

Joos, M. (1961). *The five clocks*. New York: Harcourt, Brace, & Co.

Myers, J. W. (1984). *Writing to learn across the curriculum*. Bloomington, IN: Phi Delta Kappa Educational Foundation.

Smith, F. (1983). *Essays into literacy*. London: Heinemann Educational Books, Inc.

Stauffer, R. G. (1969). *Directing reading maturity as a cognitive process*. New York: Harper & Row, Publishers, Inc.

SUGGESTIONS FOR FURTHER READING

Alvermann, D. E., Moore, D. W., & Conley, M. W. (Eds.). (1987). *Research within reach: Secondary school reading*. Newark, DE: International Reading Association.

Howard, V. A., & Barton, M. A. (1986). *Thinking on paper*. New York: William Morrow & Co., Inc.

Jensen, J. M. (Ed.). (1984). *Composing and comprehending*. Urbana, IL: National Council of Teachers of English.

Kean, J. M. (1983). *The teaching of writing in our schools*. Bloomington, IN: Phi Delta Kappa Educational Foundation.

Kroll, B. M., & Vann, R. J. (Eds.). (1981). *Exploring speaking-writing relationships: Connections and contrasts*. Urbana, IL: National Council of Teachers of English.

Petersen, B. T. (Ed.). (1986). *Convergences: Transactions in reading and writing*. Urbana, IL: National Council of Teachers of English.

Smith, F. (1978). *Reading without nonsense*. New York: Teachers College Press.

Smith, F. (1983). *Essays into literacy*. London: Heinemann Educational Books, Inc.

Squire, J. R. (1987). *The dynamics of language learning*. Urbana, IL: ERIC Clearinghouse on Reading and Communication Skills. Chapter III.

PART II

TEACHING ESSENTIAL READING
AND WRITING PROCESSES
IN THE CONTENT CLASSROOM

How does metacognition relate to reading comprehension?

How can comprehension be taught?

How do vocabulary and study skills contribute to students' comprehension of texts?

How does writing contribute to comprehension and content knowledge?

These questions relate to the essential processes of reading and writing. Comprehension is central to the reading process, as are vocabulary and study skills, yet the ultimate goal of reading is comprehension. Writing helps readers understand what they have read and communicate what they know to others.

Our Middlewood teachers face the practical problems of teaching these reading and writing processes every day. So will you. This section defines these processes and gives you teacher-tested examples of what to do in your classroom as you teach your students to use reading and writing as tools for thinking and learning.

CHAPTER THREE

Teaching Comprehension as a Thinking Skill

SCENARIO

Again we join some of the teachers at Middlewood as they prepare to leave school at the end of a busy week in late October.

"There has to be an easier way to earn a living," lamented Don as he dropped quarters in the soda machine.

"Sure, there are lots of easier jobs, but they all have their drawbacks," said John as he settled back in the old rocker in the teachers' lounge. "Why so down today, Don? You're really letting this place get to you."

Don sank wearily onto the plastic couch, rearranging himself carefully to take advantage of the only really comfortable spot left in the aging upholstery. "I'm really feeling discouraged lately, John. Why can't students see beyond what is *obvious* in their reading assignments?"

"I know what you mean," responded John. "I've been trying to ask better questions for class discussion and on tests. That inservice session on critical thinking skills we had at the beginning of the year was really helpful. Those are such important skills for science. But I'm having problems, too. My students just seem to clam up when I ask anything beginning with 'how' or 'why.' They tell me the book doesn't say anything about that stuff."

"That's it exactly," replied Don, obviously relieved to have found a sympathetic ear. "I really think I'm asking better questions. I keep hoping we'll have a really in-depth discussion, but more often than not, I'm the one coming up with all the insights, not the kids. And here it is Friday, and I'm headed home again with a briefcase full of tests to correct. The first part will be a breeze . . . all multiple choice and short answer stuff. But I dread doing Part Two. I asked both a 'how' and a 'why' question on the Battle of Gettysburg. Based on the past few weeks of class, I predict that most of the essay answers won't be very good. And there goes my weekend."

"Well, Don, you began this conversation saying there must be an easier way to earn a living. You really don't have to look for another job, you know. You could make this one a lot easier if you'd just stop asking 'how' and 'why' questions!"

―――――――――

OVERVIEW

In this chapter we'll take a close look at the factors that affect the extent to which students extract meaning from their content area reading materials. We'll again examine the current shift in focus from *product* to *process* which has significant implications for helping students read for meaning. You should begin to understand that asking good questions, while an important part of enhancing students' comprehension, is not the "cure." You will discover that in addition to asking good questions, you need to create two kinds of lessons: those that help students relate what they already know to the new information you want them to assimilate and those that will guide them in acquiring independent strategies for "actively reading" content materials.

By the end of the chapter, we hope that you will agree that Don, in fact, does not need to switch careers; he does need to understand the concepts of *cognitive theory*, *schema theory*, and *metacognition*. He needs some ideas for helping his social studies students learn to assume responsibility for their reading, to self-monitor their comprehension, and to interact with text as they read so that those "how" and "why" questions won't come as a surprise to them after they close their books.

IMPROVING STUDENT COMPREHENSION: PROCESS VS. PRODUCT

Traditionally comprehension has rested upon the premise that what (and how much) students remember or "know" after they read represents their understanding of text. We have, in other words, viewed comprehension as the *product* of the act of reading. Too often teachers have assigned readings in the content areas, conducted class lectures and/or discussions related to the topic, administered tests "covering" the material, and measured their success as well as the success of their students by the scores obtained on those tests. Students performing poorly are said to have failed to "comprehend" the material, perhaps because they did not understand the material or perhaps because they never opened the book.

What we have neglected to do is examine carefully the behaviors that lead to successful comprehension of text; we have not always looked at what good readers do in order to extract meaning from content area materials. We have too frequently, like Don, allowed our attention to focus on product (answers to questions), not process.

The Cognitive Theory: Asking the Right Questions

The landmark work of Benjamin Bloom in cognitive theory can perhaps be considered the cornerstone for contemporary research in comprehension. Bloom's taxonomy (1956) made possible the "ranking" of thinking skills associated with reading for understanding.

Early attempts to apply the cognition via taxonomy model to improve student comprehension consisted primarily of directing attention to the questioning behaviors of teachers. Numerous studies indicated that a substantial percentage of teachers' questions fell into the category of simple recall or recognition of literal level information, with very little attention to higher levels of cognition. In other words, students were too often asked to respond only to information that could be found within the text. Findings such as this led to the conclusion that teachers should "beef up" their questions, ask for responses that required the identification of the main idea, making inferences, noting sequence, and the like.

Thus, from Bloom's taxonomy of cognitive processes evolved various taxonomies (Barrett, 1972; Herber, 1978) which could be translated into classroom activities for stimulating low- to high-level thinking processes. Each of these taxonomies serves as a useful tool for the teacher wishing to ensure that classroom instruction includes attention to comprehension beyond the literal level. Teachers are advised to examine various taxonomies, try using them, and then select the one that seems most useful, perhaps combining features from one or two. In Chapter 2 we suggested the use of Barrett's taxonomy as one way to formulate questions representing various levels of comprehension. You may want to refer to Appendix 2 at this time to get a better idea of the levels of questions Barrett suggests using.

At this point it might be helpful for you to try to use this "taxonomy" approach to questioning for comprehension. Take a moment to read "A Time to Talk" by Robert Frost, and then, using the two taxonomies in Figure 3.1, see if you can think of questions that fit each suggested "level" of comprehension. Note that Barrett's taxonomy as presented here includes only the four broad levels referred to in Chapter 2. One of the advantages of using this taxonomy is that Barrett breaks down each of these levels into more specific questioning categories. This breakdown is included in Appendix 2 and is very useful, particularly for a teacher who is unsure about just how to break away from dependence on lower level questioning for discussion and/or testing purposes. Herber's taxonomy, on the other hand, rests solely on the three levels listed in Figure 3.1. Herber has suggested using these levels as a means of creating differentiated

TAXONOMIES OF READING COMPREHENSION

Barrett (1972)	**Herber (1978)**
IV. Appreciation	
III. Evaluation	III. Evaluation
II. Inferential	II. Interpretive
I. Literal	I. Literal

Figure 3.1

study guides to accommodate the needs of different ability groups within the content area classroom.

"A Time to Talk" by Robert Frost

When a friend calls to me from the road
And slows his horse to a meaning walk,
I don't stand still and look around
On all the hills I haven't hoed,
And shout from where I am, "What is it?"
No, not as there is time to talk.
I thrust my hoe on the mellow ground,
Blade-end up and five feet tall,
And plod: I go up to the stone wall
For a friendly visit.[1]

When you have created as many questions as you can for each level of both taxonomies, read the following questions carefully and try to "match" them with the various levels suggested by Barrett and Herber:

1. What is the speaker doing when his friend calls to him?
2. Why does the speaker stop what he is doing?
3. Do you think the speaker should stop as he does? Why or why not?
4. Has a friend ever called you from your work? What did you do? Should you have stopped?

Before moving on, note a few words of caution about creating questions that tap various levels of comprehension. In using any taxonomy as an assessment tool, the teacher must be careful to distinguish between questions which require convergent thinking—those for which there is one correct answer, like 1 and 2 above—and those which require divergent

---

[1]"A Time to Talk" by Robert Frost. Copyright 1916, 1923 by Holt, Rinehart and Winston, Inc. and renewed 1944, 1951 by Robert Frost. Reprinted from *The Poetry of Robert Frost* edited by Edward Connery Lathem, by permission of Henry Holt and Company, Inc.

thinking, for which several answers may be appropriate, like 3 and 4. Literal level questions (for which the answers are stated in the material) and some inferential level questioning (for which answers are not stated directly) require convergent thinking in which there is only one correct answer. Some inferential level questions, plus those at the evaluation and appreciation levels, require divergent thinking, meaning that creative responses may be possible. Multiple choice test questions should be convergent. Open-ended questions are appropriate to assess divergent thinking—if the teacher is willing to accept several answers as correct, provided that the student can state a rationale for the answer.

Questions designed to encourage class discussion should be planned carefully to include both divergent and convergent questions and as many levels of a taxonomy as possible. To use a taxonomy most effectively, teachers' questions should be designed ahead of time, not spontaneously during a discussion of a reading assignment. While not all reading material lends itself to questions at all levels, the teacher should attempt to

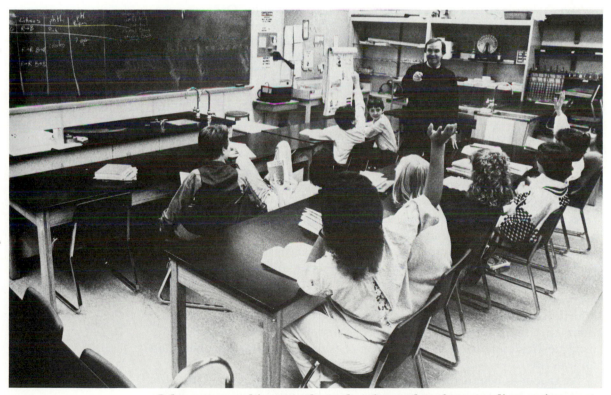

John prepares his seventh-grade science class for a reading assignment on acids and bases by discussing the concepts and asking questions about them. After students finish reading, they will check their answers to the questions and extend their study through a related lab experience.

include questions at all levels at some point during a given unit. Teachers can use a simple record-keeping system to indicate what level of questions was asked during each discussion of assigned reading. This system helps ensure that they ask students questions at all levels of comprehension.

Sometimes science and math teachers reject the notion that questions should be asked at four levels. These teachers express the view that they are concerned only with literal comprehension—that their students simply need to learn the facts. Unfortunately, this type of learning is usually not retained beyond the final examination. Think back to your own high school classes. Do you remember facts and details? Most of us remember few specific facts, but we retained general principles and concepts. Unless new information is linked in some meaningful way to prior background and knowledge, students are unable to remember what they have read except perhaps for immediate recall on a test of facts. This type of learning is forgotten all too quickly.

The taxonomy approach helps a teacher plan questions that promote conceptual integration of new material with prior learning and experiences. Inference questions can help students develop relationships between earlier learning and information in the new reading. Or these questions can help students identify cause and effect relationships, sequence of actions or ideas, and characteristics of concepts. Evaluation questions help students see how judgments on a current reading selection are related to or based upon earlier readings.

Barrett's fourth level, appreciation, is particularly important, regardless of the content area, because it taps the affective domain. Once reading material is integrated with the student's personal concerns, s/he will not forget it. A better label for this level might be "Application to a Student's Life." Application can be practical, such as a better way of keeping a ledger of one's earnings and spending in an accounting class, as well as personal, such as an emotional response to a short story in English class.

How can some reading materials, especially from science and math, relate to the affective concerns of students? While no pat answers exist, we urge teachers to find out about the personal concerns of the students through administering interest and attitude surveys such as those presented in Chapter 9, reading cumulative records, and chatting with students individually before or after class or at sports events. Making content material fit into local and national concerns is another way to relate to the affective domain. For example, in a chemistry class, students might apply their knowledge of chemical elements to discover the contents of locally used pesticides and study the effects of these chemicals on plant and animal life.

As teachers began to improve the quality of questions they ask, the shift moves from the kinds of questions to the timing of questioning. Enter the era of what Rothkopf (1982) calls *adjunct questioning*. Should questions be asked before, during, or after the reading? Rothkopf writes that questions asked before and during reading are more effective than post-reading questions because they guide the reading process. Teachers discovered that comprehension was often enhanced if students had prereading questions to consider and if they were provided with a study guide to use as they read content area assignments.

The judicious use of adjunct questioning, combined with an emphasis on including various levels of questions based on one or more of the available taxonomies, can result in sound and effective classroom activities for enhancing students' comprehension. Chapter 5 contains some examples of study guides which incorporate both the use of various levels of questions and the careful timing of questioning in content area lessons. This emphasis on proving teacher "support" to accompany reading assignments is illustrated in even more detail under the Directed Reading Activity in Chapter 11.

The Schema Theory: "Activating" Prior Knowledge

Recent cognitive research has revealed that comprehension increases if students can relate the new to the known. You are probably aware that you are able to learn more from this text than from one presenting totally unfamiliar content, such as nuclear physics. *Schema theory* (Schallert, 1982), which you first encountered in Chapter 1, postulates that we comprehend new information better if it is linked to previous knowledge. It is the teacher's job to help students "activate" prior knowledge or call it up in the process of making an assignment. Any attempt to enhance students' comprehension must be grounded in an understanding of the interaction of reader and text.

Teachers must take care to "activate" the appropriate schema. For example, it is inappropriate to talk about the library's Dewey Decimal System before assigning a reading selection about John Dewey. Some multiple-meaning words can also cause confusion if the student associates an inappropriate meaning with the new information presented in the reading assignment. One effective way to "activate schema" is to devote sufficient class time to a discussion of what students already know about the concepts covered in the reading *prior* to assigning the reading itself.

Advance organizers can accomplish this purpose. An advance organizer is a teaching device used to help students anticipate the new material that they are about to tackle (Chapter 4 contains some examples). Advance organizers might be just what Don needs in order to prepare his social studies students for the reading he assigns. He is likely to find that the time devoted to this activity before students read will have a positive effect on their after-reading performance in class discussions.

During the actual reading of an assignment, comprehension can be enhanced further if accompanying study guides include items that help students activate prior knowledge, predict meaning, and note important text structures. The goal is to move the students from dependence upon

Bev works with her seventh-grade general math class on multiplying decimals and determining percents. She is activating their prior knowledge about decimals as she begins their study of more advanced problems with percents. Note that she has written the same problem two ways: once in decimals and once in words.

the teacher to independence in associating relevant prior knowledge with the new knowledge in the reading assignment. Students need to realize how much they already know about a topic and how that prior knowledge will help them learn more from their reading assignments.

Metacognition: Thinking While Reading

As content area teachers placed more attention on providing students with questions to guide their reading, a subtle shift from product to process occurred. Despite this shift, research continued to suggest that what was happening in classrooms where comprehension was reportedly being "taught" was in fact not so encouraging. Durkin (1983), for example, concluded that too often what teachers identified as activities for *teaching* comprehension were actually *assessment* activities. Students were not in fact being shown how to comprehend but were instead being asked only (or primarily) what they had "learned" from their reading. Instead of moving away from the product-orientation of the pre-cognitive theory days, too many teachers appeared to be locked into traditional practices, failing to see that comprehension could and should be taught as a process.

Research began to reflect the close examination of what successful comprehenders do *as* they read, not *after* they read. Advice to teachers began to focus on helping all readers acquire these behaviors as research established that students of all abilities are capable of responding at the higher levels of cognition (Calfee & Drum, 1986). The era of *metacognition* as the basis for developing and enhancing reading comprehension was underway.

While the term "metacognition" is relatively new (Flavell, 1976), the basis on which it rests can be traced back almost a century (Dewey, 1910; Thorndike, 1917). In essence, metacognitive theory refers to thinking about one's own thinking—or reading—processes as applied to a specific task, in our case, the reading of content area materials.

The application of metacognitive theory to the classroom involves, among other things, a move away from dependence on asking good questions before, during, and after reading. This is not to say that the teacher's use of good questions, at all levels of whatever taxonomy one chooses to use, is no longer a valid instructional procedure. It is just that this is not enough to ensure that students will extract meaning from their text assignments. The key to metacognition is moving from teacher-directed to student-directed reading activities, a shift from teacher-developed questions to student-developed questions, questions that students ask *themselves* during the act of reading.

This is a good time for you to stop to think about what this means in terms of your own reading behaviors. How many times have you settled into a reading assignment and had the disconcerting experience of coming to the end of a chapter only to realize that you have no idea what you have been reading about? This is not an uncommon experience. (Perhaps at this very moment you are thinking that you have no idea what this chapter has been about so far!)

This also would be a good time to begin putting into practice some of the strategies that we know help readers comprehend as they read. We cannot justify the age-old excuse, "I just wasn't concentrating," for failing to understand text. Too often as we read, particularly in the content areas, we fail to monitor our own comprehension. We do not ask, at critical points in the text, "Do I understand this? Does this make sense?" This is what good readers do. This is a behavior that Don needs to help his social studies students acquire. If you do not read this way, you, too, need to acquire this skill. Teachers can encourage self-monitoring by constructing study guides which include frequent reminders to students to monitor their reading as they work through a reading assignment.

Other Text Factors That Affect Comprehension

Let's examine further the concept of metacognition as it applies to helping students understand text. It is important to consider several other salient factors that have been studied in an effort to devise effective teaching strategies for enhancing comprehension. While the cognition/taxonomy model for selecting classroom activities continues to be both popular and effective, if used prudently, there are other ways to conceptualize the teaching of comprehension.

The teacher should examine reading materials in terms of the differing demands made of the reader in the various content areas. We have already pointed out the substantial difference between the narrative materials which students become accustomed to in the early grades and the kinds of reading they are expected to do as they begin to study social studies, science, and math using textbooks as their primary sources of information.

Reading a chapter in a science book demands very different responses from those associated with reading a story in a basal reader. Sequence in a basal reader story is likely to be based on time chronology while sequence in a science chapter is not likely to be so evident, nor easily understood. Comprehension strategies that work effectively for narrative materials may not be the best ones to use for content area reading assignments. Students are not likely to know this as they move into more demanding texts; they will need careful and systematic instruction to make the transition from narrative to expository materials. Are you thinking that you could perhaps benefit from some instruction in how to read content materials more effectively? Are you thinking that in fact you read all kinds of material in exactly the same way?

It is also important to look at content area reading in terms of *explicit* versus *implicit* text (Pearson & Johnson, 1978). Helping readers develop the skill of reading in order to assimilate both types of information is a critical part of teaching for comprehension. When Don referred to his students' failure to get more than what is "obvious" from their reading assignments, he was differentiating between explicit and implicit text structures. Too often teachers make the mistake of thinking that students will read "between the lines" for implicit information simply on the basis of our asking them to respond to "how" and "why" questions. As Don lamented, this doesn't always work. Students must be taught to note "cues" for uncovering what isn't "obvious."

Directed reading instruction based on the Pearson and Johnson model is one way to help students develop this skill. Teachers can direct students' attention to particular words, phrases, or passages which are critical to content objectives or to understanding an author's style. This procedure, which is most often used early in the students' use of the text, focuses students' attention on what the author says, how s/he provides information, and what clues s/he gives to readers. Careful instruction to help students read the text with precision can help them form habits that will be useful throughout the year, or as long as that text is used. Over time, students will come to understand how scientists write, how mathematicians write, and how historians write, as well as how novelists and poets write. The differences are clear to many of us, but students need to see them through directed reading.

Finally, it is important to sort out two components of comprehension often associated with metacognitive theory. Baker and Brown (1984) have pointed out that effective comprehension involves making choices among a number of possible strategies. For example, the strategy chosen for use with a particular reading selection depends upon whether the objective is reading for *remembering* (studying for a test) or reading for *meaning* (comprehension). They suggest that reading for remembering requires that the reader organize text information via various study strategies such as outlining and note-taking, while reading for meaning involves the use of various self-monitoring strategies such as "lookbacks" (reviewing while reading) and self-questioning as one reads. Some of these strategies are described in some detail in Chapter 5, where we discuss the teaching of study skills for enhancing text comprehension.

WRITING AND COMPREHENSION

As you can see, teachers have an excellent opportunity for using writing to teach content. Divergent thinking responses lend themselves to writing beyond the "fill in the blank" and multiple-choice formats. Teachers in all content areas can construct carefully worded questions that demand written responses of more than a few words. These need not be limited to items on study guides, end-of-chapter quizzes, or examinations, though questions of this nature should be included for these purposes.

If writing is in fact to be an integral part of each content area, then it must be seen as more than a means for assessing student comprehension. As pointed out earlier, writing can be a powerful tool for learning new concepts. Writing to learn means that students record, consider, organize, explore, compare, contrast, evaluate, and analyze the ideas they are encountering in text and through various media presentations in class. By now you should recognize this as an example of utilizing all the language modes in order to maximize learning.

One especially effective means by which to encourage "writing to learn" is the use of the content journal, or learning log (Fulwiler, 1987). Students are required to keep an ongoing record of written responses to the content of a course. For example, as students study a unit on weather in a science class, they keep a daily "log" on what they are learning. The teacher might ask them to begin each class period with a few quiet "composing" minutes. The journal entry may be a response to a thought-provoking question requiring them to consider the previous day's assigned reading, a film recently viewed, or an important concept from yesterday's class lecture. Some days the teacher might ask students to predict what they might learn from the day's topic which is listed on the board; or perhaps students might be asked to write about what they already know about this topic.

An interesting alternative for learning logs is to ask students to write in the middle of a content area lesson, commenting on what they are learning, what they do not quite understand, what they wish the teacher would explain again, and what they think (or hope) will come next. Such a writing activity serves two important functions. Students have the opportunity to "stop and ponder," to actively consider the content being presented. In other words, they are forced to self-monitor their comprehension. At the same time, the teacher has the opportunity to examine what students are assimilating and to restructure, if the logs so indicate, the next lesson or lessons to clarify that which students did not understand. A third possibility is to encourage the use of dialogue journals (Danielson, 1988) in which teacher and student interact on a more personal, conversational level, about the content of a course, again raising questions about what is unclear, or perhaps even controversial. Such journals can prove a very stimulating and motivating factor in the content area classroom.

Regular log-type writing serves a number of purposes. Students come to value writing as a viable means for learning, not just as a way to show what they have learned. They learn to clarify their thoughts about new concepts. They learn that "writing it out" often helps them retain important aspects of what they've read or heard in a course.

These log writings need not be viewed as major composition undertakings requiring extensive student revisions and time-consuming "correcting" by the teacher. Instead, they should be viewed for just what they are: tools for enhancing and stimulating comprehension. They should be shared in some way, perhaps with several volunteers reading their entries aloud as a means for stimulating discussion for the day's class activity. (Students should be encouraged to make some changes if their perceptions have been incorrect or need further clarification.) But, for the most part, writings of this nature should remain rough drafts or "sloppy copies," the composing stage of the writing process described in Chapter 2.

SUMMARY

We now know a great deal about what successful readers do as they read and about what behaviors are likely to lead to effective text comprehension. We know, for example, that good readers have in their arsenal a variety of strategies from which to choose when confronted with content area materials. These readers choose the strategy that they know will work best for a particular reading task. In other words, good readers are flexible; they adjust their reading behaviors for factors such as rate, purpose, and type of text. The task for the content area teacher is to ensure that students undertake any reading assignment with a clear understanding that they can control to a great extent whether or not they read for meaning. This, of course, means teachers must provide direct instruction in and modeling of various metacognitive strategies for enhancing comprehension (Chapter 5); select and assign appropriate materials in terms of readability (Chapter 7); and build interest in the topic and provide sufficient motivation for the assignment (Chapter 9).

By now you should be convinced that making certain students read and understand reading assignments involves more than just asking questions. We've examined the shift from product to process in helping students extract meaning by considering cognitive theory, schema theory, and metacognition. We've emphasized the importance of helping students learn to assume responsibility for reading with understanding by using self-monitoring strategies. We have also emphasized once more the critical role writing can play in enhancing comprehension, particularly through the use of journals and/or learning logs in all the content areas.

As a conclusion to this chapter on comprehension, we recommend that you look carefully at the following overview (Alvermann et al., 1987) which reflects what the research tells us are the three critical elements for teaching comprehension as a thinking skill.

I. Focusing attention on the most informative parts of text through the use of enrichment activities and activation questions
   A. Enrichment activities
      1. Using analogy to illustrate relationships in text (Hayes & Tierney, 1982)
      2. Using oral previews to relate text to students' previous knowledge and experiences, to stimulate prediction, to provide necessary background, and to provide purpose(s) for reading
      3. Using written thematic organizers to define explicitly for students the central theme of the material
      4. Using structured overviews or graphic organizers (visual representation) to introduce key concepts via highlighting the logical structure students will encounter in the text
   B. Activation questions
      1. Prequestioning (before reading) to improve students' learning of target information
      2. Postquestioning (after reading) to help students acquire an overall, general understanding of text
      3. Interspersed questioning to help students monitor their comprehension as they read

II. Elaborating and organizing new material in order to commit it to long-term memory
   A. Elaborating
      1. Self-questioning strategies (for example, SQ3R as described in Chapter 5)

   2. "Looking back" or rereading when reading does not make sense
      (Garner, 1984)
   3. Reading for remembering via taking notes, generating (or com-
      pleting) outlines (see Chapter 5)
 B. Organizing via written summaries

III. Knowing when and how to use comprehension strategies
   A. Teacher modeling of comprehension/thinking strategies ("think-
      ing ahead") to show students how use of various strategies
      enhances comprehension
   B. Using direct instruction to alert students to "signals" in text such
      as the words "however," "on the other hand"
   C. Teaching strategies in meaningful context (like using content
      area texts, not isolated skill practice and unrelated materials)
   D. Encouraging students to learn new strategies by building on ones
      they know
   E. Providing teacher and peer feedback as students learn and use
      new strategies
   F. Evaluating student learning by testing on what is understood, not
      just "remembered"

REFERENCES

Alvermann, D. E., Moore, D. W., & Conley, M. W. (Eds.). (1987). *Research within reach: Secondary school reading*. Newark, DE: International Reading Association.

Baker, L., & Brown, A. L. (1984). Cognitive monitoring in reading. In J. Flood (Ed.), *Understanding reading comprehension* (pp. 21–44). Newark, DE: International Reading Association.

Barrett, T. C. (1972). Taxonomy of reading comprehension. *Reading 360 Monograph*. Lexington, MA: Ginn Press.

Bloom, B. S. (Ed.). (1956). *Taxonomy of educational objectives, handbook I: Cognitive domain*. New York: David McKay.

Calfee, R., & Drum, P. (1986). Research on teaching reading. In M. L. Wittrock (Ed.), *Handbook of research on teaching* (3rd ed.) (pp. 804–849). New York: Macmillan Publishing Co.

Danielson, K. E. (1988). *Dialogue journals: Writing as conversation*. Bloomington, IN: Phi Delta Kappa Educational Foundation.

Dewey, J. (1910). *How we think*. Boston: D. C. Heath & Co.

Durkin, D. (1983). *Is there a match between what elementary teachers do and what basic reader manuals recommend?*. Reading Education Report #44 [ED 235 470]. Champaign, IL: Center for the Study of Reading, University of Illinois at Urbana-Champaign.

Flavell, J. H. (1976). Metacognitive aspects of problem solving. In L. B. Resnick (Ed.), *The nature of intelligence* (pp. 231–235). Hillsdale, NJ: Lawrence Erlbaum Associates, Inc.

Fulwiler, T. (1987). *Teaching with writing*. Upper Montclair, NJ: Boynton/Cook.

Garner, R. et al. (1984). Inducing use of a text lookback strategy among unsuccessful readers. *American Education Research Journal, 21*, 789–798.

Hayes, D. A., & Tierney, R. J. (1982). Developing readers' knowledge through analogy. *Reading Research Quarterly, 17*, 256–280.

Herber, H. L. (1978). *Teaching reading in content areas*. (2nd ed.). Englewood Cliffs, NJ: Prentice-Hall, Inc.

Pearson, P. D., & Johnson, D. (1978). *Teaching reading comprehension*. New York: Holt, Rinehart & Winston.

Rothkopf, E. (1982). Adjunct aids and the control of mathemagenic activities during reading. In W. Otto & S. White (Eds.), *Reading expository material* (pp. 109–138). New York: Academic Press, Inc.

Schallert, D. (1982). The significance of knowledge: A synthesis of research related to schema theory. In W. Otto & S. White (Eds.), *Reading expository material* (pp. 13–48). New York: Academic Press, Inc.

Thorndike, E. L. (1917). Reading as reasoning: A study of mistakes in paragraph reading. *Journal of Educational Psychology, 8*, 323–332.

SUGGESTIONS FOR FURTHER READING

Alvermann, D. E., Moore, D. W., & Conley, M. W. (Eds.). (1987). *Research within reach: Secondary school reading*. Newark, DE: International Reading Association. Chapters 4 (pp. 33–51), 5 (pp. 52–63), and 12 (pp. 153–169).

Calfee, R., & Drum, P. (1986). Research on teaching reading. In M. L. Wittrock (Ed.), *Handbook of research on teaching* (3rd ed.) (pp. 804–849). New York: Macmillan Publishing Co.

Chall, J. S., & Stahl, S. A. (1982). Reading. In H. E. Mitzel (Ed.), *Encyclopedia of educational research* (5th ed.) (pp. 1535–1549). New York: Macmillan Publishing Co.

Fulwiler, T. (1987). *Teaching with writing*. Upper Montclair, NJ: Boynton/Cook.

CHAPTER FOUR

Teaching Vocabulary to Increase Comprehension

SCENARIO

The staff and students at Middlewood are looking forward to the first vacation break of the year. The Thanksgiving recess is about to begin.

"Hi, Marge. Join you for lunch?" asked John as he entered the cafeteria. The level of noise was more intense than ever as students enthusiastically discussed vacation plans.

"Have a seat, John. If we keep our minds on conversation, we may forget how bad this so-called Thanksgiving feast tastes," joked Marge with a wave of her hand at the empty seat across the table.

"Agreed. I keep promising myself to brown bag it, but somehow at dawn I'm not up to it."

"Ditto. What's up in your end of the science wing this week?" asked Marge.

"Not much besides the budget deadline Friday," said John. "I *am* trying to help my poor readers by teaching more vocabulary for each chapter, but it's not going well. They failed the latest test anyway. I'm really appalled by how poor their vocabulary is, Marge. I guess I had never really asked them about a lot of words in the book before. I had just assumed that they were not even trying to read the assignments."

"One thing I learned early in this game was not to be shocked by what students think words mean," responded Marge. "You know, John, it's a good thing I still teach one regular English class in this job; it helps keep me in touch with reality!"

"How so, Marge?" asked John.

"Well, I try hard to take my own advice, especially about vocabulary, but I don't always succeed," answered Marge. "Last week, for example, I assigned a short story which included the word 'barricade.' I assumed that students would know this word so I didn't preteach or preview it. Guess how I felt when I discovered that several people had missed much of the story's significance because they thought it had something to do with a flesh-eating fish!"

OVERVIEW

Does it surprise you that students might mistake "barricade" for "barracuda"? Are you thinking that this just would not happen in a middle or secondary classroom? If you are skeptical, you should find this chapter of interest. The truth about teaching in the content areas is that such "mistakes" are all too common, even among so-called competent readers. And, sadly, teachers are often unaware of just how frequently students "misread" the texts assigned to them.

This chapter focuses on vocabulary instruction, one of the three major components of reading, and it presents two ways of teaching vocabulary: as word attack skills and as concept development. Word attack skills include using context clues, structural analysis, sound patterns, and outside references like dictionaries. Concept development works with the readers' schema, using the processes of joining, excluding, selecting, and implying to build students' vocabulary.

DEFINING VOCABULARY SKILLS

Chapter 3 again focused attention on teaching reading as a language process. We talked about helping students develop skills for obtaining meaning from print through monitoring their own comprehension. Until now, however, we have purposely avoided specific discussion of vocabulary because it is so critical to comprehension that we want to give it maximum coverage. Thus, we devote this entire chapter to helping you develop strategies for teaching vocabulary as an aid to comprehension.

The Decoding Process

What is happening when students "misread" important words in the text? Let's consider Marge's "barricade/barracuda" example. At least three different possibilities suggest themselves here. Several students might hesitate when they come across the word "barricade" in an assignment, particularly students for whom the reading material is at the instructional or frustration level.

An instructional reader, for example, probably has adequately developed word attack skills which allow him to figure out, or *decode* the word "barricade." His reading "rhythm" may be interrupted temporarily, but he is likely to be able to use *word structure* cues such as syllable division (bar-ri-cade) and sound (phonic) cues such as the "silent e" at the end of the word to determine the correct pronunciation of the word.

A frustration level reader, however, for whom content material is too often very difficult, may not be able to figure out "barricade" so successfully. She may syllabicate the word successfully and try to use phonetic cues. But what if she pronounces the first syllable, "bar," as we pronounce "car"? She has not made an illogical word attack decision, has she? The difference between correct and incorrect word identification in this case rests upon the extent to which readers monitor their own comprehension as they encounter new and/or unfamiliar words in text. Reading, even at the word identification level, is a *language process*.

Do you remember from Chapters 1 and 3 the general principles of learning which apply to teaching reading? Do you recall the terms "metacognition" and "schema," our references to the importance of previous knowledge and the transfer of that knowledge to the reading of new materials? Our instructional reader likely succeeded in identifying the word "barricade" correctly because it "made sense" in his schema. If he "tried out" the word using the "car/bar sound," his "inner voice" probably told him that this couldn't be right; in fact, the word "barricade" was not really a "new" word for him at all. He had heard it spoken before but he simply had never encountered it in print. For him, then, the word "barricade" was not really a new word. (Later in this chapter we will discuss students' listening versus their reading vocabularies.) Skilled readers constantly monitor meaning; if a first "attempt" doesn't make sense, they make another, and another, until the meaning is clear. Because our instructional reader really knew the word "barricade" before he came across it in a reading assignment, he was able to use his word attack skills as an aid to reading for meaning.

What happens next for our readers, both of whom interrupted their reading rhythm for a new word? Once the instructional reader decides that he "has it right," he will likely read on until he encounters the next "hard" word. Having experienced success, he is probably willing to keep going. If the material is in fact at his instructional level, he will have trouble with about five in every one hundred words. If he can maintain interest in the assignment and not become unduly frustrated by having to hesitate so often, he will complete the assignment with at least 75 percent comprehension. But keep in mind that this is a lot of "ifs."

Our frustration level reader, on the other hand, is not likely to have success with the word "barricade," despite her attempts to utilize the word attack skills she has learned. She may well "read on" once she divides the word into syllables and "sounds it out" as best she can. But she has not successfully identified the word and the passage has likely stopped making sense to her. The word "barricade" may in fact be a new word for her, a word not in her listening vocabulary as it was in the instructional reader's. The difference between the instructional and frustration readers in content area classes is the extent to which they employ alternative strategies when they encounter problems in their reading. Frustration readers may try something when they come to a new or unfamiliar word, but they are likely just to read on (or quit altogether) when their first attempt does not yield a meaningful response.

Marge helps her English class see the differences and similarities between "barricade" and "barracuda," two words that they have confused. Pre-teaching unfamiliar words before reading an assignment helps students anticipate problems and identify words successfully when they see them.

Remember that what Marge told John, however, was not that several of her students mispronounced the word "barricade," as poor readers would likely do, but that they thought the word was "barracuda"! What happened here is the third possibility. The instructional readers in Marge's class hesitated over the word but successfully figured it out; the frustration readers either incorrectly decoded the word and kept reading or skipped it altogether. What about those who misread the word as "barracuda"? These students may well have started to decode the new or unfamiliar word as they encountered it, but they neglected to carry through on self-monitoring their comprehension. In other words, as soon as their "inner voices" came up with a word which might "work," they read on, failing to note that the story about a "barricade" didn't make sense with the word "barracuda" as a substitute. We often characterize such readers as careless and lazy. They typically come to new words and make a quick guess based on the first few letters, often only noting the first letter. Obviously they are not using reading as a language process.

How can we ensure that students develop effective strategies for identifying new or unfamiliar words in their reading assignments? How can we help them utilize both word attack skills and self-monitored comprehension as they read? Let's consider what teaching vocabulary is really all about.

Learning new, sometimes highly specialized vocabulary is a requirement for students in all content areas. In some courses learning the vocabulary means learning the content of the course! This usually happens when the new words are labels for concepts and the teacher wants to teach for concept development. This chapter deals with teaching vocabulary as concept development. Examples of other types of vocabulary development activities are also included.

Vocabulary and Meaning

Learning vocabulary, or mastering the new words in any learning situation, is perhaps the most obvious set of reading skills needed by students. Indeed, in many content areas, mastering the new vocabulary in a lesson or unit is equivalent to mastering the content. What we usually mean by "vocabulary" is that set of words or phrases which label the parts of material to be learned and which are necessary for students to use in talking and writing about the material.

Vocabulary, which represents both reading skill and content background, is cumulative: we learn new words all our lives as we learn new things. We need a constantly increasing set of words to talk about what we know. The teaching process assumes that the words we learned last week and last year can be used any time and that we will understand them. This is true for many people, but our ability to retain those words and their meanings is directly related to several principles of learning:

1. The more frequently we use words, the easier it is to recall and use them again.
2. The more ways we have used words and seen them used, the easier it is to remember them.
3. The more important or interesting words are to us, the easier it is to remember them.
4. The more we know about a whole subject, the easier it is to remember specific words that are related to that subject.

These principles, and teachers' reflections on whether their students are likely to fit them, lead to the conclusion that it is unwise to assume that all students have the same cumulative and easily remembered vocabularies. Teachers need to assess student vocabulary levels frequently.

Another factor in vocabulary development is that students (and all of us) have several different vocabularies. We have a *listening* vocabulary, a *speaking* vocabulary, a *reading* vocabulary, and a *writing* vocabulary. Our listening vocabulary includes the words we understand when we hear them. Our speaking vocabulary includes the words we use when we talk. Our reading vocabulary includes the words we understand when we read them, while our writing vocabulary includes the words we use in writing. We all develop listening and speaking vocabularies before we can read or write. Indeed, most beginning readers are given materials to read with carefully controlled vocabularies, so that they are reading only words which are already in their speaking and listening vocabularies.

Young children, and some older students, have larger speaking and listening vocabularies than reading and writing vocabularies. Sometimes in the intermediate grades or in junior high school, most students pass over the threshold into mature reading and writing. In this stage, their reading vocabulary becomes larger than their speaking vocabulary, These students can read and understand words they have never spoken or heard spoken. They can manipulate written words without first translating them into spoken form.

However, students move from using primarily a *speaking* vocabulary to using a *reading* vocabulary at very different times. Gifted students may do this earlier. On the other hand, bilingual and bidialectal students working with standard English texts may do it later; exceptional students, such as Learning Disabled or Educable Mentally Retarded students, may do it later; and students with little interest, motivation to learn, or background knowledge may do it later, or not at all.

We recommend, then, that all teachers remember the original primacy of speaking and listening vocabularies and that they present vocabulary study orally in classroom activities. The translation from written to oral and back to written is good practice for most students, regardless of their language proficiency.

An important skill for teachers is the ability to select for their students those vocabulary items necessary for understanding a particular piece of reading. In identifying words students must know, the teacher can separate them into several groups. The first group is *new words*, those words that the teacher predicts the students have never had occasion to deal with before. Teachers expect new words in a lesson or unit to be problems. After all, if students understood all those words and the concepts they represent, there would be no need to teach them. Students would already understand the material! The careful teacher will pretest students on all these new words to be sure they don't know them. This pretest serves as an on-going diagnosis of students' current stage of knowledge.

The second group of problem vocabulary can simply be labelled *familiar words*. These words should be identified by the teacher as necessary for students to know in order to understand the content. Thus, many of them are content-related. However, the teacher knows that these words have been taught and used in earlier units or previous years. Since vocabulary learning is cumulative, these familiar words should be in the students' active vocabularies, but careful teachers do not make that assumption. (Remember what happened to Marge!) Instead, they pretest students to be sure that these words are really familiar to them. This pretest has a double purpose: it provides information on who knows which words; it also provides a review and reinforcement for students. Students who have learned the words earlier but haven't used them for some time need to be helped to bring the meanings to their conscious minds.

As teachers work with the vocabulary for the unit or lesson, they should look for a third set of words or phrases—those with *multiple meanings*. Words with multiple meanings may be either new or familiar. Teachers recognize that words mean different things in different contexts in different content areas. Thus, students might be confused when they encounter these words.

Consider the word "set." Math teachers deal with this word frequently. Even a school dictionary such as the paperback *Webster's Dictionary* (1974) has nine meanings for "set" as a noun. A math teacher's meaning of "set," "a collection of mathematical elements (as numbers or points)" (page 632) is the last on the list in this dictionary. A student meeting "set" for the first time in math class may easily assume that it means the same thing in math as in other areas: stalking game (as "a dog is 'set' "); becoming hard or firm in consistency (as in "the gelatin is 'set' "); tendency or direction ("the course is 'set' "); the "set" of a play; the fruit on the apple tree is "set"; a "set" of square dancing; or a "set" of tennis. This list goes on—"set" has many meanings. In the 1980 *Random House College Dictionary*, "set" has eighty-four meanings; the math meaning is eightieth. It serves as a noun, verb, or adjective. It fits in many idiomatic expressions (set up, set in, set out, set back). Math teachers dealing with "sets" want their students to understand the precise meaning of "set" as used in math. Yet they must help students fit this meaning of "set" into the meanings they currently have for the word.

In this early planning stage, when teachers are examining the reading material before building specific activities or exercises, they must be alert to words with the potential of multiple meanings and take this into account when planning activities. Look at Figure 4.1, a seventh-grade science teacher's list of words from a unit on "The Biosphere and Its Habitats." We'll use this unit as an example later in the chapter. This teacher identified at least one meaning or use for each word in list C which could cause confusion to students. In a great many cases, the words will be used in the "Habitat" unit with different contexts than in other readings. It is this teacher's judgment that the words listed in C are the ones she must be careful to clarify for students.

CONCEPT WORDS IN "THE BIOSPHERE AND ITS HABITATS"

A. New Words		**B. Familiar Words**	
ecosystem	environments	triggers	adaptation
biosphere	abundant	migration	average
moderate	oxygen	presence	suitable
habitat	carbon dioxide	lack	adequate
niche	adapted	constant	unsuitable
moisture	organism	centimeters	context
lichens	bacteria	obtain	nutrient-poor
humus	decomposing	extend	enriched
topsoil	nutrients	determine	decaying
rodents	limited	influences	weathered
borrowers	Celsius	anchored	molds
dormant	burrow	microscopic	decimeter
plankton	polar	microorganisms	calculated
phytoplankton	enables	hazards	available
zooplankton	survive	churned	dwellers
bioluminescent	processes	varies	dissolved
predators	behavior	sewage	temporary
scavengers	migrate	organisms	absence

C. Words with Multiple Meanings			
moderate	polar	triggers	dissolved
niche	behavior	presence	anchored
adapted, adaptation	migrate, migration	constant	

Figure 4.1

Used in conjunction with V. Webster, G. S. Fichter, C. R. Coble, and D. R. Rice, *Prentice-Hall Life Science* (Englewood Cliffs, N.J.: Prentice-Hall, Inc., 1980).

USING WORD ATTACK SKILLS IN CONTENT AREA READING

Students come to content subjects already possessing some skills we call *word attack skills.* That is, these skills are designed to "attack" new words to find out what unfamiliar words mean. Our goal as readers, hence as teachers, is to identify necessary words by sight, which means that we will immediately recognize a word and attach a meaning to it.

We know that fluent readers do not read every word in a passage. They read only enough to get the meaning from it. The more background knowledge the fluent reader has, the less s/he has to read. The converse is also true, and it explains problems our weak readers have: the less a student knows about the subject and the less fluent a reader s/he is, the more likely that s/he will have to read every word in order to understand the passage. Word-for-word reading is not only much slower and less efficient; it also makes it harder to develop an overall understanding of the passage, including connections within it. Any time readers must stop their reading to identify a new word, no matter which skill they use, they may lose the train of thought. Careful readers must then go back and reestablish the thought pattern before going on.

Thus, our goal as teachers is for students to become familiar with all important words so that they don't need to stop to identify them when they occur. That's what we mean when we say that students recognize certain words by sight. The meanings have become automatic. This is an important step toward the "automaticity" discussed in Chapter 2.

Unfortunately, some students do not know by sight many words that are necessary to learning content materials. We must ask students to use their word attack skills to identify these new words in their reading. Four major groups of word attack skills are commonly taught in elementary school: (1) use of context clues; (2) use of structural analysis, (3) use of sound patterns; and (4) use of outside references. All of those skills are used by fluent readers, often in combination, but teachers need to be sure that all students can use all of these skills. Then they need to help students transfer what they know from reading class to the content material. Let's look at each of these skills.

Context Clues

The context of an unknown word is the material surrounding it. This context may be a phrase, a sentence, a paragraph, or an entire chapter. Context clues are words, phrases, or more which help the reader identify the unfamiliar word. Context clues can be classified in these categories:

1. Definition—The descriptive context defines the unknown word. For example: Tom and Dick lived next door. They were *neighbors*.
2. Experience—Students use past experience to complete the thought. For example: Jack gave his dog a *bone* to chew.
3. Comparison with known ideas—The unknown word is compared to something known. For example: You do not have to run, you can *walk*.
4. Synonym—The preceding context offers a synonym of the unknown word. For example: When the captain gave up, the crew had to *surrender* too.
5. Familiar expression—Our language is filled with expressions that are meaningful to native speakers but confusing to those learning the language. For example: If he isn't careful he's going to put his foot in his *mouth*.
6. Summary—An unknown word serves to summarize previous concepts. For example: The elephants, clowns, and cages came down the street. The *circus* had come to town.
7. Reflection of a mood or situation—For example: The clouds were black. Scarcely any light came in the window. The house was dark and *mysterious*. (See Herber, 1978; McNeil, 1987.)

We can help students learn to use context efficiently by providing practice in identifying and using context clues in reading. The seventh-grade science teacher could help her students in the unit on "The Biosphere and Its Habitats" by looking at the use of context in that chapter:

> A habitat *(HAB-e-tat) is a place where an organism lives. You may think of a habitat as the organism's neighborhood. The habitat of some organisms is very large. The habitat of whales, for example, is the ocean. Other organisms live in small habitats. Ants in an anthill are an example. What type of habitat do you live in?*[1]

In this paragraph, "habitat" is defined three times—first, as "a place where an organism lives"; second, as "the organism's neighborhood"; third, as differing by size (an ocean is large; an anthill is small). The definition of "habitat" is central to the unit; therefore the author is defining it by giving various characteristics as well as a simple one-phrase definition (the first) and a synonym (neighborhood). The characteristic, size, is a familiar concept. Thus, in this one paragraph, the context clues for the meaning of habitat include numbers 1, 3, and 4 on the Herber/McNeil list.

In a broad sense, the author of the unit "The Biosphere and Its Habitats" has used the entire unit to define "habitat" completely. That is the central topic or concept to be learned. In other situations, where the word is not a central concept but nonetheless a useful term, it is defined in a sentence and left at that: "This decaying material is called *humus*." Under the broader topic of soil, the development of "humus" is a subtopic that is valuable but not central. Thus, the definition of humus as decaying material is given once. If a student misses this clue, s/he will not be able to place "humus" in context successfully.

One way to help students practice using context clues is to provide modified versions of the *cloze procedure* (presented in detail in Chapter 8). The format of the cloze procedure when it is used for vocabulary practice allows the teacher to delete vocabulary words from a passage as they occur. The student has a list of the words necessary to fill the blanks and need only recognize the clues in the passage which give meaning to the blank. In the example given in Figure 4.2, the seventh-grade science teacher has identified the sixteen words she wants students to practice. The underlined words would be blanks for students to fill in, thirteen in all. A rule of thumb in preparing vocabulary cloze exercises is that a teacher should delete no more than one word in ten, on the average. This ratio gives students sufficient context for identifying the missing words.

Practice in using context clues can range from filling in blanks in single sentences to full paragraphs, like the example in Figure 4.2. Teachers

---

[1]From *Prentice-Hall Life Science* by Vera Webster, Geo. S. Fichter, Charles R. Coble and Dale R. Rice. Copyright © 1980 by Prentice-Hall, Inc., Englewood Cliffs, New Jersey 07632. Reprinted by permission.

CLOZE PROCEDURE AS VOCABULARY PRACTICE

<hr>

Habitats

The paragraph below talks about habitats and the animals who live in them.

Use the words listed below to complete the exercise. Each word or phrase can be used once, more than once, or not at all. Fill in each blank with the word or phrase that makes sense in the sentence.

standing	predators	temperature	moving
saltwater	water	scavengers	light
oxygen	constant	freshwater	dormant
air	soil	land	moisture

There are three kinds of habitats in our world: __land__, __water__, __air__.

The largest part of the earth's surface, almost 75% of it, is __water__. Almost all of this habitat is in the oceans which are the __saltwater__ habitat. Plankton are a common type of organism living near the surface of the oceans. In the deepest parts of the oceans are two types of animals: __predators__ who hunt and eat other animals, and __scavengers__ who feed on dead animals and plants. There are two important features of the ocean habitat. One is __light__, which helps plants to make their own food. The other is __temperature__, which determines where and at what depths animals can survive.

Freshwater habitats make up only about 3% of the earth's water. Yet we are most familiar with freshwater habitats. They may be springs, streams, or rivers (which we call __moving__ water) or ponds, lakes, and swamps (which we call __standing__ water). Some of this freshwater is always available, or __constant__. Other freshwater is only temporary. In temporary freshwater living organisms sometimes go into __dormant__, or resting, stages, when the water disappears.

Teacher Information
13 blanks; 186 words; or 1 blank/14 + words

<hr>

Figure 4.2

can find the material for cloze exercises from the assigned text or from alternative materials. Or they can write the material themselves, as this science teacher did.

The next example is a short cloze exercise developed for an Algebra I class. The math teacher has the same problems as other teachers in using new terminology in context. However, s/he has an additional concern—the use of symbols interchangeably with the words or phrases for which they stand. Kane et al. (1974) developed and validated a cloze procedure for use specifically with mathematics materials and other materials with heavy use of symbols, like chemistry and physics. In the example in Figure 4.3, the text material has been used, with a deletion pattern focusing on the concept of intersection of sets. Underlined words, phrases, and symbols are deleted in the student version.

The context exercise example in Figure 4.4 is an English teacher's exercise from a unit on mythology. Each sentence is taken from the reading material within the unit so that students can return to the larger context of the complete reading, if necessary, to find the meaning.

MATHEMATICS CLOZE EXERCISE

The Arithmetic of Sets: Intersection

The intersection of two sets consists of the elements they have in common. For example, if A = (1,2,3,4,5) and B = (3,4,5,6,7), the intersection of these sets would be (3,4,5), which could be designated set C. The symbol for intersection is __$\cap$__ (read "cap").

In words: The ___intersection___ of set A and B is set C.

In symbols:

or $\dfrac{A}{(1,2,3,4,5)} \quad \cap \quad \dfrac{B}{(3,4,5,6,7)} = \dfrac{C}{(3,4,5)}$

It should be noted that the intersection of two sets is a _subset_ of each set.

   Intersection may also be represented pictorially by closed figures called _Venn Diagrams_. The region within a _Venn Diagram_ is assumed to represent the set being illustrated. Because each of the sets used in the problem is a subset of U, U is called the universe or _universal set_.

Figure 4.3

Adapted from *Modern Algebra: Structure and Method, Book One* by M. P. Dolciani, S. L. Berman, & J. Freilich. Extra for Experts, pp. 30–31. Copyright © 1962 by Houghton Mifflin Company. Reprinted by permission.

Structure Clues

Structural analysis is the process of dividing words into their *roots* and *affixes*. A root is the part of a word that carries the base meaning of the word, while affixes are prefixes, suffixes, and infixes. *Prefixes* are those word parts added to the front of a root, while *suffixes* are added to the end of the root. *Infixes* occur mostly in old words, such as man/men and sit/sat/set, in which the differences based on number (singular or plural) or tense (present, past, or participle) are located inside the words. All four—roots, prefixes, suffixes, and infixes—are common components of English words.

   Most middle school and secondary students have been exposed to the simplest principles of word parts—prefixes and suffixes—in elementary school. However, we can't be sure that they will remember them. Linus, in Charles Schulz's *Peanuts* cartoon, once defined "prefix" this way: "Prefix means to fix something before it is broken." Think back to Marge's "barracuda" example: her students did not look beyond the first segment of the word and, as a result, misread an entire passage. Your task will be to reactivate your students' prior knowledge of prefixes, roots, and suffixes and to help them transfer that knowledge to your more complex vocabulary items. Let's now take a closer look at these word components.

   Roots are parts of words which carry the base meaning of the full word. Roots may be independent words like the root in "spectroscope." However, many roots in content subjects are of Latin or Greek origin and there is no English word using just the root, like "port" in "reporter." The meanings of such roots must be determined by the use of outside sources or references to similar words.

CONTEXT CLUES EXERCISE

Context Clues   **20 points**

Goal: To learn to use context clues to help you determine an unfamiliar word's meaning.

Explanation: Often you can get a general meaning of a word from other words in the same sentence or paragraph. These words are called Context Clues.

For example: The Indians paid *homage* to many spirits, but most of all, they worshipped the Great Spirit. Here, *homage* is "defined" by what word? _____

Directions: Underline the word or words which help you to understand the meaning of the underlined word. Then, in the blank, write what you think the word means.

_____ 1. "You murder me now, and steal my throne—but one of your own sons will dethrone you, for crime begets crime."

_____ 2. "Her white hands danced among the flax, and she worked so quickly, so deftly, that she seemed to have forgotten the loom."

_____ 3. "Poseidon smiled to himself because the sky was empty, and he knew that the impulsive Zeus had chosen it because it looked so high."

_____ 4. "The avaricious king had to have dominion over all of the kingdoms, not only ten."

_____ 5. "Her body was as pliant as a stem."

_____ 6. "They curvetted twice in the air, and plunged into the hole again."

_____ 7. "A great wailing and lamentation arose as the people lifted their faces to Olympus and prayed for Zeus to help them."

_____ 8. "If any food has passed her lips during her sojourn in Tartarus, then she must remain there."

_____ 9. "She saw a tree which had been struck by lightning: it was still smoldering."

_____ 10. "To his dismay, she was joined by a gaggle of hamadryads, mischievous girls who loved to tell tales."

Figure 4.4

Prepared by Drucilla C. Weirauch, State College, Area School District, Pa. Reprinted by permission.

Affixes have two major purposes. They may be *inflectional* or *derivational*. Inflectional affixes relate to grammatical categories: plurals, verb tense, or those that change a word from one class to another. In English, inflectional affixes are either suffixes or infixes, not prefixes. Derivational affixes change the meanings of words and may change the word class to which they belong. Students are likely to have learned inflectional affixes in elementary reading class. They will probably also have learned some basic derivational affixes, like un-, dis-, -ness, and -able. However, there are higher levels of these affixes which students won't encounter until they begin reading higher-level content materials with a wider use of Greek, Latin, and other derivatives. Consider the inflectional affixes here:

Singular		Plural
synthesis	→	syntheses
datum	→	data
formula	→	formulae

These singular-to-plural forms must be taught carefully to allow for transfer of the principle of number (singular/plural) to these new forms.

There are many more examples of derivational affixes which need to be studied in content fields. Consider the word "spectroscope," given earlier. It must be taught as relating to "spectral," "spectrometer," and "spectrum." It must also be taught as relating to "microscope," "telescope," and "oscilloscope." Each word part is seen, in this analysis, as part of a wider concept: "spectr"—related to light; and "scope"—related to seeing through or by.

An additional process students need in order to internalize a new word by structural analysis is how to use it in different contexts:

Spectroscope (noun)—an instrument for examining the light spectrum
Spectroscopic (adjective)—made or performed with a spectroscope
Spectroscopy (noun)—the study of the spectrum through the use of the
    spectroscope

The *-ic* ending transforms spectroscope into an adjective and slightly alters the meaning. The *-y* ending, meaning "study of," not only changes the meaning but turns the word into a different noun. "Spectroscopy" should thus be seen in relation to biology, botany, zoology, history, and other branches of learning.

Practice for students in developing word "families," lists of words with similar parts, is one way of assisting students in seeing the uses of structural analysis. A word of caution, however. Structural analysis is normally used to build the meaning of a word by adding together the meaning of its parts:

reporter = one who carries back (information or news)
re = back
port = carry
er = one who

This fairly simplistic process works well when the parts have clear and discrete meanings. Thus, in chemistry, the difference between "sulfite" and "sulfate" is clear and important, using this additive process:

$$sulf = sulfur$$

$$+ \text{ ite} = \text{salt of an acid ending in -ous}$$
$$sulfite = SO_3 = \text{salt of sulfurous acid}$$

$$+ \text{ ate} = \text{salt of an acid ending in -ic}$$
$$sulfate = SO_4 = \text{salt of sulfuric acid}$$

However, in areas like social studies and literature, in which word parts have multiple meanings or those meanings are less precise, the process of building meaning can be much more difficult. "Amnesty" means a general pardon, while "amnesia" means a loss of memory. The relationship between these two meanings can be explained, but it is not automatically clear to most students. (It is interesting that these words both use the Greek prefix *a-*, meaning "not," so that the original Greek word for both "amnesty" and "amnesia" is a + mnesthai or not + remember. The root of both words is the Greek word for "remember.")

A second word of caution has to do with words which look as if they have the same root but don't. A case in point: "indigent" and "indigenous." Both words are adjectives with Latin roots. "Indigent" comes from the Latin root—"egere," meaning "need." With the prefix "in," the meaning is clearly "in need." However, "indigenous" comes from the Latin word "indigena," and means "native to the country." Here are two very different meanings for two words which look alike on the surface.

As you can see, identifying a word's meaning by using structural analysis is a useful skill, but it can't be used simplistically. To avoid the pitfalls of root-affix work, students need to be aware of both judgment about the appropriate meaning of a word in context and the judicious use of a dictionary. It is also clear that working through word meanings and word families this way is time-consuming. Teachers will not find it appropriate to do this systematically unless the vocabulary items are central to the understanding of the topic or concept.

This student is working at a learning center in social studies. She has a set of word cubes with prefixes, roots, and suffixes on them. She can build words by rearranging the cubes. To her left is a flannelboard with similar word parts on velcro strips. These word parts can be rearranged physically, just like the word cubes.

The greatest problem for content teachers in using structural analysis is to help students transfer the skills learned in reading class to the content situation. In the picture on the preceding page, a frustration level reader is working with a set of materials to help her transfer the appropriate reading skill, a set of cubes with word parts on them from which she can create new words. Remember that frustration level readers often need more practice than other students; they need more concrete hands-on experiences; they are likely to have more trouble with higher level cognitive work, such as the analysis (taking words apart) and synthesis (putting words together) required here. A learning center is especially useful here, because it allows frustration level readers to spend the extra time in a highly structured activity, while other students who don't need that much practice can do something else.

The cubes used in this center are simple for teachers or students to develop. They are color coded (prefixes—gold, roots—green, suffixes—rust). The letters are press-ons; the posterboard is the kind every school has. Find some masking tape, and you are in business. Another hands-on item in this same center is a flannelboard with velcro strips and a set of word parts on posterboard with the same color coding. With these word parts, students can build new words or take words apart on the flannelboard. Also contained in the center are conventional worksheets involving work with word parts, and sets of exercises are available for each of the specific skills: roots and prefixes; roots and suffixes; roots with both prefixes and suffixes; and two-root words. The teacher can assign students to all or part of each exercise set.

Sound Patterns

The sound patterns of words, or their pronunciation, are important in developing vocabulary. Being able to pronounce new words means being able to use them orally. Thus, by using new words orally and asking students to do so, the teacher can ensure that students add new words to their speaking and listening vocabularies as well as to their reading and writing vocabularies.

Students come to content reading with some understanding of sound patterns. They are likely to be able to use phonics, the relationship of sounds to written symbols, and to sound out many words. When they encounter an unfamiliar word, they can use these phonic patterns to pronounce the word. So far, so good. Most students can recognize the difference in sound between "kit" and "kite," "cap" and "cape," "dot" and "dote." Some can even indicate what the silent -e rule is, but using such rules on words like "spectroscope" means applying rules in ways that they have never used them. Hence, content teachers must again be concerned with transfer. (Simple assessment using the Informal Reading Inventory [IRI] discussed in Chapter 8 can help teachers know how well students can use the basic phonic rules and how much they can already transfer to words in the appropriate subject.)

The application of phonics rules presents several problems for content teachers. The most important is that many new words are longer, with prefixes and suffixes. Let's use "spectroscope" again as an example. Most students facing it as a new word will not see that its root, "scope," follows the final -e rule, but it does. Thus, once the initial break between prefix and root occurs, spectro + scope, the student can apply the phonic patterns learned earlier to attempt pronunciation of the word.

Another part of pronouncing a word is establishing its intonation pattern, or where the accents fall. This is especially troublesome in words of three syllables or more. Students need to know: (1) how to break words into syllables, roughly a vowel sound and surrounding consonants; and (2) the usual accent patterns in English. Both these skills are used correctly by standard English speakers at an early age, but they may have difficulty articulating the rules they follow. Bilingual and bidialectal students will not necessarily know or follow the same rules. Hence, intonation patterns can be especially troublesome for them.

Look again at our sample words, now including their accent patterns and vowel sounds:

spec′	tro	scōpe‵	(silent)′	= primary stress
spec‵	tro	scŏ′	pic ‵	= secondary stress
spec‵	tro′	scə	py	

As we move from "spectroscope" to "spectroscopic," we drop the -e to add -ic—a familiar rule. This also means the o in scope goes from long o to short o (as in "shot"). The accent pattern shifts so that the primary stress goes from the first to the third syllable. In the move to "spectroscopy," the o is no longer in an accented syllable. Primary stress is on the second syllable and secondary stress remains on the first syllable. We know that, in English, vowels in unaccented syllables almost always have an "uh" sound, the *schwa*, represented by the upside down e (ə). Hence, in these three related words, there are three different accent patterns and three different sounds for the o in scope. The complexity in these sound pattern changes underscores the problem with vocabulary work in content areas. These word attack skills, often learned in isolation in reading class, must be applied in combination in content classes. Transfer, always difficult to achieve, is even more difficult to develop in these cases. Teachers must teach consciously and carefully in order for their students to grasp the patterns and processes appropriate in a particular subject area.

A word of caution: Applying sound patterns is important and useful in content reading. However, some new words are not derived from English and the sound patterns we teach students are useful primarily with English words. Case in point: "epitome." This Greek word breaks well into prefix + root: epi + tome. Epi = on, over, upon. Tome looks like a normal English word meaning book, following the final -e rule: pronounced tōm. Wrong. The meaning of "tome" in "epitome," while ultimately from the same Greek root, has become generalized, so "epitome" means a representative example of something, as in "Macbeth is the epitome of the troubled king." The accent patterns and pronunciation do not follow English patterns; they follow Greek patterns—i-pit′-ə-me. Teachers must be aware of the language from which vocabulary items derive in order to warn students of words which don't follow the usual English pattern.

Even with this caution, there are several rules of thumb students can use in finding the pronunciation of unfamiliar multi-syllabic words.

1. When there is no other clue in a two-syllable word, the accent is usually on the first syllable: ar′ my.
2. In inflected or derived forms of words, the primary accent falls on or within the root word: re por′ ter.
3. If de-, re-, be-, ex-, in-, or a- is the first syllable in a word, it is usually unaccented: re por′ ter.
4. Two vowel letters together in the last syllable of a word may be a clue to an unaccented final syllable.
5. Where there are two like consonants within a word, the syllable before the double consonants is usually accented: rub′ ble.
6. In words of three or more syllables, one of the first two syllables is usually accented: sy′ la ble, re por′ ter (adapted from Winkley, 1966).

Outside References

When all the other skills fail, students can, in the words of the old saw, "Look it up!" This means leaving the context of the reading and make-up of the word itself to use a glossary, dictionary, or other source of meaning. Students may well have learned to use the dictionary in earlier grades. The important problem in using the dictionary is to be sure that the meaning selected fits the context of the passage. Especially with words like "set," with multiple meanings, students cannot simply find the first meaning listed and use it. If students don't recognize the word and don't know much about the topic, it can be very difficult for them to identify the correct meaning in the dictionary. For these reasons, using the dictionary is the last resort for identifying a new word.

The glossary of the text or other reading material may be more useful to the students than the dictionary because it will not have so many meanings to confuse the reader. Early in the year, teachers must be sure students know where the glossary is and how to use it. The glossary is preferable to the dictionary as a source of information for students. Chapter 5

VOCABULARY DEVELOPMENT EXERCISE

Lord of the Flies Vocabulary Development—Chapters IX–XII
Fun with Words

In this exercise you will get to find out the meaning of the words in many different ways. Follow the directions closely and check with your group when you finish.

Chapter IX

1. indignity—p. 135b
    (1) Divide the word into syllables — How many does it have?
    (2) It contains a prefix. What is it? _____ What does it mean? _____
    (3) What does the whole word mean? _____
    (4) Write the plural form. _____
    (5) Write two other words using the same prefix. _____
        Define them. _____

        _____

2. succulent—p. 138m—From context define the word.
    (1) Answer *true* or *false* to the correct use of the word in these statements:
        _____ The steak was a succulent one.
        _____ The succulent sound hurt my ears.
        _____ Our band concert was succulent.
        _____ Although I wasn't hungry, the succulent orange tasted good.

3. demented—p. 140m—Any person who would kill another human being just for fun is *demented*.
    (1) From context clues write the meaning of demented.

        _____
    (2) Create a sentence using this word correctly.

        _____
    (3) Write an antonym for this word.

        _____

4. abominable—p. 141m
    (1) What part of speech is this word? _____
    (2) Write its suffix. _____
        Change its suffix to *ation*. _____
    (3) What part of speech is it now? _____

Figure 4.5
Prepared by Callie Kingsbury and the tenth-grade English team, State College, Pa., Senior High School. Reprinted by permission.

contains techniques for teaching students how to use a book's glossary and a dictionary.

Figure 4.5 is an example of one teacher's vocabulary guide for *Lord of the Flies* in tenth-grade English. She combines several word attack skills in her "Fun with Words" exercise for one chapter of that novel. Although she focuses on only four words, students are practicing all the word attack skills. Content teachers are well advised to build practice exercises like this one to help students use word attack skills in a meaningful situation.

TEACHING VOCABULARY AS CONCEPT DEVELOPMENT*

Concept development, a cognitive process, is widely suggested to be the goal of content teaching. This is especially true in mathematics, science, social studies, industrial arts, and home economics. It is sufficiently pervasive in contemporary content teaching to spend some time focusing on concept learning and its interaction with vocabulary development.

A concept is known by its characteristics, or components. It is, in Hafner's words, "a class of things or ideas with common elements or characteristics" (1977, p. 27). A concept, such as "chair," has certain elements which are common to all chairs. Through analysis of the concept "chair," we can determine what those common elements are. Through a synthesis of its characteristics, we can develop a composite of "chairness." Additional analysis shows some characteristics which a chair may have (for example, arms) but which are not necessary for it to be called a "chair."

Note that up to this point, we could have done all this analysis without using language. We could use pictures to illustrate the components, as in Figure 4.6. However, the word "chair" is not the same thing as the object. The word represents, or serves as a symbol for, the object. Consequently, the concept of a chair, representing not only a concrete object but its essen-

---

*The teaching materials in this section were developed jointly with Sandra L. Snyder of Pennsylvania State University.

THE CHARACTERISTICS OF CHAIRS

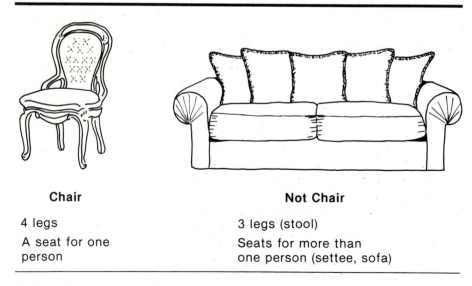

Chair	Not Chair
4 legs	3 legs (stool)
A seat for one person	Seats for more than one person (settee, sofa)

Figure 4.6

tial characteristics, is another step up the abstraction ladder. Remembering learning principles again, you should realize that students with a limited background in a particular content area, students who have limited experience with a topic, and students who have difficulty learning abstract material will have difficulty learning concepts. Add to that list students who have difficulty manipulating the standard English in which concepts are usually presented by teachers, books, and other materials. Now the reasons many students fail in concept learning is clearer. However, the need for students to learn concepts is not diminished. What emerges is a need for teachers to plan carefully to avoid or overcome some of the problems identified here.

Teachers first need to plan concept teaching to make it as concrete as possible, to provide as much first-hand experience with the actual concepts as possible. Hands-on activities are recommended, along with real-world experience on the concept in action. This includes labs in science, home economics, and shop, with students using examples of the concept in class—an actual chair or spectroscope—if the concept represents an object. If the concept is an idea, as in government, then a field trip may be required—to a city council meeting, a school board meeting, or to a government building. A trip to a living pond demonstrates several habitats to the seventh-grade science class. More vicarious experiences include movies, slides, videotapes, filmstrips, and other pictures. These are not the same as being there, but they are better than just words.

Just words. As Eliza Doolittle says in *My Fair Lady*, "Words, words, words! I'm so sick of words! . . . Is that all you blighters can do?"[2] Students often feel this way about concept learning in schools. It seems to be just words, words, words—no pictures, no visual representation of what is going on. Teachers need to plan a teaching strategy that helps students learn the words that are necessary to work with important concepts and learn to manipulate the words instead of the objects. They can begin, perhaps, by working with the actual chair, but our goal is for them to work, if they can, at the higher abstraction level required to manipulate concepts intellectually by means of language.

Henry (1974) suggests a process for conceptualizing which allows teachers to plan effectively. Conceptualizing means "to discover relations and to invent a structure of these relations" (p. 14); that is, to analyze the concept into relationships, then to synthesize the components into a whole again. Remembering Bloom's cognitive taxonomy, this means that the conceptualizing process is a fairly high-level process, subsuming the three lower levels into the process. For Henry, concept development requires four basic operations:

1) *The act of joining* (bringing together, comparing, generalizing, classifying). Its logical operator is *and* (*moreover, furthermore*). Its grammatical form is the coordinating conjunction and the connective adverb.
2) *The act of excluding* (discriminating, negating, rejecting). Its logical operator is *not* (*this . . . not that*). Its grammatical form *neither . . . nor* (exclusive, dichotomous).
3) *The act of selecting* (one or the other or both). Its logical operator is *some* (*part, few*). Its grammatical form is *either . . . or*; quantitative pronouns.
4) *The act of implying* (*if* not *this . . . then that*; cause-effect, result, necessity, proof, condition). Its logical operator is *if . . . then*. Its grammatical form is the subordinating connective adverb and the subordinating conjunction. (pp. 14–15).

These four operations can help teachers focus on concept development when they plan teaching processes.

Teaching for concept development requires a great deal of time. Topics taught this way must be central to the subject. Our example of a topic taught by concept development procedure is a seventh-grade life science unit, "The Biosphere and its Habitats," and the reading material comes from a standard text.[3]

Planning for Concept Teaching

Concept training begins when the teacher looks at the domain to be taught and chooses those topics and materials which will be his or her focus. All subject areas contain more to learn than can possibly be taught. Choosing what to teach is not easy for teachers. However, the full domain of learning is a jumble of unknown perceptions to students. Look at the potential topics given in Figure 4.7.

This looks like a disorganized mess. The teacher must make sense of it for students by identifying the items to focus on and the characteristics which make them important. In this set of nine potential topics, a teacher may choose to focus on shape and have three groups of three (circles, triangles, squares); s/he may focus on the lines and have three groups of three (vertical, horizontal, slanted); or s/he may focus on the small marks superimposed on each item, and have three groups of three ($\sqrt{}$s, xs, or os). The teacher tells students what is important by helping them focus on important items and organizing those items or showing the relations between them.

---

[3]V. Webster, G. C. Fichter, C. R. Coble, and D. R. Rice, *Prentice-Hall Life Science* (Englewood Cliffs, N.J.: Prentice-Hall, Inc., 1980).

CONCEPTS—WHICH ONE TO LEARN?

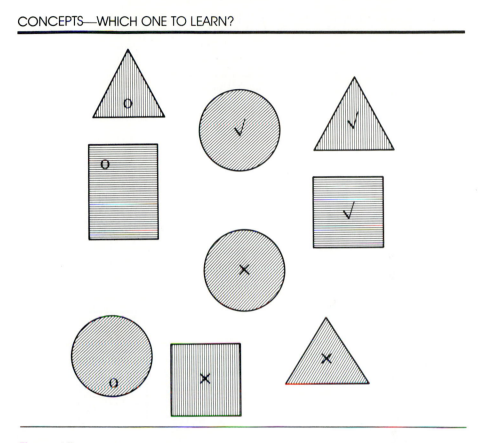

Figure 4.7

One way of helping students make sense of a unit is to provide them with an *advance organizer*, a process of giving students not only the items to be learned, but also the relationships among them. The process, first described by Ausubel (1968), is a critical first step in teaching for concept development. One effective way to provide an advance organizer using the important vocabulary for a unit is the *structured overview*. Figure 4.8 is a structured overview for the unit on "The Biosphere and Its Habitats" for seventh-grade science. The important vocabulary items here are all labels for the concepts which make up the larger concept of habitat. Students know many of these concepts, such as "oxygen," "temperature," and "light," from other units and in other contexts. So these concepts have meaning which can be added to other concepts here, such as "predators," "scavengers," and "plankton." These added concepts will probably have to be developed. The structured overview, given as a motivating and organizing preview for the unit, can help students develop what Herber calls the necessary instructional framework, or a cognitive map. They

STRUCTURED OVERVIEW FOR "THE BIOSPHERE AND ITS HABITATS"

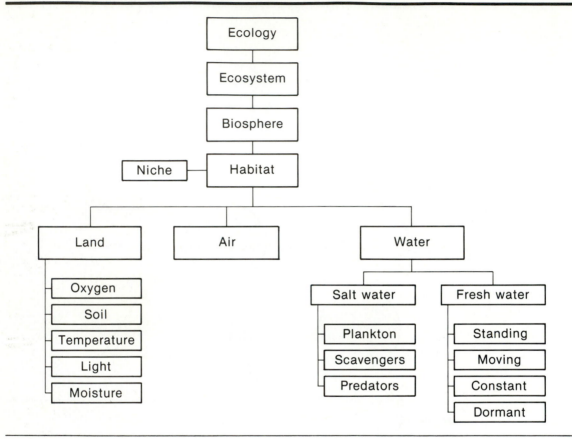

Figure 4.8

need such a framework in order to tie the specifics of each concept together to make the connections necessary to synthesize the concept of habitat.

Structured overviews are built in several steps. First, the teacher identifies the concepts and their labels which are central to the unit. Second, the graphic organization is developed. This second step can be completed by the teacher and the overview can be presented as a whole to the students. Or the connections can be developed with the students in an inquiry lesson or discovery process, using a field trip, movie, or other media to present an introduction and overview of the unit. The results of either approach are the same, however; the students enter the unit with a sense of where they are going and what they need to learn. The structured overview is an example of the first of Henry's operations, the act of joining. We used these steps to develop the overviews used in this book.

A second technique for helping students preview important vocabulary and concept labels before reading is the *semantic map* (Heimlich & Pittleman, 1986). When students help develop a semantic map, they are identifying the words they know about a new concept and developing the structure of the new concept so they can add labels as they meet them in the reading. Figure 4.9 shows a semantic map for the vocabulary introduced in the "Habitats" reading.

A semantic map may be developed before the reading. The teacher helps students list all the words they know about the central concept. Together, teacher and students create a map showing the relationships that they already know. They can also identify some areas they need to learn about, creating questions to answer during the reading. This technique helps to activate students' schemata and then helps create new and more extensive schema after the reading (Hanf, 1971).

An extension of this mapping technique is the *refocused semantic map* (Johnson et al., 1981). After reading the selection, the teacher helps students to focus the map on the specific reading they have just completed; in the process they revise, refine, and extend the map they created before reading.

SEMANTIC MAP FOR THE BIOSPHERE AND ITS HABITATS

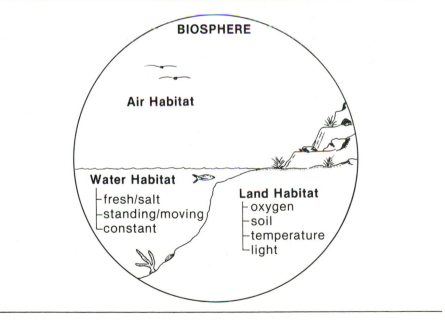

Figure 4.9

Linking Vocabulary to Concept Development

By now it should be clear that vocabulary study is inseparable from concept development. The two are essentially the same thing. However, typical exercises for providing practice in learning vocabulary will not necessarily contribute to concept learning. Memorizing the definition of a word, for example, is useful but not enough to guarantee that a student can use it in concept learning. Concept learning requires the use of the four operations Henry suggests—joining, excluding, selecting, and implying. Here are some exercises which require that students know the meanings of words but go on to use the words and their meanings in one of these operations.

Joining, or categorizing, is one way students can learn which words belong together. The example given in Figure 4.10 uses the five concepts on the structured overview which are subsumed into "land habitats"—temperature, light, moisture, soil, and oxygen. In the categorization activity given here, students must first put each word under an appropriate category; second, they must explain why they chose that category in the discussion that follows. Some words may be placed under more than one category (for example, sun relates to both light and temperature). The student is encouraged to see that some words relate to more than one concept.

CATEGORIZING

The Act of Joining

Under the list of words below there are five categories. Place each word in the category to which it belongs (may be listed more than once).

acids	deserts	extreme	nutrient-poor	
air	dim	freezing	polar regions	soak
breath	drink	humus	rain	sun
Celsius	dry	minerals	sand	tropical
clay	energy	moderate	shade	water
cold	enriched	night	snow	

TEMPERATURE	LIGHT	MOISTURE	SOIL	OXYGEN

Figure 4.10

Excluding in concept development involves learning what a concept is, as well as what it is not. Remember, the chair is not a stool, bench, or sofa, although all these words could be subsumed under the larger concept of something to sit on. Frequently, a group of four or five vocabulary words from the same unit can be organized in several ways, depending on the student's cognitive structure. Herber (1978) developed a process of selecting items which have several potential organizations. Figure 4.11 is an example of such an exercise. Here, the student must use his/her knowledge of the unit's content to relate three of four of the words in each list but to exclude one. Hence, they join the words under a higher level concept, but they exclude the one unlike word. For example, in group III, the excluded word is "oceans," which contain salt water. All the other choices represent fresh water habitats, the general concept which subsumes them all.

This type of exercise can also be varied by placing in each list words which have multiple organizations. Instead of having a single correct answer, as in the exercise above, several correct answers are possible. A

DISCRIMINATING

The Act of Excluding

Choose the one word in each group that does not relate to the others and should be excluded. Write it in the blank labeled "Exclude." In the blank labeled "General Concept" write the concept that describes the remaining words.

I. oxygen
    carbon dioxide
    temperature
    food
    sun

    1. Exclude _____

    2. General Concept _____

II. land
    forest
    air
    water

    1. Exclude _____

    2. General Concept _____

III. oceans
     ponds
     springs
     streams
     lakes

    1. Exclude _____

    2. General Concept _____

IV. phytoplankton
    zooplankton
    protists
    rodents

    1. Exclude _____

    2. General Concept _____

Figure 4.11

further variation asks the student to look at a group of words and choose the word which subsumes the other four:

assessor
taxation (subsumes the others)
customs
import
property

Choosing to exclude words from lists, as with other concept operations, can range from simple, low-cognitive level exercises to high-level exercises requiring both analysis and synthesis.

Selecting in concept learning includes, again, making choices and explaining why. Selecting suggests that we start with the whole and identify its parts, a form of analysis. One common way of practicing the selection process in vocabulary development is the use of synonym exercises. Figure 4.12 is based again on "The Biosphere and Its Habitats." In this instance, as before, the emphasis is not on finding the one right answer but in choosing several potentially correct answers and judging their worth.

In the first example, both "plentiful" and "great" are potentially correct, as are "stable" and "permanent" in the third example. The student's ear for language and his/her sense of the fine differences in meaning will be used in explaining why each is possible and which is better.

SYNONYM PRACTICE
___

The Act of Selecting

Directions: Circle the words under each sentence that could be used in place of the underlined word. Be ready to explain why each is appropriate.

1. Materials and energy needed for life are *abundant* here.
   scarce   great
   plentiful   negligible
   useful   useless

2. The desert rat *adapts* to these high temperatures by searching for food at night.
   appeals   changes
   adjusts   applies
   adopts   attends

3. These habitats are not always *constant*.
   there   stable
   pleasant   dormant
   temporary   permanent

___

Figure 4.12

Implying resides in the if-then or cause/effect relationship. The most common form of vocabulary exercise using this higher cognitive level process is the *analogy*. Analogies ask students to identify the relationship between two words, for example, "in" and "out," and then to construct such a relationship between another word and an unknown fourth word, for example, "up" and ⸻?⸻. This process requires the use of all three processes (joining, excluding, and selecting). For this reason, Gagne (1965) calls this the rule-making process and places it at a higher level than the other three. Henry's organization is based on Piaget's plan (1957). Both agree that the if-then, hypothesis-making process requires the ability to use the other three and must occur later in the learning process.

Analogies can come in many forms. The student can be given a choice of answers or s/he can be asked to recall the answer from memory. In the analogy above, in:out::up:⸻?⸻, the student is asked to recall the answer. Figure 4.13 shows some examples of analogies from the Habitat unit which require recognition rather than recall.

ANALOGY EXERCISE

The Act of Implying

Underline the word in each grouping which completes the analogy.

1. Niche: habitat as house:
   country
   cave
   neighborhood
   mansion

2. Extreme: moderate as high:
   medium
   level
   top
   below

3. Plankton: protist as reptile:
   snake
   amphibian
   mammal
   frog

4. Sewage: water as smoke:
   food
   breathing
   pollution
   air

5. Ecosystem: forest as government:
   organization
   democracy
   politics
   legislature

Figure 4.13

Analogies can be based on a number of relationships—synonyms, antonyms, part-whole, and others. Students need practice in working with the implication process, such as different forms of analogies, so that the thinking process and the format become familiar to them.

A CONCEPT-ORIENTED VOCABULARY EXERCISE

It is very important for my students to recognize the relationships between the sets of Real Numbers. The term "number" suddenly becomes vague. They need to be specific in their explanations and definitions. This assignment allows them to visualize the structure of the set. In class we would construct the tree diagram starting with Real Numbers. Important to any discussion of sets is the language involved:

Intersection   ∩
Union   ∪
Empty Set   Ø

Exercise

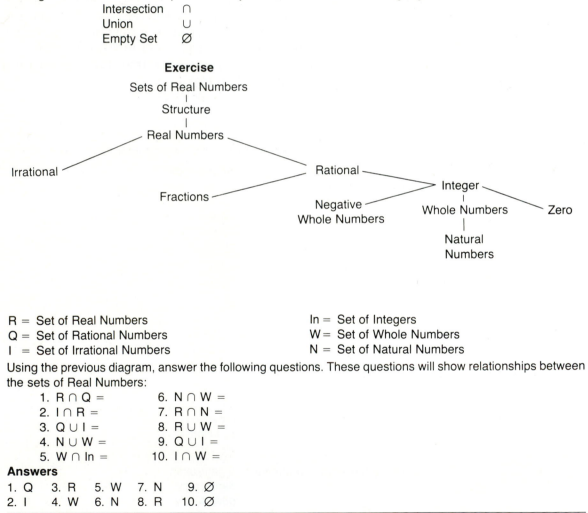

R = Set of Real Numbers   In = Set of Integers
Q = Set of Rational Numbers   W = Set of Whole Numbers
I = Set of Irrational Numbers   N = Set of Natural Numbers

Using the previous diagram, answer the following questions. These questions will show relationships between the sets of Real Numbers:

1. R ∩ Q =   6. N ∩ W =
2. I ∩ R =   7. R ∩ N =
3. Q ∪ I =   8. R ∪ W =
4. N ∪ W =   9. Q ∪ I =
5. W ∩ In =   10. I ∩ W =

Answers

1. Q   3. R   5. W   7. N   9. Ø
2. I   4. W   6. N   8. R   10. Ø

Figure 4.14

Prepared by Nancy C. Musselman, Holidaysburg, Pa., Area Junior High School. Reprinted by permission.

Let's turn from science to mathematics. A general math teacher (grades seven and eight) developed some concept-oriented vocabulary exercises for use with her students. Figure 4.14 includes her explanation and one of the exercises. This teacher introduces the topic of sets with the structured overview and exercise. She summarized the year's work with the vocabulary relationships exercise, given in Figure 4.15, in which students connect the concept labels from different units during the year, aiming for synthesis of the material covered throughout the year.

The process of concept development is complex and deserves greater discussion than is possible here. Hafner (1977), Henry (1974), and Herber (1978) all give more detail on concept learning and reading. Books on learning theory and educational psychology, like Ausubel (1968) and Gagne (1965), provide the theoretical base. Consult these sources for an in-depth discussion of these topics.

VOCABULARY RELATIONSHIPS EXERCISE

Directions: If the two words of a pair mean the same or nearly the same, or are otherwise related, write "S" on the line between them. If they mean the opposite or nearly opposite, write "O" between them. If there is no relationship between the words, write "N."

1. approximation	_____	equal
2. add	_____	subtract
3. multiply	_____	divide
4. vertical	_____	horizontal
5. circle	_____	square
6. square	_____	multiply
7. minus	_____	subtract
8. scalene	_____	equilateral
9. right angles	_____	complementary angles
10. even numbers	_____	odd numbers
11. numerator	_____	denominator
12. obtuse	_____	acute
13. ratio	_____	quotient
14. rational	_____	irrational
15. composite	_____	prime
16. complementary angles	_____	supplementary angles

Answers

1. S	2. O	3. O	4. O	5. O	6. S	7. S
8. O	9. S	10. O	11. O	12. O	13. S	14. O
15. O	16. O					

Figure 4.15

Prepared by Nancy C. Musselman, Holidaysburg, Pa., Area Junior High School. Reprinted by permission.

Effective teachers need to use both word attack skills and concept development at different times during their teaching, depending on the students, topic, and objectives. Therefore, it is important to develop a large repertoire of specific teaching techniques which the teacher can call upon whenever necessary.

SUMMARY

This chapter describes two different ways of teaching vocabulary skills. First, vocabulary can be taught as word attack skills (skills in identifying unfamiliar words): identifying words by sight, use of context clues, use of structural analysis (roots, prefixes, suffixes, infixes), use of sound patterns, and use of outside references.

The second way of viewing vocabulary, and the most common in content teaching, is to teach vocabulary as a means of concept development. Concepts are formed through four processes: joining, excluding, selecting, and implying. Vocabulary study and practice based on these cognitive processes will help students learn how to develop concepts and add to their vocabularies. Effective teachers choose the vocabulary processes that fit the objectives they have established and develop appropriate teaching plans.

REFERENCES

Ausubel, D. (1968). *Educational psychology: A cognitive view*. New York: Holt, Rinehart & Winston.

Gagne, R. (1965). *The conditions of learning*. New York: Harcourt Brace Jovanovich.

Hafner, L. E. (1977). *Developmental reading in middle and secondary schools, foundations, strategies and skills for teaching*. New York: Macmillan Publishing Co.

Hanf, M. B. (1971, January). Mapping: A technique for translating reading into thinking. *Journal of Reading, 14,* 225–230.

Heimlich, J. E., & Pittleman, S. D. (1986). *Semantic mapping: Classroom applications*. Newark, DE: International Reading Association.

Henry, G. H. (1974). *Teaching reading as concept development: Emphasis on affective thinking*. Newark, DE: International Reading Association.

Herber, H. L. (1978). *Teaching reading in content areas* (2nd ed.). Englewood Cliffs, NJ: Prentice-Hall, Inc.

Johnson, D. D., Toms-Bronowski, S., & Pittleman, S. D. (1981, November). *An investigation of the trends in vocabulary research and the effects of prior knowledge on instructional strategies for vocabulary acquisition*. Madison, WI: Center for Education Research, University of Wisconsin.

Kane, R. B., Byrne, M. A., & Hater, M. A. (1974). *Helping children read mathematics*. New York: American Book Co.

McNeil, J. D. (1987). *Reading comprehension: New directions for classroom practice* (2nd ed.). Glenview, IL: Scott, Foresman & Co.

Piaget, J. (1957). *Logic and psychology*. New York: Basic Books. Translated by W. Mays and F. Whitehead.

Random House college dictionary. (1974). Springfield, MA: G. C. Merriam.

Special issue on vocabulary. (1986, April). *Journal of Reading, 29*.

Webster's seventh new collegiate dictionary. (1974). Springfield, MA: G. C. Merriam.

Webster, V. Fichter, G. C., Coble, C. R., & Rice, D. R. (1980). *Prentice-Hall Life Science*. Englewood Cliffs, N. J.: Prentice-Hall, Inc.

Winkley, C. (1966, December). Which accent generalizations are worth teaching?. *The Reading Teacher, 20*, 224.

SUGGESTIONS FOR FURTHER READING

Alvermann, D. E., Moore, D. W., & Conley, M. W. (Eds.). (1987). *Research within reach: Secondary school reading* (pp. 64–79). Newark, DE: International Reading Association.

Hafner, L. E. (1977). *Developmental reading in middle and secondary schools, foundations, strategies, and skills for teaching*. New York: Macmillan Publishing Co.

Henry, G. H. (1974). *Teaching reading as concept development: Emphasis on affective thinking*. Newark, DE: International Reading Association.

Herber, H. L. (1978). *Teaching reading in content areas* (2nd ed.). Englewood Cliffs, NJ: Prentice-Hall, Inc.

Heimlich, J. E., & Pittleman, S. D. (1986). *Semantic mapping: Classroom applications*. Newark, DE: International Reading Association.

Jongsma, E. (1980). *Cloze instruction research: A second look*. Newark, DE: International Reading Association.

Lee, J. W. (1978, December). Increasing comprehension through use of context clue categories. *Journal of Reading, 22*, 259–265.

CHAPTER FIVE

Teaching Study Skills to Enhance Comprehension

SCENARIO

Middlewood Middle and Secondary School is back in session after a welcome and restful break for the Thanksgiving holiday. Meet a new teacher on the staff, Janet Parrish, who teaches in the Business Education department. Don MacArthur has been assigned to Janet as her mentor during her first year at Middlewood. We join them as they meet after school one afternoon.

"How's it going, Janet? Did you get to see your folks over break?" asked Don as Janet arrived in the conference room where they met each Tuesday afternoon.

"Things are going pretty well right now, thanks. And yes, I did see my folks. What about you? Did you get away at all?" asked Janet.

"Not far, but I got out to our cabin in the mountains and got in a full day of hunting, so I'm refreshed and ready for continued combat!" replied Don. "Now, what can I help you with this week?"

"Well, Don, I do need some advice, if you've got a few minutes."

"Sure do. What's up?" asked Don. He was enjoying his role as mentor for two of the new teachers on the staff. "Pour some of that coffee and pull up a chair. You wouldn't by any chance be wondering about the inservice notice we got in our mailboxes this morning, would you?"

"You've got it," replied Janet, sounding worried. "Have I missed something? I didn't even know we had curriculum review committees, and now I see I'm part of one. What in the world does the study skills review group do? I'm really nervous about spending half of our next inservice day with a committee I know nothing about."

"Not to worry, Janet," said Don. "Every new teacher gets assigned to one of our curriculum committees, usually to replace someone who has retired or been reassigned elsewhere. You'll find the others on your committee pretty helpful; they've each been new at one time. Marge is now serving on the study skills committee and I'm sure she'll be glad to brief you before next week's session. I served with that group when it began two years ago, so I can give you some background."

"Great, Don," sighed Janet with obvious relief. "Tell me what I need to know to get my feet wet."

"Two years ago we had quite a few faculty meetings that became pretty heated whenever anyone touched on the subject of teaching such things as outlining, notetaking, map and chart reading, skimming, and finding the main idea. Everyone thought someone *else* should teach all these things . . . and preferably *before* the students got to their classes! To make a long story short, the decision was made to form a separate committee to define what study skills are and to determine when each should be taught and by whom."

"Now that makes sense, Don," responded Janet. "I've been struggling to decide whether or not to teach notetaking and outlining before assigning a short investigative report to my advanced class. It sure would help to know whether they've had any of this before and if so, how it was taught, so I don't present something that might confuse my students. Is there anything in writing I could look at now, before that inservice meeting?"

"Yes, I'd suggest you ask Marge. Last year the committee put together a continuum that outlined what skills we all need to be aware of and at what grade level each one is to be introduced, reinforced, and so on. That should be helpful to you," replied Don.

Janet looked very much relieved as she gathered her things to go home. "Thanks, Don. As usual, you've been a big help. What did new teachers ever do before this mentor idea came into being?"

OVERVIEW

The need for students to learn study skills seems greater than ever before. No longer is it enough to learn dates and facts about a content area. With knowledge about our world increasing every day, we can learn and remember only a few important facts. We need to learn the skills that make retrieval of dates and facts possible. Study skills are the "learning how to learn" skills which are crucial to future learning both in school and throughout life. Study skills can make the difference between reading with comprehension and missing the meaning altogether in content area reading assignments.

Today's modern public libraries no longer rely on a card catalog, for example. To locate a particular book, we now can quickly consult a microfiche reader to find out the call numbers of the book. When we want to research a particular topic, we can use a computer search to locate information related to the topic. The ERIC (Educational Resources Information Center) system, for example, has indexed published and nonpublished articles, paper presentations, symposia, and reports by descriptors which enable us to call up these sources, providing bibliographic information as well as abstracts.

With such modern technology available to students, instruction in the skills of locating and using information from all sources becomes increasingly important. Unfortunately, in many schools, content area instruction has continued to emphasize memorization of facts which are quickly forgotten after the final exam.

Some evidence (Askov, Kamm, & Klumb, 1977) exists that teachers themselves have not mastered some of the study skills. Furthermore, students who have not been taught study skills do not seem to pick them up on their own during their elementary and secondary school careers (Askov et al., 1980). If teachers are not familiar with the skills, they either do not teach them or else do a poor job teaching them (Kamm, White, & Morrison, 1977).

Because study skills include such varied activities as reading maps and graphs, locating information in a library, and adjusting reading rate to the reading purpose and to the difficulty of the material, it is difficult to cover such an important area in depth. In addition to reading this chapter, which focuses upon the teaching of some study skills, you may wish to consult and work through the activities presented in the book *Study Skills in the Content Areas* (Askov & Kamm, 1982). These activities will ensure that you master study skills yourself. Meanwhile, as you read this chapter, you should find that the information about comprehension in Chapter 3 will begin to make even more sense as we move from the theories behind reading comprehension to the practical application of those theories in the classroom.

GOALS FOR TEACHING STUDY SKILLS

The ultimate goal of study skills instruction is to foster independent learning. Instruction and guided application should move students from dependence to independence not only in applying the appropriate study skills but also in knowing when and why particular study skills are needed. A teacher can accomplish this task by gradually phasing out the use of cues and prompts as students learn to apply particular skills on their own.

In addition to independence in learning and reading tasks, study skills enable students to learn more efficiently. The teacher acts as a model to help students see how to use study skills in learning and how they enable the teacher to gain information more quickly and effectively. Students will soon realize the long-term benefits of applying study skills, even though it may take more time to do their assignments.

Another goal in teaching study skills is to help students learn content materials. Since these are the enabling or "learning how to learn" skills, they ought to be applied to meaningful materials, such as a content unit of instruction or a textbook assignment. If study skills are taught separately from content materials, as in a learning center or learning packet, the teacher should provide guidance in applying these skills to content reading assignments.

Study skills instruction should also foster metacognitive knowledge, making students aware of their own learning processes. They need to learn which study skills are most appropriate for a given purpose with a given set of materials. They need to be able to recognize when a specific strategy will not work due to poor text organization or poorly written headings. They need to know when to write a summary—when the content is important enough to warrant the amount of time it takes. They furthermore need to learn to monitor their own reading processes so that they are aware of when their application of study skills is working and when it is not. They need to know when and how to switch strategies for optimal learning. While these seem to be ambitious goals, they should serve to guide instruction throughout elementary and secondary schools.

STUDY SKILLS AND METACOGNITION

Recent reading research has focused on the fact that in order for students to gain independence in learning, they must first develop a metacognitive awareness of what they read. (For a review of metacognition, see Chapter 3.) To get the most out of what they read, students must be able to judge which study skills will be most appropriate to a particular reading.

To this end, Paris (1986) set forth the Informed Strategies for Learning, a planned sequence of reading strategies that facilitate comprehension. The purpose of this plan is to give the student information about reading tasks, goals, and tactics, such as study skills, in interesting and usable ways. This method assumes that strategies can be taught directly to students. The teacher's job is that of a coach, providing knowledge of the reading task, motivation to apply the strategies that are taught, and feedback on the students' uses of the strategies.

This approach is different from traditional study skills instruction in that the teacher guides the students through specific reading tasks. In the past we have taught study skills, often as an isolated unit of study, and hoped that students would use them when appropriate. With the Informed Strategies for Learning approach, the teacher shows the students how to apply the study skills to the reading task. Paris emphasizes *procedural knowledge*—knowledge of how to perform the reading tasks which can be taught directly and applied through guided practice—and *conditional knowledge*—knowing when and why strategies should be applied. The teacher helps the students verbalize these types of knowledge to encourage thinking aloud about strategies for reading.

Paris's concept of "cognitive coaching" implies a different relationship between teacher and students. In this relationship, the objectives for learning (including reading a particular assignment) are shared, and learning becomes a joint responsibility. If a breakdown occurs in the learning process, both are to blame. The students often work together during guided practice. Group discussion follows, allowing teacher and student to talk about how and why particular strategies and study skills were applied.

This approach to study skills instruction teaches students not only how to organize and read content material but also when and why particular study skills should be applied. Students learn to recognize, for example, that when a reading provides main ideas with supporting details, outlining becomes an appropriate study tool. Developing this metacognitive awareness in students is important in fostering independence in learning.

INSTRUCTION IN STUDY SKILLS

Ideally, teachers of a given content area, such as social studies or science at the elementary, junior, and senior high school levels, should work together to plan study skills throughout the curriculum. They can use a list of skills found in most school district curriculum guides as a starting point to determine what skills are important in a given content area. As Don explained to Janet in our opening scenario, this is precisely what the study skills curriculum committee at Middlewood faced as its initial task.

After the crucial skills are identified, the next step is to determine appropriate grade levels for initial teaching and review for each of the selected skills. After a skill has been taught, teachers and students will need to review it. Teachers cannot assume that students will automatically apply a skill at a new level or in a new content area. They need to teach for transfer after initial instruction in the skill.

Teachers of a given content area can create a flexible scope and sequence chart of study skills showing what skills will be taught and reviewed at each grade level. They cannot rely on a textbook series to make these important decisions. Some textbooks do not provide adequate instruction in study skills but expect students to apply them in content study.

Often the reading specialist can assist in these efforts. Marge, for example, worked with the study skills curriculum review committee at Middlewood in developing a scope and sequence chart for study skills. She coordinated her reading instruction with her students' elementary teachers to determine what skills were being taught. Janet Parrish, new to the committee, will likely be asked to help develop her own scope and sequence chart as a professional growth experience for a beginning teacher. Janet will find that study skills exercises, to be most effective, should be integrated into her Business Education curriculum. A skill can be taught as it is needed in the content, or it can be taught ahead of time with a brief review at the time of application of the skill.

Consider the difference between maps and globes, for example. Don might challenge one of his social studies students to peel the skin of an orange without tearing it. If he flattens the skin, as the "skin" of the globe is flattened in making a map, he will inevitably tear the skin near the stems. Similarly, when reality on a globe is presented in the flattened form of a map, the areas at the poles are distorted. This point may be vividly demonstrated to students by having them compare the size of Greenland on a globe and map. Due to distortion at the poles, Greenland appears much larger on a map than on the truer representation of the globe. Study skills thus become meaningful to students as they use them in content subjects. Reading graphic materials, such as maps, tables, and diagrams, poses a particular problem since students will probably ignore such materials unless particularly directed to them and taught how to read them.

While research has tried to establish which study techniques, such as outlining, notetaking, and underlining, seem to produce the best learning, it is now recognized that the particular technique applied is not as

These two fifth-grade students are trying to find out whether an orange peel can be flattened without tearing it, just as Don asks his students to do. This exercise helps demonstrate how the "skin" of a globe and a flat map are related and why some areas on a map may be distorted.

important as the "depth of processing" required (Anderson & Armbruster, 1982). In other words, students tend to comprehend and retain what they have said in their own words through notetaking because paraphrasing requires a greater depth of processing, a greater involvement with the text, than, say, underlining. Underlining is most effective with material in which the interrelation among ideas is crucial. For example, material such as dates and facts, which are to be learned only at a literal level, can be underlined to highlight the points to be remembered. Just as important as teaching these study techniques to students is teaching them flexibility. As a teacher you must guide them in analyzing the demands of the reading task to decide which study strategy is most appropriate.

Let's look closely at Marge's English class. She has assigned independent research projects to her tenth-grade class. One of her students, Karen, is gathering information in preparation for constructing a model of the Elizabethan stage. Since at this point Karen is interested only in literal comprehension of facts, she is making a list of the important characteristics of the early stages described in the material. It would be a waste of Karen's time, and less accurate with this material, to require that she state everything in her own words. On the other hand, when Karen must write an interpretation of a scene from a Shakespearean play, Marge will expect Karen to restate the ideas in the play. A verbatim transcription would clearly be inappropriate.[1]

One final caution is in order. Frequently teachers ask students to apply study techniques, such as outlining and notetaking, without providing instruction in these skills. If the teacher also does not check the product of such efforts, s/he may not see a student's difficulties in applying the study techniques. For example, John Roberts asked one of his students to take notes from his science textbook, which was appropriate for his reading level. The student said that, of course, he knew how to take notes. When pressed for specifics, he blurted out, "What is notetaking anyway? Don't I just copy what the book says?" The resulting notes would likely contain unimportant as well as important information mixed together in a verbatim transcription of the textbook.

STUDY GUIDES TO TEACH STUDY SKILLS

Janet is sure to discover that one of the topics included on the agenda for the study skills review committee is study guides. Study guides provide

---

[1]Throughout this text we emphasize the importance of helping students see the value of writing as part of the comprehension process. In Chapter 6 you will read in detail a description of one way students can be encouraged to put into their own words the information they have read, heard, or seen in a content area class.

one structured approach to teaching study skills to enhance comprehension while also teaching content subject information.

The first step in developing study guides is to examine your objectives for instruction. What do you want your students to learn about the content subject in a particular reading assignment? What study skill(s) instruction would enhance comprehension of the text?

Next, be sure to consider the levels of thinking that you want to promote by the kinds of questions you ask. If the objective in reading a selection is to learn information about a subject, then literal-level reading comprehension is appropriate. Questions about facts and clearly stated main ideas encourage literal comprehension. If you want students to be able to make inferences beyond what is stated, then study guide questions should encourage inferential thinking by probing beyond what is specifically stated in the text. If you want students to be able to make critical or evaluative judgments—for example, comparing two accounts of the same event in history—then create some questions to promote critical thinking.

Teachers should try to include all levels of questioning in study guides if their objectives and evaluation include these levels of thinking. Remember that in Chapter 3 we discussed two such taxonomies, Barrett's *Taxonomy of Reading Comprehension* (1972), based on Bloom's *Taxonomy of Educational Objectives* (1956), and Herber's (1978) three-level model, which can serve as models for creating good study guides. You should also review Chapter 3 for our discussion of question placement before you read further to see how study guides might be constructed for readers at varying skill levels.

After creating a study guide, check it against your objectives for reading. Also check the guide against the evaluation to be used when study of the topic is complete. You should be able to see a clear correspondence between objectives, study guide, and evaluation. For example, if the objectives emphasize understanding of the main ideas, then the study guide and evaluation should similarly stress the main ideas of the material. Let's look at some sample study guides.

A Guide for Underachieving Readers

Our first sample study guide is intended for poor readers who are unable to read a textbook without help. The study guide in fact tells them what to read and what not to read. Most content area textbooks contain descriptive details that embellish the main ideas. Poor readers usually get lost in the details, "unable to see the forest for the trees." This type of guide enables students to read a textbook that is actually at their frustration level. Figure 5.1 gives a sample from a study guide that directs poor readers in what they should look for while they are reading an assigned selection. It also teaches the study skill of identifying the stated main ideas in paragraphs.

SAMPLE STUDY GUIDE EXERCISE FOR UNDERACHIEVING READERS

1. Read the last paragraph. This summarizes the selection.
2. Read paragraph 1. Write the main idea: _____

_____

3. Skip paragraph 2.
4. Read the first sentence of paragraph 3. How does this help you understand the main idea in the first paragraph? _____

_____

Figure 5.1

A Category Guide

Another type of study guide which is effective with all readers requires them to organize information by filling in a chart. This type of guide is particularly useful for students who do not actively read for meaning and do not organize information. The guide forces them to think about the material, thus enhancing their overall comprehension.

First the students read the material which contains descriptive details. Upon completion of the reading selection, they fill in a chart requiring categorization of information. Because they have to arrange the material into categories, they are more likely to remember the content. Figure 5.2 shows an example of a guide intended to accompany a ninth-grade science textbook (see page 106).

The textbook material describes the process of identifying trees by their leaves. John Roberts, our Middlewood science teacher, has collected specimens for his students to identify using the characteristics described in the text. Recording important details in the correct categories helps the students remember them. This type of guide is also useful if students are reading a variety of materials on the same topics. They know what types of information they must seek from either assigned materials or library research. Placing the information in categories forces students to organize reading material.

To avoid tedium, teachers should use a variety of study guides. If they use the same type of guide repeatedly, students tend either to ignore it or to copy the answer from another student simply to get it finished. A bit of humor throughout helps lighten the task. Since you know your students better than a textbook publisher, you can tailor your guides to your students in ways that questions at the end of a chapter cannot. We advise looking at textbook questions and exercises carefully. In our experience, often these questions require either rote recall or such high-level inferential/creative thinking that even the teacher is unsure of the answer! You

CATEGORY GUIDE

Leaves	Compound/ Simple	Pinnate/ Palmate/ Whorled	Opposite/ Alternate	Scientific Name
Specimen 1:				
Specimen 2:				
Specimen 3:				

Figure 5.2

can incorporate textbook questions that do seem valuable into a study guide that includes other items of your own devising.

An Open-Ended Guide

An open-ended guide is particularly useful if students are using a variety of reference sources as part of study skills instruction while engaged in investigating a common topic. The guide can focus on any study skill or set of skills. Smith (1987) recommends that open-ended questions be used rather than fill-in-the-blank answers. These questions require students to think about the material; the students cannot simply skim to find the correct answer to fill in the blank. Remember that having to write out answers that integrate the use of writing into content area instruction should enhance reading comprehension.

Smith reported that positive effects were noted in post-reading oral and written discussions with more spontaneity, participation, and longer discussions and papers when the students used open-ended rather than traditional study guides. Open-ended guides encourage responses that cannot be judged as correct or incorrect; they encourage the expression of personal feelings and solicit evaluation. Note that metacognitive responses are encouraged as students reflect upon the process of reading as they read. Figure 5.3 is an example (Smith, 1987) of this guide.

Additional study guide questions could pertain specifically to the use of study skills. For example, Janet Parrish might want to use this format with her business education students as they read an assigned chapter in their textbook. She could add the following questions pertaining to a bar graph showing changes in types of industries throughout the twentieth century: Write a short paragraph summarizing changes in types of indus-

A STUDY GUIDE FOR CONTENT AREA READING ASSIGNMENTS

1. Suggest a different title for the section you have just read. Try to capture the essence of the selection in your title, but keep it short.
2. Two key ideas or concepts in this section are:
   A. _____
   B. _____
3. Three details or facts you would like to remember from this selection are:
   A. _____
   B. _____
   C. _____
4. Did you find anything especially interesting or surprising in this selection?
5. What word or words from this selection do you think the author chose rather carefully?
6. Indicate any words, sentences, or paragraphs in the selection you would like to discuss in class or have explained:
   Page: _____ Line: _____
7. If the author of this selection were available to you, what questions would you ask or what comments would you make to him or her?
8. What, if any, mental images did you form while you were reading this selection?
9. Rate this selection by marking an X on the line at the point that indicates your evaluation.

	Very		Not Very
Interesting:			
Informative:			
Easy to Read:			

Figure 5.3

"Study Guide" from "Study Guide for Extending Students' Reading of Social Studies Material" by Richard J. Smith, *The Social Studies*, March/April, 1987, p. 86. Reprinted by permission of the author.

tries as shown in the bar graph. Given the trends shown, what do you project for the revolution of the twentieth century?

INDEPENDENT STUDY TECHNIQUES

One set of skills frequently included among lists of study skills is instruction in independent study techniques. While study guides are an excellent means of ensuring comprehension of a reading assignment, students need to learn how to study material independently. The teacher cannot always provide guidance for reading that must be done in a content area. Students may read different materials, for example, in preparing independent reports or projects. The teacher cannot possibly anticipate all reading needs with a study guide. Besides, our ultimate goal is for students to become independent learners. Study guides, if they are used, should gradually wean students from direct teacher guidance to greater independence in reading. This goal is for students to read content materials independently with good comprehension. Instruction in the use of independent study techniques can help them accomplish that goal.

The earliest and probably most widely known technique for independent study is *SQ3R* (Robinson, 1961). Others, such as *PQRST* (Spache, 1963), are variations on the original SQ3R. *REAP* (Eanet & Manzo, 1976), on the other hand, uses writing as a means to enhance reading comprehension as the students write a retelling of the selection which they then condense into a summary. *ConStruct* (Vaughn, 1982; 1984) employs multiple (three) readings for different purposes; the outcome is the construction of a graphic overview during and following each reading. Vaughan and Estes (1986) describe a variety of study techniques to be used before, during, and after reading.

All these techniques teach students the process of independent study which can be used on a short selection or a whole book. The gist of SQ3R is:

S—Survey: Quickly read through the major headings as well as the introductory and summary paragraphs to get an overview of the selection. In a book, a "survey" involves reading the Table of Contents and prefatory material that explains the intent and audience of the book. In this step the material may be deemed acceptable or rejected as inappropriate for the reader's intended purpose. This survey process is essentially the same as skimming.

Q—Question: Based on the survey, the reader formulates questions that s/he expects will be answered in the reading material. Questions may be created by converting headings or chapter titles into a question format. Initially, questions should be written down with space for answers. As students become sophisticated in applying independent study techniques, the question phase becomes internalized, with no need to put the questions in writing.

R—Read: Now the student is able to read purposefully because of the questions set forth. It is easier to grasp the main ideas and see the relative importance of supporting details.

R—Recite: The student now answers the questions that were set down in the second step. Answering the questions in writing provides a permanent record of notes. Other important details are also jotted down under the questions. If the questions have identified the main ideas of a selection, then in essence answering them becomes similar to the process of outlining. These notes should be written in the student's own words to ensure that they are meaningful.

R—Review: At a later point the student should review his/her notes to recall the main ideas and important details. Because the student has gone through the process of actively reading the material—by formulating and answering questions—the student's notes should be meaningful. In fact, rereading notes should be more meaningful than rereading the material itself.

Teaching students to use independent study techniques fits the view of the reading process presented in Chapters 1 and 2. The preparation and background that a reader brings to the reading material is considered crucial in determining how much s/he will comprehend. With the use of the Directed Reading Activity (see Chapter 11) and study guides, the teacher guides students through the material and helps them identify important points. Through the use of independent study techniques such as SQ3R, the reader guides him/herself through the task of reading. By anticipating what will be said, the reader becomes actively involved in the reading task. The reader who comprehends is not passively processing what the writer has set forth, but s/he is actively engaged in the problem-solving task of trying to answer anticipated questions.

Students usually do not readily accept the extra work involved in using independent study techniques. They prefer to read and reread material passively rather than actively trying to anticipate what the author is saying. Because this "lazy" approach is somewhat understandable, the teacher must require students to formulate and answer questions. These must be checked, as one would check a study guide, until the independent study process becomes truly independent. When students realize how much learning can be enhanced through independent study techniques, their attitudes will change and the process will become almost automatic. Effective independent study habits may indeed be the most important learning that students can take away from content area study.

Anderson and Armbruster (1982) suggest caution in using SQ3R and other independent study techniques. Sometimes a student's questions tend to be trivial if the textbook headings do not adequately state the main ideas of the sections. For example, if a heading in a social studies textbook were labelled "The Louisiana Purchase," a student might convert that heading to "What was the Louisiana Purchase?" While an answer which contains the date and extent of territory purchased for a given amount of money might be appropriate in some instances, the important point may actually be the impact that the Louisiana Purchase had on the eventual development of the United States. Therefore, students should be aware that a heading may not always form the best question if the material presented goes beyond the scope suggested by the heading.

Because independent study techniques are so important, they should be taught and reinforced by all teachers at all levels. This is the rationale behind creating an active study skills review committee at Middlewood. Janet will probably find that the staff has already made a commitment to seeing that students receive good instruction in using various study skills in all curriculum areas throughout the grades. The goals are to enhance learning in the content areas and to encourage positive attitudes toward applying the study strategies when working independently.

Janet works on outlining with her business class as part of Middlewood's study skills program. She sees the value of helping these students become independent learners.

SUMMARY

By teaching study skills teachers are giving students the means to continue learning after their formal schooling has been completed. The goals of instruction in study skills are twofold: 1) the students will learn the skills that will help them better understand the content areas being studied, and 2) they will develop a positive attitude toward applying those skills. The first goal is obviously important to content area teachers. The second goal is equally important in teaching students to use library resources and read graphic materials independently instead of ignoring them or relying on others.

Teachers can teach study skills through the use of study guides to show students what is important in content reading material. Various types of study guides help students comprehend content area textbooks. Your choice of a study guide depends upon the organization of the text and your purpose for the reader. While study guides enable you to provide direct guidance, students also need to learn how to learn independently. Study skills are taught as part of the content area studies to help students arrive at independent learning. Techniques for independent study help students apply study skills in their own reading outside class. The goal is to teach the lifelong skills that enable students to continue learning in later school years and adulthood.

REFERENCES

Anderson, T. H., & Armbruster, B. (1982). Reader and text-studying strategies. In W. Otto & S. White (Eds.), *Reading expository material* (pp. 219–239). New York: Academic Press, Inc.

Askov, E. N., & Kamm, K. (1982). *Study skills in the content areas*. Boston: Allyn & Bacon, Inc.

Askov, E. N., Kamm, K., & Klumb, R. (1977, February). Study skill mastery among elementary school teachers. *The Reading Teacher, 30,* 485–488.

Askov, E. N. et al. (1980). Study skills mastery: Comparisons between teachers and students on selected skills. In M. L. Kamil (Ed.), *Perspectives in reading research and instructions, twenty-ninth yearbook of the National Reading Conference* (pp. 207–212). Washington, D. C.: The National Reading Conference.

Barrett, T. C. (1972). Taxonomy of reading comprehension. *Reading 360 Monograph*. Lexington, MA: Ginn Press.

Bloom, B. S. (Ed.). (1956). *Taxonomy of educational objectives, handbook I: Cognitive domain*. New York: David McKay.

Eanet, M., & Manzo, A. V. (1976). REAP: A strategy for improving reading/writing/study skills. *Journal of Reading, 19,* 647–652.

Herber, H. L. (1978). *Teaching reading in content areas*. (2nd ed.). Englewood Cliffs, NJ: Prentice-Hall, Inc.

Kamm, K., White, S, & Morrison, B. (1977). A report of procedures used in the implementation of an objective-based reading program in 15 schools. *Working Paper 246*. Madison, WI: The Wisconsin Research and Development Center for Cognitive Learning.

Paris, S. G. (1986). Teaching children to guide their reading and learning. In T. Raphael (Ed.), *Contexts of school-based literacy* (pp. 115–130). New York: Random House, Inc.

Robinson, R. P. (1961). *Effective study*. (Rev. ed.). New York: Harper & Row, Publishers, Inc.

Smith, R. J. (1987). A study guide for extending students' reading of social studies material. *The Social Studies, 78* (2), 85–87.

Spache, G. (1963). *Toward better reading*. Champaign, IL: Garrard.

Vaughn, J. L. (1982). Use the construct procedure to foster active reading and learning. *Journal of Reading, 25,* 412–422.

Vaughn, J. L. (1984). Concept structuring: The technique and empirical evidence. In S. D. Holley & D. F. Dansereau (Eds.), *Spatial learning strategies* (pp. 127–147). New York: Academic Press, Inc.

Vaughn, J. L., & Estes, T. H. (1986). *Reading and reasoning beyond the primary grades.* Boston: Allyn & Bacon, Inc.

SUGGESTIONS FOR FURTHER READING

Askov, E. N., & Kamm, K. (1982). *Study skills in the content areas.* Boston: Allyn & Bacon, Inc.

Early, M., & Sawyer, D. J. (1984). *Reading to learn in grades five to twelve.* New York: Harcourt Brace Jovanovich.

Estes, T. H., & Vaughn, J. L. (1985). *Reading and learning in the content classroom: Diagnostic and instructional settings.* (2nd ed.). Boston: Allyn & Bacon, Inc.

Graham, K. G., & Robinson, H. A. (1984). *Study skills handbook: A guide for all teachers.* Newark, DE: International Reading Association.

Herber, H. L. (1978). *Teaching reading in content areas.* (2nd ed.). Englewood Cliffs, NJ: Prentice-Hall, Inc.

Paris, S. G. (1986). Teaching children to guide their reading and learning. In T. Raphael (Ed.), *Contexts of school-based literacy* (pp. 115–130). New York: Random House, Inc.

Vacca, R. T., & Vacca, J. L. (1986). *Content area reading.* (2nd ed.). Boston: Little, Brown & Co.

Vaughn, J. L., & Estes, T. H. (1986). *Reading and reasoning beyond the primary grades.* Boston: Allyn & Bacon, Inc.

CHAPTER SIX

A Practical Approach to Teaching Content Area Writing

SCENARIO

This time we find Marge preparing for her monthly meeting with representatives from each content area. She is wondering about their reactions to her latest memo. She worked long and hard on the wording, aware of how critical it is not to create antagonism among teachers already somewhat overwhelmed by the demands of a crowded curriculum. Marge is certain, however, that the time is right to urge everyone on the staff to begin implementing some of her ideas about process writing.

"Hi, Don." Marge noted with relief that Don was the first to arrive. In fact, he was several minutes early and she was glad of the opportunity to speak with him first. "How's the writing going these days?"

"Really well, Marge," replied Don. "I confess that you've made me a believer. Focusing on all those preparation stages *before* papers get turned in has made a real difference in what my kids are writing. I'm still struggling to fit it all into my schedule and the peer conferencing idea needs a lot of refining, but I'm beginning to understand why all those "experts" keep telling us that writing can actually increase the amount and quality of learning that takes place."

"I hope you'll feel free to say some of that in today's meeting, Don," said Marge with a touch of concern in her voice. "I have a feeling I'll need all the support I can muster to convince the other staff representatives that writing needs to be included in every content area. And even if I can win over all you folks here, I know it will be tough for you to convince all of your fellow staff members."

"Well, here comes Bev and I'd guess you have your work cut out for you right there, Marge. She was eager to improve vocabulary instruction and really excited about some of those strategies you demonstrated for teaching comprehension skills, but I have a feeling she will not want to go beyond the administration requirement that we include essay exam questions. And I don't envy you at all when you try to get the vocational and business departments to teach writing. Good luck!"

OVERVIEW

The purpose of this chapter is to provide a practical model for a writing-across-the-curriculum program. Three key objectives are at the heart of this model. First, teachers using the model can focus on the *craft* of writing, helping students move through the stages real writers experience as they work. Second, students are given meaningful *purposes* for all writing activities, writing for real audiences other than the teacher as often as possible. Third, students are taught various *strategies* for generating and organizing ideas.

The suggested model clearly reflects various research findings in the area of writing instruction, particularly those emphasized in the 1984 National Assessment of Educational Progress report (NAEP, 1984). The model also addresses several factors that have often meant failure for schoolwide writing projects. Its effectiveness appears to rest on two critical factors, *teacher manageability* and *student success*. Teachers using this model are relieved of the time-consuming burden of constant paper correcting while students are relieved of the frustration of compositions returned with low grades and inadequate guidance for making their ensuing efforts any better.

GETTING STARTED IN CONTENT AREA WRITING

Our Middlewood teachers have come a long way since the beginning of the school year. They have gained valuable insights into the reading process, now clearly understanding that they have a responsibility to do more than assign textbook chapters to be read. They recognize the critical role of metacognition in learning and know that they must attend to the reading process in order that students learn how to learn. Comprehension activities in their classrooms are beginning to reflect the teaching of effective comprehension strategies, not just the traditional testing of comprehension. Teachers are giving increased attention to vocabulary, but these days teachers like John, Don, and Bev focus on concept development, not just definitions.

Finally, these teachers have made attempts to integrate the four language skills into the teaching of content. Each has tried to move away from reliance on the traditional lecturer role, instead including a wide variety of instructional activities in order to ensure that all students have access to key concepts through the visual, auditory, and sensory modes. Not surprisingly, Middlewood teachers continue to struggle with the idea of writing as an integral part of content area instruction. While writing across the curriculum is beginning to make sense to them, they wonder how they can possibly fit this additional activity into an already crowded curriculum. They further wonder, understandably, how they can manage writing instruction effectively, especially correcting papers.

A SUGGESTED FIVE-STAGE MODEL

One of the models that Marge has suggested that Middlewood teachers implement in their classrooms requires that class time be set aside often for an assigned writing activity conducted in a laboratory setting. This means that students do most if not all of their writing under the direct supervision of the teacher who is available to provide instruction, encouragement and feedback at each of the five stages of the writing process we described in Chapter 2. Thus, students are not *told* to write as in the traditional writing program model; they are *taught* to write within a carefully controlled, supervised instructional environment where "experimentation with language" is both nurtured and encouraged (Lee, 1985).

Students begin to recognize that any piece of writing begins with careful attention to the *prewriting* or preparation stage, just as any instructional reading activity demands careful preparation time in order to develop the necessary concepts and establish purposes for the reading.

Prewriting activities are followed by a period of *composing* similar to the uninterrupted sustained silent reading period often suggested for classroom reading activities (McCracken, 1971). During "quiet composing time," a student should concentrate on getting all of his/her prewriting ideas down on paper without pressure for perfection of form or mechanics. Because the writing activity occurs in the directed laboratory setting, the teacher is available during this time should the composing process break down for some reason.

Composing is followed by *conferencing* with a peer and/or the teacher in order to obtain some ideas for *revision* of the initial draft. Students listen attentively to one another's pieces, first offering words of encouragement and then moving to suggestions for improvements. Writers return to their desks with ideas to consider which may make their drafts stronger.

Once revisions are completed, students address the *editing* stage, again with encouragement to utilize peer and teacher assistance. The emphasis at this point moves from revision of content to the correction of mechanics with students working together to discover each other's errors in spelling, punctuation, and sentence construction.

Many but not all edited pieces are then readied for some sort of *publication*, perhaps for a grade, perhaps for sharing with students in another instructional group. When students come to realize that only selected pieces will go into the publishing stage, the emphasis on writing in the laboratory environment truly changes from the traditional product model to that of process. And because teachers do not feel compelled to grade every piece of writing, and because those select few writings that do need to be corrected have already been revised and edited considerably through peer conferencing, one of the major stumbling blocks to content area writing is largely eliminated.

Assigned Versus Self-Selected Topics

Because writing reports and answering essay questions based on assigned topics are the kinds of tasks students face more and more often as they move through the grades, we suggest that teachers introduce this type of expository writing during the middle grades, gradually increasing the number of such activities as students approach the junior and senior high school levels.

Assigned topic expository writings generally demand a precision and discipline not always necessary in the narrative or personal story form generally used by students when they self-select their writing topics in the early grades. For example, "order" in narrative writing is usually chronological and poses little problem for the writer who must only relate the story in the order in which it happened. An assigned expository writing assignment for one of the content areas, however, might well demand that the writer make decisions as to the most effective order in which to present ideas, which ideas to include and which to eliminate, how best to persuade the reader of the soundness of an idea, and what words to choose for making an opinion sound convincing.

Do not expect students who are *learning to write* through the exclusive use of self-selected topics to learn the precision and discipline that will be needed as they move into the *writing to learn* part of the content area curriculum. That would be a miracle. Self-selection of topics is important to the development of confidence and fluency and as such should be included in the writing program at all grade levels. However, it is equally important that students be introduced to and expected to engage in assigned topic writing activities that are closely related to the content areas. They will then develop the necessary skills for an increasingly complex content-laden curriculum. Figure 6.1 illustrates one way of ensuring that all through the grades students have the opportunity to develop skills in both types of writing.

Asking Writers the Right Questions

One of the most effective ways to implement an effective writing-across-the-curriculum program is for all content teachers to become proficient in constructing carefully worded questions based on key content concepts.

A SUGGESTED "BALANCE" BETWEEN SELF-SELECTED AND ASSIGNED TOPIC WRITING

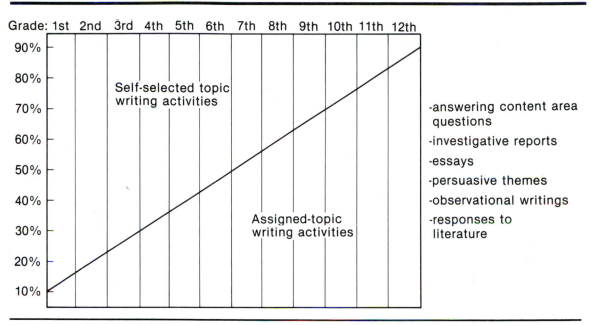

Grade: 1st 2nd 3rd 4th 5th 6th 7th 8th 9th 10th 11th 12th

Self-selected topic writing activities

Assigned-topic writing activities

-answering content area questions

-investigative reports

-essays

-persuasive themes

-observational writings

-responses to literature

Figure 6.1

Adapted from "Topic selection in writing: A precarious but practical balancing act" by Joyce W. Lee, *The Reading Teacher*, November 1987, p. 182. Reprinted with permission of Joyce W. Lee and the International Reading Association.

These questions must be worded so that students can "turn them around" to formulate clear opening statements for written essay-type responses.

Students at all grade levels can be taught a simple strategy for transforming questions into "good beginnings" (see Figure 6.2). Providing students with such a strategy generally serves to expedite that all-too-familiar classroom scenario of students wasting time and energy trying to figure out "how to begin." Students know that once the writing is under way, they can always reconsider their opening statements, revising them to catch the reader's interest and thus strengthening their writing.

Teachers in all subject areas can become skilled in constructing well-worded questions that are transformed easily into responses that demonstrate comprehension of key curriculum concepts. Then, using the five-stage process approach for teaching writing, each content area teacher can direct manageable and effective lessons that provide students with practice in assigned expository writing. In short, each content teacher assumes some responsibility for helping students make the critical transition from "learning to write" to "writing to learn."

Let's examine in some detail how one of our Middlewood teachers integrates writing instruction into a content area reading lesson. This should

THE SIX STEPS

STEP ONE: Read the question, consider possible answers, and make a
             shopping list of writing ideas.

STEP TWO: Cross out the question word(s), the question mark, and change *you*
             to *I* if necessary.

~~How were~~ the Spanish able to conquer the Aztecs and Incas?

STEP THREE: Find a possible starting word and circle it.

~~How were~~ (the) Spanish able to conquer the Aztecs and Incas~~?~~

STEP FOUR: Capitalize your starting word.

~~How were~~ (The) Spanish able to conquer the Aztecs and Incas~~?~~

STEP FIVE: Underline words in the question you want to use in your answer;
             add and/or change words.

~~How were~~ (The) Spanish *were* able to conquer the Aztecs and Incas~~?~~
because of an armor advantage

STEP SIX: Read your sentence to be sure it makes sense and is a good
             answer to the question.

*The Spanish were able to conquer the Aztecs and Incas
because of an armor advantage.*

Figure 6.2
Adapted from "What are the Six Magic Steps?" from *Writer's Lab,* 1985–86, edited by
Joyce W. Lee, p. 7. Reprinted by permission of State College Area School District.

provide you with some insights into the concept of process writing instruction as it applies to assigned topic writing, and, most importantly, with an
overview of how each stage of the five-stage process approach can be implemented in a content area writing activity.

The Prewriting Stage

Don MacArthur's sixth graders have been studying the Spanish conquest
of the Aztecs and Incas using their social studies text. Don has devoted
several days to directed reading instruction using the text chapter in a
variety of ways (see Chapters 10 and 11). Additionally his students have

viewed a filmstrip depicting several of the key concepts in the chapter. At this point Don determines that students are ready for an assigned expository writing activity designed to help them internalize some of the ideas in the unit. He is committed to the belief that their being able to "write it down" is the best indication that they have assimilated content concepts (Lee, 1985).

Don first devotes some preparation time to constructing a question for students to consider as the basis for clear opening statements. He decides to use the question, "How were the Spanish able to conquer the Aztecs and the Incas?" He then prepares a "sloppy copy" worksheet for students to use as the first part of the writing activity (see Figure 6.3).

Don then helps his students make several critical prewriting decisions. First, students must clearly establish an audience for the writing. Second, following a classroom brainstorming session, each student generates a

SLOPPY COPY WORKSHEET
_____

                                    Writer: _____

Audience: _____

Purpose: _____

Shopping List of Writing Ideas:

Possible Opening Statements:

_____

Figure 6.3

"shopping list" of possible writing ideas. Third, each develops several possible effective opening statements for the piece using Don's questions.

Teachers find that the use of the friendly letter form for writing assignments often serves to meet the important objective of defining audience. If, for example, fifth graders are going to write in response to a question about a key concept in their nutrition unit, they might decide to write letters to the cafeteria staff. Eighth graders writing in response to a question about a guest speaker's presentation in their science class might direct their letters to the speaker as a means of saying thank you for coming to their classroom. In short, students are constantly reminded that writing activities have meaningful purposes and as such demand attention to specific audiences.

Don suggests that his students direct their responses about the Spanish conquest to a fellow student who is hospitalized and trying to keep up with her classwork while recuperating from surgery. Thus his students focus on a meaningful purpose for their writing. Using their "sloppy copy" worksheets, students fill in "Sarah" as their identified audience and then brainstorm several possible ideas to include in their writings. As Don directs the brainstorming session, he records the suggested ideas on a "shopping list" on the blackboard, thereby providing students with correct spellings of several terms they may choose to use in their letters. Students record on their worksheets only those ideas they think they will use in their writings.

George is one of several low-achieving students in Don's social studies class. Because students like George often provide the most difficult challenges for content area teachers, it is helpful to take a close look at how one of these students might respond to an assigned content writing activity using the suggested model. Let's look at the first part of George's prewriting worksheet:

> AUDIENCE: Sarah
> PURPOSE: help her learn about the Spanish conquest of Aztecs and
> Incas
> SHOPPING LIST OF WRITING IDEAS:
> > armor advantage
> > weapons
> > greed for gold
> > guns and arrows
> > horses
> > cannons

Everyone in the class has received direct instruction and practice in using the six-step strategy for turning questions into clear statements (review Figure 6.2). They are all able to do the crossing out, underlining, and adding/deleting necessary for transforming Don's question into an effective beginning for their letter to Sarah. George and other low-achieving students generally find this technique particularly helpful. More capable students may not even need to participate in this part of the directed writing activity. They might be encouraged to go ahead with their composing.

Don keeps in mind some advice Marge Gottfield gave him when she helped him begin to integrate process writing with the social studies content. He is cautious in using the structured six-step approach for helping students get their writings under way. It is critical that students not "get into a rut" by turning teacher questions into opening statements that all "sound the same." It is equally important that students do not come to depend on the teacher to provide a question for them each time they must complete a written assignment. Don keeps in mind Marge's advice to maintain an environment of "experimentation" within the writing laboratory.

Many teachers using the suggested model provide students with several alternative questions. The teacher might then ask the students to use one or more of the other questions on the worksheet for devising a different opening statement independently. Students would then share their results and each would be encouraged to select one of the suggested opening statements for use in an initial draft of the assignment.

Other teachers might require that students create more than one possible opening statement using a single question. Use of this approach encourages students to experiment with a variety of possible ways to begin opening statements using the basic word structures in teachers' questions. While many students fall into the habit of beginning most of their topic sentences with the "third word" of the question, most, with careful direction from teachers, can be led toward using a wide variety of beginnings and thus to an ever-increasing sophistication in their writing style.

George's whole class has been directed to try several options using the teacher's single question, "How were the Spanish able to conquer the Aztecs and the Incas?" As a group they use the overhead projector to construct the possible opening statement, "The Spanish were able to conquer the Aztecs and the Incas for several reasons." Don then asks that they each create another possible opening statement on their individual worksheets. Students share their ideas and are encouraged to make changes on their worksheets if they get good ideas from their classmates. Thus a true laboratory environment is clearly established; the process of writing is the focus of the activity, not the finished product.

Don now helps students make their final prewriting decisions. Students must select which opening statement they will use, always aware that at any point in the writing process they may change their minds and make revisions using a different statement. Decisions about paragraphing options are also made at this point. George, for example, elects to write two paragraphs, each one to begin with one of the opening statements he has created on his worksheet, "The Spanish were able to conquer the Aztecs and the Incas because of an armor advantage"; and "The Spanish were able to conquer the Aztecs and the Incas because of a greed for gold." He and the other sixth graders are now ready to move to the second stage of the five-stage process writing model, composing.

The Composing Stage

Many teachers characterize the composing stage of process writing as similar to the daily uninterrupted sustained silent reading period. Students, as well as the teacher, spend a specified amount of time concentrating on getting their ideas down on paper without pressure for perfection of form or mechanical precision.

As in the students' silent reading period where the teacher also sits quietly for a few moments to read for pleasure, the teacher is serving as an important "model" of writing behavior. Students need to see that the skill they are developing in composing is one which they are likely to need all through their lives. Seeing their teachers at work in the writing process is a powerful means for delivering this message.

During this uninterrupted silent composing period, students are encouraged to create initial drafts that are truly sloppy copies, subject to lots of revision. This bears repeating because the concept of revision is at the

Don joins his sixth graders as they begin to compose their initial drafts of an assigned content area writing activity. The teacher can provide a powerful model for this stage of the writing process.

heart of the five-stage writing process. In a process-oriented writing program, the composing stage is clearly defined for students at all grade and ability levels as the time for getting one's ideas on paper in temporary, "subject to change" form.

In order to foster an environment conducive to composing initial drafts that really are "subject to revision," teachers need to set up various ground rules depending on grade level and student abilities. For example, during the composing stage, all students are expected to focus exclusively on getting their shopping list ideas down on paper and not to worry about spelling, capitalization, and sentence construction problems. All students are encouraged to use pencil only, to skip lines so as to allow space for revisions, and to use phonemic spellings for difficult words. Students who know that their initial drafts are really just that are likely to find the composing stage nonthreatening and therefore are likely to create initial drafts with real promise.

Don's sixth graders have been writing quietly for about twenty minutes. He has made it clear, prior to composing time, just how long they will be expected to write and what to do if they complete their initial drafts before time is up. He has spent the first part of the composing period writing on the same topic and has spent the remainder of the period circulating about the room in what has been described as the "cheerleader" role (Lee, 1985). As a cheerleader, the teacher is available to give encouragement when words don't come easily, to listen to a student's experimental sentences, and to suggest ways of getting more information into the initial draft.

As our sixth graders complete their initial drafts, Don concludes the day's work with a brief sharing period. On a volunteer basis, several students (and Don!) read aloud what they have written so far. Again Don acts as cheerleader, not as "corrector." Every student's rough draft has some redeeming feature about which the teacher can make a positive comment.

Let's examine what George has composed during the quiet composing time:

Dear Sarah,

The Spanish were able to conquer the Aztecs and the Incas because of an armor advantage. The Spanish where able to conquer the Indians because they had wepons. When the Spanish came they road on horses and had canons and guns them.

The Spanish were able to conquer the Indians because of there greed for gold. They would ride on boats for months to get gold. The Spanish would die or be shot with arrows to gold, they took hostiges and asked for ransum.

Sincerely,
George

Note that George has used both the opening statements he constructed under the direction of the teacher during the prewriting stage. He has then used his shopping list of ideas to compose follow-up sentences for each opening sentence. He has done a good job of getting his ideas down on paper. Note that he has not had any trouble spelling the words "conquer," "Spanish," "Aztec," and "Inca," which appeared in Don's question. Note that George has, however, misspelled the content words "weapons," "cannons," and "ransom." If you are already getting nervous about the other words he has misspelled, the words he has omitted, his homonym errors, or the fact that he has a run-on sentence, you've missed the point of composing initial drafts that focus on content, not mechanics.

Because George is part of a writing program that emphasizes process, he feels free to get his ideas down even if he isn't confident about his spelling, punctuation, and sentence structure. George knows that it is a long way from rough draft to published product and that lots of help will be available as he and his classmates proceed through the five-stage writing process.

The Revising Stage

As you should recall from Chapter 2, the composing stage of the five-part writing process is followed by revision. Note, however, that prior to revision, the writer is expected to conference.

It has been suggested that hearing one's initial draft read aloud is the single most effective way to ensure that positive changes will be made in the draft. Student writers understand that during the initial conference they are to *listen* to the partner's draft. This is not the time to *look* at the writing, as doing so is likely to change the emphasis from content to mechanics. Most teachers therefore suggest that conferencing partners sit across from each other so that there is no temptation to look at the writing while the focus is on content.

Conferencing differs from classroom to classroom in programs using the process approach to writing instruction. Figure 6.4 is one suggested format for conducting peer conferences as well as for student-teacher conferences. It is also an effective format to follow for teacher-conducted small group writing conferences, an efficient means for helping several students at one time.

Teachers use a wide variety of organizational plans for managing conferencing. For some writing activities students are assigned conferencing partners; at another time students are instructed to look around for another student who is ready to conference at the same time. Students may draw the name of a conferencing partner at the beginning of a writing activity. The teacher may simply assign conferencing partners, perhaps instructing students to work with the person seated at the next desk. Conferencing also gives teachers the chance to match students according

CONFERENCING GUIDELINES

FIRST: Listen! Don't look at your partner's writing yet.

SECOND: Say one nice thing about your partner's writing.

THIRD: Try to repeat what you heard your partner read to you.

FOURTH: Ask some questions to help your partner get some ideas for revision.

FIFTH: If you have time, make some helpful suggestions to your partner for revisions.

Figure 6.4

Adapted from "Conferencing Guidelines" from *Writers' Lab*, 1985–86, edited by Joyce W. Lee, p. 47. Reprinted by permission of State College Area School District.

to instructional needs, perhaps matching up students at similar levels or, for example, putting a weaker student with a more skilled one.

Teachers need to be patient as students learn how to conference effectively. Sometimes the only result of a peer conference is one partner's discovery that he or she has omitted a word; the teacher needs to recognize this as a positive occurrence. Students will get better at conferencing; they will begin to ask constructive questions that will help a partner add something significant during revision, and they will learn to listen more intently to their own work as they read it aloud. Finally, many teachers report that what they see as the most significant part of the writing conference is the "Say something nice about your partner's writing" guideline. Learning to respond in a positive way, even if it is difficult to find anything good to comment on, is a valuable lifetime skill; conferencing can provide meaningful practice in this skill.

Returning to our sixth-grade classroom, we find that the students are completing their conferences. As each conference ends, students return to their seats to work on the third stage of the five-stage process, revision. Don hopes that each student has at least one idea for revision, perhaps a sentence to add, perhaps an idea to delete, possibly only a word to change. Because students have written in pencil and have skipped lines on their initial drafts, they can make revisions easily.

Before moving to the fourth stage of process writing, let's look again at George's writing efforts. Recall that his initial draft included two paragraphs, each with a clear opening statement. During quiet composing time he was able to construct follow-up sentences using his shopping list of ideas.

George has now conferenced with Kevin, a partner he selected because they both finished their initial drafts at about the same time. Kevin listened to George's draft, commented that he liked what George said about the Spanish taking hostages and being willing to die to get gold. Following this positive comment, Kevin asked if George could "maybe say something more about the Spaniards' weapons and explain about the ransom thing." He then asked George to reread his piece and suggested that it might be even better if he would add "endings" to his paragraphs. George's part of the conference ended with his having some clear ideas of what to do next, which means that the conference was successful.

Here is George's piece following some work in the revision stage. Note that he has only made a few changes in the mechanics area, such as the spelling of "were." He apparently also "heard" his two omission errors, inserting the words "with" and "get." George has clearly focused on the revision of "content":

Dear Sarah,

The Spanish were able to conquer the Aztecs and the Incas because of an armor advantage. The Spanish were able to conquer the Indians because they had wepons. When the Spanish came, they road horses and had canons and guns with them. The Indians had never seen horses or guns so they had no way to protect themselves, the odds were 1 to 1000, the Spanish won and beet the odds.

The Spanish were able to conquer the Indians because of there greed for gold. They would ride in boats for months to get gold. The Spanish would die or be shot with arrows to get gold. They took hostiges and asked the Indians for ransum. This was another good way to get gold. If they got the ransum they killed the hostages. These are two of the ways the Spanish were able to conquer the Aztecs and the Incas.

Sincerely,
George

George has clearly benefitted from his writing conference with Kevin. He has taken seriously Kevin's suggestions to say something more about "weapons" and "ransom" and has added a concluding statement to each paragraph.

The Editing Stage

The fourth stage of our model, editing, is often what makes teachers uncomfortable about process writing. Editing (often labelled "proofreading") is the "bottom line" item for teachers committed by tradition to obtaining "letter-perfect products" from all students.

Let's look again at our sixth-grade writers and see how editing skills instruction might be included within the framework of an assigned process writing activity. Remember that George and his classmates have worked on their initial drafts during composing time and have each had the opportunity to conference with another student and/or the teacher in order to get some ideas for revisions. We have examined the revisions George has made following his conference with Kevin.

While students are finishing up their conferences and working on revisions, Don circulates around the room listening and observing what his students have written up to this point. He stops now and then to provide direct assistance to a student who is "stuck" on how to improve his or her draft, perhaps taking time to hold a small group conference with several students who appear to be having trouble with similar aspects of their writings.

Now let's look at what Don does during the next day's writing period. As he circulates among his students during their peer conferences and observes them as they work on revisions, he watches for one or two specific editing skills to use for directed skills instruction. He notes that many students, like George, are continuing to have difficulty with run-on sentences. He also notes that a number of students have neglected to include concluding statements in their drafts. Don identifies these two points as

Don holds a small group conference with three of his sixth graders who have completed their initial drafts. Each student reads his/her draft aloud, and the others offer both encouragement and suggestions for revision content.

"focus correction areas" (Collins, 1985), an idea suggested to him by Marge when he expressed dismay about the overwhelming number of errors his students were making in their writings. She urged that he identify only one common error in the mechanics area and one in the content area for each writing assignment (see Chapter 8 for a detailed explanation of focus correcting). Don will consider only these errors in grading finished papers.

Based on this "focus correction area" idea, before the students return to their writings the next day, Don conducts a directed lesson on one mechanics skill, run-on sentences, and one content skill, writing concluding statements. He asks students to look at their drafts carefully in teams of two to see if they can identify any run-on sentence errors. He has selected one student's rough draft to use for classroom practice, first securing that student's permission to use her writing for this purpose.

Using the overhead projector, Don asks all the students to examine Susan's writing for run-on sentences. Together teacher and students carefully consider Susan's use of punctuation and make the necessary corrections. Next, Don directs students to look again at each other's drafts to see if they have correctly "repaired" their run-on errors. Next Don asks the students to explain why it is important for some paragraphs to have concluding statements, perhaps asking one or two student writers to read aloud their drafts to illustrate his point.

Now Don's students are ready to edit their own rough drafts, both independently and with one or more peers. They are directed to do their own editing first, paying particular attention to the two focus areas of the day's skills instruction lesson, run-on sentences and writing concluding statements. Don reminds students that they are also expected to edit for other areas such as end punctuation, capital letters, indenting, supporting details, precise words, "action" verbs, and other skills which have been previous focus correction areas.

Most teachers using the suggested model work with students to develop editing checklists to be used during this stage of the writing process. Such checklists differ from classroom to classroom, of course, but all of them reflect the skill areas which have been previous areas of focus during directed skills instruction. See Figure 6.5 for an illustration of such an editing checklist. It is important that students help develop these checklists and that they be revised frequently to reflect current focus correction areas.

Editing is a busy time in process writing classrooms and needs to be monitored carefully in order to ensure high productivity. Most students are eager to get this part of the writing process over with in a hurry, often taking a hasty glance at their pieces and saying, "I've checked it and it's fine," long before their writings have in fact been taken to the point of "best possible effort."

Let's examine George's piece following his self-editing. Keep in mind that Don has focused on two specific areas for students to look at in their

EDITING CHECKLIST

Writer _____

Assignment _____

Two Special Areas to Check:
1. _____
2. _____

Other Areas to Check:
Clear opening statement(s)? _____

Capital letters where needed? _____

End punctuation all there? _____

Commas in right places? _____

Any sentence fragments? _____

Apostrophes for ownership? _____ For contractions? _____

Endings on all words? _____

A conclusion for each paragraph? _____

Spelling checked?
(any homonyms to check on?)

Figure 6.5

pieces: run-on sentences and concluding statements. Compare this "edited" draft with George's "revised" piece following his conference with Kevin:

Dear Sarah,
   The Spanish were able to conquer the Aztecs and the Incas because of the armor. The Spanish were able to conquer the Indians because they had weapons. When the Spanish came they rode horses and had canons and guns with them. The Indians had never seen horses or guns so they had no way to protect themselves. The odds were 1 to 1,000, the Spanish won and beat the odds.
   The Spanish were also able to conquer the Indians because of their greed for gold. They would ride in boats for months to try to get gold from the Indians. The Spanish would die or be shot with arrows to get gold too. They took hostiges and asked the Indians for ransum. This was another good way to get gold. If they got the ransum they killed the

hostages. These are two of the ways the Spanish were able to conquer the Aztecs and Incas even though they outnumbered.

Sincerely,
George

It is apparent that George has in fact attended to Don's reminder to check carefully for run-on sentences. He has corrected one of his run-on errors but has overlooked the other one. George had already written a concluding sentence for each of his paragraphs but improved his second one during editing time. He has used his checklist carefully (refer again to Figure 6.5), correcting some homonym errors and apparently looking up (or asking the teacher) several (but not all) of the content words he chose to use. Overall, George's writing has undergone several significant changes between prewriting and editing.

The students in George's class know that once they have completed their self-editing, they are expected to work with at least one other student to edit each other's pieces. George now takes his writing to a classmate, they exchange papers, and, using their editing checklists, look over each other's papers. George's editing partner points out that the word "cannons" is not copied correctly from the prewriting shopping list on the board and that the word "were" is omitted in his last sentence. George makes these corrections and is satisfied that his piece is "finished."

No, George's letter to Sarah is not "letter perfect." He still has some misspelled words. He still has a run-on sentence despite his teacher's focus on this skill area. Don, however, recognizes that George has likely taken his piece as far as he can on his own. The writing reflects George's current developmental writing stage. Of more importance than the fact that the writing is not "perfect" is Don's awareness that George is writing more than earlier in the year, he is now composing more easily and, most important, he is more willing to revise and edit his own work. In short, here is a teacher who understands what process writing is all about and is genuinely committed to a writing model in which the primary goal is to help students make their rough drafts better.

Don may or may not get around to George for a final editing conference. No teacher can meet with every student individually for each writing activity and should not try to do so. Instead, teachers should manage to see several students during one or two small group conferences during both the conferencing and editing stages while students are meeting with each other. And of course, they should circulate about the room during each stage of the writing activity, holding mini-conferences with students as they are writing.

If Don is able to see George one final time before this writing activity is brought to a conclusion, he will likely focus on the uncorrected run-on sentence. He might, for example, stop at George's desk and ask that he read aloud beginning with "The odds were 1 to 1000," to note where he "punctuates with his voice." George may or may not "hear" his mistake. If he does not, and if Don believes that further attention to this mechanics skill is appropriate, he may ask George to read the same section of his paragraph to a partner to see if together the students can correct the error. Only if Don has made a good decision about the appropriateness of having George correct this error is it likely that it will be changed on the final draft.

At this point the writing activity in our sixth-grade classroom is likely to be concluded with students being asked to prepare "good copies" to be sent to the designated audience, their classmate Sarah who was in the hospital. In this case, an assigned writing activity has gone into the fifth stage of the five-part process model, publishing. Keep in mind, however, that not every piece of writing should be taken to the publication stage.

When teachers move away from writing that focuses on every paper becoming a "finished product," the whole idea of process writing instruction becomes clear. Students need to recognize that much of what they write is for "practice" and that only selected pieces will be considered for specific publishing purposes.

The Publishing Stage

Because many writing activities in Marge's suggested model involve the use of the friendly letter form, teachers should make a real effort to see that many of these writings are received by the designated "audiences." For example, a fifth-grade class writes letters on dental care and sends them to the school's dental hygienist; sixth graders complete a letter to the author of an instructional book they have enjoyed; eighth graders write a letter to the science coordinator about what they have learned in a new science unit; and tenth graders direct letters to the new superintendent describing their perceptions of a live presentation of *Hamlet* that the school board financed. Because students are aware from the beginning of this kind of assigned content area writing that some of their finished copies will be published and read by a specific person, they are likely to invest a bit more time and effort in the writing than for an assignment with undefined purpose and audience.

Marge has helped Middlewood teachers institute monthly Spotlight Writing Awards in order to provide another publishing opportunity. Don's students are aware that once a month one writing from each content area is to be selected for a Spotlight Award. The names of all Spotlight Writers are announced over the loudspeaker, the selected writings are prominently posted on a hall display, and each Spotlight Writer receives a special certificate signed by the principal.

SUMMARY

You have now seen how one model for content area writing incorporates many of the implications from current research into the nature of the writing process. While this model is suggested as a schoolwide program, it should be clear that the program can be implemented successfully in individual content area classrooms as well. There is no reason to wait for an entire staff to implement process writing.

Even the youngest students are surprisingly receptive to the instructional procedure described in this chapter and are able to compose clear and effective opening statements for assigned writings in the content areas. Earlier than you would think possible, these students are able to write one or more follow-up sentences with ease. As they move up through the grades, they come to expect that they will be asked to write this way regularly in all curriculum areas. Eventually, their skill in composing in the organized, logical manner imposed by the careful structure of the strategy becomes an internalized response for most students.

In the upper grades, most teachers are able to use this same instructional procedure for moving students into multi-paragraph writing assignments in the content areas. The procedure lends itself particularly well to early report writing: it helps students develop a number of carefully constructed questions about their topics, and each question forms the basis of a paragraph in their reports. Thus, assigned topic content area writing activities become the cornerstone of a writing program intended to help students develop the basic skill of clear, organized writing. The leap from "learning to write" to "writing to learn" becomes a curriculum reality.

In Chapter 2 you read an overview of this current trend in teaching writing. Teachers in all content areas are moving away from emphasizing only the products of writing assignments to the use of class time for helping students learn the craft of composing rough drafts subject to revision. In this chapter you have followed one of our Middlewood teachers as he directed a social studies class through all five stages of the process writing model suggested by Marge. You have watched George, a low-achieving student, create an effective beginning for a piece of writing using a strategy for turning a teacher-question into an effective opening statement. You have followed George through the composing of his rough draft and his peer conferencing for revision of both mechanics and content to the publication of his writing for a real audience. In short, you have seen process writing in action in a content area classroom.

REFERENCES

Collins, J. (1985). *The effective writing teacher.* Andover, MA: The NET-WORK, Inc.

Lee, J. W. (1985, fall). Daily writing: A successful and manageable reality. *The English Record, 36* (1), 20–24.

Lee, J. W., Bemis, J., & Morris, C. (Eds.). (1985). *Writers' lab: A teacher's handbook.* State College, PA: State College Area School District.

McCracken, R. A. (1971). Initiating sustained silent reading. *Journal of Reading, 8,* 521–524.

National Assessment of Educational Progress. (1985). *Writing objectives: 1983–84 assessment* [#15-W-100]. Princeton, NJ: Educational Testing Service.

SUGGESTIONS FOR FURTHER READING

Fulwiler, T. (1987). *Teaching with writing.* Upper Montclair, NJ: Boynton/Cook.

Graves, D. H. (1983). *Writing: Teachers and children at work.* Portsmouth, NJ: Heinemann Educational Books, Inc.

Howard, V. A., & Barton, J. H. (1986). *Thinking on paper.* New York: William Morrow and Co.

Murray, D. M. (1984). *Write to learn.* New York: Holt, Rinehart and Winston.

Murray, D. M. (1985). *A writer teaches writing* (2nd ed.). Boston: Houghton Mifflin Co.

PART III

GATHERING INFORMATION ABOUT STUDENTS AND MATERIALS

What kinds of reading materials should teachers use in their classrooms?

How do they select and evaluate textbooks?

How well do students read, and how do we find out?

How do we know whether they learn what we teach?

What do students want to read? How do we find out?

Questions like these may be in your minds about now. We have discussed reading and writing and the processes we use in teaching them. Now we need to turn to ways of evaluating the materials we can use and the students we teach. Students are complex creatures, so we must look at their cognitive learning, through assessing what they have learned and how well they read. We must also look at their affective concerns, their attitudes and interests.

We begin this part with a discussion of materials. In our effort to match students' reading levels to appropriate materials, we must evaluate textbooks and other materials to see how difficult they are to read and whether they contain the appropriate content.

CHAPTER SEVEN

Selecting and Evaluating Reading Materials

SCENARIO

There is an air of excitement in the halls of Middlewood as the end of December approaches. School will soon close for the mid-winter break and everyone is beginning to show signs of vacation fever.

"Morning, Marge," John greeted her as she passed him in the hall. "How are your plans for the skiing holiday coming?"

"Great, John," replied Marge, her face lighting up at the thought of two weeks in the Rockies. "How did the science meeting go last night?"

"Very smoothly. We really accomplished a lot. In fact I made a note to see you some time this week about something that came up at the end of the meeting. Got a minute now?"

"Sure. I'm early today for a change," replied Marge. "What do you need?"

"It looks like the school board is looking favorably at our proposal to purchase a new textbook for the tenth-grade biology course for next fall. That's the good news. The bad news is that we'd better get to work fast to select a title if we are to make a wise selection."

"And you'd like my help?" asked Marge.

"For starters, I'd like some advice about determining the difficulty level of various texts we have to choose from. We've already received a number of really exciting-looking books, and of course all the literature that comes with sample copies is full of promises about how perfect each one is for high school students. How can we tell if the text level we'd like to use is really appropriate for the students in our classes?" asked John.

"In other words," replied Marge, "can you believe what the publishers say about readability?"

"Exactly. Is there an easy way to check out their claims?"

"I can help you there for sure, but that's the easy part of text selection. There's a lot more to matching a textbook with a group of students, however. Let me dig out some stuff from my files on readability and other factors that need to be considered. You know you have to look at things like clarity of illustrations, size of print, marginal notations, levels of questions, and use of subheadings. That's the hard part, John," responded Marge.

"Is that *all*, Marge? Whew! This sounds like a more complicated task than I anticipated," John answered with genuine dismay.

"It's a challenge, that's for sure, but not an impossible job. I'll be glad to help. I've got some sample text analysis forms we can look at which will help us define what needs to be done," Marge promised.

"Thanks for your usual optimism. You always make things sound so reasonable," said John. "You're sure you didn't leave out any of the things we need to look at in considering a new text?"

"As a matter of fact, I did. Don't forget that we also have to take a close look at community attitudes!"

OVERVIEW

This chapter concerns materials selection and evaluation: who selects the materials used in teaching and how should these materials be selected? We will dicuss five principles that are useful as a base for selecting materials. How can a teacher measure the reading level of a text? How reliable are publishers' estimates? What factors determine the difficulty of a text? This chapter also suggests the most common ways of assessing readability levels and identifies the problems in using these procedures. The goal is to develop a teacher's professional judgment in assessing the reading difficulty of texts in his/her content area.

Last, we will present a procedure that Marge might recommend to John and the science team as they consider the purchase of a new textbook. This procedure is one which you can use in evaluating any materials for use in a course, unit, or lesson.

THE SELECTION PROCESS

In this discussion, we use the term *materials* to refer to all the concrete things a teacher may use to help students learn what they need to learn. Materials include textbooks, printed items such as paperback books, magazines and newspapers, reference books, library sources, and any and all reading sources available. In addition, materials include non-print *media* of all kinds, such as films, filmstrips, slides, audio- and videotapes, maps, globes, transparencies, and an ever-increasing variety of equipment. Other kinds of materials are the hands-on items used in many classes, from science lab equipment to wood-shop equipment to the kitchen equipment in cooking class. Some classes use a great amount of hands-on equipment; others use very little. The choice of materials from all these types depends largely on the students' needs and on the content objectives of the class.

Who selects materials? In the final analysis, each teacher selects the materials that are appropriate for particular students in a particular lesson. Teachers make a professional decision to use specific materials after they know the students' needs and their own objectives for teaching. They must also decide how they will present the learning situation to students and what instructional strategies and management processes they will follow.

Before we can talk about selecting materials for lessons, however, we need to look at how materials are selected in advance to ensure that teachers have a wide variety to choose from when they are planning a unit or lesson. In many places, this process begins with *textbook adoption*.

Textbook Adoption

Textbook adoption generally refers to a school or school district choosing a text for use in particular classes. For example, the school or district needs to adopt an Algebra I text, a basic biology text, or an American literature text. Adopting a text usually means that the district, through some process, selects a text, and the school board approves that selection. Then enough texts are purchased so that each student in that class will have one to use. Think how many books that can be—from twenty copies of an advanced French or calculus text in a small high school to hundreds of copies of a book every seventh grader in one district must use in social studies or English classes.

Textbook adoption policies differ widely across the United States. Some states, like Texas, adopt a few texts statewide for a particular course. In other states, districts may choose texts, but they must provide the state with a rationale for the use of any text. Ultimately, the selection of texts is a function of the state as it regulates education within its boundaries (English, 1980). Wherever teachers teach, it is important to know what the state says about materials for use in their classrooms.

In many districts, textbook adoption is an ongoing process, as it should be. Even though the legal requirement may be to adopt texts officially every three or five years, these districts encourage teachers to be continually aware of new materials and to plan for changes in texts, if these changes would support the teaching and learning process more effectively (Farr & Tulley, 1985). In such districts, like Middlewood, a committee of teachers and administrators frequently considers texts which might be appropriate for a given course. From that committee, the selection recommendation goes through a department head or coordinator, the building principal, and the curriculum director or assistant superintendent to the superintendent. When the superintendent approves, the school board usually must consider the recommendation and officially adopt the text.

School board adoption may be *pro forma,* or it may be fraught with controversy. Community groups are becoming more and more involved in responding to professional text selections. Remember Marge's parting comment to John about the need to consider community attitudes? Indeed, the community's concerns about issues such as language, religious beliefs, and politics, as well as differing views of the purposes of education, play a large role here. Your analysis of the community will help to anticipate issues which may affect the selection of textbooks and other materials. All teachers must be concerned with textbook adoptions in their school and district. The first step is to find out what that process is. This is likely to be a priority recommendation from Marge to John and the science team.

We are dealing here, then, with a long-term process, the adoption of particular texts for use in particular courses. The adoption is for an extended period, perhaps three to five years or longer. The adoption is a formal and legal matter, a part of the state's legal concern for schools and a matter for the school board to act upon. We are also dealing here with the immediate, short-term process of a teacher selecting the readings and other materials necessary for a group of students to master an objective. An inescapable conclusion is that materials selection is a large and important process with implications for every teacher.

Principles of Selection

Certain principles underlie materials selection. These principles apply to school and district-wide long-term adoption processes as well as to the teacher's decision to use certain materials today or next week. They derive from the learning principles discussed in Chapter 1.

First, materials should encourage active learning by the students who use them. Active learning, as opposed to passive learning, means that the student's mind is engaged in figuring out what is happening, in answering questions, in providing alternatives to situations. Texts and other materials which lend themselves to higher level learning (on Bloom's taxonomy) or to higher comprehension levels (on Barrett's taxonomy) will encourage more active learning. Texts that encourage rote memorization of names, dates, and formulas will not encourage this kind of active learning.

Active learning does not mean, necessarily, that a student must be physically active. Books can engage the mind actively. However, younger students (middle and junior high school) and some types of exceptional students will respond better to concrete materials and to physical activity. All this means, for example, that doing a science lab experiment is better than merely reading about it, but students may read about it first. Making a cake is better than reading about it, but students must read the recipe to do it. Reading a novel is sometimes better than, or perhaps different from, seeing the movie. The best reading material will make the connection with the activity.

Second, teachers should select materials to suit the needs of individual students. Teachers should match appropriate materials to groups of students, based on objectives to be met. Materials within a unit or lesson need to address specific types of students. Gifted students and/or independent level readers need enrichment reading and materials for further learn-

Students need to use a wide variety of reading materials, as well as textbooks. This student is studying Elizabethan costumes, preparing to write about costuming during Shakespeare's time. Providing access to such materials is an important task for teachers.

ing—extra lab experiences, challenging math problems, and the like. Frustration level readers need alternative materials which match their reading level; reading which has a low reading level but a high interest level is appropriate for them.

Students with particular exceptionalities may require specific readings and materials. Blind and partially sighted students may need to use Braille materials or audiotapes of required readings. Bilingual students need materials based on their level of English proficiency. All these groups of learners will be described more completely, including their needs for materials, in Part IV.

Classes of heterogeneously grouped students have a wide range of reading levels. This range can be figured by using a simple formula, *if* the class has a normal IQ range (Singer & Donlan, 1985). For a tenth-grade class with an average chronological age of fifteen, these are the results:

$$
\begin{aligned}
\text{Expected Reading Range} &= 2/3 \times \text{Average Chronological Age} \\
&\quad \text{(CA)} \\
&= 10 \\
\text{Expected Reading Age Range} &= \text{CA} \pm 1/2 \text{ Expected Reading} \\
&\quad \text{Range} \\
&= 15 \pm 5 \\
&= 10 - 20 \\
\text{Expected Grade Level Range} &= \text{5th Grade–College}
\end{aligned}
$$

Using this formula, the expected Reading Age Range is 10 to 20 years. This does not mean actual ages 10 to 20. It means the reading level of average 10-year-olds, usually fifth graders, to average 20-year-olds, or college students. In other words, a tenth-grade teacher of a heterogeneous class can expect to have some students reading like average fifth graders and some reading like college students. How can a teacher cope with such widely varying reading levels? The basic task for teachers is to match readers with reading materials at appropriate levels of difficulty. We call these levels the *readability* of a text.

The third principle is that the materials should reflect student interest whenever possible. This principle speaks to the areas of interest which students tend to go through as they pass from childhood through adolescence to adulthood. Adolescence, especially, is a time of exploration. As teachers plan courses and units, they can select supplemental enrichment reading geared to the interests of the age group they are teaching and the specific interests of their students, which they can identify through interest questionnaires.

Don, for example, might provide for interest areas in his eighth-grade American history class. He could use *Your Reading* (Christenson, 1983). to identify fiction and nonfiction about American history which might suit his students. He is especially aware of adolescents' interests in biography, autobiography, and historical fiction. He should also be careful to include books by and about minority groups—blacks, Indians, and immigrants of various origins—in the period being studied. Finally, he should be sure each list includes some easy reading and some advanced reading, so students of all levels will find appropriate reading materials. As an added help to students, he might ask not only the school library, but also the public library and the local bookstore, to cooperate in making the books on his list available to students.

Interest-oriented materials are much more likely to attract and hold student attention. Materials that are career-oriented or prevocational can be used in this way, as can materials designed to encourage continued leisure reading. Students interested in biological careers may enjoy reading about the DNA researchers or contemporary biologists as well as about Antoni van Leeuwenhoek or, for chemistry enthusiasts, Madame Curie and Joseph Priestley. The argument over whether the world is round or flat comes to life when students consider Columbus and other explorers. The risk-taking involved in exploration can be connected to contemporary undersea and space exploration. The potential for vocational and avocational applications of content objectives should be explored as a highly interest-oriented activity. Reading about these possibilities is feasible for both students and teachers. Such reading is optional for those students who are interested. Teachers can handle the logistics of the readings if these are preplanned, independent activities.

The fourth principle of materials selection is that the materials suit the curriculum in the school or district and are sensitive to the needs and attitudes of the community as suggested by Marge. Its application to materials selection means that the teacher can explain his/her rationale for selecting materials, as well as content, in a way that the community will accept. No teacher or school can please all of its constituents. However, the teacher should feel confident that s/he has the support of the community.

One application of this principle is that all minorities, including women, should be included in the reading and visual materials used in a course, balanced out over time. Texts should be chosen to reflect the different ethnic groups in American society, as well as the particular state and community in which we teach. The way in which we involve minorities depends on the makeup of the community. Dealing with literature by and about blacks is appropriate in any English classroom. However, the choice of literature and the way it is presented may differ depending on whether blacks are members of the community or not. If students have no first-hand experience with black people, they will read about black experiences as an exploration of such questions as how similar or different their lives are or how similar their interests and concerns are. Students in classes including both black and white students, reading the same selection, can compare firsthand their responses to the reading.

The fifth principle in materials selection is that specific materials are selected in the appropriate order. The adopted textbook is *not* the curriculum. Teachers choose the materials that are necessary to teach the students they have and the objectives they have set.

On a practical basis, this often means supplementing the adopted textbook in several ways. First, teachers can use alternative texts. Alternative texts may differ in reading level, approach, or content. Second, the teacher can supplement, or add to, the adopted text using media of all kinds. Third, s/he can supplement the text with other reading materials (for example, magazines, newspapers, or reference materials) for information or enrichment. Fourth, s/he can supplement the text with any number of hands-on or concrete materials and experiences (labs, field trips, and the like). All of these decisions on specific materials for the lesson or unit are made only after the decisions on content and objectives have been made.

These basic principles for materials selection are a synthesis of issues raised throughout this book. The principles themselves have been discussed earlier and are here applied to the process of selecting materials. Now we can look at a basic concept in text evaluation, the readability of materials.

WHAT IS READABILITY?

Readability is a much-discussed problem in content area reading. Most teachers have experienced the problem of student readers for whom the text is too hard, with the result that these students do not succeed in reading the material. Recently, there has been discussion of the other side of the problem: the gifted or independent reader who will not read the material because it is too simplistic. As you know, a continuing problem is the reader who can read but won't, no matter what the level of his/her reading skills is. When we talk about readability, we are dealing with selecting reading materials for students to use in learning from text, whether in class or out of class.

Readability deals with matching reader and text. A more complete definition is this one suggested by Dale and Chall in their classic 1948 work:

> *In the broadest sense, readability is the sum total (including interactions) of all those elements within a given piece of printed material that affects the success which a group of readers have with it. The success is the extent to which they understand it, read it at optimum speed and find it interesting (p. 12).*

This definition holds true today and suggests that the matching process is fairly complex and should be applied individually to each reading. As Marge pointed out, there is more to matching a textbook with a group of students than just the publisher's statement about its suitability for certain grade levels. Four major components of readability are:

1. the reader's background information on the subject
2. the reader's interest in the subject
3. the aids to reading found in the text
4. linguistic factors in the text

The teacher should become familiar with the students' background knowledge and interests. If s/he doesn't know these, s/he should assess them early in the course using techniques described in Chapters 8 and 9. Generally speaking, the more knowledge students already have about the topic and the higher their interest is, the easier the material will be to comprehend. For most students, generating interest (or motivation) is important in the teacher's planning. So, too, is it important to plan to tie together material from previous learning to the material about to be read and learned. This principle is at the heart of advance organizers and pre-reading activities (see Chapters 11 and 12). Teachers can overcome or compensate for problems with background and interest by careful assessment and planning for instruction (Klare & Schumacher, 1981).

Careful text selection can help pinpoint those materials with the greatest number of reading aids for students. These reading aids include definitions of terms in context or set off in the text, effective comprehension questions, the use of sideheads and other sectioning with chapters, effective use of pictures and graphics, and other techniques that make the reading easier to comprehend.

When the word "readability" occurs in most discussions, however, the definition is limited to linguistic factors. All the widely used formulas for estimating readability levels focus on this component. Reiter (1973) identified the following linguistic factors in readability:

1. Vocabulary: How long are the words? How familiar are they to the reader? The longer or less familiar the words, the harder the reading.
2. Sentence Structure: The longer and more syntactically complex the sentences, the harder they are to read.
3. Relationships: Connections between words, sentences, or parts of sentences; these usually mean relations between concepts or ideas. The more relationships are required, the harder the reading.
4. Levels of Abstraction: Content reading becomes more abstract, less concrete. The reader must connect concrete and abstract. The more abstract the reading, the harder it is to read.

These factors, particularly factors one and two, remain the basis for the most commonly used readability formulas. For example, the Fry Readability formula, probably the one that is most frequently applied, is based entirely on word and sentence length. Factors three and four should remind you of the word attack principles presented earlier and the discussion of cognitive and comprehension levels and concept load. English teachers may call this "style." Everyone can name a writer whose prose is more complex and difficult to understand, or a writer who assumes the reader has a great deal of background and therefore doesn't provide explanations or connections.

One way of describing these concept or background points in factor three is in terms of *density*. Density refers to the number of words or phrases in a passage that relate to the topic under discussion. That is, words or phrases that may be unfamiliar to the reader. (Remember that knowing the terms is often the same as understanding the concept or topic, because the terms are concept labels.) Here is what we might call a dense passage. The most difficult words and terms are not italicized:

> ***How a Transformer Works.*** *In our explanation of* electromagnetism *it was pointed out that a* coil *of* wire carrying *a* current *has a* magnetic field set up *about it. When another* coil *of* wire *is brought close to it, the* magnetic field *is* cut *and a* current *is caused* to flow *in the* second coil. *We say that a* current *is* induced *in the* second coil. *There must be an actual* cutting *of the* lines of force. *Remember that* alternating current *changes direction frequently. Because it does, the* coil *does not have to be* moved through *the* magnetic field. *The* ebbing *and* flowing of *the* current *takes care of the* cutting *and causes the* field *to* build up *and then* collapse. *This provides the necessary* cutting *of the* field *by the* wire.[1]

The words and phrases that are not italicized above are all part of the terminology necessary to understand basic electronic technology. However, the density of this passage is roughly one content term in every three words.

Now read the following word problem from an Algebra I book, another example of density:

> *The fence enclosing the area around a rectangular pool is being constructed from prefabricated sections of uniform length. The width of the area fenced requires five sections of fence plus a 1.5-meter portion of a section. The length requires eight sections plus a 1-meter gate. The difference between the length and width is 6.1 meters. Find the length of each prefabricated section.[2]

This passage not only contains content terms but also uses symbols instead of words for some of them. Further, it assumes a knowledge of fence building in addition to mathematics.

[1]Delmar W. Olson, *Industrial Arts for the General Shop.* Englewood Cliffs, NJ: Prentice-Hall, Inc., 1973, p. 199.
[2]Clyde L. Corcoran, et al, *Scott, Foresman Algebra: First Course.* Scott, Foresman and Company 1984, p. 153.

Word problems in mathematics are often dense, as is a lot of poetry, and these two types of writing cause students difficulty because of their density. In the math problem, almost every word is necessary to solve the problem. The words are either quantities or concepts or processes. In poetry, the density reflects multiple layers of meaning, so that the reader must consider several different meanings for the same set of words.

Abstraction levels referred to in factor four may also be involved in dense writing. Consider this selection from a social studies text on the Supreme Court:

The Supreme Court is both a trial court and an appeals court. Three types of disputes have their original trials in the Supreme Court: (1) cases involving the official representatives of other nations, (2) suits between states, such as an argument between California and Arizona over water from the Colorado River, and (3) cases involving a state and the national government. Most cases, however, are appealed from a lower court.[3]

This paragraph is full of terms related to the topic. In contrast to the industrial arts text quoted earlier, this passage does not contain many concrete references. It discusses the types of cases which reach the Supreme Court, but it remains primarily at the abstract level. Students reading this passage can experience great difficulty making connections between this material and anything they already know because of the high level of abstraction.

By and large, density is not quantifiable. Teachers can assess the relationships, abstraction, and syntactic complexity levels involved in a piece of reading, but so far, no well-established process has been developed for assessing grade levels or scores. For this reason, most commonly used readability formulas, such as Fry's (1968, 1977), continue to rely on word and sentence length.

To assess density, teachers need to develop their professional judgment, their ability to separate harder from easier materials for students. As a way to do this, Singer (1975, 1985) developed the SEER technique. SEER, the Singer Eyeball Estimate of Readability, is not just tongue-in-cheek. Singer capitalizes on teacher experience and judgment to assess readability of particular materials. To use SEER, teachers are trained to assess materials by using their knowledge of the subject matter to be studied and the students who will study it to arrive at an estimate of its reading level. Clearly, the more teachers involved in making the judgment, the more reliable that judgment will be. Therefore, text selection committees considering text adoption can act effectively to judge the read-

[3]John J. Patrick and Richard C. Remy, *Civics for Americans*. Scott, Foresman and Company, 1982, p. 220.

ability of those texts if they have been trained in what to look for—the components of readability discussed here. It is possible that Marge will suggest to John that the science committee use some sort of estimate technique, such as the SEER, before recommending which new text to purchase for tenth-grade biology.

Readability Formulas in Wide Use

The linguistic factors most commonly used in readability formulas are those which seem to be the easiest to count: word length, sentence length, word familiarity, and sentence complexity (defined as number of subordinate clauses and/or prepositional phrases). Formulas use some combination of these variables.

The Dale-Chall formula (1948) probably has the greatest reputation for validity today. This formula works with two variables: average sentence length and word familiarity. Familiarity is judged by matching the words in the passage with the Dale list of 3,000 familiar words. While this formula is widely used, it has one great problem for content reading: every word that is not on the Dale list increases the reading difficulty, as measured by this formula. In many content texts, a high percentage of the words will not appear on the Dale list; hence the reading level score is high. However, if students have been adequately prepared, some of the these words are not really unfamiliar. Hence, the reading level may be artificially inflated. The same problem can occur with any formula using word familiarity as a factor, based on a general word list.

One attempt to counter this is the work of Kane, Byrne, and Hater (1974). Their formula for assessing the difficulty of mathematics books uses a word list of mathematics terms that are familiar to students at the seventh-grade level, the eighth-grade level, and so on. Their lists show that students' vocabularies tend to grow, to accrue more terms related to the subject, as they study those areas. Thus, to use word familiarity as a factor, a teacher may need to give his/her own pretest of key terms which students would know on entering the course. Generally, the more specific the word list is—to subject area (math) and to specific course (Algebra I)—the more useful it is to you as a teacher.

A second readability formula, the *Fry Graph for Estimating Readability* (1968, 1977), uses only sentence length (in words) and word length (in syllables) to measure reading difficulty, as was mentioned earlier. Figure 7.1 shows Fry's graph and instructions for using it. This formula may be the most widely used formula today, because it avoids the "familiarity" pitfall and doesn't get into syntactic issues. It is based on sampling principles, as the others are, and a random selection of three 100-word samples is used for estimating a book's readability level. Fry recommends that if the results within the three samples differ markedly, more samples should be used. Many books will be shown to have uneven readability because of uneven writing, difference in content discussed, or multiple authors. It is not safe to assume that reading level in a book goes from easier to harder, or that the level is fairly constant. Recent research (Fitzgerald, 1980) suggests that the three-sample recommendation may be unreliable, although previous research (Vaughn, 1976) shows high correlations between the Fry, Dale-Chall, and SMOG scales. Even if the Fry estimate is reliable, its validity is open to question because it deals with only two variables affecting readability (Marshall, 1979). However, the Fry graph seems to be as reliable and valid as other formulas, and it is undeniably easy to use; hence its popularity with publishers, reading specialists, and teachers. In addition, a number of computer programs are available to determine readability levels according to Fry's graph. This software makes the Fry readability even easier to determine. It is very likely that Marge will suggest that the science committee use this formula in its textbook evaluation process.

A third formula, the *Raygor Readability Estimate* (1977), is growing in popularity. It is similar to the Fry in its strengths and weaknesses. It uses the same sampling procedure and the same two variables. However, it defines word length not in number of syllables, but in number of letters. Words with six or more letters are counted as hard words and figured into the formula (Baldwin & Kaufman, 1979). Figure 7.2 shows this graph and instructions for using it.

In both the Fry and Raygor formulas, which are based on computer analysis of large amounts of text, the graph identifying reading levels shows large "gray areas" where the analysis is considered invalid. The logic of these areas is clear: to fall into them, a passage either has very long sentences and very short words or the reverse. The analysis on which the graphs are based suggests that published writers (that is, anyone whose work has been published) will not write that way. Hence, an analysis which shows such a set of data either has found a highly unusual writer or has been done incorrectly.

A fourth formula is the SMOG formula (McLaughlin, 1969) which looks at the same linguistic variables. To use SMOG, or The Simple Measure of Gobbyldegook, follow these steps:

a. Choose three sets of ten sentences from places throughout the book.
b. Count the number of words with *three or more syllables* (polysyllabic words) in each set of ten sentences.
c. Add the three numbers of polysyllabic words.
d. Develop a grade level using this formula: SMOG grade level = 3 + square root of the polysyllabic word count.

SMOG specifies the number of sentences, rather than the number of words, and defines reading level in terms of the number of long words, defined as 3 or more syllables. The authors' description of their formulas indicates that SMOG predicts comprehension of 90–100 percent accuracy,

FRY GRAPH FOR ESTIMATING READABILITY—EXTENDED

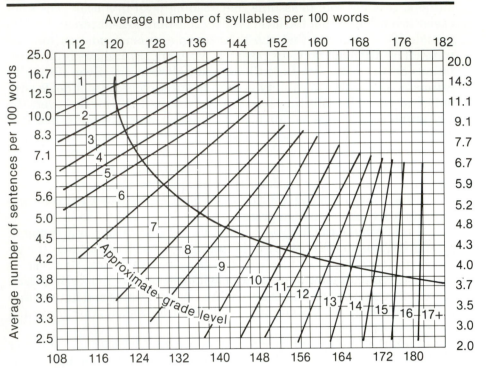

Average number of syllables per 100 words

Randomly select 3 one-hundred-word passages from a book or an article. Plot average number of syllables and average number of sentences per 100 words on graph to determine the grade level of the material. Choose more passages per book if great variability is observed and conclude that the book has uneven readability. Few books will fall into gray area, but when they do, grade level scores are invalid.

Count proper nouns, numerals and initializations as words. Count a syllable for each symbol. For example, "1945" is one word and 4 syllables and "IRA" is 1 word and 3 syllables.

EXAMPLE:	SYLLABLES	SENTENCES
1st Hundred Words	124	6.6
2nd Hundred Words	141	5.5
3rd Hundred Words	158	6.8
AVERAGE	141	6.3

READABILITY 7th GRADE (see dot plotted on graph)

From Fry, E. (1977). Fry's readability graph: Clarifications, validity, and extension to level 17. *Journal of Reading, 21*, 242–243.

Figure 7.1 Continued:

Expanded Directions for Working Readabilty Graph

1. Randomly select three (3) sample passages and count out exactly 100 words beginning with the beginning of a sentence. Do not count proper nouns, initializations, and numerals.

2. Count the number of sentences in the hundred words estimating length of the fraction of the last sentence to the neartest 1/10th.

3. Count the total number of syllables in the 100-word passage. If you don't have a hand counter available, an easy way is to simply put a mark above every syllable over one in each word, then when you get to the end of the passage, count the number of marks and add 100. Small calculators can also be used as counters by pushing numeral "1," then push the "+" sign for each word or syllable when counting.

4. Enter graph with average sentence length and average number of syllables; plot dot where the two lines intersect. Area where dot is plotted will give you approximate grade level.

5. If a great deal of variability is found in syllables count or sentence count, putting more samples into the average is desirable.

6. A word is defined as a group of symbols with a space on either side; thus, "Joe," "IRA," "1945," and "&" are each one word.

7. A syllable is defined as a phonetic syllable. Generally, there are as many syllables as vowel sounds. For example, "stopped" is one syllable and "wanted" is two syllables. When counting syllables for numerals and initializations, count one syllable for each symbol. For example, "1945" is 4 syllables and "IRA" is three syllables and "&" is 1 syllable.

Figure 7.1

NOTE: This "extended graph" does not outmode or render the earlier (1968) version inoperative or inaccurate; it is an extension.

or what we will call the *independent* level, while the Fry predicts 50–70 percent accuracy, or what we will call the *frustration* level.

Another point to make about these formulas is that they are designed to be used with prose, rather than poetry or other formats. As the text format moves away from straight prose, the formulas may not accurately reflect reading difficulty. Math, science, industrial arts, and music texts are most likely to demonstrate this problem, but many others will find it occasionally. Kane, Byrne, and Hater (1974), working with readability of math texts, identified some of the reasons why: 1) students who were required to move from word to symbol and back (since d=rt, the distance=20 mph × 4 hours) had more trouble reading; 2) when the reading did not move smoothly from left to right, as you are doing now, but instead

THE RAYGOR READABILITY ESTIMATE

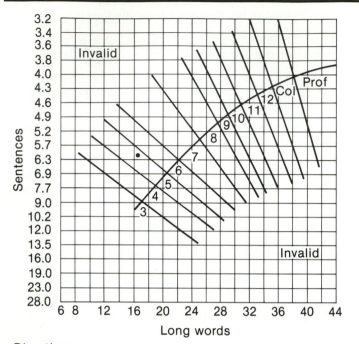

Directions:
Count out three 100-word passages at the beginning, middle, and end of a selection or book. Count proper nouns, but not numerals.

1. Count sentences in each passage, estimating to nearest tenth.
2. Count words with six or more letters.
3. Average the sentence length and word length over the three samples and plot the average on the graph.

Example:

		Sentences	6 + Words
Note mark on graph.	A	6.0	15
Grade level is about 5.	B	6.8	19
	C	6.4	17
Total		19.2	51
Average		6.4	17

Figure 7.2

"The Raygor Readability Estimate" by Alton L. Raygor from *Reading: Theory, Research, and Practice* edited by P. David Pearson. Copyright © 1977 The National Reading Conference, Inc. Reprinted by permission.

moved up, down, and sideways, readers had more trouble reading:

$$r = \frac{d}{t},$$

3) formulas and other symbols generally add to the density of the writing. That is, it takes many more words and more space to say something in words than is necessary when symbols are used:

$$x_1 = 4 \pm \sqrt{y-6}$$

or

x sub one equals four plus or minus the square root of y minus six.

While these problems are not neatly quantifiable, they can be assessed generally by the teacher. The more symbols and formulas given in a text, the less likely that a standard readability rating (for example, the Fry graph) will be an accurate estimate of reading difficulty. This is another argument for the use of teacher judgment, as in the SEER technique, in combination with one or more readability estimates.

What can we conclude about the use of readability formulas on content materials? First, we always want to know which formula was used and what variables were assessed. Second, we always consider the teacher's own evaluation of the materials and his/her knowledge of student background and interest more important than readability estimates. Third, we know that, if they are used judiciously and with knowledge of their strengths and weaknesses, readability estimates can be useful in providing a wide range of materials for students to use. Marge will probably suggest that, as one part of an overall selection process, John and the other science teachers should use one or two readability formulas on the texts they are considering. Used judiciously, the estimates they obtain should be helpful in making a final decision.

Other Uses for Readability Assessments

Readability assessment goes beyond identifying textbooks for selection processes. Here are several ways to use readability assessments effectively:

1. Texts frequently differ in difficulty from one section to another. Sometimes these differences come from the topics covered and the terminology used to discuss them. Sometimes differences arise from different authors or writing styles. A careful assessment of different chapters or sections of a text will allow teachers to plan for effective teaching for more difficult sections.

2. Questions and follow-up activities in texts may have different readability levels from the text itself. Therefore, assessment of those sections will alert teachers to potential difficulty. This can be done quickly as teachers are examining the cognitive and comprehension levels of the questions and activities (using Bloom's and Barrett's taxonomies).

3. Assessment of teacher-made materials, both study materials and tests, is a useful activity. The difference between the level used by the teacher and the text level should be intentional. Teachers may choose to write study materials that are easier to read than the text, especially if the text is fairly difficult. However, teachers need to become sensitive to the difficulty level of their own writing and be careful that their materials are not more difficult than necessary.

EVALUATION OF TEXTS AND PRINT MATERIALS

All teachers evaluate print materials. A school's evaluation procedure may involve a single teacher or an entire department or grade level. An effective method is to organize a committee to evaluate specific texts. Each teacher will have input, but a representative committee can undertake the formal evaluation and comparison of the materials available for adoption. Kuykendall (1980) synthesizes the evaluation procedure into five basic questions.

1. Does the material do what it says it does?
2. Is the material supported by a solid rationale?
3. Is the content of the material sound and well balanced?
4. Is the material designed for learning as well as for teaching?
5. Is the material geared to the abilities and interests of the students intended to use it?

A committee dealing with textbook adoption, formed in advance of the time the book will be used, would do well to answer these five questions for each potential text and then compare the answers.

However, these general questions, while important, do not cover all the concerns generally expressed by the various levels of professionals who deal with text adoptions. Administrators need to know about items like durability and cost, and a thorough presentation to the school board would need to include this information.

A second concern is for quantification of the results. Comparison between texts is often easier if the analysis can be given a numerical value. The text analysis procedure in sections A and B of Figure 7.4 provides one way to make such a comparison. Each characteristic is given a rating, using a Likert-type scale, from 0 to 6. The sum of these ratings provides a total score for the text. A committee can rate several texts, develop an average score for each one, and report to the faculty their joint evaluation by giving a set of comparison scores.

A third consideration is that a single text frequently cannot be evaluated or adopted in isolation. Math, grammar, reading, and foreign language texts are usually adopted by series. The series may range from two years (such as Algebra I and Algebra II) to four years (such as grammar books, grades 9 to 12) to the full reading series, grades kindergarten through eight. When teachers are evaluating texts which are part of a larger program, they must look at evaluations of all books in the series. A numerical rating scale makes these comparisons more useful.

A final consideration is that many texts and series now published are accompanied by audio-visual materials, a testing program, workbooks, computer programs, and other materials in addition to the basic text. These materials are important in evaluating the full impact of the text or series. When the committee compares such programs, it must have some way of looking at the full range of materials available.

The Program-Series-Text Analysis Outline in Figure 7.4 is one way to meet the multiple demands for text evaluation and adoption. Evaluators respond to the statements within the outline on a scale from 0–6 and then add up the ratings by sections as described above.

It is important to note page references where evaluators find the elements listed in the analysis and to make notes indicating why each item is rated as it is. Such references are useful for group discussion of each text. Remember that Marge promised John she would show the science committee a text analysis form they might be able to use? The Program-Series-Text Analysis Outline is an example of that form. Now let's look at evaluating different types of materials for class use.

USING READING AND MEDIA TO TEACH CONTENT

Throughout this book, we encourage teachers to use a wide variety of materials in their teaching. This section provides additional principles for selecting media beyond reading materials. As a beginning, consider Dale's "Cone of Experience" (1969) as a basis for selecting media for teaching. This cone, given in Figure 7.3, moves from materials with the broadest application and the widest use, but the least personal involvement, to materials with the most immediate personal application, but the narrowest and least efficient use of teacher and student time.

Reading fits at the top of the cone, under verbal symbols. Verbal symbols are abstractions and tend to be the least personal of all the media available to the teacher. Reading is also efficient in many ways—it is low-cost and efficient in time, and it allows the student to go back and study material over again. At the other end, direct experience is a great teacher with enormous potential for student motivation. However, it is costly and relatively inefficient in use of time. Generally, one chance is all you get, so students have no chance to repeat the experience. The teacher also has limited control over what happens during the experience.

As an example, consider the study of government. A teacher may use any medium to present the concepts and information. If s/he uses reading, s/he can be sure that all relevant information is covered. However, students may have difficulty relating the abstract principles of government to their lives. At the other end of the scale, a field trip to see govern-

DALE'S CONE OF EXPERIENCE

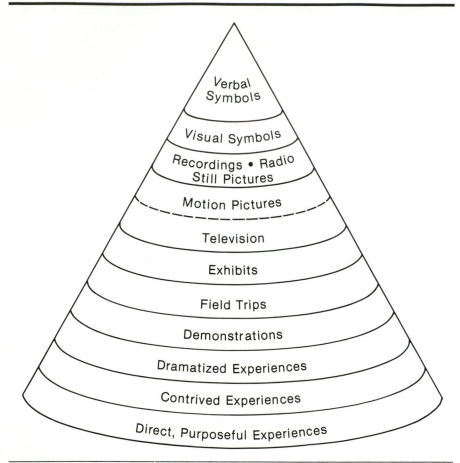

Verbal
Symbols

Visual Symbols

Recordings • Radio
Still Pictures

Motion Pictures

Television

Exhibits

Field Trips

Demonstrations

Dramatized Experiences

Contrived Experiences

Direct, Purposeful Experiences

Figure 7.3
"Dale's Cone of Experience" from *Audio Visual Methods in Teaching*, 3/E, by Edgar
Dale. Copyright © 1959 by The Dryden Press, a division of Holt, Rinehart and Winston,
Inc. Reprinted by permission of the publisher.

ment in action may be very useful—a trip to Congress, the state legislature, the city council, or school board. However, the teacher can't be sure
anything during the students' visit will demonstrate the principles neatly. It would take many hours of watching, for example, to see a bill move
through Congress to become a law. At one extreme on this scale, the
teacher would form a government and have the students take roles in
various situations or actually govern themselves, as in student government. The problem, again, is efficiency in time and resources and control
over the content learned.

PROGRAM-SERIES-TEXT ANALYSIS OUTLINE

Name of analyst _____

Name of program or text to be analyzed _____

Author(s) of program or text to be analyzed _____

Publisher of program or text to be analyzed _____

Date of publication _____ Edition _____

Grade level(s) for which the program or text is primarily intended _____

Subject area(s) for which the program or text is primarily intended _____

Product Characteristics

A. What does the author consider the most appropriate length of time in weeks or years for use of the whole set of materials?

_____ Weeks   _____ Years

Check which of the following items are covered in this analysis. If any listed in a through g are unavailable, list as such and why they are unavailable.

Present Cost

a. Student text
b. Teacher's guide
c. Audio-visual materials
d. Testing program
e. Workbook
f. Rationale
g. Computer programs
h. Other (explain)

B. Check which of the following are included in the program or text:

a. Complete table of contents
b. Full index
c. Complete glossary
d. Useful references for additional reading
e. Appropriate print size
f. Emphasis in bold print, color, etc.

Content

1. The physical and technical durability of all materials in the program.
2. Pictorial sources, maps, graphs, charts, tables, and other illustrative material are integrated and used with text narrative and questions.
3. Key terms and concepts are defined for the student.
4. Adequate data are available for students to use in answering questions.
5. Factual data and interpretations of data seem to be accurate.
6. A multi-ethnic approach is integrated into the program.
7. A multi-ethnic approach is sensitive or suitable to the needs of ethnic groups within your school population.

Figure 7.4 Continued:

8. Women are portrayed adequately in the program.
9. The portrayal of women is sensitive and suitable to the needs of females within your school population.

Score: _____,_____ (maximum: 54)

Special Note: Identify which levels of comprehension are required to answer questions in the text. Give one example of each level you find.

_____ Literal
_____ Inferential
_____ Evaluation
_____ Appreciation

The Cognitive Domain

The acquisition of knowledge which includes concept formation (the many meanings which can apply to one word such as "horse," "war," or "revolution") and the development of basic study skills and critical or analytical thinking skills are generally referred to as cognitive processes.

10. The author states and defines his/her cognitive objectives clearly in the teacher's manual.
11. Student materials and/or suggestions in teacher's manual include learning processes, such as the following (List pages on which each one is found):

_____ a. Observing or perceiving.
_____ b. Listening.
_____ c. Discussing.
_____ d. Defining and expanding the meanings of key terms or concepts.
_____ e. Reading.
_____ f. Writing.
_____ g. Contrasting and comparing to note similarities and differences.
_____ h. Locating, gathering, and classifying information.
_____ i. Interpreting globes, maps, or other types of map projections.
_____ j. Making maps.
_____ k. Interpreting tables, graphs, or charts.
_____ l. Making tables, graphs, or charts.
_____ m. Recognizing a problem for further study.
_____ n. Drawing inferences, making tentative conclusions, or stating hypotheses.
_____ o. Testing the validity of hypotheses.
_____ p. Forming generalizations.
_____ q. Synthesizing information from a variety of sources.

12. The author's emphasis on memorization of data is low and emphasis on critical or analytical thinking is high (as in 11, m-q, above).
13. The teacher's manual includes specific teaching strategies and additional lessons for use with these kinds of students:

_____ a. Slow students
_____ b. Average students
_____ c. Gifted students

Score: _____ (maximum 132)

Figure 7.4 Continued:

The Affective Domain

Learning concerned with a closer look at one's attitudes and values, empathizing, and any behavior which causes a student to be willing to perform as a responsible person both inside and outside the classroom (social participation) is part of the affective domain.

14. The author states and defines his/her affective objectives clearly (in the text or teacher's manual).
15. Student materials or suggestions in the teacher's manual encourage students to explore, clarify, and act

    _____ a. on their own values.
    _____ b. on values held by others.
    _____ c. on the presentation of alternative and conflicting points of view.

16. The author's values and attitudes are not imposed on readers.
17. The teacher's manual includes specific teaching strategies and additional lessons within the affective domain for use with these kinds of students:

    _____ a. Slow students
    _____ b. Average students
    _____ c. Gifted students

        Score: _____ (maximum 48)

The Testing Program

18. The testing program provided with the text tests students for factual recall.
19. The testing program tests for basic skill development (as listed in question 11, a-l).
20. The testing program tests for critical or analytical thinking skill development (as listed in question 11, m-q).
21. The testing program tests for concept development.
22. The testing program tests for attitudes and values.
23. The testing program takes into account the learning abilities and capacity for learning of the slow student.
24. The testing program takes into account the learning abilities and capacity for learning of the average student.
25. The testing program takes into account the learning abilities and capacity for learning of the gifted student.

        Score: _____ (maximum 48)

The Author's Rationale

26. The author's rationale is clear, is found explicitly in the text or other materials, and has guided the development of the program.
27. The analyst agrees with the author's rationale.

        Score: _____ (maximum 12)

Figure 7.4 Continued:

Summary

28. Suppose the following types of students were to be in the grade level for which this program or text is intended. Imagine, too, that these students asked: "What good is spending a year on this program or text going to do me?"

_____ a. It would greatly benefit a slow student or a student with reading problems.
_____ b. It would greatly benefit an average student who reads at the grade level for which the program or text was intended.
_____ c. It would greatly benefit a gifted student who reads above the grade level for which the program or text is intended.

29. Considering the grade level for which this program or text is primarily intended, this program or text would be very suitable for meeting the needs of the following kinds of students:

_____ a. Slow students
_____ b. Average students
_____ c. Gifted students
_____ d. Other types of students, including exceptional students

30. This program/text is highly recommended for use at the designated grade level.
31. The analyst believes this analysis represents the materials very adequately.

Readability Review:

Develop a readability review by using the three readability procedures given here:

a. The Fry Graph for Estimating Readability (1977)
b. The Raygor Readability Estimate (1977)
c. The SMOG formula (McLaughlin, 1969)

or develop a readability analysis using a computer program with three or more formulas.

Interpret the readability data in one or two paragraphs. Remember, the Fry level predicts a student reading at this level will read this material at 50–70 percent accuracy in comprehension while the SMOG formula predicts 90–100 percent accuracy in comprehension. The Fry is roughly the frustration level; the SMOG is roughly the independent level.

Conclusion

Write a one- to two-paragraph conclusion in which you summarize the strengths and weaknesses of the program or text and your judgment about with what kinds of students and in what kinds of situations you would use the book.

Total Score: Content _____
The Cognitive Domain _____
The Affective Domain _____
The Testing Program _____
The Author's Rationale _____
Summary _____

TOTAL _____

Figure 7.4

The conclusion, then, is that to provide the best coverage of content within reasonable time and resources, the teacher's best choice is a variety of media which contribute to student learning. This choice is based on the needs of the students, the objectives, the grouping patterns, and teaching strategies. All of these professional decisions will be made by the teacher during the planning process.

As a general guide to making appropriate choices, the matrix in Figure 7.5 can be useful. One axis represents common types of objectives. The other axis is common types of media. High, medium, and low levels relate to the effectiveness of the media type in helping students with particular kinds of learning. For example, a history teacher teaching the Civil War finds that textbooks are fine (rated medium) for providing dates, names, and places of battles. However, if s/he wants students to learn concepts of battle tactics or the influence of geography on the war, s/he will use TV or film (rated high). A shop teacher may choose a demonstration to teach a skill, like using a specific tool; the same teacher may provide written instructions for shop procedures and mount them on the wall.

One final note on the process of choosing media and reading: Many types of media besides texts and supplementary readings require students to read. Programmed instruction, by computer or any other form, requires

THE RELATIONSHIP OF INSTRUCTIONAL MEDIA SELECTION TO LEARNING OBJECTIVES

	Types of Learning Objectives					
INSTRUCTIONAL MEDIA TYPE:	**Learning Factual Infor- mation**	**Learning Visual Identifi- cations**	**Learning Principles, Concepts, and Rules**	**Learning Procedures**	**Performing Skilled Perceptual- Motor Acts**	**Developing Desirable Attitudes, Opinions, and Motivations**
Still Pictures	Medium	HIGH	Medium	Medium	low	low
Motion Pictures	Medium	HIGH	HIGH	HIGH	Medium	Medium
Television	Medium	Medium	HIGH	Medium	low	Medium
3-D Objects	low	HIGH	low	low	low	low
Audio Recordings	Medium	low	low	Medium	low	Medium
Programmed Instruction	Medium	Medium	Medium	HIGH	low	Medium
Demonstration	low	Medium	low	HIGH	Medium	Medium
Printed Textbooks	Medium	low	Medium	Medium	low	Medium
Oral Presentation	Medium	low	Medium	Medium	low	Medium

Figure 7.5
From "Research in Instructional Media and Art Education" by William H. Allen, *Final Report of the Uses of Newer Media in Art Education Project,* August 1966 by the National Art Education Association, 1916 Association Drive, Reston, Virginia 22091. Copyright © 1966 by National Art Education Association. Reprinted by permission.

a great deal of reading. Many filmstrips, slides, and other forms of still pictures have accompanying study guides, worksheets, or other reading materials. Therefore, the teacher who is carefully matching materials to students' needs to look at the amount and kind of reading required by the medium. Generally speaking, materials with more visuals (still or motion pictures, TV, charts, graphs, and maps) are easier to comprehend than those that consist mostly of words. Concrete objects and experiences are easier to comprehend than more abstract activities.

The choice of teaching materials is a complex and important activity for teachers. Even though this choice comes late in the professional planning process, it remains critical in its effect on student learning. The wise teacher provides multiple materials for students to use in mastering important objectives, so that individual assignments are possible.

Sources of Media

All sorts of media materials for teaching, like print materials, are being produced at a rapid rate. Keeping up with what is available is a formidable task for any teacher. To be sure they have considered all possible materials in building a unit, teachers should check with their librarian and audiovisual specialist. Catalogs from publishing companies and media sources, plus reviews in professional journals (such as *The Mathematics Teacher, The Science Teacher, The English Journal*), are good sources of information on media. Check state, regional, and local school agencies for rentals of films and other media. It is important to order new materials early enough to preview them before they are used in class.

Selecting Materials for Lessons or Units

As we stated earlier, each teacher is responsible for selecting materials for use in the classroom at a specified time. The final selection may well take into account the text, program, or series adopted for use in the course. However, the teacher makes the final decisions as to what is useful in the adopted text and what alternative and supplemental materials should be used.

The areas for consideration are the same ones given for planning a unit or lesson: the content to be covered; the specific needs of the students in the class, especially reading levels; the grouping patterns planned for the unit; and the teaching strategies planned for the unit.

An example of how a teacher might select materials for a unit in eighth-grade social studies underlies the need for careful selection of materials which reflect multiple reading levels. Even without additional information, the average eighth-grade class, grouped heterogeneously, can be expected to include students reading at fourth- to twelfth-grade levels.

Don MacArthur, our Middlewood social studies teacher, knowing this wide range was possible, collected American history books for several different reading levels. When he gathered reading data on his students, he discovered that they had standardized test reading scores (*California Test of Basic Skills*) ranging from nearly non-reader to adult (percentile scores of 10–99). He therefore developed a basic reading system of three groups:

Group	Reading Level	Basic Text
I	Grade Level 0–5	*The American Nation*, by J. D. Hicks, G. E. Mowry, and R. E. Burke, 5th edition (Boston: Houghton Mifflin Co., 1977).
II	Grade Level 6–8	*Liberty and Union*, by D. H. Donald (Boston: Little, Brown and Co., 1978).
III	Grade Level 9 & up	*The Free and the Brave*, by J. Cornwell (New York: Leisure Books, 1978).

In addition, he provided study guides with each reading assignment and learning centers incorporating slides, filmstrips, and additional reading activities.

Teachers who are planning and teaching units should develop an annotated bibliography of potential materials for the unit. This bibliography should include the following information: 1) title, author(s); 2) publisher, place of publication; 3) edition, copyright date; 4) media available (text, primary source, filmstrip, lab manual, workbook, slides, etc.); 5) grade level of student for which it is designed; 6) readability level and formula used, if applicable; and/or 7) annotation (one to two paragraphs) describing strengths and weaknesses, unique features, special instructional or reading help for students, and other relevant comments. This bibliography can be placed on 5″ × 7″ cards or in another format that is easy to keep and easy to find whenever it is necessary to use it.

ANTICIPATING CHALLENGES TO CLASSROOM MATERIALS

Teachers and school districts have experienced a marked rise in challenges to their adopted teaching materials and practices in the past few years. These challenges come from many directions within the community, although the largest number have come from traditional and fundamentalist religious groups, who have challenged literature selections from Shakespeare, *Catcher in the Rye,* and *Huckleberry Finn.* Social studies materials dealing with social issues like nuclear war, population control, and family living have been challenged. Science topics like evolution have been challenged, as has the concept that the world is round, which has been challenged by the Flat Earth Society (Association of American Publishers, 1981; Jenkinson, 1986). Sex education, drug and alcohol abuse, death and dying . . . the list is long. What can teachers do to avoid or overcome challenges to teaching materials and practices? Here are some guidelines to follow:

1. Teachers should be certain their schools and districts have a well-defined and approved materials selection process. A number of processes like the one given earlier may be used. The important point is that the school board has reviewed and approved the process.

2. Teachers and administrators can include community representatives in the selection process—as an advisory board, as part of a district-wide committee, or just as interested parents.

3. Teachers must follow the approved selection process. It must be more than a "paper process." They should also remember that taking shortcuts can be a problem, no matter how convenient it is.

4. The district should have an approved process for reconsidering materials selections—that is, a process to receive community challenges to materials and deal with them systematically. This process should ask, among other things, whether the challenger has read the entire book or selection.

5. Teachers should file their rationale for using a text with the building principal, curriculum coordinator, or other administrator. Such a rationale should be based on the curriculum, specific objectives, teaching strategies, philosophical position, community needs, and state or national requirements. The philosophical positions behind adoption should be those that are endorsed by the department and bolstered by professional associations. For example, teaching evolution in a biology class is supported by the National Science Teachers' Association. Community needs can be demonstrated by community surveys, test results, and the like. State and national requirements come from accrediting agencies. For example, many states require the teaching of sex education and ways to avoid drug and alcohol abuse. These supports mean that the individual teacher is not deciding to teach a topic. Instead, the topic is part of a professionally appropriate curriculum.

SUMMARY

The process of materials selection is complex. It involves analyzing texts and reviewing all types of media. Teachers need to understand text adoption in its broadest sense as well as the selection of materials for particular units and lessons. It is especially important to keep materials selection in context: top priority is assigned to the objectives to be met and the students' needs. Teachers select materials that meet these basic requirements.

Four factors are of importance in assessing reading difficulty in content materials: the reader's background information, the reader's interest, the aids to reading found in the text, and linguistic factors. Teachers should assess all four factors in determining the readability of a text.

Readability formulas are widely used to estimate reading level, but they deal primarily with linguistic factors only. The Fry and Raygor Readability Estimates are suggested as reasonably valid, reliable, and easy to use. The goal of this chapter has been to develop teachers' professional judgment in assessing the difficulty level of reading materials.

Materials, including media, should be evaluated as they are selected to be sure they will meet students' needs. Using a wide variety of materials is the best way to keep students interested while teaching instructional objectives.

REFERENCES

Association of American Publishers. (1981). *Limiting what students shall read*. Washington, D.C.: Association of American Publishers.

Baldwin, R. S. & Kaufman, R. K. (1979). A concurrent validity study of the Raygor Readability Estimate. *Journal of Reading, 23,* 148–153.

Christenson, J. (1983). *Your reading: A booklist for junior high and middle school students*. Urbana, IL: National Council of Teachers of English.

Dale, E. (1969). *Audiovisual methods in teaching*, (3rd ed.). New York: Holt, Rinehart and Winston.

Dale, E., & Chall, J. (1948, January–February). A formula for predicting readability. *Educational Research Bulletin, 27,* 11–20, 37–54.

English, R. (1980, December). The politics of textbook adoption. *Phi Delta Kappan, 62,* 275–278.

Farr, R., & Tulley, M. A. (1985, November). Do adoption committees perpetuate mediocre textbooks?. *Phi Delta Kappan, 66(7),* 467–471.

Fitzgerald, G. G. (1980). Reliability of the Fry sampling procedure. *Reading Research Quarterly, 15,* 489–503.

Fry, E. (1968). A readability formula that saves time. *Journal of Reading, 11,* 514–515.

Fry, E. (1977). Fry's readability graph: Clarifications, validity and extension to level 17. *Journal of Reading, 21,* 242–243.

Jenkinson, E. (1986). *The schoolbook protest movement*. Bloomington, IN: Phi Delta Kappa.

Kane, R., Byrne, M. A., & Hater, M. A. (1974). *Helping children read mathematics*. New York: American Book Co.

Klare, G. R. (1984). Readability. In P. D. Pearson (Ed.), *Handbook on reading research* (681–744). New York: Longman, Inc.

Klare, G. R., & Schumacher, G. M. (1981). Student behavior while reading from text. *ERIC, #201957.*

Kuykendall, C. (1980, May). What's new in teaching materials. *The English Journal, 69,* 77–78.

McLaughlin, G. H. (1969). SMOG grading: A new readability formula. *Journal of Reading, 12,* 639–646.

Marshall, N. (1979). Research: Readability and comprehensibility. *Journal of Reading, 22,* 542–544.

Raygor, A. L. (1977). The Raygor Readability Estimate: A quick and easy way to determine difficulty. In P. D. Pearson (Ed.), *Reading: Theory, research and practice,* 26th Yearbook of the National Reading Conference (259–263). Clemson, SC: National Reading Conference, Inc.

Reiter, I. (1973). *The reading line.* New York: Cambridge Book Co.

Singer, H. (1975). The SEER technique: A non-computational procedure for quickly estimating readability level. *Journal of Reading Behavior, 7*(3), 255–267.

Singer, H., & Donlan, D. (1985). *Reading and learning from text.* Hillsdale, NJ: Lawrence Erlbaum Associates, Inc.

Vaughn, J. L. (1976). Interpreting readability assessments. *Journal of Reading, 19,* 635–639.

SUGGESTIONS FOR FURTHER READING

Holdzkom, D. (1987). Readability. In D. E. Alvermann et al. (Eds.), *Research within reach: Secondary school reading.* Newark, DE: International Reading Association.

Jenkinson, E. (1986). *The schoolbook protest movement.* Bloomington, IN: Phi Delta Kappa.

Singer, H., & Donlan, D. (1985). *Reading and learning from text.* Hillsdale, NJ: Lawrence Erlbaum Associates, Inc.

CHAPTER EIGHT

Assessing Students In Content Area Reading And Writing

SCENARIO

The school year is approaching the halfway point. Students and staff at Middlewood have returned to their classrooms after a long and restful two-week winter vacation. They have exchanged tales of exciting vacation adventures, warm family reunions, and sumptuous holiday feasts. Life has returned to its normal hectic pace for Marge and her colleagues. We find Marge offering some helpful advice to Janet.

"Thanks for stopping by to see me, Marge," said Janet as Marge entered the business education office.

"I was glad to get your note, Janet. You may recall that last fall I urged all our new staff members to contact me if they needed any help in teaching reading and writing skills in their content classes."

"Yes, I remember that note and I confess that I tossed it aside as something that had little if anything to do with me," said Janet, looking a little embarrassed.

"No need to apologize, Janet," assured Marge. "A great many teachers enter this profession thinking that they don't have to be concerned with teaching reading and writing. They assume that the English teacher does all that. I know, because I used to be on the English staff full-time. And you know I still teach one English class each year to keep me honest!"

"Yes, I did know that. And I admit that now that the year's half over, I realize that I need some help from you. My classes have gone fairly well so far, but I really run into trouble when I try to assign chapters from the textbook or when I ask students to write anything that requires more than a few words. Help! What am I doing wrong?"

"Let's start by looking at your textbook," replied Marge. "Have you made any attempt to determine whether or not your students can read the book? And have you ever tried to assess their writing skills to get an idea of the quality of written responses you can reasonably expect from them?"

"You've got me there. No to both questions," said Janet. "It never occurred to me to check out students' reading and writing skills. I guess I have no idea whether they can read the book or not, and I have no idea what I should be expecting in the way of writing. And here it is almost the middle of the year. I guess I really *do* need some help, don't I?"

"Don't take it so seriously," Marge said. "It's not too late to remedy the situation. There's a fairly easy way to determine how appropriate the text is for your students. It's probably fine for most of them, too easy for some, and too hard for the others. Once you find that out, we can talk about some ways of grouping for any instruction that is related to reading assignments."

"That sounds reasonable. What about writing?" asked Janet. "How do I find out what they can do and what I should be expecting in reports and on tests?"

"One thing at a time," said Marge. "First let's take a look at your textbook and work on an assessment tool that will give you some critical information about your students' abilities to read and understand assignments."

OVERVIEW

This chapter presents some general information about the assessment process, with an emphasis on the uses of various tests for obtaining practical information about students' abilities to read content area materials. A distinction is drawn between norm-referenced and criterion-referenced tests, with suggestions for using each type. You will learn how to construct a group-administered skills inventory for assessing students in the specific reading skills needed to acquire information from any textbook in any content area. You will also discover a method for checking the compatibility of a writer's style with a learner's reading ability. This method is called the "cloze technique." Scores from these two informal diagnostic tools will assist you in making decisions about instruction.

The chapter concludes with a brief look at assessing writing in the content areas. Some options for scoring student work are presented, including holistic scoring and focus correction. Last, we look at peer evaluation and other suggestions for assessing writing in the content classroom.

DEFINING SOME TERMS

It is important for middle and secondary teachers to recognize that some students, even those who may have been "good" readers in elementary school, may have difficulty reading content textbooks. Each content area provides unique challenges to readers. Specialized vocabulary, new concepts, a different writing style—such factors can spell disaster for students as they encounter more and more school tasks directly related to their ability to read and comprehend content area texts. It is fairly easy to recognize the advantage students bring to content area classes when to some extent their background experiences "match" the reading material they are assigned. One student might have an extensive background in a particular content area such as industrial arts. Another might excel in geography, having traveled widely across the United States. But, just as teachers cannot assume that students have equal background experiences in a content field, neither can they assume that the reading abilities of their students are equal.

Since a major goal for each content area teacher is helping students learn as much as possible about curriculum content, it makes good sense to conduct a preliminary assessment of student reading abilities in each class. Obviously some content area courses rely more on reading than others, but all teachers expect students to comprehend assigned reading. Assessing students' comprehension, therefore, is the first step in ensuring that students will succeed in content area classes.

The *Dictionary of Education* (1973) defines *individual assessment* as a process by which as many data as possible are gathered and used to evaluate a person more accurately. Many elementary schools routinely conduct an assessment of reading skills as an integral part of the developmental and remedial programs. It seems, however, that the further a student moves from the early grades, the less often his/her reading is assessed. In high school these assessments generally stop altogether unless a student persistently demonstrates a serious learning problem. Too often teachers assume that by the time students reach the middle or secondary schools, they have attained the level of reading ability necessary to comprehend any assigned content area text. They assume that assessment of students' reading skills has been done often enough by someone else and if anything were "wrong," that someone would have undertaken appropriate remediation. Finally, teachers of older students often fail to recognize that reading continues to be a developmental process beyond the early elementary years. What do teachers in the content areas really know about their students' reading abilities? How much data do they collect to get an accurate concept of these abilities? Too often the answer to both questions is "very little."

Before we discuss formal and informal evaluation, let's clarify a few more terms. As Gronlund (1985) points out in his concise text entitled *Measurement and Evaluation in Teaching,* there is often confusion about the terms "assessment," "evaluation," "measurement," and "testing." We have defined *assessment* as a data-gathering process used for evaluation. Gronlund suggests that *evaluation* is the systematic process of collecting, analyzing, and interpreting information for the purpose of determining the "extent to which pupils are achieving instructional objectives" (p. 5).

Evaluation thus answers the question "How well?". *Measurement* is defined as the process of "obtaining a numerical description of the degree to which an individual possesses a particular characteristic" (p. 5). Measurement can be said to answer the question "How much?". Finally, a *test* is an instrument or systematic procedure for measuring a sample of behavior. A test answers the question of how well the individual performs, either in comparison with others or in comparison with some domain of performance tasks.

The primary usefulness of tests is to help teachers make sound instructional decisions. Within this context, tests can be used in placement decisions, selection decisions, grading decisions, diagnostic decisions, and so on. There are commercially available reading tests which are appropriate for all of these purposes.

FORMAL TESTS

Formal testing is most often conducted by a reading specialist, reading supervisor, or guidance counselor. There are two basic types of formal tests. *Norm-referenced tests* (NRTs) are the most common type. These are standardized tests designed to compare the achievement of a local group of students to that of a national or state sample of students at the same academic level. The Scholastic Aptitude Test (SAT) is an example of a norm-referenced test.

Because their function is to make comparisons, these tests are carefully standardized. They cover a large domain of learning tasks with a few items measuring each specified task. NRTs are useful for survey testing, which emphasizes discrimination among individuals. Performance results on norm-referenced tests are most often reported as *grade equivalents* (for example, 10.9 or tenth grade, ninth month) or *percentiles* (for example, the 44th percentile, which means that the student scored as well as or better than 44 percent of the others in the group to which s/he is being compared).

A second type of test are *criterion-referenced tests* (CRTs). These tests are tied very closely to the local curriculum. CRTs compare students, not to their age or grade mates, but to how well they perform in learning a specific set of objectives. These tests focus on a limited number of learning tasks and often have a large number of items measuring each task. CRTs are often used with mastery or outcome-based learning. Scores are therefore reported most often in terms of percentages obtained for each subskill, with an indication of what is considered mastery of each skill. CRTs are therefore said to emphasize description of what a student has and has not learned within the local curriculum.

Both NRTs and CRTs are useful for formal assessment. They both may use the same type of test items and the same rules for writing those items. Also, they are both judged on their validity (the test actually measures what it purports to measure) and reliability (the consistency of results from one measurement to another). A technical bulletin, which indicates the validity and reliability of any formal test, should be available from the publisher to help teachers judge both types of tests.

INFORMAL TESTS

Formal tests play an important role in helping teachers make some general decisions about instruction. They are limited by their nature, however, when it comes to helping teachers make decisions about individual students in their classrooms. Therefore, content teachers should develop their own informal tests in order to diagnose individual and group strengths and weaknesses. Informal testing for the purpose of diagnosis will enable teachers to determine whether students can use written curriculum materials successfully. It is not unusual in a seventh-grade social studies classroom, for example, for some students to be functioning at a third-grade reading level while others are functioning at the eleventh-grade reading level. In fact, it has been estimated that as many as 50 percent of secondary school texts may be beyond the comprehension of the students to whom they are assigned (Estes & Vaughn, 1978).

Another reason to use informal diagnostic tests is to determine specific reading and study skills for both groups and individuals. Although proficiency in specific reading skills is related to general reading ability, these skills should be assessed by the content teacher in order that appropriate group placements and reading assignments can be made. One tool for informal diagnostic testing is the criterion-referenced group reading inventory.

THE CRITERION-REFERENCED GROUP READING INVENTORY

The informal group reading inventory (GRI) has proved to be a useful diagnostic tool in content area reading. It yields information about a student's general reading ability and his/her proficiency in those specific skills needed to read the materials in any content area. The GRI is very similar to an individual reading inventory (IRI), which is administered to elementary students in order to determine at what level directed reading instruction should begin.

The data from both these informal measures indicates to what extent students can comprehend the concepts and vocabulary of the material they are expected to read in class. In the early grades, a student generally reads from narrative passages of increasing difficulty, stopping at the level where s/he can no longer read fluently (on oral passages) or where his/her comprehension falls below 70 or 75 percent. As students enter the middle or secondary grade levels, IRIs are unlikely to be administered and, in fact, if based on narrative passages, are unlikely to yield the most useful information to content teachers. At these upper grade levels, teachers need to know how proficiently students process expository reading materials in their particular content areas, and, perhaps more importantly, they need to be able to assess whole classes of students at one time. The group reading inventory (GRI) meets both these criteria.

The group reading inventory for the content area classroom needs to go beyond the scope of the traditional IRI. In addition to measuring whether or not students can process the actual "text" part of a book, a GRI should assess such common skills as using parts of the book. For example, a test should include questions regarding the table of contents, index, and glossary, as well as questions on vocabulary skills, such as identifying word meanings in context, dividing words into syllables, and picking out frequently used roots and affixes. In addition to finding a student's reading rate, the test assesses comprehension skills by requiring the student to read a particular section from the textbook. The test also assesses a student's ability to scan to locate specific information and to skim to obtain a general overview.

Informal reading assessment can help content teachers determine students' ability to understand specific reading materials. Above, students work on an informal group reading inventory (GRI).

Teachers may also consider assessing the graphic skills unique to their content areas. For example, social studies teachers might include assessment of map reading skills while science teachers might assess the interpretation of tables and graphs. Home economics teachers, on the other hand, might focus on students' abilities to read charts and diagrams.

The difficulty with the group informal reading inventory, as described by Shepherd (1978) and others (for example, Burmeister, 1978; Singer & Donlan, 1985), is the lack of sufficient items to provide a reliable measure of skill attainment. Therefore, we propose that content teachers create group reading inventories that are also criterion-referenced; that is, each section of the GRI reflects a particular objective and provides sufficient items to assess that objective. Creating a GRI takes time, but it may be the most important activity a teacher can do to ensure students' success in the content classroom.

Developing a Criterion-Referenced GRI

Following is a simple six-step process for developing a criterion-referenced group reading inventory. As you read each step, refer to the sample GRI in Figure 8.1.

1. First, the teacher selects a section of a textbook or other reading material s/he wishes to use for instruction. The passage should be four to six pages in length. It should be relatively self-contained, if possible, and the information should not be highly dependent on prior reading or experience. A section that includes some sort of closure or ending is ideal for use in a GRI.

2. Next, the teacher writes a series of comprehension questions using one of the taxonomies suggested previously. S/he begins by creating ten to twelve literal level questions which emphasize recall of important facts from the reading. Then s/he develops ten to twelve questions at the inference level which require students to "read between the lines." These questions should be text dependent; a student should not be able to answer these questions by using other background knowledge. Finally the teacher asks students to determine the meaning of about ten to twelve vocabulary words from the passage. Students should be able to determine meanings by using the context of the selected passage.

3. The teacher now decides which subskills are important by examining the selected content passage very carefully. Different content areas emphasize different skills. For example, a social studies teacher may include comprehension skills involving sequence and map reading skills on a GRI while a mathematics teacher may focus on specialized vocabulary and/or graph reading skills. The idea is to assess students' abilities in areas that will be vital to their reading success in a particular content classroom. Approximately four to six subskills may be selected for assessment.

4. The teacher now writes ten to twelve items which will assess each skill. If 80 percent is the mastery level when scoring student responses, eight correct responses out of ten would be considered acceptable. Teachers are often surprised at the results of this part of a GRI. It usually becomes clear when examining the class results that some students need work in some of the subskill areas in order to really comprehend their reading assignments.

5. The teacher writes explicit directions for each part of the GRI, making it clear that s/he can help students understand the task required of each section but that they will have to do the reading.

6. Last, the teacher administers the group inventory and emphasizes that it is not a test. S/he tells students that s/he is trying to obtain an accurate representation of their strengths and weaknesses in various skills needed for reading the textbook successfully. Creating unnecessary test anxiety will not further this purpose. S/he allows as much time as necessary to complete the inventory.

SAMPLE GROUP READING INVENTORY

General Directions: This is a survey to help me evaluate skills you will be using in this course. This is not a test to see what facts you know and you will not be given a grade. Read each question carefully and give the best answer you can find.

Part I. Reading Skills—Comprehension

This part of the Reading Inventory will help me see how much you understand of the material you will be reading during this course. Turn to page 227 of your science book (*Prentice-Hall Life Science* by V. Webster et al., Englewood Cliffs, NJ: Prentice-Hall, 1980) to the section called "Plant Structures." Begin reading at that point on page 227 and continue to read over to but not including "Flowers and Cones" on page 235. When you are finished reading, raise your hand so that I may record the time it took you to read this section. (Don't hurry; read at your usual speed for this type of material.) After I have noted your time, then answer the questions. You may now turn to page 227 and begin reading.

Directions to students: On the lines in each of the following sentences, write the word that best completes the sentence. Notice that one of the sentences asks for two words but the remainder of the sentences only require one-word answers.

1. The seed plant has _____ main parts.

2. Roots, stems, and _____ provide the day-to-day needs of the plant.

3. _____ anchor the plant in the soil.

4. There are _____ main types of roots.

5. _____ help to support the plant and display the leaves and flowers.

6. Most plants have stems that are _____.

7. Many plants have green stems. Green stems contain _____.

Figure 8.1 Continued:

8. With few exceptions, _____ _____ occur in the leaves of seed plants.

9. Most leaves are flat and _____.

10. Most leaves have _____ parts.

Directions to students: Answer the following questions about the material you have read. Use complete sentences.

11. If a seed plant lost its reproductive parts, it would not die; however, what would happen to future generations of seed plants?

_____

_____

12. Some of the large cacti may contain enough water in their stems to supply their needs for several years. Why is this a good adaptation in a desert environment?

_____

_____

13. Bulbs contain both stems and leaves. Onions are examples of bulbs that you can eat. What would happen if you put an onion in a pot of moist soil?

_____

_____

14. What would happen to a plant if its leaves were not arranged in a spiral around the stem and why?

_____

_____

15. Why might it be an advantage for cacti to have thin spines instead of broad leaves?

_____

_____

16. In measuring one rye plant, biologists found that the roots measured 608 km in length! Since a rye plant has an underground root system, how were the biologists able to measure the root system?

_____

_____

17. Plants you may have heard or read about are air plants, such as orchids. These do not have roots that anchor them in the soil. How do you suppose these plants get the minerals they need to grow?

_____

_____

18. What time of year is best for observing the branching pattern of a tree and why?

_____

_____

19. What might happen to a seed plant that lost the root cap and why?

_____

_____

Figure 8.1 Continued:
Part II. Reading Skills—Vocabulary

This part of the inventory will show me how well you understand the meaning of words by using context clues. Context clues help you get the meaning of new words by using the words around them.

Directions to students: On the lines in front of each of the following sentences write the letter of the phrase that best matches the italicized word or words in the sentence.

_____ 1. The *epidermal cells* protect the root cells from being injured as the root grows.
    A. cells that transport food to the plant stem
    B. cells that cover the root cap
    C. cells that photosynthesize sunlight

_____ 2. It is through the *root hairs* that the plant absorbs water and minerals.
    A. cells that take in food for the plant
    B. cells that cover the root cap
    C. cells that transport food to the plant stem

_____ 3. Some kinds of plants have one large root called the *taproot*.
    A. a root that taps water from the ground
    B. a type of plant that has one big root
    C. a type of plant that has many roots growing under the ground

_____ 4. Roots that are slender and are all nearly equal in size are called *fibrous roots*.
    A. a plant with one main root
    B. a plant with only two roots
    C. a plant with many roots

_____ 5. Some plants have *tendrils* that wrap around plant stems or other objects for support.
    A. slender projections from the stem that are used to help a vine stand up
    B. slender projections from the stem that are used to absorb water
    C. slender projections from the stem that are used to catch insects

_____ 6. Some plants have stems called *stolons* that creep over the ground.
    A. stems used to gather food for the plant
    B. stems used to reproduce new plants and roots
    C. stems used to move up walls and other vertical objects

_____ 7. One kind of an underground stem is called a *rhizome*.
    A. the leaves of a plant that help it grow
    B. the part of the plant cell that is underground
    C. a stem that does not grow above the ground

_____ 8. Large swollen structures at the end of underground stems are called *tubers*.
    A. big growths at the base of a plant stalk
    B. big growths at the very tip of a root cap
    C. big growths at the end of underground stems

_____ 9. the *stalk* attaches the leaf to the plant stem.
    A. a part of the root system
    B. a part of the stem
    C. a part of the leaf

_____ 10. The *blade* is the flat, thin portion of the leaf.
    A. a part of the stalk of a leaf
    B. a part of the stem of a plant
    C. a part of the leaf of a plant

Figure 8.1 Continued:

Note: To avoid testing fatigue, the remainder of the inventory should be given as separate tests on different days.

Part III. Knowing Where to Look

This part of the Reading Inventory will tell me how familiar you are with the different parts of your book.

Directions to students: On the line in front of each of the following phrases write "T" if information could be found in the table of contents. Write "G" if it could be found in the glossary and "I" if the information could be found in the index.

T - table of contents
G - glossary
 I - index

_____ 1. What page Unit 1 starts on.

_____ 2. Definition of "crustaceous."

_____ 3. Page number on the topic of rocky mountain spotted fever.

_____ 4. How many chapters does Unit 5 contain?

_____ 5. How many syllables does the word "multicellular" have?

_____ 6. Page numbers that deal with the reproduction of plants.

_____ 7. How do you pronounce "antennae"?

_____ 8. How many units does the book contain?

_____ 9. How many meanings are used in our textbook for the word "conjugation"?

_____ 10. How many pages long is Chapter 7?

_____ 11. Where could you find a pronunciation key?

_____ 12. A respelling of the word "spiracles."

_____ 13. Key words used as examples of the respelling symbol "/zh/."

Part IV. Vocabulary Skills—Prefix Meaning

This part of the Reading Inventory will tell me how well you can figure out the meanings of words when you know what the prefixes of the words mean.

Directions to students: Study the chart below. Then put together the meaning of the prefixes bio, de, geo, and in, to match each word with its meaning.

Prefix	Meaning	Example
bio	life, of living things	biology
de	to break down or remove	deregulate
geo	earth, of the earth	geochemistry
in	no, not, without	incomplete

Figure 8.1 Continued:

Write the letter of the meaning from List II that matches each word given in List I. The words in parentheses () are given to help you.

LIST I

_____ 1. biochemistry
_____ 2. decomposer
_____ 3. geology
_____ 4. inorganic
_____ 5. invertebrates (backbone)
_____ 6. bioluminescent (light)
_____ 7. desalination (salt)
_____ 8. geothermal (temperature)
_____ 9. involuntary

LIST II

A. not living
B. having the ability to produce light
C. study of chemical make-up of living things
D. heat energy from the earth's crust
E. not under conscious control
F. organism that breaks down dead matter
G. animals without backbones
H. process that removes salt
I. study of the earth
J. to remove the backbone of

Part V. Using Visual Aids

Each of the following exercises was designed to show me how well you can use the pictures and diagrams in your science book.

Directions to students: Read each of the following questions and follow the directions given. Then answer the questions that are asked. You may look at the picture or diagram for as long as you like.

1. Turn to page 170 and look at figure 5.13. Which is the largest biome found on the North American Continent? (biome — a major division of the earth having distinct climate and vegetation). _____

   _____

   In which biome do we live primarily? _____

2. Turn to page 216 and look at figure 7.9. What is the third stage of mitosis called?

   _____

3. Turn to page 221 and look at figure 7.15. Several organs join together to form a(n) _____
   _____ (complete the sentence).

4. Turn to page 237 and look at figure 8.17. What parts of the flower make up the stamen?

   _____

5. Turn to page 253 and look at figure 9.1. What is another name for your hipbone?

   _____

6. Turn to page 258 and look at figure 9.8. In what layer of skin is the oil gland found?

   _____

7. Turn to page 296 and look at figure 10.4. What is the chemical symbol for Mercury?

   _____

8. Turn to page 307 and look at figure 10.10. What are the deficiency symptoms that result from a lack of vitamin C? _____

9. Turn to page 348 and look at figure 12.12. In what ways is water returned to the atmosphere?

   _____

Figure 8.1 Continued:
Part VI. Getting the Main Idea

This section of the Reading Inventory will tell me how well you can get the main idea from paragraphs that you may be reading in your Science book.

Directions to students: Read the following paragraph, noting the underlined sentence.

<u>There are more species (about 700,000) of insects than of all other animals combined.</u> Imagine, it has been estimated that the total weight of all the ants on the earth is greater than the total weight of all the other land-dwelling animals combined!

The sentence that has been underlined can be called the main idea of the paragraph. It tells us what the paragraph is about. The remainder of the paragraph supports the main idea or helps further explain what the paragraph is about. Any idea or sentence that supports the main idea is called a supporting detail. Now, read the next paragraph.

There is a greater variation in body forms and habits among the insects than among any other group. <u>But there are also several common features that are shared by all insects.</u> An insect body has three parts: head, thorax, and abdomen. Most insects have one pair of antennae on the head. They all have three pairs of legs attached to the thorax. Some insects are wingless, but most have two pairs of wings. (An exception: flies have only one pair of wings.) Now that you know these basic characteristics, see if you can name five insects.

As you can see, the main idea of a paragraph is not always contained in the first sentence. Below, in outline form, I have rewritten the paragraph using only short sentences and phrases.

I.   **Main Idea—Common features of all insects**
  A. supporting detail—body has three parts
     1. head
     2. thorax
     3. abdomen
  B. supporting detail—most have one antenna
  C. supporting detail—all have three pairs of legs
  D. supporting detail—most have two pairs of wings

Now read the next paragraph.

Almost all insects are land-dwellers. Some may live in fresh water, but none are considered marine, or sea-dwelling.

II.   **Main Idea—Almost all insects are land-dwellers.**
  A. supporting detail— _____

_____

You should have answered something similar to: *Some may live in fresh water, but none are considered sea-dwelling.* Now read the next paragraph. The main idea and some of the supporting details have been identified for you. Please complete the outline by filling in the remaining supporting details.

Insects breathe through spiracles. These are holes along the sides of the thorax and abdomen. These holes lead into air tubes called trachea. The tubes have many branches that extend into the body tissues. Oxygen is taken into the body through the spiracles and reaches every cell of the body through the trachea.

Figure 8.1 Continued:

III. Main Idea—How insects breathe

    A. supporting detail—breathe through spiracles
    B. supporting detail—(1) _____
    C. supporting detail—air tubes called (2) _____
    D. supporting detail—(3) _____

Now read the next paragraph and try to complete the outline by yourself.

    For young insects to become adults, they must change from one stage of development to another. The changes may result in forms that look very different from one another. This changing is called "metamorphosis." Most kinds of insects have four stages in their metamorphosis: egg, larva, pupa, and adult. Some insects go through all four stages in a few days. Others require years to complete their metamorphosis. The insect may change both in appearance and habits in each stage. A caterpillar, for example, is the larval stage of a butterfly.

IV. Main idea—(4) _____

    A. supporting detail—(5) _____

    B. supporting detail—four stages of development

    1. (6) _____

    2. (7) _____

    3. (8) _____

    4. (9) _____

    C. supporting detail—(10) _____

    D. supporting detail—(11) _____

When you have finished, turn your paper in.

Figure 8.1
Prepared by Rodger L. Smith, Radio Park Elementary School, State College, Pa. Reprinted by permission.

Using a Criterion-Referenced Group Reading Inventory

Usually the GRI is administered at the beginning of the school year to enable the content teacher to determine students' reading ability using given materials. It can also be administered again at the end of the school year to assess growth in skill development. The teacher should not set time limits; students should be encouraged to do their best work. The following steps are recommended in administering the inventory.

    1. The teacher asks students to read silently the preselected four to six pages of the content textbook or other reading material. They should be given any necessary background to help them understand the selection, but the teacher should not introduce new vocabulary. To determine each student's reading rate, the teacher should ask students to raise their

hands as they finish reading, noting the time. Later s/he can convert this to words read per minute.

2. When students have completed their reading, the teacher gives them the criterion-referenced group reading inventory. First, they should answer the literal and inferential comprehension questions over the selection they have just read. They should also answer vocabulary questions dealing with words in context immediately after reading the material. Students may refer to the reading selection if necessary in answering questions. At another time, the teacher may check students' memories or recall comprehension by having them close their books before answering comprehension questions.

3. Next, or at a later time, students answer the subskills portion of the test. During this portion they must use the textbbook to answer items. The teacher collects the papers upon completion.

The scoring procedure for the inventory is as follows:

1. The teacher first calculates the number correct for each of the following: literal comprehension questions, inferential comprehension questions, and vocabulary meanings derived from the context. S/he then enters these figures on a grouping chart such as the one in Figure 8.2.

2. The teacher next calculates the total percent correct of the combined literal, inferential, and vocabulary questions and enters it on the grouping chart. Using the criteria suggested by Singer and Donlan (1985), the

RESULTS OF THE GROUP READING INVENTORY

Students	Part One		Part Two	TOTAL	Part Three	Part Four	Part Five	Part Six	TOTAL
	Literal 1-10	Inference 11-19	Vocab Context 1-10	Parts 1 & 2	Parts of Book 1-13	Prefexes 1-9	Visual Aids 1-9	Main Idea 1-11	Parts 1–6
Robert	9	7	8	24/29	10	5	9	8	80%
Sue	10	9	8	28/29	12	5	9	5	83%
Helen	6	3	6	15/29	10	3	8	2	54%
Sara	7	4	5	16/29	9	3	8	3	55%
Matthew	10	9	9	28/29	8	4	3	3	65%
Victor	5	5	5	15/29	7	3	7	5	52%
John	9	9	7	25/29	10	8	8	9	90%
James	4	5	6	15/29	7	3	5	4	48%
Andrea	9	8	4	21/29	9	7	8	8	75%
Tina	2	6	9	17/29	6	5	5	4	52%

Figure 8.2

teacher finds that scores above 90 percent indicate that the reading material is most likely at a student's independent level, meaning that that student can read on his/her own. Scores between 70 to 90 percent correct indicate a student's probable instructional range, where s/he will likely need some teacher guidance. Scores below 65 percent correct indicate that the reading material is likely at a student's frustration level and therefore too difficult for use in instruction. The teacher should examine carefully all scores between 60 and 70 percent, since the difference between frustration level and instructional level is important. Teachers are advised to assess further the students scoring in this range in order to determine whether or not they are really weak in specific skill areas.

3. The teacher should calculate the number of correct items for each subskill that was assessed. Enter each on a grouping chart such as the one in Figure 8.2. From the grouping chart the teacher can see the general reading level of the students as well as strengths and weaknesses in skill acquisition. If most students in a class score at the independent level, the teacher should probably select more challenging supplementary study materials. If most students score at the frustration level, the teacher should attempt to find alternative reading materials written at an easier level. If these are unavailable or limited, the teacher needs to consider techniques for adapting the textbook or using study guides to help students focus on the important elements in the textbook.

Stop to Think

Let's pause here to determine how well you are comprehending this chapter. Using the sample grouping chart in Figure 8.2, answer the following questions about the students whose names and scores appear on the chart. When you have completed this activity, compare your answers to those found after the questions.

1. Which students appear to be the strongest in determining vocabulary meanings from context?
2. Which students appear to need some instruction on using various parts of the textbook?
3. Which students appear able to read the textbook independently?
4. For how many students does the text appear to represent instructional level reading material?
5. Which students appear to be the overall weakest readers; i.e., for whom does the textbook appear "impossible"?

Your answers to these questions should look like this:

1. Matthew (97 percent) and Tina (97 percent) are the strongest students in determining vocabulary from context.

2. Victor (54 percent) and James (54 percent) encountered the most difficulty with using various parts of the text.
3. Matthew and Sue are the only students able to read the text independently. Both of these students, however, need assistance in working with prefixes, and Matthew needs help in using visual aids.
4. The text is at the instructional level for John, Andrea, and Robert.
5. The text may be impossible for James, Tina, Victor, Sara, and Helen.

THE CLOZE PROCEDURE

Another informal teacher-developed technique for determining students' reading level is the *cloze procedure*. A teacher-constructed assessment tool, the cloze procedure is often used in conjunction with a GRI to corroborate and enhance diagnostic information for grouping purposes. While readability formulas may provide teachers with general estimates of textbook difficulty, they do not account for the individual student's background knowledge in a content area, language ability, interest level, ability to draw inferences, and so forth. The teacher who uses standardized reading test scores to match students to reading material will have some success. However, a standardized test score in reading does not indicate the student's knowledge and prior experience in a particular content area. Since comprehension is greatly influenced by a student's prior knowledge and experience, the criterion-referenced group reading inventory, used along with a cloze procedure instrument, may permit a teacher to match students to reading materials more accurately.

The term "cloze" relates to the concept of closure. Fluent readers do not read every word; our eyes stop along a line of print to take in one or two words. The mature reader comprehends by reading a sampling of the words rather than laboriously reading every word (Smith, 1983). With the cloze procedure, words at regularly spaced intervals (for example, every fifth word) are omitted. The student uses the surrounding context to supply the missing words. The use of the cloze procedure to estimate reading levels has been well established (Jongsma, 1980). If a passage from the content area textbook is used, then the teacher can estimate a student's reading level in relation to that material.

Developing a Cloze

Teachers select a passage of approximately 250 words from the content textbook or other required reading materials. The first sentence is left intact, with no omissions. Beginning with the second sentence, every fifth word is deleted from the passage, for a total of fifty deletions. All blanks

SAMPLE CLOZE TEST

Directions to students: Fill in the blanks in the following selection with the word that has been left out. Try to supply the exact word the author used. Only one word has been deleted from each blank. You will have as much time as necessary to complete this exercise.

In the early 1800s the French biologist, Jean Lamarck, proposed his theory of evolution, or gradual change in organisms. Lamarck's theory was based (1)_____ the idea that organisms (2)_____ change to fit into (3)_____ environment. He believed that (4)_____ organism can acquire certain (5)_____ that will better adapt (6)_____ to the environment and (7)_____ these acquired traits can (8)_____ passed on to the (9)_____.

For example, Lamarck believed (10)_____ all giraffes developed long (11)_____ because they needed to (12)_____ for food in trees. (13)_____ a giraffe kept stretching (14)_____ neck, the neck would (15)_____ longer. The offspring, then, (16)_____ inherit this acquired trait (17)_____ be born with a (18)_____ neck. The offspring would (19)_____ slightly different from its (20)_____ but would be better (21)_____ to the environment. Lamarck (22)_____ that in this way, long-necked (23)_____ gradually evolved.

Likewise, Lamarck (24)_____ that if certain parts (25)_____ the body were not (26)_____, these parts would eventually (27)_____. The offspring, then, would (28)_____ born without these parts.

Lamarck's (29)_____ has never been proven (30)_____ be true. In fact, (31)_____ is highly criticized by (32)_____ people. One reason for (33)_____ his theory incorrect is (34)_____ present-day knowledge of genes (35)_____ hereditary factors. For body (36)_____ to change and to (37)_____ these changes passed on (38)_____ offspring, the genes of

should be of equal length so as not to provide students with clues about word length.

The cloze exercise (it is not a test) can be somewhat frustrating for all students. It is helpful if students are prepared for this activity with a few practice examples. Students should be instructed to do their best but not agonize over each blank. They should be allowed as much time as needed to complete the cloze.

Figure 8.3 Continued:

(39) _____ organism must change. Even (40) _____ the giraffes could stretch

(41) _____ necks to become longer ((42) _____ like people who lift

(43) _____ and develop their muscles), (44) _____ genes would not be

(45) _____. And the genes determine (46) _____ an organism's offspring will

(47) _____ like. Why won't a (48) _____ with well-developed muscles produce

(49) _____ child with well developed muscles?

In (50) _____ mid-1800s Charles Darwin proposed a different theory of evolution. He developed

his theory as a result of observations he made during a voyage around the world.

Answers:

1. on	18. long	35. as
2. can	19. be	36. parts
3. their	20. parents	37. have
4. an	21. adapted	38. to
5. traits	22. believed	39. an
6. it	23. giraffes	40. if
7. that	24. believed	41. their
8. be	25. of	42. much
9. offspring	26. used	43. weights
10. that	27. disappear	44. their
11. necks	28. be	45. changed
12. reach	29. theory	46. what
13. if	30. to	47. look
14. its	31. it	48. person
15. get	32. many	49. a
16. would	33. believing	50. the
17. and	34. the	

Figure 8.3

Rodger L. Smith, of Radio Park Elementary School in State College, Pennsylvania, the same teacher who constructed the criterion-referenced group reading inventory on the seventh-grade life science book, also created a cloze test on the same book. This cloze test determines reading levels quickly in relation to the textbook and helps a teacher form tentative groupings within the class (see Figure 8.3).

Scoring the Cloze

In scoring a cloze test, the teacher must decide whether s/he will accept only the exact word that was deleted as correct or whether a synonym is also acceptable. If the student must supply the exact words, then the instructional range is usually considered to be 44 to 57 percent correct (Bormuth, 1968). Students scoring in this range probably can comprehend the material if given teacher guidance before, during, and after reading. Scores below that range may indicate that the material is too difficult. That is, the reading material is at the frustration level for students scoring below the minimum cutoff score. Scores above that range indicate the independent reading level, and more challenging supplementary materials are probably needed.

If the teacher chooses to accept synonyms for the deleted word, then scores of approximately 50 percent correct (as a minimum level) would indicate suitability of the material for instruction (Dupuis, 1980). Acceptance of synonyms makes scoring more difficult since each choice must be considered for acceptability. While a teacher can speed the scoring process by accepting only the exact word, this policy goes against principles of flexibility and variety of word choice.

Obviously, a criterion-referenced GRI is more useful than the cloze procedure in assessing diagnostic information about skill attainment. However, an observant content teacher can draw some conclusions about students' language skills. If, for example, a student inserts a verb where a noun belongs, or if a sentence no longer makes sense, then the student probably is not deriving meaning from the reading selection.

Since cloze tests are so easily constructed and scored, teachers can create them for all reading materials to ensure that students are using appropriate materials. For example, if several resources are available on the same topic, a cloze test using a passage from each resource could indicate which students should be reading which resource. Thus, reading level in relation to content materials may be determined by both the criterion-referenced group reading inventory and the cloze procedure. Skill attainment, however, is best measured by the criterion-referenced group reading inventory since the student is required to use content materials in the application of the skills.

LIMITATIONS OF INFORMAL TESTING

Although standardized norm-referenced tests do not yield diagnostic information, they do have the virtues of usually being valid and reliable. Validity and reliability are problems inherent in informal testing. In norm-referenced tests, items are typically reviewed by content experts to be sure that they cover a broad sample of material. Most tests have also been field-tested with large numbers of students to ensure that the results are reproducible (that is, reliable). Teacher-made informal tests, however, do not indicate whether students miss an item because they have not grasped what it is measuring or because it is a poorly written item. Likewise, the test may not emphasize what is covered in instruction (that is, it is not valid), or the results may not be reproducible.

A teacher can take several steps to overcome the shortcomings of informal teacher-made tests. First, teachers may systematically review their objectives for instruction and write items to measure attainment of those objectives. In other words, they may create a criterion-referenced test which measures whether or not students have mastered a particular objective stated in behaviorial terms. Mastery level (for example, 80 percent correct) should be determined by a realistic level of performance.

Next, the teacher should review the items for appropriateness in measuring the objective; this can be done by other teachers of the same content area. Kubiszyn and Borich (1987) suggest aspects of objective tests that are appropriate to consider: teachers should express test items clearly; they should use words with precise meanings; and they should avoid complex or awkward word arrangements.

ASSESSING AND EVALUATING STUDENT WRITING SKILLS

In earlier chapters, we have made a strong case for including a writing component in every content area course. We have established both a research and practical application basis for writing across the curriculum. At this point, then, we need to turn our attention to how content teachers can effectively manage assessment and evaluation of student writing. This would be a good time to check your own comprehension of this chapter by asking yourself if you understand the true distinction between these two terms. If you are unsure, look back to the section "Defining Some Terms."

Just as it is important to gather data about the reading skills students bring to each content area classroom, it is important to assess their writing skills as they enter various content courses. Likewise it is important that content teachers know how to evaluate their students' writing efforts as they proceed through these courses.

The discussion of assessing reading skills contained both formal and informal measures, with attention given to both the value and limitations of each. In the area of writing assessment, teachers rely heavily, if not entirely, on informal measures. As the writing across the curriculum movement gains momentum, more and more tools for obtaining standardized, norm-referenced measures of writing skills are becoming available. Yet for most content area teachers, informal measures remain the more practical alternative.

One of the authors, Dr. Joyce Lee, has worked extensively with teachers in the development of an informal measure for assessing student writing abilities. One of the promising implications of this work is that teachers *can* construct fairly valid and reliable criterion-referenced informal inventories of writing skills that serve the purpose of assessing student writing skills in an efficient manner (Showers, 1987).

Remember that during the elementary school years, it is likely that a student's reading level is assessed several times, particularly if s/he has any kind of learning problem. Such assessment of reading levels has two limitations which middle and secondary teachers need to keep in mind. First, reading assessment in general tends to decrease as students move up in the grades, so that in fact the middle and secondary teacher may find little or no recent information on reading levels in student files. Second, reading assessment in the lower grades often focuses only on establishing reading levels, not diagnosing specific skill strengths and weaknesses. A third limitation relates directly to assessing writing abilities. Assessment of reading skill in the lower grades almost always involves having students read from sample narrative passages; as discussed previously, it becomes more and more critical that teachers assess students' reading in terms of their ability to comprehend content area materials which are written almost exclusively in expository style.

Middle and secondary school teachers may find some information about writing skills in student folders, but this information may be of limited value for the same reasons that information about students' reading during their elementary years may not be very helpful in grouping and planning for content area instruction. For example, this data may indicate a general "writing level" for a student or group of students, but it may show little or no indication of the specific writing skills demonstrated. Further, as is often the case with reading assessment, the writings on which the indicated "level" is based were likely of a narrative nature, not the kind of writing which content area teachers will demand of students.

Each content area teacher should, then, construct a criterion-referenced informal measure for assessing incoming students on their ability to tackle the kinds of writing which will be expected during the year. This measure need not be elaborate and certainly will not have the scope of the criterion-referenced group inventory outlined for assessing various content area reading skills. Instead, the teacher need only require that students produce a "sample" piece of writing at the beginning of the year, presenting the activity in exactly the same format as assigned writing will be presented throughout the year. For example, if a teacher includes essay-type questions on tests, the initial writing assessment could be a sample essay with the criteria s/he expects to be met clearly indicated. Students should be told that this "sample" will not be graded but will be used to help the teacher plan for instruction.

One practical way to combine both reading and writing assessment at the beginning of any content area course is for the teacher to add a sample writing activity to the group reading inventory that s/he constructs using the textbook or other reading material from the course. This sample writing activity will give the teacher a good idea of how skilled students are in writing about that kind of reading material.

Keep in mind that at this point we are discussing *assessment* of writing skills, not *evaluation*. Content area teachers can look carefully at a group of sample writings as described here and draw a number of conclusions about students' writing skills. If specific criteria have been established, the teacher can, for example, conclude that fourteen students in a social studies class appear able to write a clear paragraph supporting an opinion; eight students appear to have no idea how to construct a paragraph with any logical organization; seven appear able to identify key ideas but do not express themselves clearly. This same teacher might also note which students appear to have mastered the basic mechanics of writing (sentence structure, punctuation, capitalization, spelling) and which appear to be weak in some or all of these areas. The information obtained from a sample writing activity could then be added to the grouping chart suggested earlier.

If writing across the curriculum is to become a reality in the middle or secondary school, a starting point for each content area teacher is the collection of data which helps in making instructional planning decisions. Later, you will find practical suggestions for grouping for instruction based on data gathered through the informal measures described here.

EVALUATING STUDENT WRITING

Just as important in considering students' writing skills is 1) determining how well they write in comparison to others, and 2) assigning grades or "rating" their writings as part of content area assignments and tests. Note that evaluation of student writing is a somewhat controversial issue, particularly among those who are proponents of teaching writing as a process. Many believe that as teachers move away from emphasizing writings only as final products, traditional grading of written assignments becomes a contradiction in terms. Many have long argued that it is impossible to measure and grade something as intangible as writing. Murray (1968) is often quoted as saying, "The student who gets a grade on his paper will look at the grade, he will not look at anything else; and the grade never diagnoses his problem, never shows him how to solve it" (p. 138).

Conversely, others insist that writing *is* a tangible and that evaluation of writing serves a useful purpose both for teachers and students. Graser (1983) suggests that evaluation is necessary to the improvement of student writing so long as evaluation standards are based on clearly identified qualities of good writing. Similarly, Holdzkom et al. (1984) argues that assessment of student writing samples at all stages of the process can and should enhance the instructional process.

The fine points of evaluating student writing constitute subject matter for an entire volume. For our purposes, it seems sufficient to look at evaluation under three broad categories: 1) holistic scoring, an alternative to the traditional letter grading of writing composition; 2) traditional grading, with some suggestions for making grading more meaningful; and 3) focus correcting, which might be considered a practical combination of the first two categories.

Holistic Scoring

Holistic scoring methods for evaluating writings are, in simplest terms, quick rating procedures most often used for ranking sets of writings rather than assigning letter or percentage grades (Cooper & Odell, 1977). In other words, holistic evaluation provides the teacher with a general picture or impression of student performance. The intent of using holistic scoring is for raters to be able to move quickly through large numbers of writings, getting a first impression score or rating based on the whole paper. The scorer does not analyze each piece of writing for errors, make suggestions for change, or in fact, comment on any specific parts of the writing. As described by Trost (1984), the evaluator reads the piece as a whole, looks only at certain features, and assigns a score or rating immediately.

If a teacher wishes to utilize holistic scoring rather than traditional grading for writing evaluation, it should be noted that under the general label of holistic scoring you may utilize more specific procedures such as general impression marking, primary trait scoring, and analytic or dichotomous scale scoring.

General impression marking is the simplest holistic procedure. The rater scores writings by deciding where each piece fits within the range of all papers to be evaluated for that assignment. *Primary trait marking* requires that the rater specify a set of criteria for the assignment. Each paper is then rated or scored according to whether or not the writer has met the established criteria, for example, "the writer includes at least three different reasons for buying a domestic car." All other factors are ignored. *Scale scoring* involves using a yes/no rating (dichotomous scale) for a series of questions about specific expectations for a set of papers, for example, "Does the writing include a concluding statement?" The rating for each paper would thus be a summation of *yes* responses. Use of *analytic scale scoring* means delineating a list of prominent features or characteristics a teacher expects to be present in a set of papers. These features or characteristics are described in some detail. For example, "The writer includes a clear rationale for the signing of the peace treaty." Often a "scoring line" is included for each identified feature, allowing the rater to assign high-medium-low points for each. Graser (1983) suggests that a summed score of each feature rating represents a valid holistic impression of a piece of writing.

Traditional Grading

While holistic scoring is an appealing alternative to traditional grading of written composition, many teachers remain uncomfortable with rating procedures which do not easily translate into language students and parents can understand. The reality of the real school world is that teachers are responsible for assigning grades or percentages, and they believe that in general students perform better when they know they will be held accountable for their written work. Accountability for writing assignments in the content areas will therefore likely continue to depend to a great extent on teachers taking the time to grade essay questions, reports, and other written assignments.

A great deal has been written about the pros and cons of assigning letter grades to student writings. Teachers bemoan the time involved in red marking every error in an effort to explain the grade assigned; researchers conclude that students for the most part ignore teachers' red marks and comments and that such markings have little or no effect on subsequent writing efforts.

Another dilemma for teachers in grading written work is the distinction between content and mechanics. What about students who have good ideas, present these in logical order, make good word choices, and/or write in an interesting style, but who turn in papers with errors in punctuation, capitalization, and/or spelling? A single letter grade cannot possibly give the student a clear message that what he or she had to say was excellent, spoiled only by mechanical errors.

One solution to this dilemma is to assign two grades to each piece, one for content, the other for mechanics. In the above example, the student would likely receive an *A* for content and a *C* for mechanics. While the student can obviously average the two and conclude that the paper in reality is a *B*, the teacher has sent a clear message that excellence in content is recognized, an important principle of process writing.

Remember that teachers using the process approach are encouraged to assign grades only a few times per year, not for each piece of writing. It is also a good idea to permit students to select a "best piece" from their writings to submit for a grade and to encourage students to revise previously submitted pieces whenever possible.

Focus Correction

Teachers might consider the combination approach to evaluating student writing suggested by Collins (1985) and referred to as *focus correcting*. Dr Joyce Lee has had considerable experience using this approach and notes that teachers, students, and parents find the system understandable and, most important, they note improvement over time in student writing in the content areas.

In brief, focus correcting refers to teachers beginning the year by identifying one or two main areas of writing to emphasize, such as effective introductions and complete sentences. The first writing turned in for a grade is evaluated only on the basis of whether or not the student has created an effective introduction and has written in complete sentences. The teacher ignores all other features. Thus an *A* paper is one that meets the two focus correcting requirements, a *B* paper meets only one of these, a *C* meets neither.

Obviously such a grading system creates its own set of pros and cons. How can a conscientious teacher overlook sixteen spelling errors and four misplaced apostrophes? What happens when the paper goes home and parents note that the teacher failed to red mark the misuse of the pronoun "me"? On the "pro" side, focus correction, like holistic scoring, takes much less time and frees the teacher from the tedium of red marking every little error. Another plus for focus correcting is that students are able to see more readily what they did right.

The critical question to ask, of course, is whether or not the use of focus correction leads to improvement in student writing. The jury is still out on this question, and we must leave it to future researchers to determine whether a steady diet of focus correcting rather than traditional grading will make a real difference. The alternative procedure is a practical means for evaluating student writing through the continued use of grades while eliminating some of the negatives long associated with traditional procedures.

Here are a few other ideas to contemplate as we conclude our discussion of assessing and evaluating student writing. First, teachers using focus correcting are advised to communicate clearly with parents (and, of course, students!) about the system in order to avoid misunderstandings about assigned grades on essay tests, reports, and other writing assignments. An effective way to handle this is to prepare a cover sheet for each written assignment which lists the focus areas that were considered for a paper.

Second, use the two-grade-per-paper idea presented earlier under traditional grading. The teacher identifies specific "expectations" for both content and mechanics, listing these in separate columns and grading each individually. Again, it is important to communicate clearly to parents and students what features are expected in each area and that the two grades represent two separate but integrated elements of written discourse.

Next, teachers should make focus correction a collaborative effort with students. Teachers and students can work together to determine which focus areas are appropriate for assigned writings.

Finally, focus correction areas should be made cumulative over time. That is, if on the first assignment students are graded for *effective introductions* (in the content column) and capitalization (in the mechanics column), then on the next assignment they should be held accountable for these focus areas as well as for one or two new areas.

SELF AND PEER EVALUATION

Lest you lose sight of our commitment to the process approach for teaching writing, remember two important ideas. The goal of any writing program, whether a part of the English curriculum or a vocational agriculture course, is to promote independent writers capable of finding their own strengths and weaknesses and working toward improving their own writings. Dr. Joyce Lee opens every workshop on teaching writing with the statement, "The goal of any writing activity is to help students learn to make a rough draft better."

Therefore, before any writing assignment is considered ready for teacher evaluation, students should be expected to look at their own work and judge it against the standards by which it will be evaluated. Teachers can prepare a form listing the qualities they will use in evaluating. Do not expect students to become skilled in self-evaluation overnight. Teachers using the process approach report that this is a skill that takes a great deal of practice and patience on the part of teachers reluctant to use class time this way. The most effective way to help students acquire skills in self-evaluation is to model the process as a whole class activity—and to do so often.

Graves and others who have led the process writing movement point out that students will often note that a section or sentence does not "feel right," but they may be unable to identify exactly what is wrong. It is suggested that students be asked to underline the part they are uncomfortable about and then ask for peer or teacher assistance in revision and/or editing (Gaskins, 1982). Gradually students should become more skilled at discovering and correcting their own errors.

Following self-evaluation by the writer, each piece of writing should be examined by at least one peer or a group of peers. Peer evaluation helps student writers become aware of the importance of audience as well as helping them note how different people approach the same or similar writing assignment. Again, teachers are advised to move slowly in helping students learn to evaluate each others' work, often conducting model peer evaluations for the entire class. In Chapter 6, a detailed description of peer conferencing for revision and editing was presented. This would be a good time to go back for your own review of this essential part of teaching writing as a process.

Finally, the authors suggest that effective writing programs, particularly in the content areas, use all three evaluators: teacher, self, and peer. In combination, these evaluation modes should encourage and enhance student growth in writing in all areas of the curriculum.

SUMMARY

In this chapter, we have looked at the need for and distinction between assessment and evaluation for both reading and writing skills. The value and limitations of formal and informal measures have been considered with the suggestion that teachers rely heavily on their own criterion-referenced reading/writing measures for assessment of students at the beginning of the school year. These measures should be constructed using sample materials from each content area in order to obtain useful data about how well students can read and write about a particular subject area. A description of several approaches to evaluating student writing has also been presented with practical suggestions for easing the paper-correcting workload of the teacher while enhancing the chances of students' improved writing performance.

Emphasis has again been placed on the concept that effective teaching of reading and writing rests on an understanding of the underlying processes involved in each. The products of reading (what has been learned and remembered) and the products of writing (summaries, essays, and reports) should become less the focus of instruction as teachers use practical assessment procedures to determine what students do (or do not do) as they read and write. Thus assessment can be used effectively as teachers plan meaningful content lessons which focus on helping students develop those reading and writing skills that they need in each content area.

REFERENCES

Bormuth, J. R. (1968). The cloze readability procedure. *Elementary English, 45,* 429–436.

Burmeister, L. E. (1978). *Reading strategies for middle and secondary school teachers* (2nd ed.). Reading, MA: Addison-Wesley Publishing Co., Inc.

Collins, J. (1985). *The effective writing teacher: 18 strategies.* Andover, MA: The NETWORK, Inc.

Cooper, C., & Odell, L. (Eds.). (1977). *Evaluating writing: Describing, measuring, judging.* Urbana, IL: National Council of Teachers of English.

Dupuis, M. M. (1980, September–October). The cloze procedure as a predictor of comprehension in literature. *Journal of Educational Research, 74,* 27–33.

Estes, T. H., & Vaughn, J. L. (1978). *Reading and learning in the content classroom.* Boston: Allyn & Bacon, Inc.

Gaskins, I. (1982, November–December). A writing program for poor readers and writers and the rest of the class, too. *Language Arts, 59,* 854–863.

Good, Carter V. (Ed.). (1973). *Dictionary of education.* New York: McGraw-Hill Book Co.

Graser, E. (1983). *Teaching writing: A process approach.* Dubuque, IA: Kendall/Hunt Publishing Co.

Graves, D. H. (1983). *Writing: Teachers and children at work.* Portsmouth, NH: Heinemann Educational Books, Inc.

Gronlund, N. E. (1985). *Measurement and evaluation in teaching* (5th ed.). New York: Macmillan Publishing Co.

Holdzkom, D., Reed, L., Porter, E., & Rubin, D. (1984). *Research within reach: Oral and written communication.* Washington, DC: National Institute of Education.

Jongsma, E. (1980). *Cloze instruction research: A second look.* Newark, DE: International Reading Association.

Kubiszyn, T., & Borich, G. (1987). *Educational testing and measurement* (2nd ed.). Glenview, IL: Scott, Foresman, and Co.

Murray, D. (1968). *A writer teaches writing.* Boston: Houghton-Mifflin Co.

Shepherd, D. L. (1978). *Comprehensive high school reading methods* (2nd ed.). Columbus, OH: Merrill Publishing Co.

Showers, D. (1987). Developing an effective analytic scale to evaluate student writing. Unpublished Master's paper, Pennsylvania State University, University Park, PA.

Singer, H., & Donlan, D. (1985). *Reading and learning from text.* Hillsdale, NJ: Lawrence Erlbaum Associates, Inc.

Smith, F. (1983). *Essays into literacy.* London: Heinemann Educational Books, Inc.

Trost, M. A. (1984). *Teaching and evaluating student writing.* Evanston, IL: McDougal, Littell & Co.

SUGGESTIONS FOR FURTHER READING

Graser, E. (1983). *Teaching writing: A process approach.* Dubuque, IA: Kendall/Hunt Publishing Co.

Murray, D. (1985). *A writer teaches writing* (2nd ed.). Boston: Houghton-Mifflin Co.

Singer, H., & Donlan, D. (1985). *Reading and learning from text.* Hillsdale, NJ: Lawrence Erlbaum Associates, Inc.

Smith, F. (1983). *Essays into literacy.* London: Heinemann Educational Books, Inc.

Trost, M. A. (1984). *Teaching and evaluating student writing.* Evanston, IL: McDougal, Littell & Co.

CHAPTER NINE

Assessing Student Attitudes and Interests

SCENARIO

"Hi, Don," called Marge as she walked into the office one particularly icy January morning. "I got your note about Andy Stabler and Jenny Covington. Tell me more while I try to thaw out by this heater. I've never worked with either of these students. What's the problem?"

"Andy and Jenny really have me puzzled," replied Don. "They're in my highest achieving ninth-grade social studies class and seem as capable as any of the rest of the kids. But neither will do the readings I assign. I'm beginning to wonder if they *can* do the assignments. I've been assuming that they *won't* do the work. When I wrote you that note I guess I was feeling a little guilty."

Marge laughed. "It's guilt that gets a lot of things done, I guess. You're right to recognize that there's a difference between *can't* and *won't*, and it is important to find out which is the real issue for both these students. If either of them has a reading problem, we need to know that and provide some remedial or corrective service. We may even need to ask Bob Diaz to do a psychological evaluation for us if it looks likely that either of them might have a more severe learning problem. On the other hand, if Andy and Jenny *can* but *won't* read, then we may have uncovered an attitude or motivation problem."

"How do we determine what the true situation is?" asked Don, backing away from the office heater to make way for other staff members. "I would feel terrible if one or both of these kids were being asked to read materials that really are too difficult for them."

"Put your guilt on hold for now, Don. Just fill out two reading assessment referrals and I'll make a quick check of their records to see what recent test scores we have on them to get an idea of where they've been performing. Then I'll schedule them each for an informal reading inventory to get an estimate of their current instructional levels. This should help us decide whether or not they have the skills for reading your assignments. Maybe they've just been too cold to comprehend these past few weeks," Marge joked as she too headed out of the office to face the day.

"That's a distinct possibility," Don answered. "Thanks for your help. By the way, if you conclude that one or both of them *can* read the material, where do I go from there?"

Marge stopped on her way out the door. "Then we probably have a slightly more complex issue to consider. Negative attitudes aren't easy to change in any situation, but among adolescents, with the power of peer groups, we sometimes find ourselves up against tough odds. Let's take one thing at a time, Don. You get the ball rolling with those referrals and I'll schedule some time with Andy and Jenny during their study halls next week. Have a good day and stay warm!"

OVERVIEW

At the beginning of this book, we stated that we were concerned about your willingness to involve yourself in teaching necessary reading skills to your students. This concern centers on your attitude. Our assumption was (and is) that we can present a lot of information to you in this book, but if your attitude is negative, you will learn little from the experience. Do you remember Marge's comment in the Chapter 8 scenario about content teachers who persist in believing that the teaching of reading and writing is the job of the reading teacher or English teacher? Unless you begin this book believing that all teachers share the responsibility for teaching reading and writing, or unless you have become a believer in this principle, then much of what we've had to say has likely had little impact. The same thing is true with students' attitudes toward reading and writing. This chapter deals with ways you can work with students' attitudes and interests so you can plan activities that will be of maximum interest to them.

ATTITUDES AND READING

Why do we need to be concerned about students' attitudes? McNeil (1987) reminds us that students "have perceptions and feelings about themselves as readers that affect their performance" (p. 92). He goes on to describe the impact of negative attitudes: if students feel that they cannot succeed, based on past experiences of failure and frustration, it is more likely that they will not succeed with their current reading tasks, even if their reading achievement level suggests that the material is appropriate for them.

Kubiszyn and Borich (1987) define attitudes as "descriptions of how people typically feel about or react to other people, places, things or ideas" (p. 156). They add, "attitudes can be thought of as fairly consistent and stable ways that people feel, behave, and are predisposed to feel and behave in the presence of various stimuli" (p. 156). Reading and writing are examples of the kinds of stimuli about which people, especially students, often have very strong feelings. Concern about attitudes falls into the affective domain and includes students' attitudes toward school and education in general, as well as reading. (This concern may be related to a student's cultural background, as will be discussed in Chapter 12.)

In addition to their attitudes toward education, teachers need to care about the students' attitudes toward the subject. For example, in science, do they have positive memories of science from past years? Do they enjoy scientific procedures? Do they watch TV programs related to science? Teachers can develop a list of questions related to their own subject area to find out how their students feel about their content area.

However, this book is about reading and writing in content areas. This chapter deals primarily with attitudes toward reading, especially those attitudes of students beginning with fifth grade. We are concerned with attitudes toward writing, too, but we are focusing here on attitudes toward reading because there is a stronger research base for our discussion. Most of the ideas presented could also be used to deal with attitudes toward writing, based upon the limited research available in this area.

Attitude Factors

Timing and age are important in attitudes. Students who have mastered basic reading skills are more likely to feel good about reading in general. They are more likely to read material that teachers ask them to read. Students who have not yet mastered basic reading skills are more likely to feel that reading is unpleasant, something to be avoided. These students may simply not read what teachers ask them to read. This is why Marge suggests to Don that the first step in determining why Andy and Jenny aren't reading the assignments is to find out if they are able to read the material.

Several important educational variables are related to attitudes. Self-concept, a student's perception of self and his/her worth, is related to reading attitude. A student with a low self-concept frequently expects to fail and usually lives up to his/her own expectations. A student who has done poorly in reading in earlier grades will likely expect to fail in later years, a self-fulfilling prophecy. School achievement is often related to attitude. Frequently, students who succeed in school or in particular subjects demonstrate better attitudes than those who are less successful. Also, parental example and involvement in students' reading and school activities seem to correlate with positive student attitudes. Parents who read a lot, talk about reading with their children, and have reading materials around seem to help their children develop better attitudes toward reading.

Another variable related to reading attitude is the teacher and the classroom climate created by that teacher. A positive atmosphere "is one in which learners are accepting of one another and in which a group spirit prevails" (Alexander & Filler, 1976, p. 10). Peer attitudes and actions in the classroom, as well as the teacher's behavior and talk, are important. The "Pygmalion" theory of Rosenthal and Jacobson (1968) is applicable here: Teachers' expectations for students' success or failure will likely be met. Similarly, teachers who expect their students to be uninterested and nonreading will probably find them to be that way. Thus, teacher enthusiasm and positive thinking are important in developing and nurturing positive attitudes (Good & Brophy, 1986).

Other variables have often been related to attitudes: sex, socioeconomic level, and intelligence. Research has suggested that the traditional wisdom in these areas may not be accurate. Teachers assume that girls have more positive attitudes toward reading than boys. However, some studies do not support this. The same caveat applies to socioeconomic level. It is inappropriate to assume that students from lower socioeconomic levels have less positive attitudes than those from higher socioeconomic levels. Intelligence as a factor in reading attitude works the same way. Reading achievement correlates highly with intelligence, but reading attitude does not. On these three factors—sex, socioeconomic level, and intelligence—the teacher is well advised to make no assumptions. (For further discussion on attitudes, see Corno & Snow, 1986.)

"Not making assumptions" may be translated into two kinds of action. First, teachers who don't make assumptions don't label a class the "dummies" and expect them not to read homework assignments or take part in class. The same teachers don't label another class "my good class" and assume they will always read and take part in class. These teachers treat all students as potential learners with equal value to themselves, the class, and the world at large.

Second, teachers who don't make assumptions try to find out in each class just who does care about reading and who doesn't. Don is such a teacher. He has a genuine desire to find out what's behind Jenny's and Andy's problems. This vital information must come from the students themselves. Attitudes may change during adolescence, and attitude data are less reliable than achievement data. Therefore, previous attitude assessments are less useful and it is necessary for teachers to develop their own data for their own students.

Obviously, some students at any grade level and in any subject will have positive attitudes toward reading and some will not. In middle and junior high schools, especially, it is fashionable among some students to talk down reading, writing, and studying with their peers. Indeed, peer pressure plays an important role in dealing with reading and writing.

These two activities are at the heart of school (and academic) activities, but peer pressure makes it easier for students who have few positive adult role models in reading and writing outside of school to dismiss them as being of no value on the street. Teachers of such students must work very hard to make reading and writing connect with life outside of school.

Another attitude problem, which our scenario teachers found with Jenny and Andy, are those readers who "can read, but won't." Such "can read, but won't" readers generally have average or above average achievement scores in reading and other areas. They simply don't want to read. Sometimes it is hard to identify these students from those who have real reading difficulties, because they hand in blank test papers. Sometimes these students respond well to materials in areas of high interest to them. Sometimes the school's reading teacher can find ways to work with them. A very small number of these students have serious psychological problems requiring a counselor and outside help. A student who may be a "can read, but won't" reader needs some special attention from the teacher and referral to other specialists for more help.

Student Interests

Educators traditionally separate attitude from interest, although the two are closely related and both are part of the affective domain. Interests change fairly frequently as students grow up, especially during adolescence, so that records of student interest easily become out of date. Interests can change from June to September. Thus a careful teacher wants up-to-date information on student interests to assist in selecting alternative materials, projects, and enrichment activities.

Student interests are usually defined as what they like or don't like: what they want to read and what they avoid reading. Carlsen (1980) has suggested that the topics or types of books students most often choose are grouped by ages—early adolescence (ages eleven to fourteen), middle (ages fifteen to sixteen), and late (ages seventeen to eighteen) adolescence. However, even Carlsen's categories leave much room for individual variation. Figure 9.1 lists the topics given as most often of interest to these age groups.

A careful review of these types of reading suggest that many are especially appealing to a particular age group but may remain appealing to some students for long periods of time. For example, a student's interest in mystery stories may begin at an early age with the "Choose Your Own Adventure" or "Choose Your Own Ending"-type series. Some students read a few of these and go on to other things. A few may retain an interest in mysteries and move on to Sherlock Holmes, Agatha Christie, and Erle Stanley Gardner.

Teachers need to be aware of student reading interests in general. However, they are most interested in student interests related to their

READING INTERESTS OF ADOLESCENTS

Early (11 to 14)	**Middle (15 to 16)**	**Late (17 to 18)**
animal stories	nonfiction adventure	search for personal
adventure stories	biography and	values
mystery stories	autobiography	social significance
supernatural tales	historical novels	strange and unusual
sports stories	mystical romance	human experience
growing up around the	stories of adolescent life	transition to adulthood
world		
home and family life		
stories		
slapstick humor		
settings in the past		
science fiction		

Figure 9.1

Adapted from Carlsen, G. R., *Books and the Teenage Reader* (2nd rev. ed., New York: Harper & Row, Publishers, Inc., 1980).

subject area. Social studies teachers may review the chart in Figure 9.1 and decide that an American history unit for grade 10 or 11 will need enrichment reading, including historical novels, biographies, and autobiographies of people studied in the unit, as well as first-person nonfiction accounts of the events studied. A biology teacher whose students are in the transition from early to middle adolescence (grades 9 and 10) would be wise to look for enrichment reading in many areas: animal stories for students still in the early stage, biographies of biologists, and nonfiction accounts of biological discoveries for those who have moved to the middle period. Science fiction is valuable for biology, too.

Many good book lists are available for teachers to use as references. The school librarian is an excellent resource for books on particular topics at particular levels. Carlsen (1980) and Fader (1981) are good sources, as are *Books for You* (Gallo, 1985), a senior high list, and *Your Reading: A Booklist for Junior High and Middle School Students* (Christenson, 1983), published by the National Council of Teachers of English. Other titles from NCTE and the International Reading Association are available. All are updated regularly to reflect new titles in the field. Professional journals are sources in other content areas (Alvermann, 1987).

Assessment Procedures for Attitude and Interest

Assessing attitude and interest is a tricky process, primarily because the source of information is the student. There are three major forms of assessment we can use: the teacher can assess a student, a student can assess another student, or a student can assess him/herself. All three of these are subjective, can be unreliable, can be faked, and are generally "soft" data. However, students are usually interested in finding out what they believe and what they like. Thus, a teacher who prepares students well for such an assessment, and who has a positive rapport with the students, can feel reasonably confident about the results obtained. Multiple measures of the same kind will demonstrate the reliability of the assessment, but many teachers feel they don't have time to give the same assessment two or three times. (For further suggestions on how to counteract the possible problems in assessment procedure, see Kubiszyn & Borich, 1987, pp. 155–80.)

Teachers can assess student attitude and interest by direct observation. This can range from a barely conscious assessment that "Jack isn't interested" (that is, he isn't paying attention in class) to more structured methods. The widely used forms of teacher assessment include:

1. Anecdotal Record: A statement of what the student did or said, given time and situation. These anecdotes are useful if the same behavior occurs over and over—and is recorded carefully.
2. Rating Scales: The teacher rates the student on an item using a 3 to 5 point scale.
3. Checklists: The teacher uses a list of acceptable or unacceptable behaviors and checks off their occurrences.
4. Interview: The teacher asks a set of questions of the student and makes observations of his/her reactions. This combines both teacher observation and student self-assessment.

Students may be asked to rate other students, using rating scales and checklists, on such items as their contributions to a group discussion, their common interest in certain topics, or their involvement in a group project.

Assessments which ask students to provide information on their own attitudes and interests are most commonly of four types, ranging from more subjective and unstructured to more objective and structured.

More subjective More unstructured			More objective More structured
1 Open-ended	2 Paired choice	3 Summated	4 Semantic differential

Open-ended assessments ask students to fill in or complete statements or to answer questions:

What do you read most?
Reading is _____
I like to read _____

Such items reveal students' thoughts fairly well. However, answers are hard to quantify and compare among a class.

Paired choice assessments ask students to choose between a given set of items:

> Would you rather:
>   play or read
>   do a science lab or read
>   watch TV or read

This approach is more structured than the open-ended items. However, students sometimes feel frustrated because they don't like the choices, or they either like or dislike both choices.

Summated items, developed most notably by Likert (1967), ask students to agree or disagree with a given statement. For example, a statement used with a Likert scale might say, " I like to read magazines" or "Most textbooks bore me." Summated items remain popular with teachers, who use a four- or five-point scale most frequently:

a. strongly agree
b. agree
c. don't care
d. disagree
e. strongly disagree

Students must choose which level of response represents their feelings. Answer *C* allows students to avoid choosing, since they can opt not to respond and still answer the question. Teachers can avoid this by forcing the choice, omitting *C*, and offering only four possible choices.

Semantic Differential. Osgood et al. (1957) developed the semantic differential technique to provide both structure and depth to the assessment of attitude. This technique uses a single word or statement, and sometimes several sentences, to establish the topic or issue to be rated. Under that is a set of bipolar adjectives (good-bad, strong-weak) and a five-, seven-, or nine-point scale. Osgood preferred a seven-point scale. The student rates the topic or issue on each set of adjectives:

Reading the newspaper?
good   ____ ____ ____ ____ ____ ____ ____ bad
useful ____ ____ ____ ____ ____ ____ ____ useless

Going to the library?
happy   ____ ____ ____ ____ ____ ____ ____ sad
important ____ ____ ____ ____ ____ ____ ____ unimportant

These techniques should be used carefully, so that the results are reasonably reliable and useful in classroom planning. Several good examples of scales on attitudes toward reading can be found in Fader (1981). Figure 9.2 is an example of a reading questionnaire developed by high-school

English teacher David Petkosh. This questionnaire contrasts student reading preferences in school and out of school. Petkosh developed his questions so that he could discuss the results with the entire class and with individual students. In his class, reading stories was compared with watching movies and TV, so the answers were directly related to the curriculum; one of the advantages of teacher-made assessments is that they can be related immediately to class content. Petkosh also adjusted the item types so that sometimes students could choose "other" and specify a different answer from the choices given—another advantage of teacher-made assessments.

Published attitude scales for reading are not plentiful, especially for content area reading, but more have been published recently. General attitude scales, like the *Warncke Attitude and Interest in Reading Inventory* (Warncke & Shipman, 1984), can be useful. A teacher who is assessing all his/her students, across a number of ability and/or achievement levels, may find an inventory like the WAIRI helpful. The WAIRI combines a checklist of preferences with open-ended items. It provides multiple levels, a way to develop student and class profiles, and suggestions for ways to develop groups based on student interest. Marge may suggest the use of such a measure in Don's class to help him better understand all of his students, especially those like Andy and Jenny whose behavior puzzles him.

Very simply, reading is a part of school and life which is very much affected by attitude. The best teaching plans are of no avail if the students refuse to attend to the topic. Understanding students' attitudes toward reading and writing is the responsibility of every teacher. What can teachers do to make it more likely that students will make a positive attempt to learn? That is the essence of motivation and techniques teachers can use to increase it.

MOTIVATION THROUGH ATTITUDES AND INTERESTS

> *The best way to motivate teenagers to read is to allow them to read books based on their needs, interests, and abilities. . . . The difficulty for the teacher is in organizing a curriculum that will help students learn necessary skills, concepts, and ideas while they are reading books based on their individual needs, interests, and abilities (Reed, 1985, pp. 195–196).*

The problem of motivation is central to teaching in most content classes. Wherever teachers gather, they discuss motivation, usually phrased as "how to motivate students." (We've already overheard our Middlewood teachers discuss the topic on several occasions!) Motivation is a matter of attitude, an affective concern. Students who are motivated

READING QUESTIONNAIRE

Check the answer which best describes what is true for you.

1. Outside of classwork, what kind of reading do you do most?
   _____ A. newspapers
   _____ B. magazines
   _____ C. novels
   _____ D. short stories
   _____ E. nonfiction (biography, personal accounts, diet-plans, etc.)
   _____ F. other _____

2. When you have adequate time and money, what kind of reading do you enjoy most?
   _____ A. newspapers
   _____ B. magazines
   _____ C. novels
   _____ D. short stories
   _____ E. nonfiction (biography, personal accounts, diet-plans, etc.)
   _____ F. other _____

3. When do you read "nonclasswork" literature most often?
   _____ A. study halls
   _____ B. library
   _____ C. evenings at home
   _____ D. weekends
   _____ E. summer or vacation

4. When you read leisure material or classwork, how do you ordinarily read?
   _____ A. in absolute silence
   _____ B. with music playing
   _____ C. with the TV on
   _____ D. other _____

5. When you read leisure material (only), how long do you ordinarily read?
   _____ A. 15 minutes at a time
   _____ B. 30 minutes at a time
   _____ C. 1 hour at a time
   _____ D. more _____ (how long?)

6. When you read classwork (only), do you ordinarily read for
   _____ A. 15 minutes at a time?
   _____ B. 30 minutes at a time?
   _____ C. 1 hour at a time?
   _____ D. more? _____ (how long?)

7. How many books of your own do you have?
   _____ A. none
   _____ B. 1-5
   _____ C. 6-10
   _____ D. 11-20
   _____ E. more than 20

Figure 9.2 Continued:

8. If you were stranded on an island alone with one object, what would you prefer?
   _____ A. a book
   _____ B. a game
   _____ C. a pocket calculator
   _____ D. a diary and a pencil
   _____ E. some method of playing music

9. Do you feel more at ease
   _____ A. reading?
   _____ B. writing?

10. Do you enjoy reading for leisure or pleasure sometimes?
    _____ A. Yes   _____ B. No

11. Do you ordinarily finish what you begin to read eventually?
    _____ A. Yes   _____ B. No

12. Do you ordinarily read what you think your parents would approve?
    _____ A. Yes   _____ B. No

13. Do your parents give you complete control over what you read?
    _____ A. Yes   _____ B. No

14. When you read for pleasure, do you read as closely and carefully as you do (or should) for classwork?
    _____ A. Yes   _____ B. No

15. Have you ever reread a book for pleasure?
    _____ A. Yes   _____ B. No

16. Do you prefer TV and movie stories to reading stories?
    _____ A. Yes   _____ B. No

17. Is it possible for a book to be "better" than a TV or movie adaptation?
    _____ A. Yes   _____ B. No

18. Are books ever a topic of your conversation with others (in the way movies are)?
    _____ A. Yes   _____ B. No

19. If you were desperate for something enjoyable to read (not to look at), could you find one good book in our school library?
    _____ A. Yes   _____ B. No

20. If a friend were in the hospital, in prison, or held captive, could you think of two thoroughly entertaining books to send to him/her?
    _____ A. Yes   _____ B. No

    If you can, name two below.

    _____   _____

Name: _____   Sex: _____
Grade: _____   Class: _____

Figure 9.2
Prepared by David Petkosh, former English Department Chairman, Manheim Central High School, Manheim, Pa. Reprinted by permission.

have a desire to learn, to achieve in class. Or they have a desire to succeed in something for which a class is prerequisite. For example, a student is interested in biology, so she works hard, learns well, succeeds, and achieves in class. Another student is not particularly interested in biology, but he needs good grades to get into college, so he works hard, learns well, and succeeds in that class. The observable result is the same for both students, but the motivation was quite different for each. Indeed, like other affective concerns, motivation is highly individual, depending for each student on what matters to him/her.

Educational psychology discusses extrinsic and intrinsic motivation. *Extrinsic motivation* includes motivators outside the student—grades, for example, or prizes, or free time. All sorts of rewards can be used to motivate students extrinsically. *Intrinsic motivation* includes personal satisfaction for learning something or from working through a long, hard problem. Intrinsic motivation also refers to students satisfying their curiosity about something that interests them; or gaining a sense of success at mastering a skill or a task that has been difficult. Teachers usually believe that intrinsic motivation is more lasting and valuable than extrinsic techniques, but grades and other parts of the current educational system are still useful as extrinsic motivation.

Now let's turn specifically to reading and consider motivation to read. Earlier we said that attitudes toward reading provide increasing problems as students move into secondary school. Students who have difficulty reading will not choose to read voluntarily, just as most of us will not choose to do something that we do not do well. This attitude toward reading is a problem for any teacher who asks that students read not only in reading class, but in health, math, or social studies classes as well.

Other people, some of them excellent students, can be motivated negatively by reading. Independent level readers and really gifted students are sometimes turned off because they are not challenged by what they are asked to read. They are bored by low-level reading that doesn't go beyond literal comprehension and minimal cognitive levels. These are students who quickly answer questions of "who," "what," and "when." They want to spend time discussing "how" and "why."

Another related reason why students are not motivated is that they resent requirements. That is, they may well be willing to read a book or study a topic, but because it is required, because they have no choice, they lose their motivation.

This discussion is but a brief overview of the problems of motivation that teachers face. Our purpose is not to analyze the problem psychologically as much as to present some suggestions for encouraging positive motivation and minimizing negative motivation. In the next section, we concentrate on intrinsic motivation. Extrinsic motivation, like grades and college admission, is always there. Teachers should work most seriously with intrinsic motivators.

TECHNIQUES FOR MOTIVATING STUDENTS TO READ IN CONTENT CLASSES

Effective motivation comes from knowing the students well, planning well, and teaching well. It is surely true that no teacher will successfully motivate all 150 students every day, but s/he can come closest to doing that by using professional judgment to plan appropriate learning experiences for students. This section includes some suggested techniques for teachers to use in the classroom. These suggestions, by the way, might be just as useful for Don's two "problem students" mentioned in the opening scenario. If Marge concludes that they can but will not read, she may well suggest that Don try one or more of these ideas for motivating secondary students to read in the content areas:

1. Match students' reading requirements to their reading levels to promote success. Matching student reading levels to the content materials means that students are much more likely to succeed. And success begets motivation to do it again. Not only will students learn more if the materials are on the right level; they will also want to learn more.

2. Encourage students to control their own learning. Whenever possible, allow students to become more independent, more self-directing in their learning. (Chapter 11 suggests a number of ways to do this: learning centers, learning packages, independent study, laboratory experiments, practical work in industrial arts or home economics or physical education.) Students can organize the time and learning situation to some extent so that they do it themselves.

3. Encourage students to make choices. Even if the teacher prescribes the content and the general procedures, students will be more motivated if they can choose from among two or three things. They could choose the topic for a report from a list the teacher prepares; they can select one of two or three novels to read; they can choose whether to give the report orally or in writing; or they can choose one of three woodshop projects. In many cases, teachers can provide several choices within a unit, in projects, reading, and reporting situations.

4. Provide as many hands-on experiences as possible. Concrete activities tend to be motivating, especially for students who prefer not to read. Growing plants, repairing a lamp, putting up a bulletin board, drawing a poster, making a collage, building a model . . . . The list could go on. If hands-on activities are included as choices within a unit, students can opt to do things most attractive to them and, usually, things with which they are more likely to be successful.

5. Cater to student interests, but don't just allow student interests to operate (they will anyway). After assessing student interests, a teacher can develop a list of projects, areas to study, and books to read that reflect them. Many interests are fairly standard; they recur year after year. A student who is a car buff and has little academic motivation must still

Don MacArthur works in the library with two of his social studies students. They are reviewing a series of books about American Indians and their cultures. Allowing students to choose their own reading from a list prepared by the teacher increases motivation to read.

study world cultures. However, he might be interested in transportation in China, Africa, or wherever. Other interests of a more esoteric nature may require the teacher to seek help from the librarian or other resource person.

6. Group students to encourage motivation. Grouping students may help or hinder motivation. Some students work well together, others get on each other's nerves. If your purpose is motivation to accomplish a task rather than some socialization goal, the groups should be formed to reflect that purpose. Students who are task-oriented and organized may work well together. Students who are creative and thoughtful may work well together. However, pairing a task-oriented student with a creative one in a problem-solving situation may frustrate both of them. In junior high school especially, the teacher must be alert to which groups work well together. Sometimes allowing friends to work together encourages accomplishment of the task. Other times, groups of friends just giggle and waste time so that they don't accomplish the task. Some students work better if they can work alone. Generally, working in small groups, where everyone shares the task and responsibility for completing it, can help motivation.

7. Relate content reading and learning to students' needs and to the real world. A common complaint from unmotivated students is that school is not relevant to their lives. This complaint may sometimes be overstated. However, we know from learning theory that learning is facilitated when the student can tie it to his/her past experiences or immediate needs. Where can the student see the topic in his/her world? Can s/he use it or see its use? If not in the student's real world, can the teacher show it in action on film or in pictures? This principle is so basic to learning that we sometimes come to see it as elementary or simplistic, but it remains as important in high-level learning as in the lowest. Our definition of the "real world" can change, though, as our learning becomes more sophisticated. The seventh-grade life science student's real world is the tree from which s/he gets the leaves for her leaf collection. By the time s/he gets to advanced biology, s/he can relate the real world to the microorganisms s/he sees under the microscope. It is also true that as the content becomes more complex, it also becomes more abstract (consider the binomial theorem, for example). So the problem of relating learning to the real world is complex. Teachers should review carefully both their students' needs and their unit plans to identify the real world connections. Such connections should become a standard part of all teaching.

Motivation is so important that teachers need to plan for it during every unit. The unit begins with a motivational experience, which should introduce the topic and provide a preview of what is coming. It should pique the students' interest in the topic, using one of the techniques listed earlier in this chapter.

This emphasis on intrinsic motivation techniques is not meant to exclude extrinsic techniques. Teachers still give grades. They can give extra credit or bonus points; they can give free reading time to students who finish the assignment early. They can hold contests or award certificates. These techniques will not harm motivation and may encourage some students. However, they are not sufficient to motivate a student who isn't already fairly well motivated. We believe the more serious motivation problems must be attacked by systematic planning to provide maximum positive motivation in content and reading instruction.

SUMMARY

Attitudes must be a central concern for content teachers as they plan instruction. Building motivational activities into units and lessons is the best way to encourage students to read. Students with lower reading levels and less intrinsic motivation will need more attention than those with greater motivation. Teachers should assess their students' attitudes and interests to anticipate problem areas and prepare teaching plans that will maximize motivation.

Techniques to encourage motivation to learn will match reading to students' reading levels, encourage students to control their own learning, encourage them to make choices, provide hands-on experiences, cater to their interests, use grouping patterns that fit student preferences, and relate their reading and learning to their real-world needs. Careful planning can make the difference in influencing students to turn to learning.

REFERENCES

Agee, H. (1984). *High interest—easy reading: For junior and senior high students*. (4th ed.). Urbana, IL: National Council of Teachers of English.

Alexander, J. C. & Filler, R. C. (1976). *Attitudes and reading*. Newark, DE: International Reading Association.

Alvermann, D. E. (1987). Developing lifetime readers. In D. E. Alvermann et al. (Eds.), *Research within reach: Secondary school reading* (pp. 25–36). Newark, DE: International Reading Association.

Carlsen, G. R. (1980). *Books and the teenage reader* (2nd rev. ed.). New York: Harper & Row, Publishers, Inc.

Christenson, J. (Ed.). (1983). *Your reading: A booklist for junior high and middle school students*. Urbana, IL: National Council of Teachers of English.

Corno, L. & Snow, E. R. (1986). Adapting teaching to individual differences among learners. In M. C. Wittrock (Ed.), *Handbook of research on teaching* (3rd ed.) (pp. 605-29). New York: Macmillan Publishing Co.

Fader, D. (1981). *The new hooked on books*. New York: Berkley Publishing Group.

Gallo, D. R. (Ed.). (1985). *Books for you: A booklist for senior high students*. Urbana, IL: National Council of Teachers of English.

Good, T. L. & Brophy, J. E. (1986). School effects. In M. E. Wittrock (Ed.), *Handbook of research on teaching* (3rd ed.) (pp. 570–602). New York: Macmillan Publishing Co.

Kubiszyn, T. & Borich, G. (1987). *Educational testing and measurement*. Glenview, IL: Scott, Foresman and Co.

Likert, R. (1967). *The human organization: Its management and value*. New York: McGraw-Hill, Inc.

McNeil, J. D. (1987). *Reading comprehension: New directions for classroom practice*. (2nd ed.). Glenview, IL: Scott, Foresman and Co.

Osgood, C. E., Suci, G. J. & Tannenbaum, P. H. (1957). *The measurement of meaning*. Urbana, IL: University of Illinois Press.

Reed, A. J. S. (1985). *Reaching adolescents: The young adult book and the school*. New York: Holt, Rinehart and Winston.

Rosenthal, R. & Jacobson, L. F. (1968, April).) Teacher expectations for the disadvantaged. *Scientific American, 218*, 19–23.

Warncke, E. W. & Shipman, D. A. (1984). *Group assessment in reading*. Englewood Cliffs, NJ: Prentice-Hall, Inc.

SUGGESTIONS FOR FURTHER READING

Agee, H. (1984). *High interest—easy reading: For junior and senior high students*. (4th ed.). Urbana, IL: National Council of Teachers of English.

Alvermann, D. E. (1987). Developing lifetime readers. In D. E. Alvermann et al. (Eds.), *Research within reach: Secondary school reading* (pp. 25–36). Newark, DE: International Reading Association.

Fader, D. (1981). *The new hooked on books*. New York: Berkley Publishing Group.

Kubiszyn, T. & Borich, G. (1987). *Educational testing and measurement*. Glenview, IL: Scott, Foresman and Co.

PART IV

ORGANIZING FOR INSTRUCTION IN CONTENT AREA READING AND WRITING

How can we plan lessons and units of study to encourage student learning?

Where do reading and writing fit into lesson and unit plans?

How can we plan for different student reading levels?

How can we plan for students' different linguistic and cultural characteristics?

How can we plan for students with different exceptionalities?

It's time to plan for teaching lessons and units for your classroom. Reading forms the core of many lessons and the central material for many units of study; that is why this part of the book considers ways to build lessons and units to ensure that students comprehend content. The effective teacher has a repertoire of teaching techniques to use with different groups of students. Different techniques work most effectively with independent, instructional, or frustration level readers. Readers of differing cultural groups and with differing dialects and language groups require lessons they can comprehend. Students with differing exceptionalities will need other types of lessons.

Teachers make the judgments about what each student needs. Most of the time, students can be grouped within the classroom to make the teacher's job manageable while still meeting these student needs. This part of the book identifies some basic instructional strategies for your teaching repertoire.

CHAPTER TEN

Organizing for Instruction:

PLANNING AND GROUPING

SCENARIO

Our Middlewood teachers arrive one blustery February morning to find this notice posted above the staff mailboxes:

FACULTY MEETING: WEDNESDAY 3:30

Please be prompt and please be prepared to discuss the article on grouping for instruction found in your mailboxes. Other agenda items will include attendance; change in lunch schedules for grades 6 and 7; use of the gym during study halls; and plans for our Valentine's Day staff party. We will meet in the library.

"Morning, Sally," said John as he entered the office. "How's that four-wheel drive performing on these snowy days?"

"Haven't been stranded yet, John," replied the office secretary cheerfully. "Here's that article Dr. Watkins wants you to read before Wednesday's faculty meeting."

"Thanks, but be prepared for possible strong language as folks pick up their mail today," warned John. "This is definitely a hot topic you're handing out. Morning, Bob. You picked a good day to spend at Middlewood. The big issue in the air today is grouping for instruction."

"Morning, John," replied Robert Diaz, the school district psychologist, as Sally handed him a copy of the article. "I think I'll stick around when I finish my testing schedule here this morning. I'd like to say my two cents' worth in the faculty room at lunch today. I'm always recommending small group instruction for students with special needs, and I know the idea is not usually warmly welcomed."

"That's an understatement, Bob," replied John. "If I were you, I'd head for the next school on your schedule and avoid the indigestion you're sure to get by staying around here today."

"No wonder Dr. Watkins handed these to me and then headed downtown to the central office!" said Sally, as she finished putting copies of the article in mailboxes.

"That's right," replied John. "He knows he's in for a heated discussion. Any time you mention 'grouping' to middle or secondary teachers, you can stand back and watch the sparks fly. Most teachers think breaking classes up into small groups for instruction belongs only in the elementary schools."

"Glad I'm just in charge of phone calls, first aid, and office management," answered Sally as she continued to sort mail. "I don't think I'd enjoy faculty meetings!"

OVERVIEW

The instructional unit plan has been utilized in the classroom for decades. It is the classroom teacher's tool for organizing content systematically and for customizing content to fit the needs of individuals, small groups, or entire classes. Instructional units typically center around some major theme, concept, or topic. This approach has been a valuable means of integrating substance and process in content area learning. It represents a teacher's most complete conceptualization of what students will accomplish within a given block of time.

There are many frameworks for developing an instructional unit. This chapter contains one which begins with a consideration of the goals of a school district and ends with an evaluation plan. It includes the following components: background and rationale; content outline, goals, and objectives; materials and resources; and student evaluation.

Secondary teachers tend to organize their instruction for large group format. However, because of the range of reading abilities at the secondary level, we find that within-class grouping for small group instruction is effective and should be included as a strategy when developing any instructional unit. Grouping by reading level, skill level, interest level, or some other criterion should facilitate learning and enhance the teacher's chances of conveying important concepts.

WHAT IS AN INSTRUCTIONAL UNIT?

There are extremes with regard to the meaning of the word "unit." Some teachers take it to mean teaching a single concept that requires a day or two, while others might consider it a year-long endeavor. Thoughtful teachers use the unit method in order to conceptualize a whole year of instruction. Without seeing the big picture, instruction could become a hodgepodge of disconnected events. Consider the English teacher who teaches the semicolon one day, *The Red Pony* the next, the complex sentence the next, and public speaking the next. Without a unifying concept, snippets of instruction can be confusing.

Obviously many concepts or skills can be incorporated into an instructional unit, but this kind of integration requires long-range planning. Math and science teachers may have less flexibility than English or social studies teachers, but all of these content area teachers can plan more easily by using instructional units.

For our purposes, an *instructional unit* is an organized study of a topic or concept in a content area which lasts from 3–8 weeks and incorporates objectives in both reading and writing. It is thematic. It should give students some sense that there is a beginning, a middle, and an ending to an area of study. Such a sense of closure often helps learners to organize important concepts.

Planning and the Instructional Unit

When creating an instructional unit, it is necessary to consider numerous other factors along with the curriculum. Do students have the prerequisite skills and background to complete the unit successfully? Are students interested in the topic or theme? Are you interested in the topic or theme? Are there ample materials and resources available to teach the unit effectively? Will the unit topic promote a diversity of activities for students?

All of these factors must be taken into account when teachers plan instructional units. One of our colleagues, Robert Neuhard, suggests that good planning is done on the seat, not on the feet. He really means that the most effective planning is deliberate and well thought out. Given the hundreds of decisions that teachers have to make each week, planning is not one that teachers can afford to make spontaneously. Unfortunately, some teachers do just that. The result is often the hodgepodge mentioned previously, but also an inappropriate focus for their instruction. Spontaneous planners often ask the question, "What should I do tomorrow?", focusing on how to spend time. A more effective focus is guided by a more important question, "What do I want my students to learn?" The instructional unit begins to answer the more important question in the broadest sense.

Aside from being a very effective method of instruction, unit construction requires that teachers analyze and understand the concepts of reading and writing in the content areas. It increases their awareness of purpose and allows them to make a systematic assessment of their students' progress. Finally, unit construction increases the use of content area reading and writing strategies in classroom teaching (Pearce & Bader, 1986).

Too often teachers rely solely on the textbook to determine a unit topic and related content. Surely most texts are good resources, but the ultimate decision for planning focused and balanced instructional units resides with each classroom teacher. Because they are written for a general curriculum, textbooks are not synonymous with comprehensive unit plans nor do they incorporate the teaching of reading and writing skills as suggested in this book.

Curriculum Guides

Instructional units are not created out of thin air nor are they spelled out in the teachers' manual of most textbooks. They are the broadest foundation of a teacher's planning, guided by many factors. One of the most important factors is the set of educational goals adopted by the school district. Instruction in most school districts draws its theoretical base from this set of goals. They may have been adopted from a statewide set of goals or they may have been adapted from educational research, but they usually serve to guide the curriculum and the sequence of instruction. From these goals, teachers can form general objectives to guide each program at the secondary level. Consequently, one goal and general objective from each subject area may appear as follows:

MATHEMATICS
Goal: A quality education should help every student become proficient in mathematics.
General Objective: Students will understand multiplication.

ENGLISH
Goal: A quality education should help every student acquire skills in listening, speaking, reading, and writing.
General Objective: Students will apply the skills of good writing.

SOCIAL STUDIES
Goal: A quality education should help every student learn the history of our nation.
General Objective: Students will comprehend the reasons for the War between the States.

SCIENCE
Goal: A quality education should help every student acquire an understanding of science and technology.
General Objective: Students will remember the names of all the planets in our solar system.

While the number of goals that guide a district-wide curriculum may be as few as 10 to 15, there may be hundreds of general objectives which guide each subject area. When general objectives are specified and put into a sequence from grades K–12, the curriculum is said to be *articulated vertically*, or organized by successive grades. When general objectives are specified and put into a sequence by individual grades, they are said to be *articulated horizontally*, or organized at a given level. The product of specifying and arranging objectives is often referred to as a curriculum's scope and sequence.

Good curriculum guides provide a broad picture of what is to be taught and at what grade level. They also allow for teacher decision-making with regard to the arrangement of daily instruction. Goals and general objectives are loose prescriptions for instruction, but ultimately the issues of when during the school year, and for how long, concepts and skills will actually be taught is up to each classroom teacher. This is where unit planning comes in.

THE SOLAR SYSTEM

Introduction and Rationale

This unit is designed to help the students understand the similarities and differences of the planets in our solar system, including earth, and lesser bodies, such as the moon.

The unit will be introduced by showing the film "A World is Born." The film will be followed by a discussion period. The unit is one in a series of units in the science curriculum. During the unit the students will work on the following reading skills:

1. Vocabulary
2. Comprehension
3. Sequence of Events
4. Cause and Effect Relationships
5. Study Skills

These skills will be incorporated into the unit through the use of the following:

1. A Structured Overview
2. A Directed Reading Activity
3. A Learning Center
4. A Learning Activity Package
5. Specific Skills Lessons

This unit will be used in a special education class. The students range in age from thirteen to seventeen. Their reading ability range is much greater. The students are in ninth and tenth grade, but their reading ability ranges from third grade to the tenth-grade reading level. Due to this great range in reading ability, many activities and materials will be provided so each student has the opportunity to be successful in this unit. The unit should be completed in four weeks.

Figure 10.1

Prepared by Stephen Caruso, Keystone Central School District, Lock Haven, Pa. Reprinted by permission.

Components of an Instructional Unit

There may be no single best format for a unit plan, but there are components which are essential if a plan is to be comprehensive. What follows is an explanation of the components that make up an instructional unit.

1. *Background and Rationale.* This is a description of the unit's general organization, time allotment, and target audience. This section contains information about the unit's theme or central focus. It often explains how the concepts fit into the curriculum at a given point and why the unit is appropriate for a specific grade level or student group. Included in the rationale are important generalizations as well as the major concepts to be addressed in the unit. The examples in Figures 10.1 and 10.2 illustrate the background and rationale statements for two units.

2. *Content Outline.* After writing a comprehensive background and rationale for the unit, the teacher should list, in outline form, all of the content s/he wants to teach. The advantage of using an outline is that learning hierarchies can be established through subordination. Task analysis is often useful in planning a unit. The more comprehensively written the content outline is, the easier it will be to plan the rest of the unit. Figure 10.3 on p. 225 is an example of a good content outline.

A *task analysis* is often useful in planning a unit. Doing a task analysis involves sequencing instruction to students' thinking processes. The important question is what prerequisite knowledge or skills will students need to learn these concepts successfully? The following sequence was developed by Sabre Martin and Karen Swoope at Washington State University (Orlich et al., 1985):

1. Begin with a [unit] goal or objective.
2. Define the learning and its critical attributes.
3. List every step in mastering the learning. (Ask the question: Can the learner. . . ?)
4. Examine each step and keep only the essential steps.
5. Sequence steps in order of difficulty:
   a. Simple to complex
   b. Concrete to abstract
   c. Pictures to words
   d. Saying to writing
   e. Paragraph to whole story (p. 67)

The example in Figure 10.4 on p. 226 shows what a task analysis might look like in a science unit.

3. *Goals and Objectives.* As explained earlier in this chapter, school curricula are guided by goal statements from which programs derive objectives. These objectives need to be written at two levels of specificity.

The first level, or general objective, is more specific than a goal, but not so specific as to be stated in measurable behaviors. For example: "Students will understand multiplication" has been suggested as a general objective in mathematics. It is composed of three component parts:

1. The learner term—students
2. The process term—will understand
3. The content term—multiplication

This general objective (GO), written in terms of the student and not the teacher, serves to direct subsequent Specific Learning Outcomes (SLO). SLOs are the second level of specificity mentioned above. Outcomes are measurable because they are written in behavioral terms. For example: "Given ten three-digit multiplication problems, the student will compute the answers with 90 percent accuracy." Specific Learning Outcomes (SLO) have five basic parts:

1. The learner term—the student
2. The behavior—will compute
3. The content—three-digit multiplication problems
4. The conditions—given ten problems
5. The criteria—with 90 percent accuracy

or

After a Directed Reading Activity (DRA), the student will answer literal and higher order questions about a news article. Seven of eight literal answers will be stated correctly and two higher order answers will be defended.

1. The learner term—the student
2. The behavior(s)—will state/will defend
3. The content—questions about a news article
4. The conditions—after a DRA
5. The criterion—seven of eight/two defended

General Objectives (GOs) and Specific Learning Outcomes (SLOs) are sometimes difficult or tricky to write. Their usefulness is that they require teachers to think clearly about what they intend for the learner. For help with writing objectives, please consult *Educational Testing and Measurement* (Kubiszyn & Borich, 1987) or *Measurement and Evaluation in Teaching* (Gronlund, 1985). Since learning outcomes are the heart of instructional planning, a teacher should make every effort to become skillful in specifying objectives. Figure 10.5 on p. 227 presents some samples of both GOs and SLOs from the unit on using the newspaper, "Read All About It!" You read the rationale for this unit in Figure 10.2.

READ ALL ABOUT IT!

Introduction and Rationale

This unit is designed for students at the middle school level; however, this unit can be adapted easily for high school or adults. Students should be identified according to performance level (frustration, instructional, or independent).

This unit should last approximately six weeks (five 45-minute class periods per week); but it may be expanded to a double period per day, with a teaming of social studies or language arts teachers, to allow for in-depth coverage of the process of reading a newspaper.

This unit has been designed to provide a flexible framework which can be utilized to teach students the reading and study skills necessary for reading the newspaper. Heavy emphasis is placed on these reading and study skills. The curriculum utilizes teacher modeling, controlled exercises, and an application of skills to the current newspaper. Students will work in homogeneous groups, heterogeneous groups, and individually. They will be evaluated both as a group and individually. Points are assigned to each requirement and students falling below expectations may contract to do additional work for extra credit. Individual conferences are held to discuss grading scale and develop contracts.

The rationale for selecting the newspaper is that it is contemporary, has something of interest for everyone, covers a wide spectrum of subjects and reading levels, guides critical thinking, is inexpensive, and is used in almost every home. The student who is "turned off" by textbooks, either because they are too hard or too easy, may find motivation in using the newspaper. In addition, students are exposed daily to current events either through the various media such as the newspapers, television, or radio; or through conversations with their parents, teachers, or peers. Therefore, they should already possess some background knowledge of the events covered in the newspaper. Also, students will be encouraged to increase their background knowledge through nonreading activities such as television and radio.

Although the primary goal is learning reading and study skills, other intrinsic goals such as socialization and civic responsibility will be addressed. The reading and study skills necessary to read the newspaper also provide skills that can be applied in many other areas.

The structure of a news article, with the main idea and facts being given in the headline and first few paragraphs, will guide the frustration reader as well as build his confidence. Familiarity with the content and availability of nonwritten sources such as television, radio, and verbal communication will also be useful. The instructional reader can be challenged by the concepts and critical thinking required. The independent student can use the newspaper as a foundation to expand his knowledge of current events, and s/he can be encouraged to learn more through magazines, library research, interviews or other sources. The structure of this unit allows for grouping by both ability and interest, as well as for individualized instruction.

One problem encountered in the design of this unit was the amount of fragmented materials already available on the use of the newspaper. Most of the material is either not deep enough or provides for the use of the newspaper as a supplement to curriculum. Another problem is the complex sentence structure and use of many three-plus syllable words, which provide a high readability estimate on many articles. This problem can be overcome by the students' knowledge of current events and motivation provided by this unit.

Studying the newspaper at the middle school level will hopefully begin (or expand upon) a basic life-long skill which is fundamental to our society being informed. Reading and study skills will blend with socialization and civic responsibility through the use of this very useful tool.

Figure 10.2
R. D. Mike Kemp, Hollidaysburg, Pa., Area School District. Reprinted by permission.

CONTENT OUTLINE

THE WONDER OF THE WATER CYCLE

I. **Nature's Water Cycle**
   A. The water cycle is one of nature's most important processes.
      1. The Water Cycle:
         a. water evaporates into the atmosphere
         b. falls to the earth as rain or snow
         c. runs to the ocean
         d. begins the cycle again
   B. Earth's energy to keep the cycle moving smoothly comes from the sun.
   C. Sun, air, water, and the force of gravity work together to keep the water cycle going.
   D. Major steps in the cycle include:
      1. the *evaporation* of water by the sun's heat
      2. the *transpiration* of water by plants
      3. the *condensation* of water vapor by cold air
      4. the *precipitation* of water by gravity
      5. and the *return* of water by gravity to oceans

II. **The Water Supply Problem**
   A. World distribution of water—distribution of precipitation
      1. *Too much rain* falls in many tropical regions every year, producing steaming jungles.
      2. *Too little rain* falls on about half the earth's land, producing deserts and near deserts.
      3. *Sudden downpours* can drench regions that seldom get enough rain, causing landslides.
      4. *Drought* can strike regions that usually get enough rain, baking the moist earth dry.

III. **Water Pollution—occurs when wastes are dumped into the rivers, lakes, oceans, and other bodies of water.**
   A. Sources of water pollution:
      1. Industrial wastes—mainly chemical waste
      2. Sewage—consists of human wastes, garbage, water which has been used for laundering or bathing
      3. Agricultural chemicals and wastes—rain water flowing from farmland into streams carries chemical fertilizers and pesticides that have been put into the land
   B. Control of water pollution:
      1. Sewage treatment—using processes, primary treatment, secondary treatment, and advanced treatment
      2. Pretreatment of wastes—industries can reduce pollution by treating wastes to remove harmful chemicals before dumping the wastes into water
      3. Drinking water standards—in 1974, the U.S. Congress passed the Safe Drinking Water Act to help protect the nation's public water supply against pollution

Figure 10.3

LEARNING HIERARCHY FOR A SCIENCE TOPIC

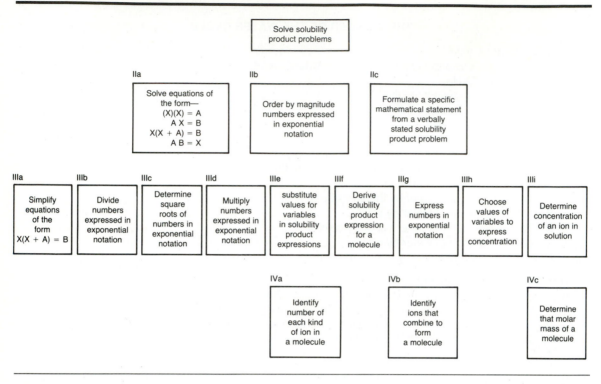

Figure 10.4

From "Revision of a Science Topic Using Evidence of Performance on Subordinate Skills" by James R. Okey and Robert M. Gagne, *Journal of Research in Science Teaching,* Vol. 7, #4, 1970, p. 323. Reprinted by permission of John Wiley & Sons, Inc.

A teacher should list objectives in the appropriate order of teaching. They should be guided by the three domains of learning as well as by the levels represented in those domains. Check back in Chapter 1 to remind yourself of these domains. Appendix 3 lists some sample behaviors for the *process term* in the GO and the *behavior term* in the SLO on the various levels of the affective, psychomotor, and cognitive domains.

4. *Activities.* As a teacher organizes objectives, activities should come to mind. These include the specific writing problems, laboratory experiments, demonstrations, and other events that will provide students with experience. These then form the basis for detailed lesson plans for everyday use.

The first activity for any unit should serve to introduce the unit to the class in an interesting and motivating manner. It should create anticipation among students, activate prior knowledge, and encourage predictions. In other words, this activity helps "set the stage" for the unit.

GENERAL OBJECTIVES AND SPECIFIC LEARNING OUTCOMES

General Objectives (GOs)

1. (affective domain) Students will demonstrate interest in reading the newspaper.

2. (cognitive domain) Students will demonstrate reading and study skills, given teacher instruction.

3. (cognitive domain) Students will develop knowledge in current events.

4. (affective domain) Students will demonstrate ability to interact with a group, assign leadership roles, and delegate responsibility.

5. (psychomotor domain) Students will demonstrate creative ability by participating in the news skit.

Specific Learning Outcomes (SLOs)

A. Given teacher-guided questioning, students will be able to state sources of news. This objective will have been met if the class gives newspapers, television, radio, adults, and peers as sources of news.

B. Given teacher demonstration, students will demonstrate ability to fold a newspaper properly. This objective will have been met when each student performs the task.

C. Given a guided discovery lesson, students will identify the major types of news articles and information available in the newspapers. This objective will have been satisfied upon completion of a teacher-made worksheet.

D. Given directed reading activity, students will be able to answer literal and higher level questions by reading news articles. This objective will have been satisfied upon completion of a teacher-made worksheet.

E. Given a teacher-designed learning center, students will use classified advertisements in the newspapers to locate information. Students completing this activity will choose another activity until they complete a total of five, or until they complete the period by reading the newspaper.

F. Students will work effectively in small groups by choosing topics, writing a script, and preparing illustrations for a news skit in an area of their interest.

Figure 10.5

R. D. Mike Kemp, Hollidaysburg, Pa., Area School District. Reprinted by permission.

Creative teachers use a variety of engaging activities in order to accomplish their objectives. Ideally the unit will include a large number of activities for small group, large group, and individual work. These activities would suggest grouping and regrouping students in a variety of ways (by reading ability, by interest, by attitudes, etc.). They should also take into consideration different learning styles or learning modalities, such as auditory, visual, or kinesthetic. The culminating activity of any unit is intended to summarize the unit or in some way bring the unit to a close. Figure 10.6 contains a sample of activities keyed to objectives. This information is taken from the unit referred to earlier, "Read All About It!"

5. *Material and Resources.* When developing this component, a teacher should consider all of the logistics of the unit: gathering materials,

SAMPLE ACTIVITIES KEYED TO OBJECTIVES FOR "READ ALL ABOUT IT!"

Day 1: Objectives (SLOs) A, B, C (motivation-convergent)
 1. Have bulletin boards up to create atmosphere.
 2. Have variety of newspapers available.
 3. Introduce unit with speaker.
 4. Use questioning strategy to define news, value, and purpose of a newspaper and sources of news.
 5. Write student suggestions on board.
 6. Allow students time to browse through today's newspaper.

Day 2: Objectives D, E, F (motivation-demonstration)
 1. Distribute structured overview.
 2. Discuss structured overview.
 3. Use questioning technique to elaborate on structured overview.
 4. Distribute newspapers.
 5. State procedure for getting newspapers before class and returning them after class.
 .6. Demonstrate how to unfold and fold newspaper.
 7. Have students practice folding and unfolding newspaper.
 8. Distribute newspaper habit survey.
 9. Have students complete newspaper habit survey.
 10. Assign students to ability groups.
 11. Have students read newspaper on completion of assignment.

Day 3: Objectives G, H (guided discovery-convergent)
 1. Use questioning technique to discover types of articles and information in the newspaper.
 2. Write student suggestions on board.
 3. Use questioning technique to classify the types of articles and information according to their purpose (inform, influence, entertain).
 4. Write student suggestions on board.
 5. Distribute teacher-made worksheet.
 6. Have students work on teacher-made worksheet.
 7. Work with each group.
 8. Have students read newspaper on completion of assignment.

Day 4: Objective I (guided discovery-convergent)
 1. Distribute teacher-made worksheet.
 2. Use questioning technique to define newspaper layout and aids to guide reader (i.e., headline, index, by-line, etc.).
 3. Write terms on board.
 4. Have students work on teacher-made worksheet.
 5. Work with each group.
 6. Have students read newspaper on completion of assignment.

Figure 10.6
R. D. Mike Kemp, Hollidaysburg, Pa., Area School District. Reprinted by permission.

SAMPLE LIST OF MATERIALS AND RESOURCES FOR SOLAR SYSTEM UNIT

Books

A Close Look at the Moon
The Earth and Space
Exploring the Sun
Introducing Children to Space
The Moons of Our Solar System
Pictorial Guide to Planet Earth
Practical Science
Project Earth
Science: The Solar System
Space Travel

Charts

Aerospace
Weekly Reader
The solar system
Pictures of the planets
The space shuttle

Audio-Visual Materials

A World Is Born—film
The Age of Space Exploration—film
The Asteroid and the Dinosaur—film
"The Solar System"—tapes
"Destination Mars: The Red Planet"—transparency
"The Planets"—transparencies
"Relative Size of the Planets"—transparency

Other Materials and Resources

Overhead projector
Tape player
Drawing paper
Paper-mâché
Scissors
Art supplies—paint, glue, brushes, etc.
Telescope
Cardboard
Compass—to help draw circles
String
Flashlight
Different size balls

Figure 10.7

Stephen Caruso, Keystone Central School District, Lock Haven, Pa. Reprinted by permission.

planning for any new locations, arranging field trips, ordering special equipment, creating exhibits or inviting guest speakers. Of particular importance is a list of all media to be used in the unit. Reading materials fit into this section of the unit, as well as the films, pictures, library materials, and other supplementary materials. As you may remember, materials should: 1) encourage active learning; 2) suit the needs of individual students; 3) reflect student interest; 4) be aligned with curriculum; and 5) be selected systematically. See a sample of a materials and resource list in Figure 10.7, from the unit, "The Solar System," which we introduced in Figure 10.1.

6. *Student Evaluation.* Well-written objectives should provide guidance and direction for the methods to be used in assessing students as they progress through the unit. A teacher can also use tests, quizzes, worksheets, observations, and other means to evaluate a student's performance during the unit. Appendix 4 provides some common types of test items and indicates for which domains (cognitive, affective, or psychomotor) and on which levels each item type is useful. It is a good idea to have the evaluation scheme worked out before the unit begins. Making students aware of the evaluation procedure is motivational; it clarifies a teacher's expectations for their achievement. A teacher should give students a chart before starting the unit so they may record their own progress. This often enhances their performance. They should not use a class chart for public viewing, however, as this may prove embarrassing to students who are doing poorly.

One important aspect of student evaluation is the paper and pencil test. While tests are not the sole means of assessing student progress, they persist as the major source of deriving student grades. Therefore, test development is a critical step in evaluating a unit. One suggestion for developing a balanced, comprehensive test is to begin with a table of specifications or a test blueprint (Kubiszyn & Borich, 1987). A good test blueprint ensures that assessment matches the objectives that were taught. It will provide direction for creating items for the test. Writing items appropriately requires skill and knowledge. If you have not had instruction or experience in writing test items, consult *Educational Testing and Measurement* (Kubiszyn & Borich, 1987) or *Measurement and Evaluation in Teaching* (Gronlund, 1985).

GROUPING STUDENTS FOR THE INSTRUCTIONAL UNIT

Earlier you read that unit plan instruction should include whole class and small group activities. When reading is considered a key variable in successfully teaching content, the small group format is logical, because students can be grouped according to their reading needs.

Grouping students within the classroom is much more common in elementary settings than in secondary schools. In elementary schools, students are grouped for reading and mathematics. They often work in small groups for many activities and projects. Learning centers, interactive bulletin boards, and educational games often occupy a portion of a student's time in grades 1–6.

Grouping patterns often change when students reach seventh grade. There is comparatively little within-class grouping. While forty-five- or fifty-minute periods are not always conducive to using small group strategies, a teacher can utilize within-class grouping with significant payoffs for student learning. Many secondary teachers have experienced success using small groups. Estes and Vaughan (1980) have suggested that "nothing is so unequal as the equal treatment of unequals" (p. 1).

Grouping Patterns at the Secondary Level

At the secondary school level, the most common pattern of horizontal structure is departmentalization, where knowledge is usually classified into the categories of math, science, social studies, language, and fine arts. Within this departmentalization exists a form of horizontal organization called homogeneous grouping or tracking. This means that students are classified according to ability based upon some standardized intellectual criteria, such as reading scores, intelligence test scores, achievement test scores, or some other measure. The assumption behind tracking is that it diminishes the range of students' intellectual abilities within a given group and therefore makes instruction more efficient (Grant, 1983). Homogeneous ability grouping or tracking is more common in secondary schools than in elementary schools, and in larger school districts than in smaller districts (Findley & Bryan, 1975). It is almost universal at the high school level (Foster, 1984).

An enormous amount of research has been done on the practice of tracking. It remains a controversial issue. Proponents claim that this grouping practice makes teaching more manageable. Slower students do not hold up the rest of the class when tracking is used. Others, however, feel that this form of ability grouping has ill effects on students' self-concepts. Some feel that this practice may be undemocratic and elitist. Still others feel that instruments to measure a student's "ability" cannot be developed. The phenomenon of tracking remains popular because it fosters the idea that there are no individual differences in students who are grouped that way. This idea is dangerous if teachers assume that they can teach all learners as though they were identical.

Regardless of how students are placed in classes, there are individual student differences within any group. These differences remain even when students are grouped according to performance on a battery of standardized tests. Differences in reading ability may exist from subject to subject. Sometimes the best way for a classroom teacher to detect these differences is through administering informal, subject-specific reading tests as described in Chapter 8. When teachers discover the differences, they may find that within-class grouping is the most effective way to accommodate the reading needs of students. Unlike tracking, within-class grouping is flexible, needs specific, and potentially healthy for students' self-concepts.

Secondary teachers typically do not use within-class grouping. The predominant strategies in the secondary classroom involve whole class instruction. With as many as six different classes a day, within-class grouping may seem like an unmanageable task for some teachers. But for classes with students who vary in their knowledge of content, their language background, their interest, and their reading ability, whole group instruction using the same learning materials almost ensures that some students won't succeed.

Teachers often avoid working with small groups because they worry about student behavior problems. However, teachers who have tried small group instruction often have fewer discipline problems because students are not bored with the pace or frustrated with the materials. They enjoy taking responsibility for their own learning. Most prefer interaction to the traditional lecture method. Secondary teachers should experiment with small groups, and here are a few ideas for using the strategy.

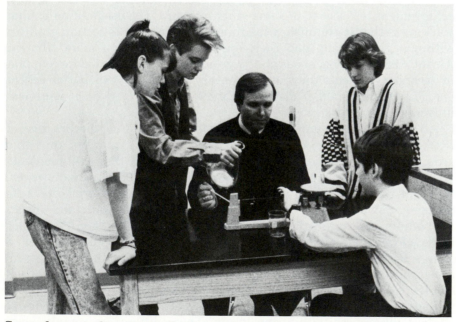

Secondary teachers typically do not use within-class grouping because they believe that it is difficult to manage. However, using small groups is an effective strategy for accommodating individual learning needs. Here, John helps a small group of frustration level readers through a science experiment.

Grouping by Reading Levels

As you know, the group reading inventory (see Chapter 8) yields three reading levels—independent (those scoring above 90 percent correct), instructional (those scoring from 70 to 90 percent correct), and frustration (those scoring below 65 percent correct). These divisions form logical groupings for working with assigned reading materials. The cloze test (Chapter 8) also yields these three levels—independent (those scoring above 57 percent correct); instructional (those scoring between 44 and 57 percent correct); and frustration (those scoring below 44 percent correct).

Figure 10.8, for example, presents a sample of a grouping chart which organizes the information obtained by diagnostic testing with a criterion-referenced group reading inventory. Look at Jane's scores in the example. Her score of 83 percent correct, found in the shaded column, is clearly within the instructional range of 70 to 90 percent correct on literal and inferential comprehension and vocabulary in context combined. The reading material should be appropriate for Jane. She is, however, weak in three skill areas. George, on the other hand, has mastered the skill areas of reading maps, tables, and graphs, but he is generally weak in reading.

GROUPING CHART FORMAT

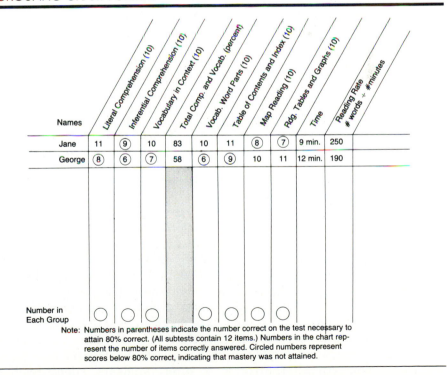

Names	Literal Comprehension (10)	Inferential Comprehension (10)	Vocabulary in Context (10)	Total Comp. and Vocab. (percent)	Vocab. Word Parts (10)	Table of Contents and Index (10)	Map Reading (10)	Rdg. Tables and Graphs (10)	Time	Reading Rate # words ÷ # minutes
Jane	11	⑨	10	83	10	11	⑧	⑦	9 min.	250
George	⑧	⑥	⑦	58	⑥	⑨	10	11	12 min.	190
Number in Each Group	○	○	○		○	○	○	○		

Note: Numbers in parentheses indicate the number correct on the test necessary to attain 80% correct. (All subtests contain 12 items.) Numbers in the chart represent the number of items correctly answered. Circled numbers represent scores below 80% correct, indicating that mastery was not attained.

Figure 10.8

GROUPING

Criterion-Referenced Group Reading Inventory

Name	I Parts of Book	II Resources	III Charts & Graphs	IV Vocab- ulary	V Main Idea	VI Compre- hension
Mastery Level	7	5	5	5	2	5
Adrian	7	4	6	2	1	0
Faye	5	3	5	3	3	3
Michele	7	5	4	5	2	4
Sharon	6	3	4	2	1	1
Jackie	6	2	2	4	0	2
Mike	5	4	3	3	1	1
Carol	7	5	5	5	2	2
Vickie	6	2	2	2	1	2
Wendy H.	6	2	3	2	1	2
Marie	6	2	4	1	1	1
Deanne	7	5	5	5	2	5
Kathleen	7	5	5	5	2	4
William	7	5	5	5	2	5
Jeffrey	6	2	3	2	2	0
Cynthia	6	1	3	1	0	0
Robert	3	3	3	2	1	1
Roger	4	4	4	2	1	1
Tina	3	2	2	1	1	0
Martin	7	4	5	5	2	4
Donna	5	3	5	2	0	3
Thomas	7	5	4	5	2	4
Wendy	7	5	5	4	2	4
Cindy	6	2	3	3	1	1

The materials appear to be at George's frustration level and should not be used with him without adaptation.

Jane and others in the instructional group should be guided in their reading through the directed reading activity approach as described in detail in Chapter 11. Before an assignment is made, the teacher provides background for the students, first creating interest in the topic of study, introducing new vocabulary in the context used in the reading selection, and filling in concepts or understandings that would help students grasp the reading material. Guide questions are given to direct students' reading so that they know what is important for them to gain from the selection. After they have read the selection, the teacher discusses the answers to the guide questions in addition to her questions at various levels of comprehension. An alternative is to direct students' silent reading

Figure 10.9 Continued:
Grouping by Skills

Parts of Book

Faye	Jeffrey
Sharon	Cynthia
Jackie	Robert
Mike	Roger
Vickie	Tina
Wendy H.	Donna
Marie	Cindy

Use of Charts and Graphs

Michele	Jeffrey
Sharon	Cynthia
Jackie	Robert
Mike	Roger
Vickie	Tina
Wendy H.	Thomas
Marie	Cindy

Main Ideas

Adrian	Marie
Faye	Cynthia
Sharon	Robert
Jackie	Roger
Mike	Tina
Vickie	Donna
Wendy H.	Cindy

Use of Resources

Adrian	Jeffrey
Faye	Cynthia
Sharon	Robert
Jackie	Roger
Mike	Tina
Vickie	Martin
Wendy H.	Donna
Marie	Cindy

Vocabulary

Adrian	Jeffrey
Faye	Cynthia
Sharon	Robert
Jackie	Roger
Mike	Tina
Vickie	Donna
Wendy H.	Wendy
Marie	Cindy

Literal and Inferential Comprehension

Adrian	Jeffrey
Faye	Cynthia
Michele	Robert
Sharon	Roger
Jackie	Tina
Mike	Martin
Carol	Donna
Vickie	Thomas
Wendy H.	Wendy
Marie	Cindy
Kathleen	

Figure 10.9

Prepared by Robert G. Sealy, Penns Valley Junior-Senior High School, Spring Mills, Pa. Reprinted by permission.

through the use of a study guide. The study guide for instructional readers would need to focus more on the literal level of comprehension initially than does the guide for independent readers. The teacher's questions after reading, however, should also focus on higher levels of comprehension.

The frustration level readers like George should not be asked to read the assigned reading material unless special guidance is available. If alternative reading material on the topic of study, written at an easier level, is not available, several options exist. (These are described in detail in Chapter 13.) One alternative, for example, is a detailed study guide which would direct students to skip some portions of the textbook, to read headings, opening and summary paragraphs, and to study graphic materials. Care must be taken to make the study guide simple enough that it can be used successfully by disabled readers.

The teacher may ask the independent readers to read longer sections at a time, perhaps using a study guide to ensure comprehension. This study guide—or teacher's questions after reading—can focus primarily on higher levels of questioning rather than primarily on the literal level of

DIAGNOSTIC GRID

Sentence Structure

	Bob	Leo	Sam	Joyce	Mary	Efram	Jennifer
Complete Sentences	X	X	X	X			
Run-On Sentences			X		X	X	
Ample Modifiers		X		X			X
Parallelism		X			X	X	
Voice	X	X					X

Small Group Instruction for Sentence Structure

Complete Sentences	**Run-On Sentences**	**Modifiers**
Bob	Mary	Joyce
Leo	Efram	Jennifer
Sam	Sam	Leo
Joyce		

Parallelism	**Voice**
Mary	Bob
Efram	Leo
Leo	Jennifer

Figure 10.10

comprehension. This independent group may also be assigned further work to gain greater depth in the topic which could be shared later with the rest of the class. Additional study might involve research, explorations in the community, or projects developed after independent research. While this group can operate more independently than the others, the teacher must be sure to guide these students in their work, focusing on higher level comprehension and study skills. Through sharing their research, this group can enrich the study of the other reading groups.

Probably the best strategy for using within-class grouping as described here is to seek variety. Sometimes the teacher may work with the frustration level readers; sometimes an independent reader can assist with the frustration level group; sometimes pairs can participate in peer tutoring; sometimes a teacher can rewrite portions of the textbook; a listening station may contain a tape of the essential portions of the tests in use. Use of grouping plans based on criteria other than reading level also avoids this problem.

Grouping by Skill Needs

The criterion-referenced group reading inventory also yields information about each students' skill mastery. From studying the number of correct items in the vocabulary section, for example, the teacher knows which students need additional work in that area in order to use the assigned reading materials effectively. Often skill groupings, particularly in the study skills, may include students from all three reading levels. In the example presented in Figure 10.8, both Jane from the instructional level group and George from the frustration level group demonstrated a weakness in inferential comprehension. The group stays together only as long as the various members have not mastered the skill being taught. Therefore, grouping by skill needs is yet another type of grouping that prevents a stigma from being attached to group membership by reading levels. Teachers should move students to new groups as soon as they master the particular skill. This usually takes no longer than several weeks. Groups are then reformed for new skill needs.

One junior high school teacher, using a criterion-referenced group reading inventory in his American history class, formed the groups in the chart given in Figure 10.9. Since most of this teacher's class displayed weaknesses in literal and inferential comprehension, the teacher plans to devote time in class to discussions of assigned mterials. He may need to review or teach comprehension skills, such as getting the main idea. The skills should be taught and applied using the textbook. Study guides may also be useful to help students read assigned materials at home. Structured overviews as well as prereading guide questions may be helpful in introducing new units of work. (These techniques and others for improving comprehension were presented in Chapters 4 and 5.)

Skill grouping can also work for writing. In the same way that an informal group reading inventory yields areas of strength and weakness, some teachers use a diagnostic grid to assess writing. After giving a writing assignment, teachers may identify group skill needs by focusing on several variables. In the areas of sentence structure, for example, teachers may wish to determine if there are complete sentences, run-on sentences, ample modifiers, or other key structural characteristics. See Figure 10.10 for an example of such a grid. The diagnostic grid may be used to assess many areas, such as vocabulary development, organization, morphology, and mechanics. Each area would produce different grouping patterns. This strategy addresses individual differences effectively.

Other Types of Grouping

Teachers may also use other types of criteria to group students. For example, students may be grouped by interests, such as various sports, to do math problems. Teachers can then create word problems pertaining to football, baseball, basketball, tennis, and running to emphasize the skill being taught, such as fractions. Students work the problems pertaining to their chosen sport. Grouping by interests tends to enhance interest and motivation in the content area study.

Students may also be given choices in studying certain aspects of a unit, such as transportation, customs, or discoveries. Members of each study group can be given reading material appropriate to their reading levels. Within the same group an independent level reader may be reading a rather technical textbook while a member of the frustration level group may be reading a pamphlet or viewing a filmstrip in order to make a contribution to the topic chosen for study by the group. Independent readers may also be able to provide leadership to the group, helping the group to function effectively.

Students may also be grouped by prior background, such as experiences with certain tools before working in an industrial arts class. For example, students who, through previous experiences, have worked with a lathe would not need basic instruction in using one in a construction project. Students who have traveled extensively might be grouped together, or perhaps interspersed within groups in a social studies class. Through hobbies, students may have extensive knowledge related to a content area. An interest in astronomy, for example, that has led to extensive independent study may provide background for a physical science class.

A third type of grouping is that of students with similar language abilities. Teachers who have students of different language backgrounds within the same class usually try to group across language groups to promote socialization among groups. They should not, however, group by ethnic groups because one goal of education is integration of diverse groups. Students for whom English is not a native language should be mixed with native English speakers as much as possible. On occasion, however, grouping Limited English Proficiency (LEP) students together may be necessary. They may need some extra instructional help if they are having difficulty grasping the content due to language problems. Grouping LEP students together in the content classroom should be on a special needs basis only, or perhaps to use special bilingual materials. They should be mixed with native English speakers in other types of groupings as much as possible to enhance their English-speaking abilities.

One junior-high English teacher with students from families of different cultural groups who had settled in the same rural valley grouped students by their elementary school in a study of their "roots" or ancestry. Although she usually grouped across elementary schools to promote socialization, grouping by previous schools meant that students are grouped with others of similar cultural backgrounds. This grouping was appropriate in the study on their ancestry.

Grouping within the content area classroom can individualize instruction. While it is impossible for a content teacher to tailor instruction for each individual, it is realistic to accommodate group needs. Grouping by

It is sometimes impractical for middle school teachers to work with individual students. Within-class grouping offers a manageable alternative to accommodate individual differences. Here, Bev works individually with a frustration level reader.

reading levels is typical in the elementary school reading program, and this grouping should continue in the secondary school when different materials are used for the different reading levels.

Groups may become stereotyped if formed only on the basis of reading levels. Grouping by skill needs, interest, prior knowledge, and background prevents the formation of stereotypes. Variety in groupings also helps maintain interest in content area study. A teacher should incorporate small group instruction when organizing for instruction, beginning slowly until s/he becomes skillful in managing small groups. A good resource for small group instruction is Chapter 7 of *Teaching Strategies* (Orlich et al., 1985).

SUMMARY

Organizing for instruction is an important part of teaching, especially the organizing of teaching units. This kind of planning allows content teachers to take into account the differences among students while attending to the content objectives necessary to each subject. A typical unit has six components: a statement of background and rationale, a content outline, goals and objectives, activities, materials, and evaluation procedures.

Grouping students for the instructional unit should be aimed at increasing their chances of success in learning the material or mastering the objectives. While homogeneous grouping, or tracking, may seem to simplify the teaching process, the range of student reading abilities within even a homogeneously grouped class will make within-class grouping a necessary strategy.

Grouping strategies vary within content classes. Grouping by reading assessments, the group reading inventory, or the cloze procedure is often useful. Independent, instructional, and frustration reading levels yield groups of students who can be given instruction appropriate to their reading ability measured against the class text. Other groups can be based on reading skill needs. Students can also be grouped by criteria other than reading level, such as interest, content knowledge, experience, language ability, or other individual characteristics. Instruction designed for these groups will make it more likely that students will succeed, which is the goal of all teachers.

REFERENCES

Estes, T. H., & Vaughn, J. L. (1978). *Reading and learning in the content classroom: Diagnostic and instructional strategies*. Boston: Allyn & Bacon, Inc.

Findley, W., & Bryan, M. (1975). *The pros and cons of ability grouping*. Bloomington, IL: The Phi Delta Kappa Educational Foundation.

Foster, S. G. (1984). A system in which 'the better get the best?'. *Education Week, IV*(1), 30–31, 58.

Grant, C. A. (1983). *Bringing teaching to life: An introduction to education*. Boston: Allyn & Bacon, Inc.

Gronlund, N. E. (1985). *Measurement and evaluation in teaching*. New York: Macmillan Publishing Co.

Kubiszyn, T., & Borich, G. (1987). *Educational testing and measurement* (2nd ed.). Glenview, IL: Scott, Foresman and Co.

Orlich, D. C., Harder, R. J., Callahan, R. C., Krauss, C. H., Kauchak, D. P., Pendergrass, R. A., & Keogh, A. J. (1985). *Teaching strategies: A guide to better instruction*. Lexington, MA: D. C. Heath and Co.

Pearce, D. L., & Bader, L. (1986). The effect of unit construction upon teachers' use of content reading and writing strategies. *Journal of Reading, 30*(2), 130–135.

SUGGESTIONS FOR FURTHER READING

Gronlund, N. E. (1985). *Measurement and evaluation in teaching*. New York: Macmillan Publishing Co.

Kubiszyn, T., & Borich, G. (1987). *Educational testing and measurement* (2nd ed.). Glenview, IL: Scott, Foresman and Co.

Orlich, D. C. et al. (1984). *Teaching strategies: A guide to better instruction*. Lexington, MA: D. C. Heath and Co.

CHAPTER ELEVEN

Teacher-Directed and Student-Directed Reading and Writing Activities*

SCENARIO

On a Friday morning in late March, the math, science, and social studies teachers are gathering in the library for a half-day inservice program. As they mingle over coffee and donuts prior to Marge's presentation, we overhear the following bits and pieces of conversation.

"Any idea what this program will be about?"

"Vaguely. Remember that questionnaire we filled out last fall on topics we'd most like to have addressed on inservice days this year?"

"Yes, but I don't recall seeing 'Independent Reading and Writing Activities' listed as a possible topic."

"Morning, Phil. Ready to get geared up with ideas for setting students loose on their own?"

"Right, Joe. About now I'd welcome some suggestions for doing just that! Good thing next week is spring break."

"Welcome back, Denise. We've missed you. Hope you're feeling strong enough to return to all of this."

"Thanks, Mark. I'm finally feeling human again, just in time for a week off for break! I came back today just to hear what Marge has to say. She has really been helpful to me as a new teacher. Almost everything she has suggested has worked out well. She sent me the outline for today's program while I was still in the hospital and I was determined to be up and around to join all of you today."

"Anyone here know what a LAP is? That's on the agenda for today under student-directed activities. Never heard of it."

*This chapter was written by Sandra L. Snyder of The Pennsylvania State University.

"I'm not sure what a LAP is or how to put one together, but I do know that Bill and Judy have been using LAPs in their tenth-grade biology classes and say they like the idea. So . . . we may be getting some really useful information this morning."

"Hope you're right, Rick. Frankly, after almost seven months of being in the director's chair, I'm about ready to turn over some of the responsibility for learning to my students."

OVERVIEW

In this chapter, we take a closer look at why many students fail to complete (or even attempt) content area reading assignments. We present a practical strategy, the Directed Reading Activity (DRA) (Stauffer, 1969), for ensuring that students can complete assigned readings. Over time, this strategy should not only result in improved assignment completion, but it should also have a marked effect on the degree of class participation. The teacher's role gradually diminishes as students internalize the process so that they can use it on their own. Students who use this process should begin reading with increased comprehension. They should come to class prepared, and the teacher can then devote his/her time to extending the concepts covered in the assigned reading.

Moving students from dependent learners to independent learners is an ongoing task for all teachers. While the teacher's prime responsibility is organizing for instruction, students may take an increasingly active role in arranging their own learning experiences. Student-directed reading and writing activities allow for variation in learning pace, methodology, and topics to be explored. When students direct their own learning, teachers may accommodate individual interest, need, and ability. However, independent learning experiences need not be viewed as "turning students loose on their own," and within-class grouping need not be chaotic if properly managed.

Activities involving the use of contracts, learning activity packages, learning centers, and instructional games allow for varying degrees of student direction. Each type of activity can be used within the framework of an instructional unit. By integrating such activities within a unit design, the teacher avoids using them as "add-on" activities unrelated to the major focus of instruction.

THE DIRECTED READING ACTIVITY

The Directed Reading Activity (DRA) is a basic strategy designed to guide students' reading. It is the antithesis of what typically occurs with reading assignments at the secondary level. Traditionally, secondary teachers assign reading with little or no introduction or directions for students. The scenario might go something like this: "Tonight for homework read pages 115 to 135." (The class groans.) "Well, okay, how about pages 115 to 130. You can't say I have no heart."

This approach to assigning homework reading does not maximize the chance that students will benefit from the reading. In order for independent reading to be effective, students need to be prepared. They need guidance in formulating purposes for doing the reading; they need to have the opportunity to make predictions and preview new vocabulary concepts. And teachers can learn a great deal about their students when they actively participate in assigned readings. Teacher participation, through the DRA, conveys the message that readings are worthwhile and important.

Perhaps the best way to examine the Directed Reading Activity (DRA) is through using an example. Let's go through the process together using an article titled "Dyslexia: Help for Victims of a Puzzling Ailment" from *U.S. News & World Report* (November 7, 1983) shown in Figure 11.1. The DRA will teach you something about an important issue in education as well as help you practice the strategy we hope you will use in your classroom.

Step 1: Establishing Background

In this step, the teacher leads a discussion through which students relate relevant experiences to the reading material, which they have not yet read. To start the discussion, the teacher can use a transparency containing the following questions, which are based on the *U.S. News & World Report* article. The transparency's primary function is motivational.

- For many children and adults, __?__ is a source of humiliation and frustration.
- As many as 15 percent of all school children are hampered by __?__ .
- Schools are becoming sensitive to the plight of __?__ .
- Testosterone may be linked to __?__ since six times as many males as females are affected by it.
- Cells located on the left side of the brains of __?__ children are not in their proper place.

To begin class discussion for *establishing background*, the teacher might ask: "Can you think of a word that would in some form fill the blank? It is the same word in each case. Do you think you know the word? If you guessed "dyslexia," you are correct. Do you know what dyslexia really is? Do you know anyone who is dyslexic? What are a few of the symptoms?" The idea here is to encourage student contribution and discussion as well as to determine how familiar students are with the concept on a personal level.

Step 2: Building Vocabulary

At some point in the prereading discussion, the teacher may move from an eliciting mode to more of an information-giving mode. She can further develop ideas that students contributed, or she can introduce new words that appear in the passage to be assigned. Take the term "dyslexia," for example. The teacher might ask: "Can you use the word attack skills to determine the real definition? 'Dys-': a prefix which means bad or abnormal; '-lex-': a root which means words or vocabulary; '-ia': a suffix meaning things derived from or related to. 'Dyslexia' is an abnormal condition related to words or vocabulary. It is known simply as a language disorder."

Other words from the article which might be introduced in a similar way are "multisensory," "reinforce," "exempt," and "testosterone." The extent to which you work with vocabulary in Step 1 of the DRA depends on the levels of readers with which you are working.

Step 3: Establishing a Purpose for Reading Through Prequestioning

Teachers can begin the prequestioning process by asking students to skim the passage to be read. Using pictures, illustrations, maps, headings, and subheadings, teachers might ask, "What would you like to know about this passage?" or "What seems important to understanding this reading?" (Be prepared for at least a wisecrack or two.) This is also an opportune time for introducing or reinforcing the first two parts of the SQ3R technique (see Chapter 5). The teacher may want to begin by demonstrating or modeling the process of generating prequestions, gradually asking students to assume this responsibility. Some of these questions might include: "After skimming the article, what would you say is the main idea? How do you think youngsters with dyslexia cope? What is the fail-safe method? Why is this issue important for future teachers? As you read the article, see if you can answer these questions."

Step 4: Silent Reading

After students reach this point, the teacher might assign the reading for homework. Students now have some background, they are familiar with the technical vocabulary, and they have a real focus on the purpose for reading. They have invested something of themselves in reading the assignment. To continue our simulation, read the article in Figure 11.1 on pages 248 and 249.

Step 5: Post Questions

After the reading, the class or group reviews the prequestions. This is an opportunity for teachers to check for student understanding. If differences of opinion arise during the review, this provides an excellent opportunity for the teacher to model making inferences, skimming to find information, and/or predicting outcomes.

After reviewing the prequestions, the teacher may ask a series of questions that are consistent with the objective(s) of the reading by using one of the taxonomies suggested in Chapter 3. Some of the questions should be convergent (both literal and inferential), while others would be divergent (evaluative and appreciation level). This is a good time to monitor how well students think critically. If they are writing the answers, the teacher can use the results to diagnose poor comprehension. For example, here are some appropriate sample questions which might be used with the article on dyslexia:

Literal Level

1. Are dyslexic students retarded?
2. What does Margaret Rawson call this multisensory technique for treating dyslexia?
3. What is the Landmark Plan?

Inferential Level

4. What kind of problems might a dyslexic person have when driving an automobile?
5. What does Sally Smith mean when she says "reading is a passport in this society"?

Evaluative Level

6. Is there enough detail in this article to help new teachers? Explain.
7. Would it be appropriate to include dyslexics in a normal secondary classroom? Why or why not?

Appreciation Level

8. How is this kind of news reporting good or bad for education?
9. Do you think that this passage smacks of sensationalism? Why or why not?

DYSLEXIA: HELP FOR VICTIMS OF A PUZZLING AILMENT

Once thought of as retarded, youngsters with a serious reading impairment are learning to cope—and excel.

When Elias Johnson, a bright and studious history major at Brown University, takes a written exam, he nearly always feels confident that he can answer the questions correctly.

But his thoughts, more often than not, end up in a jumble of misspelled words—some with entire syllables missing—that he is helpless to correct. "I'd like to present myself in the best possible light," he sighs, "but I know that it will never work out that way."

What troubles Johnson, as well as millions of other adults and as many as 15 percent of all schoolchildren, is a language disorder known as dyslexia. Despite their usually average to above-average intelligence, these people will write *was* for *saw*, mistake the letter *b* for *d*, and skip over words such as *not*, totally changing a passage's meaning.

As a result, reading becomes a torturous chore, and school performance often lags. In some instances, such students are branded as "lazy" or even classified as retarded.

Increasingly, though, schools and colleges are becoming more sensitive to the plight of dyslexia sufferers. Among the steps being introduced:

• Brown University lets such students take untimed or oral exams, as well as lighter course loads each term.

• A recent Massachusetts law exempts these students from taking standardized aptitude tests to enter any of the 12 state colleges and universities.

• In the Alief public schools near Houston, dyslexic students are paired with other youngsters who make carbon copies of class notes and assignments for them.

Still, for many children and adults, dyslexia remains a source of humiliation and frustration. Says Sally Smith, founder and director of the Lab School of Washington: "Reading is a passport in this society, and if you can't read, you're considered dumb."

In recent years, scientific research has begun to shed fresh light on the disorder that has affected some of the world's greatest minds, including Albert Einstein and Woodrow Wilson.

Studies begun in 1979 at Beth Israel Hospital in Boston have found that cells located on the left side of the brains of dyslexic children are not in their proper place—a scrambling that occurs when the brain is formed during the 16th to 20th weeks of pregnancy.

Scientists also are examining how the male hormone testosterone may be linked to dyslexia, since the trait affects six times as many males as females.

Step 6: Incorporating a Reading Skill

Teachers can instruct students on reading skills as part of the DRA. They can also emphasize specific vocabulary, comprehension, or study skills through content reading assignments. In fact, in any carefully planned DRA, students would be expected to demonstrate various comprehension skills, such as recognizing inferences, understanding main ideas, or anticipating outcomes as part of the early steps. It is always useful to point out to students that these *are* reading skills so they become conscious of the task they are engaged in.

Figure 11.1 Continued:

Further research may enable high-risk mothers to be detected early so that their children can be helped soon after birth. Without a medical cure, Dr. Albert Galaburda, a researcher, observes, "Education remains the most important approach."

"Fail-safe method." The most effective learning method now being tried is a multisensory approach that teaches children to break down words into letter sounds by using several of their senses simultaneously—seeing how the letter looks, hearing how it sounds and feeling how it is shaped in writing.

Margaret Rawson of Frederick, Md., a veteran teacher in the field of language-learning difficulties, calls this technique "a fail-safe method that gives the student other senses to fall back on when certain ones fail."

At the Renton public schools outside Seattle, primary-grade students trace large patterns of letters as they recite the phonetic sounds aloud. In Prince George's County, Md., middle-school students chant, "Loop, drop stroke, anchor, turn," as they write the cursive letter *l* on a blackboard. The exercise reinforces how each letter "feels," to prepare students for better note taking.

The multisensory approach has had dramatic results for Regina Neal, a high-school senior in Prince George's County. "Hearing the word, writing it and seeing it all at once have helped me to remember," she says.

The approach has proved so effective that it is being used to teach reading to all Prince George's pupils in kindergarten through the second grade.

In higher education, Erskine College in South Carolina is among 20 post-secondary schools in the Southeast with special programs for dyslexic students. But those who expect easier classes quickly learn otherwise. The school demands equal work from these students and makes that goal attainable by providing daily tutoring for an extra $2,000 a year.

Landmark plan. In an unusual move, the Landmark preparatory school in Prides Crossing, Mass., is trying to start a four-year, liberal-arts college for dyslexic students in Putney, Vt. Such a school would "assist those kids who have the intellect or motivation to go on to professional schools but who don't have the language skills to deal with the enormous mass of material required," says Landmark Headmaster Charles Drake.

One of the toughest problems remains convincing dyslexic students that they can learn. Before 18-year-old Trey Roski of Los Angeles found success three years ago at the Gow School for dyslexic boys in South Wales, N.Y., he seemed headed for failure. He recalls: "I would try to do my homework, but it took me so long and I always got it wrong, so I finally stopped doing it."

Some schools bring parents of dyslexic students into the process. At the Diagnostic Learning Center of the University of Houston, parents get tips on how they can help, such as by proofreading homework for errors.

Yet it is in the early grades, educators say, that new learning skills must be introduced to spare dyslexic students the humiliation of being bright but unable to read well.

Figure 11.1

Other reading skills, such as reading charts and graphs, using the index or glossary, or outlining a passage, may be incorporated in the DRA at this time. Focusing on one or two skills in each DRA would be enough to create a systematic approach to teaching reading through a content area.

For our simulation, an exercise in outlining may be appropriate. Outlining is a useful study skill: it gives one a sense of organization and often makes it easier to locate main ideas. One way to teach outlining is through the use of *partial outlines*. In this technique, the teacher provides the outline's format and fills in several items. Students can see the structure and fill in the remaining blanks. This partial structure should gradually lead students to provide complete outlines of their own.

Using our passage, complete this outline.

I. Fail-safe method
   A. Multisensory approach
      1. seeing the letter
      2. _____
      3. feeling how the letter is shaped
   B. Gives students other senses to fall back on
   C. Prepares students for better note taking
   D. _____ _____ _____ _____
II. Landmark plan
   A. _____
      1. assist kids who have the intellect and motivation
      2. _____
   B. _____
      1. _____
      2. _____

Word attack skill reinforcement is another possibility for incorporating a reading skill in this part of the DRA. The word "dyslexia" is a good example for this. How about analyzing other words that begin with 'dys-' (or dis), or that end in "ia." The possibilities for extending vocabulary are endless. This, in fact, brings us to the final step of the DRA.

Step 7: Enrichment

Students should have some choices about the kind of enrichment activity they participate in as a result of the DRA. Group projects, further reading, or special writing activities related to the DRA are appropriate. Enrichment activities may even act as a springboard for building background for the next DRA, and the process could begin again.

Possible enrichment activities for our DRA are unlimited. Here are two ideas:

Write a dialogue between a dyslexic student and a classroom teacher. Imagine that neither the teacher nor the student knows about dyslexia. Make the setting for the dialogue the classroom, five minutes after a unit test.

Hold a mirror upright on a piece of writing paper. Using a pencil or pen, try to write your name by looking only in the mirror. Then write a short paragraph about how it felt to write under these conditions.

Writing is involved most frequently in the enrichment section of the DRA. Many different types of writing, creative and expository, are appropriate in the enrichment process. Teachers should consider the post-reading suggestions in Chapter 6 as they plan a DRA so that they consider the wide variety of writing activity possibilities. Other writing activities to consider as part of reading assignments include answers to study guide questions, journal or learning log entries, and persuasive essays.

There has been some discussion about just how long a DRA should last. Some teachers manage the entire process in one class period while others take two or even three days to complete a cycle. Regardless of the duration, the DRA offers a structure teachers can employ to provide guided practice. Giving students a purpose for reading, creating anticipation, posing thoughtful questions, checking students' understanding, and incorporating a specific reading skill can maximize the chances for comprehension of assigned content area material.

THE DIRECTED READING/THINKING ACTIVITY

The Directed Reading/Thinking Activity (DRTA) was developed by the same educator who created the DRA. Dr. Russell G. Stauffer (1969) designed the DRTA to enhance comprehension when students read literature. This strategy is very useful when students read short stories since it involves students in predicting outcomes based on the content of a story. The rationale for using the DRTA is to foster the student's independence when reading. It engages students in an active process where they must use their reasoning abilities and their own ideas. By using the DRTA, students learn to set purposes for their reading and adjust their reading rates accordingly through repeated use of the activity.

The steps in the DRTA are similar to the steps in the DRA. The major difference in the two approaches is that the DRTA allows for more independence by the reader. It also encourages more critical thinking when reading literature. The following are the five steps suggested for the DRTA as proposed by Stauffer.

Step 1: Identifying the Purposes for Reading

Students are asked to skim the story to find any clues which might help in understanding the plot. They may predict what is meant by the title. They may read subtitles. They are encouraged to study pictures or illustrations in order to find out about the story prior to reading.

These clues can be used as the basis for setting a purpose or purposes for reading. The clues may generate questions or heighten curiosity. Teachers should encourage students to predict outcomes using their own experiences and background. In group discussion, similar experiences and common interests should emerge. The substance of the reading acts as a catalyst for this sharing and prediction-making process. During this prereading discussion, the teacher can record all predictions by writing them on the chalkboard. This is also a good time for introducing vocabulary.

The teacher's role is that of guiding the discussion and heading off any misunderstanding about the story as the students make predictions. Through examining clues, sharing experiences, and discussing possible outcomes in the plot, the teacher can guide the class toward the purposes for reading the story.

Step 2: Guiding the Reading Rate

Varying the reading rate to fit the purpose for reading is an important skill for all students. *Skimming*, the ability to read swiftly and lightly, is necessary when trying to locate information. *Scanning*, the ability to read carefully from point to point, helps students understand main ideas. *Studying* is also a specific reading skill that requires students to read and reread. It often requires considerable critical thinking. The teacher should discuss with students which rate is appropriate for particular reading assignments, so that students can use that rate. The DRTA asks teachers to guide students' practice with various rates during reading.

Step 3: Directing the Silent Reading

The teacher should determine appropriate points in the passage to stop the reader, and together they can verify or eliminate some of the original predictions. Some predictions may be reformulated at this time. New predictions may be considered. At any rate, the reading should not involve too many breaks; in general, one or two should be enough depending on the length of the story. The teacher might observe that students will make their own breaks as they verify their predictions. Opportunities for individual help will arise because of this discovering process. Teachers should encourage students to ask for help as they read silently.

Step 4: Developing Critical Thinking Through Questioning

This time is generally devoted to using one of the taxonomies, but limiting the number of literal questions. The emphasis should be on inference and evaluation questions. This is an opportunity for discussing student predictions and for extending the story through divergent, higher-level questioning. It is also a time to check for student understanding. There may be concepts or vocabulary that require clarification. Questions asking *why* and *what if* require critical thinking. Concept labels and relationships among concepts can require critical thinking. Questions asking students to compare and contrast, or to evaluate the process used or the choices made, require critical thinking.

Step 5: Enhancing Reading Skills

Since the DRTA is aimed at developing students' thinking, teachers should concentrate on such skills as determining reality from fantasy, drawing conclusions, making generalizations, and formulating propositions. Activities that relate to student judgment and reasoning are appropriate. Fiction can be ideal for encouraging students to consider levels of meaning, for recognizing word connotations, and for analyzing various elements in a story.

THE LANGUAGE EXPERIENCE APPROACH IN THE CONTENT AREA CLASSROOM

A third teacher-directed technique for individualizing instruction is the *language experience approach*. The language experience approach has often been advocated as a technique for teaching beginning reading. As described by Stauffer (1970), Van Allen (1976), and others, it is based on the premise that students can best learn to read if they see that reading is merely "talk written down." For this reason, the language experience approach has often been considered the natural way to teach young children to read since the reading materials consist of their own language products. The following suggestions are drawn from an article (Askov & Lee, 1980) pertaining to the use of the Language Experience Approach in content area classes.

Briefly, the language experience approach consists of the following steps:

1. A stimulus idea or activity, selected by the teacher or student, is discussed spontaneously.
2. The teacher then directs students to record their ideas on chart paper, a chalkboard, or a transparency.
3. The students dictate their ideas to the teacher who writes them, usually on a chart, while the students watch.
4. The students read what they have dictated.
5. The chart may be put into more permanent form (perhaps bound into a "book" with other experience stories) or transcribed and copied to be reread and shared with others.
6. The story may become the basis for skill development, such as teaching vocabulary skills.

The language experience approach has been used successfully with older students, primarily in remedial settings rather than in content area classrooms. For example, Wilson and Parkey (1970) report its use in a middle school reading program with poor readers. Girdon (1973) used the approach with severely disabled junior high school students, while Abbott

(1966) applied a modified language experience approach with culturally disadvantaged high school students. Chapter 13 suggests additional uses of the language experience approach with exceptional learners.

The language experience approach can be used effectively in content area classrooms. All readers, whether disabled or not, can benefit from the procedures. The technique is particularly useful in adapting difficult content materials for those students who are unable to read them successfully.

Some stimulus ideas or activities that might be used in the language experience approach in content area classrooms are pictures, slides, films, filmstrips, experiments, demonstrations, oral reading by the teacher, audio- or videotapes, records, news events, art, and music. The concepts related to the content are brought out during the discussion which follows the stimulus activity. Let's look at some examples of uses of the language experience approach in content area classrooms:

English
—The teacher reads aloud a piece of literature (for example, a short story) that would be too difficult for the students to read independently. After a discussion the students dictate a summary. The teacher later transcribes the student-dictated material to a ditto master for use in teaching the skill of writing plot summaries.
—Students dictate letters to friends and relatives who live far away. As the teacher writes the dictated letters in the proper format, she teaches students the correct form for a letter.

Social Studies
—News events which the students have heard on radio or seen on television are dictated to the teacher during the study of current events. The charts for one day may be bound together to form a daily "newspaper." Those collected over a period of time may be bound together to show how history may be recorded.
—The teacher tapes a chapter of a difficult textbook which the students listen to at a listening center while they follow along in their textbooks. After all have completed the chapter, they dictate the main ideas to the teacher who records them on a chart and then on a ditto master. This rewritten version in effect becomes the students' textbook, written in a version that is readable to the students. Rewritten portions of the textbook (on ditto) may be used the following year with students who are unable to read the textbook.

Science
—The teacher conducts an experiment. The students dictate the steps or procedures followed while the teacher records them on a chart or ditto master. The chart or dittoed sheet serves as the guide when students perform the experiment themselves.

—After viewing a film, the students dictate the main ideas presented. These are placed on a ditto master which aids in reviewing the science concepts presented in the film.

Mathematics

—The teacher presents a problem to some students, using only numbers. The students create a word problem which the numbers might represent. The word problem is then placed on a chart or ditto master for other students to solve. The challenge is to get the same answer as in the original problem.

—As students read a word problem, they dictate the important facts, omitting irrelevant details. The dictation, which is placed on a chart, helps them understand the process of solving word problems.

Home Economics

—The teacher discusses the procedures for preparing to cook safely in school. The students then dictate these rules, which are written on a chart to serve as a reminder throughout the cooking experiences.

—Similar to the science example above, the teacher may demonstrate procedures (such as for cutting out a pattern) to the class. The students dictate the step-by-step procedures which they are then to follow in working with their own materials.

Industrial Arts

—The teacher reads portions of difficult technical manuals to the students. After discussing these, the students dictate the directions in a simplified form which are placed on a chart or ditto master to guide students in their use of the machinery.

Foreign Language

—The students dictate a brief dialogue or play, using current vocabulary words. After the dictation is placed on a ditto master, the students re-read it for additional practice.

Music or Art

—The teacher plays a record of a musical selection or shows a picture or slide of a work of art. After students discuss the mood created, they dictate their ideas which are written on a ditto master to help them remember the work.

—The teacher plays a melody on the piano. Some students dictate lyrics which would fit the tempo. These are placed on a ditto master and duplicated for all students to sing.

—When students are learning a selection in music class which is related to a folk tale or other story, the teacher may ask the students to dictate the story for a chart. The story is then put into the form of a "script" for choral reading to be used in the next music class for an introduction to the song or in the content classroom for follow-up or reinforcement.

The language experience approach has been particularly successful with frustration level readers, those students who mind the textbook too difficult to understand. While all students may participate in the stimulus activity and subsequent discussion, the dictated discussion becomes the "textbook" for the poor readers. If it is placed on a ditto master, this version may become the "textbook" for poor readers in future years.

Rewriting Materials

The key to effective use of the language experience approach is that materials are written in the students' own language. This means that disabled readers or others with reading problems can read materials at their own levels. Using the language experience approach, the student writes the reading materials for him/herself and other students to read.

What can a teacher do with other difficult materials when the language experience approach is not the appropriate strategy? One possibility is for the teacher to rewrite critical parts of the materials for student use. The process of rewriting sounds simple, but it is time-consuming. Therefore, teachers need to be sure that the rewritten materials are of broad usefulness this year and for years to come.

The teacher can use the following outline for this task:

1. Select the material(s) to be rewritten.
2. Systematically sort out concepts, key words, and phrases which must be included in the simplified form. Rewrite to shorten sentences and word length, being sure to include those key words and phrases.
3. Use a readability formula (provided in Chapter 7) to check readability levels before and after rewriting.
4. Aim for a reading level appropriate for the group reading the material. For example, ninth-grade biology students may need sixth-grade reading level material as measured by formal or informal testing. Rewritten materials should aim for fifth-grade level, one grade level below the students' assessed reading level. This rule of thumb should allow students to read the material with minimal difficulty and maximum comprehension.
5. Check out rewritten material with students and let them help edit it to encourage comprehension.
6. Be sure to use visuals whenever possible—pictures, drawings, tables, graphs, diagrams, figures, and maps.

Figure 11.2 is an example of how teacher Donna D. Gibbons of the State College, Pa., School District, rewrote a tenth-grade home economics textbook to the sixth- and third-grade reading levels. Students functioning at these different levels could read the same content. The first passage, written at the tenth-grade level, is directly from the textbook.

REWRITING THE TEXT

Tenth-Grade Reading Level

CALORIES:

Calories are a unit of measure, like pounds and inches. In nutrition and related sciences, calories express the amount of energy it takes to perform certain tasks. Calories also measure the energy value found in foods.

Needs for Energy

You need energy for three different operations, all taking place at the same time. First, you need energy to run your body processes—to breathe, to circulate blood, and so on. This energy is used no matter what else you do. Second, you need energy for each and every one of your activities. These include walking to school and sitting in class as well as riding a bicycle and playing ball. Third, you need energy in the growing process. It takes calories to lay down muscle tissue and to lengthen your bones. When you have attained your full growth and development, this final need will be satisfied.

Your Calorie Needs

How can you tell how many calories you need each day? The exact amount is difficult to determine, but some guides based on scientific experiments are available. The first need, to supply energy for normal body function, is called "basal metabolism." Studies have shown that individuals will vary in the number of calories needed. Generally speaking, it has been found that a large person needs more calories to keep going than a small one, and that boys need more than girls. There are also additional individual influences.

Some studies have shown how many calories are required for various activities. For example, it takes more calories to ride a bicycle than to talk, to go upstairs than to go down, and so on. Studies of this kind are lengthy and expensive, and much more information is required. Table A shows the recommendations of the Food and Nutrition Board of the National Research Council for caloric needs of young people aged 11 to 14.

CALORIE NEEDS OF BOYS AND GIRLS

	Age Years	Weight [kg]	Weight [lbs]	Height [cm]	Height [in]	Calories
Boys	11–14	44	97	158	63	2800
Girls	11–14	44	97	155	62	2400

Table A

Caloric Content of Foods

Almost all foods contain calories. Some contain few, if any. It is the proteins, fats, and carbohydrates that supply calories. Proteins and carbohydrates provide four calories per gram and fats nine calories per gram.

There are several influences on the number of calories in a food. Because fat is concentrated and has more than twice as many calories as protein or carbohydrates, naturally the amount of fat in a food will make a difference—the more fat, the more calories. In contrast, water does not contain any calories, so watery foods, like green leafy vegetables or fruit juices, are low in calories. What you add to food can increase the number of calories, such as butter or margarine on a slice of bread, mayonnaise on salad, or sour cream on a baked potato.

From EXPLORING FAMILY LIFE by Henrietta Fleck & Louise Fernandez. Copyright © 1977 by Prentice-Hall, Inc., Englewood Cliffs, New Jersey, 07632. Reprinted by permission.

Figure 11.2 Continued:

Table B shows the calories in some common snacks. Note the wide range in caloric value. Identify other nutrients found in each food. Some have few, if any, that will contribute to your diet. Some items, such as pancakes and waffles, have additions, usually of butter or margarine and syrup or preserves. Are you surprised at the few calories in some of the snacks?

CALORIES IN SOME COMMON SNACKS

Food	Calories
Apple, 1 medium	70
Banana, 1 medium	88
Brownie, 1 (made from mix)	85
Carrot, 1, 5½-in.	20
Celery, 1 stalk	5
Chocolate pudding, ½ c.	130
Chocolate malted milk, 1 c.	502
Corn, sweet, 1 ear, cooked	70
Cola-type beverage, 12 fl. oz.	145
Danish pastry, 1 oz.	120
Doughnut, 1 cake type	125
Frankfurter and roll	290
French-fried potatoes, 10 pieces	155
Pancake, 1, 4-in.	60
Pizza, 5½-in. sector	185
Popcorn, with oil and salt, 1 c.	40
Popsicle, 1, 3 fl. oz.	20
Sherbet, ½ c.	130
Pretzel, Dutch, twisted	60
Spaghetti, with meatballs and tomato sauce, canned, 1 c.	260
Waffle, 1, 7-in. diameter	210

Table B

Most American foods have been analyzed so that we can tell approximately how many calories each contains. Although calories are important, other nutrients in foods are also of interest.

Sixth-Grade Reading Level

CALORIES:

Calories are a way to measure, like pounds and grams. In nutrition and other sciences, calories tell how much energy it takes to do tasks. Calories tell how much energy you get from foods, too.

Needs for Energy

You need energy for three things that take place at the same time. First, you need energy to run your body functions—to breathe, to circulate blood, and so on. This energy is used no matter what else you do. Second, you need energy for all of your activities. These include walking to school and sitting in class as well as riding a bicycle and playing ball. Third, you need energy for the growing process. It takes calories to lay down muscle tissue and to lengthen your bones. When you have stopped growing, you will no longer have this need.

Figure 11.2 Continued:

Your Calorie Needs

How can you tell how many calories you need each day? You look at guides to find out. The first need, to fuel your body functions, is called "basal metabolism." Studies have shown that each person has his/her own calorie needs. It has been found that large people need more calories than small people, and boys need more than girls.

Some studies have shown how many calories you need for some activities. For example, it takes more calories to ride a bike than to talk, to go upstairs than down, and so on. More studies of this kind need to be done. Table A shows the calorie needs of young people aged 11–14.

Caloric Content of Foods

Most foods have calories. Some have quite a few. It is the proteins, fats, and carbohydrates that give us calories. Proteins and carbohydrates have four calories per gram and fats nine per gram.

There are a few things which affect the calories in a food. Fat has two times the calories as protein or carbohydrates so that the more fat in a food, the more calories. Water does not have any calories, so foods with lots of water like green leafy vegetables or fruit juices are low in calories. If you add fats like butter or oil to a food, you raise the calories of that food.

Table B shows the calories in some snacks. Some snacks have lots of calories while others have few. Look for the nutrients in each food. Some have few, if any, that will help your diet. Are your surprised at the few calories in some of the snacks?

Most foods have been tested so that we can tell how many calories each one has. Calories are important but so are the nutrients in foods.

Third-Grade Reading Level

CALORIES:

Calories are a way to measure. In nutrition, calories tell how much energy it takes to do things. They tell how much energy you get from foods, too.

Needs for Energy

You need energy for three things. First, you need energy to do work for your body. Your body works when you breathe and when your blood flows. You do not need to think about this work. Second, you need energy to work and play. You use it to play ball, ride a bike, and sit in class. Third, you need energy to grow. You use the calories you get from food to build strong bones and muscles.

Your Calorie Needs

A calorie guide can tell you how many calories you need to eat each day. You might not need to eat the same things as your friend. If you are big, you might need to eat more calories than if you are small. If you are a boy, you might need to eat more things than if you are a girl.

You use calories to do most things. If you ride a bike you use more calories than if you just talk. You use more when you walk up steps than when you walk down steps. Table A shows the calories you use to do things.

Caloric Content of Foods

Most foods have calories. Some foods have a lot. Some foods have few. It is the proteins, fats, and carbohydrates in foods that give us calories. These things in our foods tell how many calories there will be. The more fat in a food, the more calories it will have. Water does not have calories at all. Foods with lots of water like greens or fruit juice are low in calories.

Table B shows the calories in some snacks. Some snacks have lots of calories. Some snacks have few.

Tests have been done on most foods. We can tell the calories in each one. Calories are important but so are the nutrients in foods.

Figure 11.2

USING TEACHER-DIRECTED STRATEGIES

By definition, teacher-directed strategies are organized and controlled by the teacher. The teacher determines which strategy will best suit a particular class or group of students. The DRA or DRTA can be used with a whole class. They can also be implemented by one group within a class, often the instructional level readers, while other groups are using other strategies. Chapter 13 will describe some specific strategies for independent and frustration level readers. However, the Language Experience Approach and rewriting activities are most often useful with frustration level readers.

The task is to find ways to motivate students to complete reading assignments. Teacher-directed activities offer teachers alternative ways to structure classrooms and organize materials to make it more likely that students will read assignments. At the same time, teachers retain control of the students. They can encourage practice, both guided and independent; they can develop an anticipatory set. They can conduct formative evaluation throughout the lesson.

As teachers plan their units of instruction, they can structure lessons to introduce the primary reading assignments using the DRA or DRTA. These lessons may well introduce the important vocabulary and concept labels for the unit. They may also focus on delivering the necessary background for students to attempt more student-centered activities, described later in this chapter, and more writing activities in response to unit content.

STUDENT-DIRECTED ACTIVITIES

Teacher-directed reading and writing activities are an important part of a skilled teacher's repertoire of strategies. Student-directed activities, while somewhat more intricate to manage, also are important and rewarding strategies to employ. To demonstrate their potential use within a unit, the student-directed activities described in this part of the chapter will focus on examples taken from an eleventh-grade American history unit titled "Urban Growth and Development in the Post-Civil War Period." Although it is not necessary (and may not be desirable) to include all forms of student-directed learning within a single unit, presenting the activities in this way should help you visualize their use in the classroom.

The following figure depicts a timetable for the unit in which four types of student-directed activities are integrated.

Six-Week American History Unit Urban Growth and
Development in the Post-Civil War Period

Week 1	Week 2	Week 3	Week 4	Week 5	Week 6
Contract		Learning Activity Packages	Learning Centers		Games

On the following pages, each of the activities included in this table will be discussed in the order that they would appear in this sample unit.

CONTRACTS

Used at the beginning of a unit of study, the contract encourages students to take responsibility for their own learning. The contract is a document in which the student specifies his/her goals, course of study, methods, and materials to be used, and the means of evaluating learning. While the contract is a concrete product, its development can be the result of a valuable process involving both reading and writing. The teacher might use the following steps to construct a contract for this unit on urban growth:

1. The teacher identifies the unit topic.
2. Using a journal, the student spends ten minutes writing an entry in which s/he discusses what s/he already knows about the topic and describes his/her interest in the topic.
3. The student examines the journal entry to determine areas where s/he lacks knowledge.
4. The teacher provides a list of materials designed to provide background information and generate interest.
5. The student selects materials s/he wishes to read.
6. The student plans a reading schedule and writes a preliminary contract depicting:
   a. Reading schedule
   b. Description of the means of recording knowledge acquired through reading
7. At the end of one week, the student writes a final contract that:
   a. Further details a reading schedule
   b. Describes a plan for receiving teacher feedback
   c. Describes a project that will be used to demonstrate learning (research paper, oral presentation, role play, etc.)
   d. Specifies a due date for the project

The preliminary contract, described in step 6 above, encourages students to begin investigating topics but allows for the planning time necessary for writing a workable contract. For this unit, the teacher is interested in getting students to consult primary source materials. In this instance, it is likely that a teacher would use contracts for all students in the class. The teacher can guide students to appropriate sources of information while allowing students to pursue individual topics presented through a variety of sources (newspapers, magazines, books, speeches, personal interviews, etc.).

In other situations, teachers might choose to use contracts with only certain students in order to individualize for students with specific learning needs (the disabled, the gifted, etc.). Teachers may want to assess the degree of students' self-direction prior to using contracts.

Learning Activity Packages

Once the contract is developed, the teacher in this unit can direct students to other student-directed activities that will assist them in meeting their contracted assignments. One such activity is the Learning Activity Package (LAP). LAPs are like mini-textbooks and workbooks combined. Teachers prepare LAPs that "speak" to students. They provide carefully written directions, selected content, skill development, and evaluation procedures. You may recall the reference to LAPs in our chapter scenario. Two of the teachers in the science department were reportedly using LAPs with success.

The LAP that was developed for the urban growth unit (see Appendix 6) was designed to assist students in their reading of primary source materials. The teacher directs students through exercises that help them note:

1. differences between fact and opinion
2. descriptive words
3. points of view

In the introductory exercises, the subject of the selected reading material (current movie and record album reviews) is intended to get the attention of adolescent students. At this stage, students are guided toward recognizing the difference between fact and opinion, noting descriptive words, and contrasting different points of view. Next, students are given practice in using these skills in reading an excerpt from an 1898 political speech. Finally, the packet focuses on the issue of governmental corruption via political machines through the commentaries of George Washington Plunkitt and Lincoln Steffens. These selections present students with opposing points of view on a topic appropriate for the larger unit. This LAP may be appropriate for all students in the class or may be needed only by students who lack the critical reading skills needed to read from primary sources.

Developing a Learning Activity Package

The first step in developing a LAP is to *determine the purpose* for it. Purposes can range from providing needed skill instruction to providing a collection of carefully selected reading materials and accompanying activities for independent study. As the teacher reflects on where it is most appropriate to include instruction through the use of LAPs, s/he should consider the following purposes. LAPs serve to:

—facilitate learning in areas where the student has a weakness
—facilitate small-group and individual work in the same classroom
—free the teacher to give more individual attention
—place responsibility for learning with the student
—provide alternative methods by which a student can meet objectives

—guide the student as s/he learns

—encourage the student to evaluate his/her own educational progress

After deciding that a LAP serves a particular purpose within a unit plan, the teacher writes *three or more instructional objectives* that clearly describe the expected learning outcomes. These objectives should focus on content to be learned as well as the reading and writing development expected. Following the writing of objectives, the teacher can take about ten minutes to *write down all the ideas s/he has for the LAP*, including in this "free write" (or brainstorming on paper) any possibilities that come to mind about the content and materials to be included and the methods to be used to help students meet the objectives. When this step is complete, s/he sets it aside. These ideas can be rewritten later and used as an introduction.

The major task in writing a LAP is to *develop appropriate instruction* aimed at assisting the student in reaching the objectives. To begin this process, the teacher should *collect appropriate materials* that focus on the students' age and ability levels. Where materials are unavailable, teachers may want to create their own. While most materials are likely to be written, it is always appropriate to include information via audio and visual selections. Such material can be contained in learning centers with the LAP used as the guide that directs students to the resources provided in the centers.

Once the materials are selected, the teacher must determine how they will be used to meet objectives. *Choose a variety of teaching methods.* The only restriction is that the directions for proceeding must be conveyed through print. Students can be asked to read passages for content; they can be guided to discovery learning; and they can be taught to read critically and to write clearly. While the LAP is designed to be completed independent of the teacher, interaction with a teacher is always possible through checkpoints where the teacher can check on student progress.

Learning Activity Packages should always include several alternatives from which students can choose. They should allow for student selection of both method and material. For example, a student might be asked to choose reading material from a list provided in the LAP, be permitted to choose the means by which practice or evaluation will be achieved, and determine the pace of completing the LAP. If a LAP is to place responsibility on the learner and encourage independence, such options must be provided.

Following the development of instruction, the teacher will need to *decide how s/he will evaluate student learning*. The LAP should include some means of preassessment. A written pretest is the most commonly used method of determining student knowledge or skill level. The teacher should look over the objectives and decide in which areas s/he needs to gather information about students prior to instruction. To assess reading or writing ability, s/he may wish to use one of the procedures described in Chapter 8.

There are two primary approaches to assessing knowledge of content. One approach is to determine the extent of prerequisite knowledge. For example, some areas of learning in a math class could not be completed by students lacking computation skills necessary for the introduction of higher level mathematics. In this case, the pretest should be designed to ensure that all students using the LAP are ready for it. Another approach is to design a pretest to single out those students who don't need the instruction contained in the LAP. Some students already may be proficient in the skill being taught or be knowledgeable about the content. This type of pretest would be similar to a posttest. If the students do sufficiently well on it, they don't need the instruction, and the teacher should provide other work for them. Thus, when the teacher has determined what to assess, s/he can *write the pretest* and be certain that it tests what s/he wants it to test.

After writing the pretest, the teacher should *develop the means to assess cumulative learning*. This assessment may be in the form of a test, a project, a paper, or any other means of determining if students have met the objectives. Between the pretest and the final evaluation, any number of formative evaluation techniques might be used to assess progress. The teacher should be careful, however, not to spend too much time evaluating. Since a LAP is designed for no more than a week of instruction, it is more productive to devote most of the time to instruction and practice.

To determine how well students have accepted the LAP, the teacher should *include a student evaluation form*. This form should be made up of questions for students to answer upon completion of the LAP to assist the teacher in revising or developing other LAPs. Questions should range from those that ask students to reflect on their attitudes toward the LAP as a method of instruction to those that focus on the specific aspects of the LAP.

To record the evaluation of student learning, the teacher should *develop a teacher evaluation form* that indicates clearly which activities in the package will be used to evaluate the extent to which the student met the instructional objectives. This form will be used to make the student aware of evaluation procedures as well as to report final evaluations at the end of instruction.

Finally, the teacher should *write an introduction to the student*, explaining the purpose of the LAP and providing an overview of the LAP's contents and procedures. The teacher can start with the "free write" from the beginning of the planning process and rewrite it so that it accurately introduces the student to the final product. The introduction should speak to an individual student explaining how the LAP will be used, the scope of the topic, the time frame for instruction, and the equipment and materials that will be used.

Use the following checklist to complete each step in developing a LAP. Have you:

_____ defined your topic and purpose?
_____ written three or more objectives?
_____ done a free write in which you included all initial ideas?
_____ selected potential materials at appropriate levels?
_____ developed instruction designed to help students meet objectives?
_____ included a variety of teaching methods?
_____ provided for student selection of materials, methods, and pace?
_____ decided upon appropriate evaluation procedures?
_____ written a pretest?
_____ developed a means of evaluating cumulative learning?
_____ written a student evaluation form?
_____ developed a teacher evaluation form?
_____ rewritten your original ideas paper to form a student introduction?

LEARNING CENTERS

Learning centers not only serve to provide individualized instruction that allows for student-direction, but they are useful for varying the physical makeup of the classroom. A classroom that contains centers of varied appearances that are designed for various instructional purposes provides a workplace environment that fosters active learning. In addition to providing useful instruction that meets the needs of individual or small groups of students, action-oriented centers contribute to enhancing student motivation to learn.

Physically, the classroom containing learning centers can take on a number of appearances, from the room where all space is used for a collection of centers to the more typical room where student desks are arranged in the center of the room with learning centers placed along walls and in corners. The physical makeup of each center can range from a table on which a collection of teacher-selected reading materials are placed to a small laboratory that might include media equipment, computers, or lab equipment.

In the content classroom, learning centers serve two basic functions: to develop thinking/languaging processes and to serve as information sources. To exemplify centers that serve both of these purposes, the following discussion will focus again on the unit on urban growth and development. The examples will be grouped under language development headings and will describe uses consistent with the two purposes:

1. Centers that develop language and thinking processes
2. Centers that serve as an information source

Thinking/languaging centers contain activities intended to develop thinking and language processes both as ends in themselves and to contribute toward the development of concepts presented in a unit. In the urban growth unit, the teacher designs centers that equip students with the skills needed to use and comprehend primary source materials and to further develop their understanding through writing and speaking.

Information centers hold a collection of materials that provide information related to the unit of study. The materials include, but are not restricted to, print materials. While the primary purpose of these centers is to deliver information, language learning is likely to be an outcome of these centers, too.

Reading Centers

Reading centers are those designed to develop reading skills appropriate for the print materials that will be used for acquiring information on a unit topic. A reading center that contributes to learning how to use primary source materials is the center titled "That's News to Me," developed

These students are working on the learning center, "That's News to Me." They have heard the opening audiotape and are working on the color-coded activities that are included in the center.

by Andrea Lee and Gillian Craig (Appendix 6). The content concerns learning about the newspaper, its parts, and its functions. Since newspapers provide a valuable source of accounts of historical events, learning about newspapers helps students make good use of this source of information.

The center is introduced by a short audiotape which directs students on the procedures for using the newspapers and worksheets in the center. The motivation-readiness device is a quick look at six or eight newspapers gathered into the center, ideally including national and local papers and daily and weekly papers. The reading selections are color-coded by the kinds of articles; for example, news in red; sports in blue. Students come to the center in groups and pick up a worksheet and an assignment ticket telling them which colors to work with in which order. This eliminates everyone's reading the same articles and avoiding topics they know nothing about.

Reading comprehension is developed through the reading of news articles and responding to questions contained on assignment cards. The reading selections and questions increase in difficulty in each section. Teachers may allow free choice to students in determining difficulty levels or they may assign students to levels according to diagnostic information.

A reading center that serves the purpose of delivering information would include a collection of various print material. For this history unit, the teacher might arrange a table that holds newspapers, transcripts of speeches, articles from journals and magazines, and several textbooks. To provide for different reading levels, the materials can be grouped by level of reading difficulty.

Writing Centers

Writing centers are places where students engage in the process of writing both to develop thinking and to communicate with an audience. These centers can be made up of a table and chairs with written guides that help them focus on a writing task. The guides may direct students to discuss their writing with other students and engage in peer editing. A center could also contain personal computers where students use word processing to write numerous drafts of a paper. For example, students using the LAP from the urban growth unit could work on the essay on the boss system at a writing center.

Another type of writing center that uses computers is one that contains a selection of computer software designed to develop writing. Interactive software programs allow students to practice sentence and paragraph construction, use descriptive words, or organize ideas into essays. The software provides information that is instructional in the composing process.

Listening Centers

Listening centers that serve the purpose of developing listening skills aim to teach students to attend to the organization of a spoken message in order to enhance comprehension. Students studying the urban growth unit will be expected to gather some information from recorded speeches. A listening center can prepare students to listen through the use of audio-tapes in combination with worksheet exercises. Once the student completes the center that provides listening instruction, s/he is ready to listen to speeches related to urban growth and gather relevant information.

Speaking Centers

The development of oral communication skills is frequently overlooked in the content classroom. Thought and communication probably occur more frequently through talk and listening than through written language. For this reason, speaking centers should be used to provide instruction in numerous speaking activities. Students can be taught to organize spoken messages to participate in group discussion, debates, role playing, and formal speech making.

Speaking centers with audiotapes and recorders can be used to exemplify well-organized speeches and to provide students with the opportunity to develop and listen to their own speech production. Students studying the urban growth unit might be asked to role play by delivering an actual speech of a city official or to create and deliver their own speeches on a topic relevant to the unit.

Other speaking centers can be used as a space for roundtable discussions. Students using these centers could be presented with a list of possible solutions. For example, the discussion center for the urban growth unit could involve a small group of students sharing their opinions about the contrasting views of "machine politics" presented by George Washington Plunkitt and Lincoln Steffens.

Instructional Games

Instructional games are an enjoyable way for students to practice skills and review important content. Practice in language skill can be achieved through crossword puzzles, word searches, words with scrambled letters, and board games developed by the teacher. Competitive games that involve pairs or teams can review details of content through a series of trivia questions that give students practice in recall of information.

The teacher of the urban growth unit might make a game out of the development of *cinquains*, a five-line poem with limited line lengths. After students write their individual cinquains, they would be placed in groups to engage in an activity that Vaughn and Estes (1986) call "Pro-

These two eighth graders are working at a listening center in mathematics class. They are working with a set of geometric shapes and manipulating them according to the directions of the audiotape.

gressive Cinquains." In this activity, the group constructs a cinquain that combines the best ideas of the group members. Each group presents its cinquain to the entire class and a vote is used to determine the best one.

The specific teacher-directed and student-directed activities included in this chapter encourage teachers to organize specific teaching activities directed to enhancing students' comprehension of the unit content. In addition, these activities are aimed at moving students toward more independence in learning and less dependence on teacher direction as they mature. Because students have different levels of maturity as well as different reading levels, we anticipate that teachers will need to use within class grouping, as described in Chapter 10. In addition, specific groups of students, those with identified needs, will need special instruction, as described in Chapter 13. Careful planning by teachers using their assessment data will enable them to meet students' needs and accomplish content objectives successfully.

SUMMARY

Teacher-directed activities are the heart of most content classes. The Directed Reading Activity (DRA) and its corollary, the Directed Reading-Thinking Activity (DRTA) are the most flexible and useful strategies for directing students' reading and responding to text. The DRA allows teachers to focus on critical concepts and vocabulary included in the reading as a means of enhancing comprehension. The DRA also focuses on purpose as critical to student comprehension.

The Language Experience Approach is presented as a technique to use with students, especially frustration level readers, who need to talk through difficult material before they read it. By writing down what students say about the topic, teachers create a text from students' own language, a much easier text for them to read.

Text rewriting is also an alternative for teachers. In this case, teachers rewrite the text to a level students are more likely to understand. This technique is time-consuming, but it is especially useful for difficult texts on critical topics.

Student-directed activities include contracts, learning activity packages, learning centers, and instructional games. These activities allow students to become involved in the direction their learning will take. Students are encouraged to take responsibility for their learning, work at their own pace, focus on needed skill development, choose methods and topics, and vary information sources. Like the teacher at the end of our scenario, at some point you must turn over some of the "directorship" of the classroom to students. Teachers need to structure student-directed activities in a way that ensures the sound development of skills integrated with the learning of content. Use of student-directed learning activities maximizes the potential for lifelong learning.

REFERENCES

Abbott, M. K. (1966). An experience approach in a senior high school reading lab. In S. W. Webster (Ed.), *The disadvantaged learner: Knowing, understanding, educating* (pp. 553–537). San Francisco: Chandler.

Askov, E. N. & Lee, J. W. (1980). The language experience approach in the content area classroom. *The Journal of Language Experience, 2,* 13-20.

Girdon, M. B. (1973). Helping the disabled reader. *Elementary English, 50,* 103–105.

Stauffer, R. G. (1969). *Directing reading maturity as a cognitive process.* New York: Harper & Row Publishers, Inc.

Stauffer, R. G. (1970). *The language experience approach to the teaching of reading.* New York: Harper & Row Publishers, Inc.

Van Allen, R. (1976). *Language experiences in communication.* Boston: Houghton Mifflin Co.

Vaughn, J. W. & Estes, T. H. (1986), *Reading and reasoning beyond the primary grades.* Boston: Allyn & Bacon, Inc.

Wilson, R. M. & Parkey, N. (1970). A modified reading program in a middle school. *Journal of Reading, 13,* 447–452.

SUGGESTIONS FOR FURTHER READING

Askov, E. N. & Lee, J. W. (1980). The language experience approach in the content area classroom. *The Journal of Language Experience, 2,* 13-20.

Conley, M. W. (1987). Teacher decision making. In D. E. Alvermann et al., *Research within reach: Secondary school reading* (pp. 142–152). Newark, DE: International Reading Association.

Vaughn, J. W. & Estes, T. H. (1986). *Reading and reasoning beyond the primary grades.* Boston: Allyn & Bacon, Inc.

CHAPTER TWELVE

Cultural and Linguistic Differences In Students' Reading and Writing

SCENARIO

You may recall that Middlewood's social studies teacher, Don MacArthur, agreed to serve as mentor for first-year teacher Janet Parrish. Don and Janet are now having their weekly chat in the staff conference room.

"What's up, Janet?" asked Don. "Your note sounded urgent."

"I was feeling a little frantic when I wrote that note," said Janet. "But this does seem urgent to me. Here it is March already and I realize what a poor job I'm doing with my second-language students. I had no idea that I would run into this when I was hired last fall, Don. When I did my student teaching, all my kids came from middle-class English-speaking homes. Now I'm faced with such a variety of cultural backgrounds that I'm overwhelmed. And I'm just beginning to see how much language differences influence learning."

"It may make you feel better, Janet, to know that most of us came to the job unprepared to deal with this problem," replied Don. "Our college textbooks said nothing about cultural and language differences in the classroom. Fortunately our administration has provided us with a lot of support as our population here has become more diversified. Are you aware, for example, that the school district will cover most of your expenses to attend next month's State University conference on cultural diversity in the schools? And do you have any of these pamphlets on teaching second-language students?"

"No, I had no idea about the conference or that I could attend. And I've never read much about English as a second language," answered Janet, obviously relieved to have found a sympathetic ear. "I'm afraid I've had to struggle just to keep one step ahead of my classes so far this year. I assumed that because so many of these students were receiving service in the ESL program that I had no responsibility for their language difficulties. I'm afraid I really didn't look into the situation as I should have."

"How well I recall that frantic first year in the classroom, Janet," responded Don. "Believe me, it will get better. Now, tell me a few specifics about what's bothering you."

"Well, for starters, I'm not sure how well second-language students read in English, so I wonder how appropriate my assignments are. I've really given some of them a hard time about not doing their work. I'm also beginning to feel really uncomfortable about my own attitudes toward those students whose backgrounds differ so significantly from my own. I sense their antagonism. Yesterday I really blew it. I returned papers to my seventh-period class and mutiny almost broke out because I had corrected what I considered poor grammar. You wouldn't believe what some of those kids said . . . ."

OVERVIEW

What does this scenario mean to you? Primarily it means that you and all teachers will need to understand and teach students from a variety of minority groups. This chapter will explore some of the issues you will face and suggest some teaching behaviors and activities that you may find useful in your classes.

The culture students bring to school with them—what difference does it make? What about their language? This chapter concerns both the culture and language of students and what teachers need to consider about students whose language differs significantly from that of their peers. Considering the differences in *dialect* and *register*, two important concepts first discussed in Chapter 2, teachers can assess their students' language differences and plan their instruction to deal with these differences. This chapter focuses on three examples of linguistic differences: students who speak black English, students who speak rural white English, and Hispanic bilingual students. You may well find students from a variety of other minority groups in your classes, but much of what we discuss using these three examples will apply to other groups of students as well.

WHAT ARE STUDENT DIFFERENCES?

Students differ in all sorts of ways—height, weight, race, sex, socioeconomic level. We are concerned with those differences—primarily cultural and linguistic differences—which may affect how students respond to reading and writing in school. These differences will cause you to rethink and sometimes to change both what you teach and how you teach it.

First, what sorts of differences can you expect in schools between now and the year 2001? Harold Hodgkinson (1985) has studied that question with great care. Here are some of the differences he sees for the U.S. school system:

1. More children entering school from poverty-stricken households.
2. More children entering school from single-parent households.
3. More children from minority backgrounds.
4. A larger number of premature babies, leading to more learning difficulties in school (this results in large part from larger numbers of children born to teenage mothers).
5. A continuing increase in the number of black middle-class students.
6. Increased numbers of Asian-American students, but with more from Indonesia and with increasing language problems (p. 10).

Minority enrollment in the schools will continue to grow. Already minority students are a majority in California. The enrollment of minority students in more states, from New York to Florida and west to Arizona, will approach 50 percent in the next 15 years. Blacks especially, and Hispanics in growing numbers, are attaining middle-class status and moving out of the central city into more affluent, and traditionally white, suburbs.

Valdivieso (1986) paints a clear picture: Hispanics are the youngest and fastest growing population in the country. Their rapid growth is due to the youthfulness of this cohort and their high birth rate. For example, while the white population has reached a 1.8 percent birth rate, the Hispanic population continues to grow at a rate of 6.1 percent a year. The Bureau of Census (1987) indicates that while the national population is decreasing, the number of Hispanics is increasing, and they will surpass blacks as the largest minority group in the country by the end of the century.

Cultural and linguistic differences among students are concerns which teachers have long discussed. These concerns have become more visible in recent years, in light of the federal court ruling known as the Lau decision (Teachner, 1977). This decision holds that students whose native language is not English are entitled to receive an education appropriate to their linguistic proficiency. This decision and federal legislation regarding bilingual education suggest that content teachers must understand the issues involved and be sensitive to the teaching of non-English-speaking children in their classes.

The issue of language differences in schools was extended legally to include black English speakers by an Ann Arbor, Michigan, court decision. The Ann Arbor case found that students who spoke a dialect different from standard English, in this case black English, were not receiving equal educational opportunities because their teachers did not adjust their teaching to take these language differences into account (*English Journal,* September 1980). Again, this decision has required, as a minimum, that teachers come to understand the significant dialects spoken by students, so that they can provide instruction appropriate to the students in their classes. Remember what happened in Janet's class? This chapter provides background information for content teachers on identifying and assessing students' cultures and language.

CULTURAL COMPONENTS AND STUDENT DIFFERENCES

One difference among students is the culture and language they bring with them to school. By and large, neither culture nor its component, language, can or should be changed materially by the teacher on his/her own. Thus, our primary concern is coming to understand the culture the students live in and the language they speak and hear.

As individuals make their way in the world, many forces impinge upon them and contribute to shaping them. These forces are concrete (space, material objects); human (relations with others, the concept of self); and abstract (time, ideas, the spiritual world). If several individuals react in much the same way and generally react in that way, then they may be said to be part of a culture or ethos. It is easy to see, then, that these seven forces can become the components of an ethos or culture and an examination of behavior along these lines can become a description of the culture (Searles, 1980).

In the concrete realm, humans behave in a *spatial dimension* and divide space into territories they can manage, both within a group and as an individual. They spend much effort and material in defining and defending the boundaries of that territory. As an example, the predominant American culture pattern defines personal space in an unusual way. Persons seem to live in an envelope of space, occasionally penetrating it as they shake hands. The extent of the feeling about space is measured by the fact that we apologize for bumping into someone—we've violated that envelope of space.

The concrete realm has a *material dimension*: the resources which can be used to provide a quality to life. The material dimension of the American ethos is based on an abundance of material goods to the degree that yesterday's luxuries are today's necessities. The cultural norm is that of acquisition as more and more people try to possess more and more goods. With this proliferation come the demands, real or imagined, dictated by fads and fashions. Needs and wants become confused; choice becomes more difficult.

Any culture has a tangled web of human relationships, which we call the *human realm*. Any social organization from the most simple and primitive society to the most complex civilization is built on the premise that no man is an island. Behaviors are learned in order to lubricate the frictions of social life. The American society, with its political dedication to individual freedom, is constantly wrestling with the problem of finding an equilibrium between that freedom and the common good.

Within the human realm is a *cultural dimension* in which humans operate within rules and patterns established by the common group. Along with this is a *power dimension* in which humans operate within power structures.

There is a *personal dimension* to this realm also. In the interplay between the individual and the group, which is a hallmark of modern living, the individual is called upon to play many roles. These roles place many complications in the way of personal identification—resulting in the age-old question "Who am I?"

The human mind is blessed (or cursed) with the ability to deal with abstractions—mental constructions organized by a process which, like the traces of an electron, are visible only by their product. We call this highly sophisticated mental process, which is poorly understood at best, "thinking." The whole idea of ideas is vastly abstract; it is difficult to think about thinking. It is doubly difficult to describe the idea of thought. This *abstract realm* has four dimensions. A *temporal dimension* explores the rhythms of the days and cycles of the lives that humans live. An *ideational dimension* provides descriptions of the language, the methods of acculturation, and ways in which a culture explains the world. The search for beauty is examined in the *aesthetic dimension* of this realm. Finally, the expressions of faith are explored in a *spiritual dimension*. Within the *ideational dimension*, humans have the marvelous capacity to construct and communicate ideas beyond palpable realities. The ideas are expressed in language, which differs from culture to culture and even within cultures. Language in turn becomes a medium for the way in which the cultural heritage is continued through generations in the institutions of acculturation/education. This heritage is a determining factor in the ways in which people explain their world—using superstitions, myths, or perhaps some rational logic.

As Edward Hall (1977) suggests, a teacher's first problem is to understand the culture of the community in which s/he is teaching:

> *Each culture is not only an integrated whole but has its own rules for learning. These are reinforced by different patterns of overall organization. An important part of understanding a different culture is learning how things are organized and how one goes about learning them in that culture (p. 131).*

The teacher's job becomes one of discovering and respecting how a person learns something in that culture. Then s/he can understand how a student has learned how to learn. This process occurs throughout a student's life, usually without him/her being conscious of it. It is likely that Don will urge Janet to register to attend that conference on cultural diversity as a first step in helping her understand her students.

One way many cultures, or subcultures, in this country learn to learn is by *oral transmission*. That is, people pass on the local news, history, and opinions on topics of importance by talking with each other. This talking may occur at the general store, the local fire hall, a church meeting, or any other gathering place. Astute observation by a new teacher in the community can help him/her identify where the word is passed and who is influential in passing it.

These influential members of the culture are the models for students as they move toward adulthood and full membership in the culture. Adolescents pass through a period of initiation into adulthood by rites established in their culture. These rites may be formal, such as religious rites of confirmation and bar or bat mitzvah, which lead to full adult membership in the church. The rites may be legal, such as the legal age to drive, drink, marry, and do other things presumably reserved to adults. In a very real sense, graduating from high school (or leaving it in another way) is a rite of passage. After that event, a person is presumed to be independent, self-sufficient; able to marry, raise children, hold a job; and be responsible for him or herself.

Teachers become significant models for many students. This has led to expectations, historically and presently, that teachers will behave in ways that are culturally acceptable in the community. It may be worth considering the extent to which teachers serve as models for students, especially in areas related to reading and language. A teacher's oral language reflects his/her own cultural background. How similar or different s/he is from the students and the community is worth noting.

The community's attitude toward education in general includes the value of education as perceived by the community. Is it important to do well in school or to aspire to schooling beyond high school? Is schooling seen as primarily of functional value? Or is schooling a liberating process of developing students' talents? Is it academic or vocational?

It is important to identify the value of reading and "booklearning." Oral cultures, those whose history and news are transmitted orally, may see little value in having students read well. They may not value reading literature, favoring practical reading materials only. They may also see little value in writing. These cultural values can be identified by asking such questions as these: What do the adults in the community read? What is the public library like and who uses it? Do these adults write much? Letters? Reports at work? Other kinds of writing? It is safe to assume that if students do not see models of reading and writing at home, they will be less inclined to read or write themselves. In the absence of such models, teachers can serve as models of wide reading and effective writing. Teachers can also seek out and use other influential people in the community—the clergy, business people, government officials, and the like—who see reading and writing as important.

Overall, the important issue regarding culture and the school is that culture provides the framework in which the school must operate to touch the lives of its students. Janet has been finding this out the hard way!

THREE STUDIES IN LANGUAGE AND CULTURE

Cultural and linguistic characteristics are a part of each of us. Many groups in this country retain specific cultural identities and unique languages. Thus, it is not possible to describe all the different sorts of cultures a teacher may face. We have chosen to focus on three separate groups—black communities, rural white communities, and Hispanic communities—for several reasons. First, they represent fairly large groups in our society and in the schools. Second, they have a concern for their own culture and language and a determination to retain them. Finally, they have been fairly well described in the professional literature.

Black Language and the Black Community

Is there a black English dialect? Much research conducted in the late 1960s and early 1970s by Labov (1972), Shuy (1967), Baratz (1969), and others found that there is a distinct black English dialect. However, some linguists feel that black speakers' English differs little from that of standard English speakers. Certainly we cannot say all blacks speak black dialect, just as we cannot say all whites speak standard dialect. For example, in his research on northern cities, Shuy lists only three linguistic forms which would distinguish a northern black from a northern white speaker and require special attention for cross-cultural material (Baratz & Shuy, 1969).

Variable	Standard English	Black English
negation	doesn't have	ain't got no
Past conditional	He asks if I ate	He asks did I eat
negative + be	When I am there he isn't afraid	When I there he don't be afraid

Alexander (1985) identifies three facts about black dialect which can help teachers understand it and work with it in the classroom:

1. Black people who use a form of black dialect do not use all of the black dialect features at *all* times. Use of these features may vary from sentence to sentence.
2. The type of black English used is determined by sex, age, socioeconomic status, geographical area in which one spent formative years, the speaker's purpose, setting, topic, and audience.
3. Black English dialect is a legitimate linguistic system with rules (pp. 21–22).

Does black English hinder the learning process? Is black English inferior to standard English or is it merely different from standard English? This is part of the "deficit or difference" debate that raged hotly in the 1960s. Educators like Englemann and Jensen felt that black English speakers were definitely inferior in intellect as a result of their language, or inferior in language development as a result of their intellect (Williams, 1970).

Labov (1972), on the other hand, showed that black English is equal to, but different from, standard English. The concept of verbal deprivation has no basis in social reality. In fact, Labov felt that black children in the urban ghettos receive a great deal of verbal stimulation, hear more well-

Black students come from all segments of American society, and teacher attitudes are critical to their success in school. Teachers can focus on students' similarities as well as their differences. This student, like other students, plays the piano as a hobby.

formed sentences than middle-class children, and participate fully in a highly verbal culture. They have the same basic vocabulary, possess the same capacity for conceptual learning, and use the same logic as anyone else who learns to speak and understand English. Labov's stand has more credence today than that of Jensen and Englemann. As Roger Shuy, (1973) points out, linguists say that all languages and dialects are of equal merit and that good language is simply language which produces the desired effect with the least trouble for the user.

Most research suggests that black dialect speakers are not seriously hampered in reading standard English (Holloway, 1985). From an early age black English speakers are exposed to standard English. Most movies and television and radio programs are still in standard English, although some programs like "The Jeffersons" have used a form of black English. With exposure to actual standard English, students learn to comprehend it adequately enough to enjoy the story, even though they may not use the language themselves. With at least five years of exposure to school English and to books written in standard English, which they have seen since they learned to read, most black English speakers are likely to comprehend written and spoken standard English adequately by junior high school age.

If it is true that black English need not interfere with the learning process, what are the disadvantages to black English speakers? The most important one is *attitude*. Standard English speakers often tend to look down on black English speakers as being less capable intellectually. This applies to teachers, particularly to white teachers, but as Gladney (1973) showed, to middle-class black teachers, too. The Ann Arbor, Michigan, decision mentioned earlier was aimed primarily at this factor.

Some teachers react adversely to children who speak black English. It is extremely important that this reaction be faced by teachers themselves. It may well be that black English has more effect on the education of children, because of teachers' attitudes, than it has on the children's ability to either communicate or understand (Shuy, 1973b).

If teachers have negative feelings about the language their students bring to school, it is difficult for them to work objectively with these students. They may try to turn disadvantaged black children into middle-class children who will fit the curriculum, and they may try to teach standard English as a replacement dialect rather than an alternate dialect.

Prejudice against black English speakers occurs outside the classroom as well. The highest percentage of unemployment is among young blacks, and this may be due, in part, to their language. These children need to learn standard English for vocational, social, and academic success. As long as the school curriculum is based on the ability to speak standard English, it is necessary for academic success. Stated another way, black children need to learn standard English so they can be successful whenever they have to function in the dominant middle-class culture.

Rural White Cultures

The cultural group being described here is the large group of white rural people who live throughout the eastern United States, especially in the hilly areas. Many of these attributes are true of rural people throughout the country. The people who live in general farming and self-sufficient rural areas are characterized by fierce independence, traditionalism, and fatalism. These rural people face danger with seldom-paralleled bravery, but fear being separated from family and community. They conceive goals in terms of relationships within the community, not material goals. Rural areas are characterized by low-density population, homogeneous and informal social groupings, integrated roles, and a traditional orientation. Some researchers have found that children reared in rural areas exhibit a tendency to be more fearful, more shy, more suspicious, and more self-deprecating than urban children.

One Pennsylvania valley is a good example of such a community. Farming is the major industry in the valley, though a percentage of the men, and a much larger percentage of the women, drive into nearby towns to work. The population is sparse and tightly knit, the older established families having been there for over two hundred years. However, the community is by no means isolated from outside influences, since all areas receive at least one television channel.

Does this valley have a rural dialect as such? Probably not a distinct, clearly defined dialect, but because of their culture, and to some degree their inwardness and isolation, they tend to lack a wide range of registers. This is true in many communities today, but it is more noticeable in a rural situation. There seem to be few register shifts—everyone from the principal to the youngest student in the school is addressed in much the same way in public. This may be a part of the closeness of the community; no one needs to be "talked up to" or "talked down to."

Read this short transcript of an eighth-grade boy's statement about fishing, a favorite pastime in his Pennsylvania valley home.

I fish down here at Penn's Creek. They'll be stockin' it here next month, I think, whenever the ice thaws out. Do you know where the Contress road is down here? Well, you go down that there until you get down to the stop sign and then you'll be able to see the creek right there. My uncle lives right along it, along the creek. I go fishin' down there by his house. That's where you go in to pay for fishin'. They got a board up there; if you fit under that it's half price and then I can't fit under the board and so then I'll have to pay $3.50 and my dad has to pay $3.50. You're allowed to keep four fish. They got blue gill, eel, and catfish, trout. What it is is just a private pond like. They got a great big pond and they divide it up in sections and put different fish in different places.

Well, my sister thought she caught an eel 32 inches long. That was down here at the Coburn part of the tunnel. So my mom she was with us. She don't like it to go fishin', but we were camping and stuff so we went down there and my sister was fishin' and my mom seen it. She pulled it up out of the water and my mom seen it and it was a black snake so she hurried up and ran into the truck and then Kathy she gave the rod to my dad because my dad he knew how to bring eels in and so he brought that in and we took pictures of it and stuff.[1]

This boy's use of language is consistent and typical of the rural area he lives in. His dialect includes using the past participles instead of the simple past ("my mom seen it") with some irregular verbs. He also used the double subject ("my mom she," "Kathy she," "my dad he"). These features, and others in this speech, are common in rural areas. The specifics of the dialect in central Pennsylvania differ somewhat from those of rural Kentucky, Kansas, or Georgia, but there are many common characteristics.

White rural children have the same need to learn to read and write standard English that black children have—to be successful in the dominant middle-class culture. However, these children face an additional dilemma. If teachers are successful in encouraging these rural children to aspire to college and careers requiring further education, they must often leave home for college and for the careers they seek. In this culture, close family ties are important. Hence, leaving home is not a valued goal for parents or children, and encouraging such aspirations is not always looked upon positively within the community.

Hispanic Communities[2]

A third group of linguistically different people are the Hispanic-Americans. This group is comprised of four distinct subgroups: Mexican-Americans, Puerto Rican-Americans, Cuban-Americans, and other Hispanics which include Central and South Americans. The Hispanic population is the largest growing minority in the United States. The Bureau of the Census (1987) reports that this population has increased by 30 percent since 1980 to approximately 19.6 million.

The Mexican-American, or Chicano, population is mostly found in four states in the Southwest of the United States: California, New Mexico, Arizona, and Texas. Mexican-Americans are a mixture of Spanish and Native American people (Hispanic Policy Development Project, 1984). Mexican-American and Mexican immigrants who populate the country are mostly agricultural workers. Most of the school children are American-born and therefore American citizens. Mexicans who come to the United States as illegal aliens or as temporary agricultural workers are

[1]Interview with Mary Dupuis.
[2]This section was prepared by Dr. Joseph O. Prewitt Diaz, Associate Professor of Education, Director of Bilingual Education Programs, The Pennsylvania State University.

often not found in the public schools but are served by the Migrant Education Program.

The second group of Hispanics is the Puerto Ricans. This group is comprised of American citizens whose native language is Spanish and whose culture is Hispanic. Many have migrated to the mainland to work in low paying jobs in the large northeastern cities such as New York, Newark, Hartford, and Philadelphia. While recent migration has included significant numbers of professionals, most Puerto Rican migrants have been poor and unskilled. This population has faced major culture shock upon its arrival in the United States (Hispanic Policy Development Project, 1984). Since this group is composed of American citizens, schools must provide access to the mainstream of educational opportunities.

The third subgroup is comprised of Cuban-Americans. This group, all political refugees, has received generous and comprehensive federal relocation support. Since most Cubans were from upper and middle classes, they rapidly created an economic infrastructure which has permitted Cuban-Americans to maintain their language as well as their culture. In the early 1980s, a second immigration of Cubans took place. This group, the Marielitos, are not as affluent as those who had settled earlier in the United States. However, they have been well accepted by the receiving communities. Most Cubans are located in Florida, New Jersey, New York, and Illinois. As opposed to the Mexican-Americans and the Puerto Ricans, they are older, more educated, and more upwardly mobile.

According to the Bureau of the Census (1987), during the last five years, the American population of Central and South American origin has increased to 2.1 million. This population, refugees from Central America, includes children who have experienced displacement due to war. It is important to note that most recently the large numbers of persons from Central America have come to the United States illegally and have settled around the largest cities. There is currently little information available about this group; however, one thing is sure: they are sending their children to school and will in the next decade add to the large number of Spanish-speaking children in the schools. The Nicaraguans have been granted refugee status, therefore their children will be eligible for services under aid for refugee children. Most of the children will need to develop vocabulary as well as social skills which are necessary to cope in a more modern society, such as that of the United States.

In the "other" category, we find persons from Spain and persons who consider themselves "Spanish," "Hispanics," or "Latinos." Generally, this group has entered the United States legally, has fewer children, and many of them consider themselves political refugees (Hispanic Policy Development Project, 1984).

Several factors make the Hispanic population likely to become one of the most influential factors in American education. In the first place, the geographic concentration of Hispanics in a number of urban areas (e.g.,

Los Angeles) will cause them to become the majority of the school population and the eventual majority of the work force in these areas (Valdivieso, 1986). Second, the type and level of literacy in Spanish as well as English will fluctuate between groups and geographic locations. Third, the school system has not provided easy access to academic programs in the schools. This situation is compounded by the high mobility of the Mexican-Americans and the Puerto Ricans.

In 1967, Congress enacted the Bilingual Education Act. Title VII, as it is known, was revised in 1984 (Public Law 98-511). The purpose of this act is to provide assistance to children whose native language is not English. Bennett (1986) reported that there are approximately 3.6 million children who have limited English proficiency. All these children are American citizens, but they represent 106 language groups. Currently about one million children are receiving services from Title VII. About 70 percent of these children are of Hispanic background. Bilingual education provides a program of instruction to assist a child in achieving competence in English. Most bilingual programs serve children in the larger school districts.

Now let's take a look at the needs of the Puerto Rican population. We have selected this population because it represents the largest number of native born American citizens of Hispanic background. Also, their migration is an internal migration, which can be compared to the migration of blacks from southern cities to the northern industrial centers.

For most immigrants to America, the schools have played a central role in their adjustment to American life. Schools have served as the link between newcomers and the established society, and they have been a factor in the newcomers' adjustment to the ideas, motivations, and styles of American life (Fitzpatrick, 1987). For Puerto Rican immigrants, the role of school in their adjustment has been changing in the last decade. In addition to a lack of knowledge of the English language, Puerto Rican parents have not understood the school well. This lack of communication has created discrepancies among the children, the parents, and the school which have had their roots in the use of native language and culture (Prewitt Diaz, 1987; Fitzpatrick, 1987). In addition, parents are struggling with their own adjustment to life in the United States. Therefore, parents find it difficult to deal with a system that lacks the personal relationships characteristic of the Puerto Rican culture.

Laosa (1982) suggests that the experience of the Puerto Rican child in the schools in the United States is part of a process of resocialization that will eventually modify family relationships, especially between mother and child. As the mother becomes familiar with the schooling process, the achievement of the child improves. As the school begins to include the parents in the planning process and keep them informed of the child's progress, the conflict between home and school is resolved (Fitzpatrick, 1987).

This Puerto Rican brother and sister are reading from a bilingual text. One page is written in Spanish and the facing page contains the same text in English. Content texts that are organized like this can help Hispanic students read in both Spanish and English.

Migration is one of the characteristics of Puerto Rican Americans. Approximately 43 percent of Puerto Ricans living on the island of Puerto Rico have migrated to the mainland at least once in their lifetimes. The decision to migrate is caused by poor economic opportunities in Puerto Rico, in the large cities in the Northeast, and often in the smaller towns of the mid-Atlantic states. Since the parents are attempting to resolve their economic situations when they decide to migrate, their children are not consulted and are uprooted without much notice (Prewitt Diaz, 1987).

The children then become involuntary migrants. These children will experience homesickness and the feeling of not belonging. Each migration process is characterized not only by a feeling of loss, but also by a transformation in the roles of family members. The Puerto Rican family is an extended family where intimate relationships with the kinship system are of high value and a source of pride and security. In contrast, the socio-legal system of the United States addresses itself to the nuclear family. The conflicts which arise in in-school behavior in the United States are often the result of adjusting family structure from an extended family pattern to a nuclear family pattern (Fitzpatrick, 1987).

The intellectual capacity of Puerto Rican children seems to be affected initially by their inability to adapt to accepted classroom behavior in the United States. Consequently, many students are referred to vocational subjects or the lower academic tracks. One of the academic ways to help the recent migrant adjust to the mainstream of American society is through reading. Reading provides equality of access to society.

The classroom teacher must be aware that new migrants are going to encounter linguistic and sociocultural differences. For most recent migrants, the major problem in reading will be the gap between what they know and the language and content of texts (Eskey, 1987). Most students will suffer from deficiencies of knowledge in one or more of the major categories of knowledge: linguistic, pragmatic, and cultural. As greater knowledge is acquired through reading, the recent migrant acquires proficiency in reading, has to dedicate less attention to identification of words, and can spend more time on processes required for interpreting texts (Eskey, 1987).

It is important that recent migrants be exposed to activities that foster vocabulary development as soon as possible. Carrell (1987) suggests that since second-language learners do not always acquire the full range of meanings that a given word may have, they may assign a single meaning to the word and may misinterpret that word when it appears in a context where a different meaning is required. While we advocate the teaching of aural/oral skills (ESL) to recent arrivals, we believe that children should begin to read as soon as possible and that the reading activity should be a class period in itself. The point of the reading class must be reading, not the reinforcement of oral skills.

Grabe (1987) has suggested that linguistic and sociocultural factors have a major impact on transfer to second-language reading. Students who read well in the native language may not transfer those abilities to the second language. Grabe also notes a number of points to consider in learning to read in the native language and in the second language:

1. Cognitive capacity and organization may be shaped culturally, which affects metacognitive patterns or schema;
2. Second-language reading can be subject to interference from first language assumptions, knowledge, and expectations;
3. Second-language reading requires a reasonable grammatical and lexical base upon which to build;
4. Reading recognition and lexical access which is needed for an adequate linguistic base must be addressed by direct instruction and extensive reading; and
5. Reading in a second language can be taught through a reading curriculum which can lead the second-language readers to read in a manner approximating that of a native reader (pp. 32–33).

This section suggests that there are sociocultural and linguistic factors which affect the achievement of Puerto Rican children in the schools of the United States. We suggest that content teachers consider the option of providing instruction and reading materials either in the student's native language or in English, at the level the student can understand. A Puerto Rican student who can read Spanish may be able to read a text in Spanish at his/her grade level, but that does not necessarily mean that the student is able to read an English text at the same level.

A Puerto Rican student who can read neither Spanish nor English at or near grade level is at an even greater disadvantage. Teachers of these students need to know how well students can read in both English and Spanish. If they read well in Spanish but not in English, the teacher may elect to use Spanish texts for the content information. If they read only in English, however poorly, teachers must find English materials at the appropriate knowledge and comprehension levels.

THE ROLE OF THE TEACHER

What is the role of the teacher in dealing with speakers of different dialects? First, the teacher must realize that their English is not inferior to standard English. But students need to learn standard English in order to understand and be understood outside of their own domain, so that when they speak or write, their thoughts and feelings are communicated widely. We are not suggesting here that a student's dialect be replaced. That would be a pointless, and hopeless, job. A dialect is a sign of belonging, a part of group membership, and to take it from students is to deprive them of their own culture, their own roots. Rather, students should be taught a second dialect, an alternate dialect, to be used for certain purposes, in certain situations. For example, black students may need to develop standard English to use in job interviews and on the job. However, they retain their black dialect among family and friends.

What we as teachers need to undertake is helping students develop a *variety of registers*. The nature of language is strictly functional; its purpose is to promote communication. Whatever forms of language facilitate clear, concise, and accurate communication may be defined as "good language"; whatever forms of language fail to communicate clearly or lead to ambiguity may, for practical purposes, be defined as "bad language." In one situation, the casual register communicates well; in another, the consultative may be more appropriate.

Language, Culture, and the Teaching of Reading

The language a student uses affects his/her ability to read. *The closer the tie between a student's own language and the words s/he reads in print, the easier s/he will find the reading to be.* This is true at all ages and stages of reading. Even within the same basic dialect, a student who uses only a casual register may find difficulty in reading texts which are written primarily in a formal or at least consultative register, to use Joos's (1961) terminology. This is all the more true by junior high school age, when content area textbooks usually contain a high vocabulary load of words and a linguistic style with which students are not familiar.

What can the teacher do? Simplistically, there are two possibilities: (a) teach the students the formal language of content area textbooks; or (b) rewrite the texts in casual language. Perhaps the best solution lies between the two. Teachers who are aware of the lack of match between their students' own language and the language style they are expected to use for reading and writing are likely to make efforts to help students cope. Janet certainly seems willing enough to give this approach a try, provided she can get the information she needs to understand the problem. Dealing with this issue is no easy one-shot task, but with a concerted effort it is possible for a school to teach its students the formal language to be found in reading. The same formal language is also the expected norm in the students' written work. And for a more immediate answer, teachers can help their students "translate" the formal language into something they can comprehend themselves. Helping students restate textbook material into their own language, perhaps through a modified Language Experience Approach (see Chapter 11), could provide links between the two registers. Such links help students move toward the formal level to the point that they can read formal language and process it for understanding without going through the cumbersome translation.

Some Specific Strategies

Use students as a resource. If you have a Spanish student, help him/her to prepare some information about his/her culture to present to the class, i.e., photos, typical music, or native games. Plan a special day when native foods could be prepared. Help a non-native student develop pride in his/her culture, and encourage other students to appreciate cultural differences.

If differences center on dialect (for example, black dialect), *develop an activity that points out differences between standard English and black dialect*—but that doesn't teach that the dialect is necessarily "wrong." Perhaps have all students collect samples of expressions common in their neighborhood or home and then share them with the class. This is a perfect time to talk about registers. Teachers generally will come into contact with three registers in the school environment—formal, casual, consultative. The key is to teach that there is an appropriate "time and a place" for each register.

Develop a buddy system if there are students unfamiliar with American culture and language. Encourage American-English-speaking students to help students whose first language is not English.

Involve the parents of students in the learning process as much as possible. Whether it is a parent from France, or one from the outer farming areas of the community, encourage them to play an active role in their child's education. Especially if the parents feel threatened or hostile towards academics, it is important to be aware of attitudes so that you can deal with their child's feelings most effectively. Parents and teachers should be in agreement concerning general education philosophy.

Use the Language Experience Approach. This approach uses student language in class. For example, you might read an excerpt from a book, and then ask a student to retell the excerpt in his own words. You can transcribe on an overhead projector and then talk about the language. This technique enhances students' self-concept, gives them practice in oral skills, and allows you to determine how well they comprehended the material. Most students enjoy this activity.

Incorporate writing into your class. If you have a student who speaks a foreign language, ask him/her to translate a brief piece of content area reading into his/her native language so that students can both see and hear another language. An activity that would fit into an English class involves reading an excerpt from a book and having students "retell" it in their own words using the casual register.

SUMMARY

Teachers need to be aware of their students' cultural and linguistic backgrounds. They should be able to use these backgrounds to help students learn the necessary content. They should also identify any dialects in the students' language. An additional concern is the registers used by the students in and out of school. Teachers need to assess the registers they use in teaching and the demands they make on students.

Many different language and ethnic groups are part of American schools. We've looked at black English speakers, rural white English speakers, and Puerto Rican Hispanic speakers as examples. Teachers' assessments of the groups in their classes enable them to use students' strengths in planning instruction while they encourage students to try to overcome weaknesses. To do this, teachers can increase student work with oral activities and greater sensitivity to potential reading and writing problems.

REFERENCES

Alexander, C. F. (1985). Black English dialect and the classroom teacher. In C. Brooks (Ed.), *Tapping potential: English and the language arts for the black learner* (pp. 20–29). Urbana, IL: National Council of Teachers of English.

Baratz, J. C. & Shuy, R. M. (1969). *Teaching black children to read*. Washington, D.C.: Center for Applied Linguistics.

Bennett, W. (1986). *The condition of bilingual education in the United States*. Washington, D.C.: U.S. Department of Education.

Brooks, C. (Ed.). (1985). *Tapping potential: English and the language arts for the black learner*. Urbana, IL: National Council of Teachers of English.

Carrell, P. L. (1987). Text as interaction: Some implications of text analysis and reading research for ESL composition. In U. Connor & R. B. Kaplan (Eds.), *Writing across languages: Analysis of L2 text* (pp. 47–56). Reading, MA: Addison-Wesley Publishing Co.

Eskey, D. E. (1987). Theoretical foundations. In F. Dubin, D. E. Eskey, & W. Grabe (Eds.), *Teaching second language reading for academic purposes* (pp. 3–23). Reading, MA: Addison-Wesley Publishing Co.

Fitzpatrick, J. P. (1987). *Puerto Rican Americans*. Englewood Cliffs, NJ: Prentice-Hall, Inc.

Gladney, M. R. (1973). Problems in teaching children with nonstandard dialects. In J. L. Laffey & R. W. Shuy (Eds.), *Language differences: Do they interfere?* (pp. 40–46). Newark, DE: International Reading Association.

Grabe, W. (1987). The transition from theory to practice in teaching reading. In F. Dublin, D. E. Eskey, & W. Grabe (Eds.), *Teaching second language reading for academic purposes* (pp. 25–48). Reading, MA: Addison-Wesley Publishing Co.

Hall, E. (1977). *Beyond culture*. Garden City, NY: Anchor Books.

Hispanic Policy Development Project. (1984). *Make something happen*. Washington, D.C.: U.S. Hispanic Policy Development Project.

The Hispanic population in the United States. (1987). Series P-20, No. 416. Washington, D.C.: U. S. Bureau of the Census.

Hodgkinson, L. (1985). *All one system: Demographics of education—kindergarten through graduate school*. Washington, D.C.: Institute of Educational Leadership.

Holloway, K. F. C. (1985). Learning to talk—learning to read. In C. Brooks (Ed.), *Tapping potential: English and the language arts for the black learner* (pp. 12–19). Urbana, IL: National Council of Teachers of English.

Joos, M. (1961), *The five clocks*. New York: Harcourt, Brace and Co.

Labov, W. (1972). *Language in the inner city: Studies in the black vernacular*. Philadelphia: University of Pennsylvania Press.

Laffey, J. L. & Shuy, R. W. (1973). *Language differences: Do they interfere?* Newark, DE: International Reading Association.

Laosa, L. M. (1982). School, occupation, culture and family: The impact of parental schooling on the parent-child relationship. *Journal of Educational Psychology, 74,* 791–827.

Our readers write. (1980, September). *The English Journal, 69,* 68–74.

Prewitt Diaz, J. O. (1987). The enculturation/deculturation process of the Puerto Rican child and its effect in school performance. In T. D. Yawkey (Ed.), *Bilingual early childhood, parent education and family literacy: Curriculum development, programs and evaluation* (pp. 1–11). State College, PA: The Pennsylvania State University.

Searles, J. E. (1980). *Components of culture*. University Park, PA: The Pennsylvania State University.

Shuy, R. (1967). *Discovering American dialects*. Urbana, IL: National Council of Teachers of English.

Shuy, R. (1973a). Nonstandard dialect problems: An overview. In J. L. Laffey & R. W. Shuy, (Eds.), *Language differences. Do they interfere?* (pp. 3–16). Newark, DE: International Reading Association.

Shuy, R. (1973b). The linguistic problems of teachers. In J. S. DeStefano (Ed.), *Language, society and education: A profile of black English* (pp. 196–200). Worthington, OH: Charles A. Jones.

Valdivieso, R. (1986). *Must they wait another generation? Hispanics and secondary school reform*. New York: ERIC Clearinghouse on Urban Education.

Williams, F. (Ed). (1970). *Language and poverty: Perspectives on a theme*. Chicago: Markham Publishing Co.

SUGGESTIONS FOR FURTHER READING

Brooks, C. (Ed.). (1985). *Tapping potential: English and the language arts for the black learner*. Urbana, IL: National Council of Teachers of English.

Dubin, F., Eskey, D. E., & Grabe, W. (Eds.). (1987). *Teaching second language reading for academic purposes*. Reading, MA: Addison-Wesley Publishing Co.

Joos, M. (1961). *The five clocks*. New York: Harcourt, Brace and Co.

CHAPTER THIRTEEN

Alternative Strategies For Exceptional Learners

SCENARIO

The school year is more than half over. Spring is in the air. Marge and the new teacher, Janet Parrish, are in the local supermarket.

"Hi, Marge. Am I glad I ran into you tonight," said Janet as she narrowly missed colliding with Marge's shopping cart.

"I'm glad you really *didn't* run into me! What's up? You look a little worried," replied Marge.

"I hate to bother you with a school problem at the supermarket, but I really am worried about a note I got from the guidance office this afternoon just as I was leaving the building," responded Janet. "The school psychologist has recommended that a new student be added to my third period class, and you know that's the class that's already so big. Not only that, but this girl is listed as being newly 'mainstreamed.' I'm not sure what that means."

"No wonder you almost ran me down with that cartload of groceries, Janet! I wish I had been there when you got the notice. We could have looked over this girl's records and done some preparing for her arrival tomorrow. Without her file, I can't really help you much except to reassure you that Bob Diaz wouldn't be putting her into your class unless everyone involved in her case is confident that she's ready to be in the regular education programs. She has likely been in a learning disabilities resource room or some other special program and has made good progress this year. That's basically what mainstreaming means."

"I guess you're right about why she's being moved into my class, but I can't help feeling apprehensive," lamented Janet. "It is always hard to add someone to a class partway through the year, especially someone who might really demand a lot of individual attention. With that third period crew of mine, that would be a disaster."

"I don't blame you for feeling that way, but just remember that somewhere out there is a girl who is even more nervous than you are about third period tomorrow!" replied Marge with a warm, comforting smile. "Go home and get a good night's sleep. I'll meet you in the office before school starts and we'll take a look at the records so you'll have some idea of what to expect. Then you should arrange to meet with Bob and the special teacher who has been working with this girl to get some guidance about how to help her adjust to the new placement."

OVERVIEW*

Law PL 94-142, which was passed in 1975, is clear about the role of content teachers in the education of handicapped students. It states:

> *It is the purpose of the Act to assure that all handicapped children have available to them, within the time periods specified, a free appropriate public education which emphasizes special education and related services designed to meet their unique needs (PL 94-142, 1975, section 3c).*

The requirements of PL 94-142 make content teachers responsible for dealing with a wide variety of exceptional students in their classrooms. What problems arise? How can these students be accommodated and taught? How are reading and writing related to the exceptional student? This chapter discusses some ways of dealing with exceptional students and gives special attention to their potential reading and writing problems.

Since 1975, when PL 94-142 became law, content teachers have been involved with the entire educational system in finding ways to provide instruction to growing numbers of exceptional children. The number of these students is growing in two ways. First, under the law's assessment provisions, more students with special needs are being identified. Second, more exceptional students are being returned to the regular classroom for part or all of their instruction.

Content teachers are now faced with the need to understand the various handicapping conditions, to develop positive attitudes toward their exceptional students, and to feel confident that they know how to work successfully with exceptional children in their classrooms. We will briefly discuss these three issues in this chapter. However, each of them could easily require a complete book in its own right. Our discussion will be limited to key elements, with references to additional reading for greater depth.

*The authors gratefully acknowledge the assistance of Barbara Van Horn in writing the first section of this chapter.

HANDICAPPING CONDITIONS AND CLASSROOM PLACEMENT

PL 94-142 has made it a federal mandate to provide an "appropriate public education" to all students identified as exceptional. In addition, this education is to be available from age three to twenty-one for such an exceptional student. These two features of the law have special significance for secondary teachers. For many years, special education classes have been common in elementary schools. They have been less common at the secondary level. In the years before PL 94-142, by the time exceptional students reached high school age they either had dropped out, transferred to special private institutions or vocational schools, or been assimilated into the lower tracks of high school classes. Those teachers who have taught for several years can recall a few "slow learners"—a few students who just could not seem to learn to read, a few who were seriously maladjusted. But these students were not made visible; teachers pitied them and taught them as best they could.

PL 94-142 no longer allows teachers this attitude. Because the age limit has been raised to twenty-one, the parents of any exceptional student may request that administrators keep that student in school until that age. As teachers identify more students with special needs, they find that most teachers at all levels have several students in their classes who are identified as exceptional. The challenge is to understand these students and develop empathy for them.

We are speaking only of those students for whom an *Individualized Educational Program* (IEP) has been developed. The IEP, which is required by law, defines the student's special needs and sets forth objectives for the student to master during a given school year. The IEP may indicate specific content areas for emphasis, or it may deal with skills. On the basis of the IEP, the student is placed in an educational situation which meets his/her special needs. The IEP will determine which situation is, for that student, the *Least Restrictive Environment* (LRE). LRE is an important concept with PL 94-142. LRE says, basically, that handicapped children must be educated as much like their non-handicapped peers as possible, unless it can be shown that the student will benefit more from an alternative service. LRE includes a wide range of alternatives and educational services to an exceptional student:

- Regular class
- Regular class in a regular school with supporting services
- Special education program in a regular school
- Special education in a special facility
- An approved private school program
- A state school program
- At-home instruction

This list moves from least restrictive (regular classroom) to most restrictive (a state school or at-home instruction). The IEP team determines for each student what the LRE is. The IEP team usually consists of the teacher, a school representative (often a counselor or school psychologist), the parents, and, with older students, frequently the student. A teacher may be asked to serve on such a team, either for students in his/her home-room or as a result of a parent or counselor request. It is possible, however, for students to be in regular classes (mainstreamed) for part of the day but not all of it, or for a few subjects but not all of them. The decision is based on the student's needs.

Definitions of Handicapping Conditions

Even though mainstreaming is only one facet of least restrictive environment, content teachers are more involved in mainstreamed cases than any other section of PL 94-142. In order to refer a child for special services and to educate the exceptional child properly, it is necessary to understand the various exceptionalities. The following definitions are for explanatory purposes only. No one child should be considered to exhibit any particular description. (Cartwright, Cartwright, and Ward (1981) is an excellent source for further discussion of these conditions.)

The exceptional student is difficult to define because s/he represents many different medical and psychological groups of students. An exceptional student is one who deviates intellectually, physically, socially, or emotionally from what is considered to be normal growth and development. This deviation must be so great that the student cannot receive maximum benefit from a regular school program and requires a special class or supplementary instruction and services.

1. The Intellectually Exceptional Student: This phrase encompasses two large groups. At one extreme are students who are characterized by high mental ability (gifted); at the other extreme are students who are referred to as mentally retarded.
   A. The Gifted Student: These students have measured intelligence which exceeds an intelligence quotient of 130. Such students constitute about 3 percent of the population. Definitions of giftedness differ widely. Some broaden the areas of giftedness to the gifted and talented, including:
      1. general intellectual ability
      2. specific academic aptitude
      3. creative or productive thinking
      4. leadership ability
      5. visual and performing arts
      6. psychomotor ability (Gallagher, 1975).
      The PL 94-142 definition generally used in schools emphasizes high intelligence as primary.

B. The Educable Mentally Retarded (E.M.R.): These students have intelligence quotients between 55 and 80.

C. The Trainable Mentally Retarded (T.M.R.): These students have intelligence quotients between 30 and 55.

D. Severely and Profoundly Mentally Retarded (S.P.M.R.): Individuals with an intelligence quotient lower than 30. They must also be evaluated by a physician prior to any placement.

2. Learning Disabled Student: A deficiency in the acquisition of basic learning skills, including, but not limited to, the ability to reason, think, read, write, spell, or do mathematical calculations, as identified by an educational and psychological evaluation. A student is assigned to a program for the learning disabled when the evaluation clearly indicates the s/he can demonstrate average or above average intellectual functioning on an appropriate intelligence measure.

3. Brain Damaged: A moderate to severe injury to the brain, as identified by a neurological examination, resulting in severe behavior and learning disorders.

4. Hearing Impaired: A hearing loss ranging from mild (hard of hearing) to profound (deaf), as identified by an audiologist and otologist, which interferes with the development of the communication process and results in failure to achieve full educational potential.

5. Blind: Those students in whom there is visual acuity of 20/200 or less in the better eye with correcting glasses or peripheral vision so limited that the widest diameter the student can see includes an angle no greater than 20 degrees. (A student with 20/200 vision is not totally blind.)

6. Speech and Language Impaired: Communications disorders or impaired language, voice, fluency, or articulation to such a degree that academic achievement is affected and the condition is significantly handicapping to the affected person. This is determined by a speech clinician.

7. Socially and Emotionally Disturbed: A condition exhibiting one or more of the following characteristics over a long period of time and to a marked degree: an inability to build or maintain satisfactory interpersonal relationships with peers and teachers; inappropriate types of behaviors or feelings; a general and pervasive mood of unhappiness or depression; or a tendency to develop physical symptoms, pains, or fears associated with personal or school problems. Such a student must be identified in writing by a board-certified or approved psychiatrist. No person shall be assigned to a program for disciplinary reasons alone.

8. Physically Handicapped: Orthopedic and/or other health

impairments of sufficient magnitude to limit a student's classroom accommodation and educational performance. Physically handicapping conditions include cerebral palsy, muscular dystrophy, spina bifida and other spinal defects, and impaired motor ability as a result of accidents or other disease.

ATTITUDES TOWARD EXCEPTIONAL CHILDREN

Teacher and student attitudes toward exceptional individuals are formed through involvement in the society at large. The attitude of many people has been that exceptional people—handicapped people—should be separated from the rest of us. In order to comply with PL 94-142, and to provide for more humane acceptance of exceptional students in our classes, teachers must consider their own and their students' attitudes toward these exceptional students. It may be understandable that we have some negative attitudes, but it is no longer acceptable.

Teacher Attitudes**

Our first task is to identify our own attitudes toward particular handicaps and toward the students who bring them to our classes. Test yourself in the following exercise.

You are teaching a ninth-grade class in your subject area. This morning, Bob Diaz, the school district psychologist, came to see you and told you that there are six exceptional children who might possibly be candidates for mainstreaming in your content area class. He said that he has come to you rather than some of the other teachers since he felt that you might be more sensitive to the needs of these exceptional students. He believes that mainstreaming these students into your class would really be to the students' benefit, and he wants to know how you feel about the idea. He left the following list of six names with you and asked you to indicate your feelings about each one. Please indicate your feelings by ranking the students in order, beginning with the one you would most like to have mainstreamed (place a 1 before that student's name) and ending with the one you would least like to see mainstreamed (place a 6 before that student's name).

Rachel is physically handicapped. She had both legs amputated after an automobile accident and also has some facial disfiguration. She is average in ability.

**This section was prepared by James Nolan of The Pennsylvania State University.

JoAnn is socially-emotionally disturbed. She is prone to periods of severe depression, is normally very withdrawn, and has exhibited aggressive behavior on a few occasions.

Mark is educable mentally retarded. He is shy, lacks social skills, and has great difficulty reading. He is seventeen years old and is determined to get a diploma.

Rick has a mild to moderate hearing loss and a severe speech impediment which makes it extremely difficult to understand him. He is above average in ability.

Lori is a gifted student. She has failed at least three subjects each year and seems to use her intelligence only to challenge the teacher.

Todd suffers from muscular dystrophy. He is in a wheelchair, has control only of gross motor movements, and has some speech slurring, but he is very bright and likes school very much.

When you have finished this exercise, ask yourself why you ranked the students as you did. Are you more concerned about students' cognitive ability? If so, you may be challenged by Lori, the gifted student, but less willing to work with Mark, the mentally retarded student. Are you fearful of JoAnn's potentially aggressive behavior? Are you repelled by Rachel's physical appearance or Todd's lack of motor control? We all have feelings like this, but we must learn to control them. What we need most as teachers are understanding, patience, and faith in these students' ability to learn, even though it may be in a different way and at a different pace from other students.

Classroom Attitudes

Our second task is to foster a positive and helping attitude toward exceptional children in our classrooms. Just as we may have negative feelings about certain handicaps, we may find that some students react negatively toward handicapped students in the classroom. Students may feel uncomfortable when faced with handicapping conditions that they do not understand. It is the teacher's responsibility to build tolerance in other class members for the physical and mental handicaps of exceptional children. Teachers should develop a positive climate in which exceptional children feel comfortable interacting with their other classmates.

Students may want to know how to assist their classmates but might be afraid to ask. Although it is important for you to encourage handicapped students to become or remain as independent as possible, you can discuss types of assistance that are needed and how members of the class can help. For example, a student can act as a helper for a physically handicapped student by holding and manipulating materials, from turning pages to handling laboratory equipment. A helper may also assist the student's mobility, such as moving a wheelchair or setting up materials so the student can handle them on his/her own. One student may be assigned to read materials to a visually handicapped class member or to record information dictated by a student who is unable to write on his/her own.

WHERE DO READING AND WRITING FIT IN?

Content teachers, especially at the secondary level, face many students whose reading and writing abilities are lower than average. Not all of these students are handicapped as defined in PL 94-142. We are talking here only about students who have an IEP, providing legal evidence to the teacher that they need individualized instruction. In addition, some students with IEPs, especially gifted students, may well have superior reading and writing abilities and need enrichment rather than remediation.

Reading and writing fit into instruction of mainstreamed students, then, as you might expect: each student's needs must be evaluated individually. It is highly likely that an IEP will speak specifically to the student's needs in reading and writing, however, as well as other basic skills. In these cases, the primary concern of both parents and the school is emphasis on the student's acquiring reasonable competence in reading and writing, especially in the case of students who are functioning at a lower level. The IEP will determine how reading and writing are treated in an individual student's program.

It is dangerous to generalize about groups of students, regardless of their exceptionality; however, a few broad guidelines may help shape the content teacher's planning. The categories are those given earlier in this chapter.

1. The Intellectually Exceptional Student
   A. The gifted child may have very good reading and writing skills, but s/he may also read on grade level or below. On the continuum of reading and writing levels, the gifted student may be anywhere; hence, careful diagnosis is important. A gifted student who reads and writes well can be treated like the independent reader, as described in the next section. The gifted child who reads and writes on grade level is still functioning below his/her capacity. The gifted child who reads and writes poorly needs attention to motivation and general attitude problems. S/he may have poor skills but high creativity; s/he may need challenge and a high level of personal attention.
   B. Educable mentally retarded students will have limited educational goals in secondary content subjects; that is, they will not usually aspire to algebra, chemistry, or physics, to

literature like *Moby Dick* and *Hamlet*, or to a study of Russian political structure. However, these students will become, with help, productive members of our society. They have reason to learn how to do basic arithmetic; to understand consumer and life science; to read short stories, poetry, newspaper and magazine articles; to write personal notes and fill out forms; and to understand government and take part as a citizen in democratic processes. The reading and writing level of EMR students is likely to be limited. They are likely to need alternative reading materials with controlled reading levels and structured writing activities, as described later in this chapter.

C. Trainable mentally retarded students are unlikely to be mainstreamed into content classrooms, especially at the secondary level. If a content teacher has a TMR student, s/he should contact the counselor and special education resource teacher immediately for guidance.

D. Severe and profoundly mentally retarded students are unlikely to be placed in a regular classroom.

2. The Learning Disabled Student

Many of the mainstreamed students in content classes are LD students. Their average or above average intelligence suggest that they have the capacity to learn in content classes. However, their problems with symbol systems make it likely that reading and/or writing will be a problem for them. LD students show a wide variety of problems. This means that the individual students' IEPs must be the content teacher's guide to their strengths and weaknesses in reading, writing, and other skills. LD students may need to learn through sources other than reading or writing, through concrete and hands-on experiences, and through carefully structured activity.

3. The Brain-Damaged Student

Teaching a brain damaged student requires careful consultation with the school psychologist, counselor, and other resource teachers. Brain damage is likely to result in serious problems with learning, frequently including reading and writing. Brain-damaged students may decode reasonably well, but they have great difficulty in comprehending. They may also have difficulty in writing logically using correct word choice. Few brain-damaged students will be found in content classes, especially at the secondary level.

4. The Hearing-Impaired Student

These students may well be placed in content classes throughout the school. There is no necessary connection between hearing loss and reading and writing ability. However, many hearing-impaired students do not have the language development expected of children their age. Students may need to sit in front of the room, near the teacher's voice, or to have a fellow student help explain oral assignments. If these students can lipread, teachers can face them when speaking. Again, it is important for content teachers to consult with the school's specialists and resource teachers to determine the student's potential for reading and writing.

5. The Blind Student

    Students with visual problems will clearly have difficulty with reading and writing. Since vision problems have a wide range, content teachers must be careful to determine the student's specific problem. Reading difficulty may result less from inability to comprehend what is read than from inability to see the text. A student whose vision is corrected with glasses may need larger print books. S/he may need more time to read if reading causes his/her eyes to tire. But s/he may be able to complete much of the reading necessary for the class. Such students may profit from sitting closer to visual materials—the chalkboard, wall maps, etc. On the other hand, a student who is legally blind will need to learn through sources other than texts—Braille texts or audio sources, for example.

    These students may find it easier to write if they have access to a typewriter or computer with Braille keypads. Computers equipped with synthesizers allow students to hear what they have written while using a word processing program. Students may also prepare audio-taped rather than written reports, or they may dictate reports to a student assistant.

6. The Speech and Language Impaired Student

    Because oral speech precedes reading and writing in the development of the language skills, it is common for students who have speech problems to also have reading and writing problems. However, this is by no means an automatic connection. Content teachers must, again, look at the specific provisions of each student's IEP. If reading is a problem for these students, it is likely that the content teacher will need to use alternative or rewritten materials with controlled reading levels to provide the student with information. Teachers should implement alternative writing assignments to build a student's confidence in written communication and to develop his/her vocabulary. These speech-impaired students also need opportunities to speak to their peers as any other student might. Although it may be difficult, the teacher must create a classroom climate in which these students feel comfortable speaking in small groups or within a wider classroom discussion.

7. The Socially and Emotionally Disturbed Student

Students with emotional problems severe enough to warrant identification and the resulting IEP will need individualized teaching in content classes. These students will vary widely in their interest, attitudes toward school, and attitudes toward particular classes. However, there is no necessary reason to think that they have problems with reading and writing. Emotionally disturbed students may refuse to read or write or take part in classroom activities, but these problems may be more attitudinal and emotional than skill related. Over a period of time, perhaps years, a student with emotional problems can miss a large amount of skill instruction. Thus, in later years the emotionally disturbed student may be below the expected reading/writing level in content classes. As a result, the careful teacher will look at all aspects of the students' background and current skill levels before designing instruction for them. Close coordination with the school psychologist and counselor is necessary in making appropriate assignments.

8. The Physically Handicapped Student

Students who are identified as physically handicapped may suffer from any number of limitations. By definition, these physical handicaps are not necessarily connected to intellectual functioning. However, multiple handicaps are fairly common, especially with cerebral palsy. The connection between physical handicaps and reading and writing is also cloudy. Some handicaps, like cerebral palsy, may well suggest problems with reading and writing because students have difficulty with the required coordination. Some students who can read and write will not be able to handle the texts and to manipulate the materials physically. However, handicaps from accidents or progressive diseases like muscular dystrophy will not necessarily impair reading or writing ability. Advances in technology, such as computers, can assist physically handicapped students with reading and writing activities.

TEACHING INDEPENDENT LEVEL READERS

Who are independent readers? Some of them, of course, are intellectually gifted students working at their capacity level. Gifted or not, independent readers are the students who scored above 60 percent on a cloze test or above 90 percent on an Informal Reading Inventory (see Chapter 8). These readers can handle a textbook without systematic reading instruction. On the basis of their informal test scores, the teacher will need to check their permanent records for a full picture of their achievement and their performance in other areas.

Let's consider some alternatives in an interpretation of independent students' reading levels.

1. Independent readers can read the text without much assistance. However, they still need instruction to learn the content. Being an independent reader doesn't mean a student already knows the material. It simply means that s/he can read the material as a means of learning the content.

2. Some students are independent readers because they have a high interest in the subject and a great amount of background knowledge about it. The teacher might find that these students' records may show average to above average achievement in other subjects but high achievement in his/her subject. These students are not gifted in a broad sense, but may be high achievers for him/her.

3. Some independent readers are truly gifted students, as their records will show. They may be highly skilled in academic subjects and need the challenge of a demanding curriculum.

4. Some independent readers are capable in reading but not particularly interested in a subject or in school. Some capable readers develop negative attitudes and are labeled "underachievers," since their classroom achievement doesn't match their capabilities.

All of these interpretations are possible, given only the results of informal reading assessments. Those students who are identified as gifted under PL 94-142, and who are involved in the special education program, are academically talented students. In many districts, a gifted student will be eligible for special instruction or assistance through the special education program. In that case, a teacher can seek help in preparing an individualized program for each gifted student, using the information available in the student's file. The gifted specialist or Special Education Resource teacher provides assistance in carrying out the student's program.

Gifted students need to be challenged to use their special talents. Sometimes this challenge is to learn the same content as other students but to do it faster. This leads to accelerated classes in which students cover more material in the same length of time. The impact of accelerated classes on reading is that students may be asked to read a great deal in a short time. For example, accelerated English classes may ask students to read two novels in a grading period in which the regular class reads one.

Another way to challenge gifted readers is to give them a more demanding text. In American history, for example, an advanced class may use a text designed for college level classes. The students may respond to the content, but the teacher must be sure that the reading level of the advanced text is still within their reading range. Remember that Don Neely used three different texts to meet the needs of all his eighth-grade history students (see Chapter 7). When he wanted to challenge his most advanced readers, he gave them a text designed for freshman college history courses. This approach works if the reading level is appropriate and the students' background knowledge is sufficient. In order to be prepared to use this approach, teachers should identify textbooks at several levels of difficulty in advance of the time students may need to use them.

Instructional Strategies for Independent Level Readers

Gifted students need to be challenged by learning activities clustered at the higher levels on Bloom's taxonomy: analysis, synthesis, and evaluation. This translates into reading comprehension at the inferential and evaluation levels of Barrett's taxonomy. They still need to learn the literal information, but they can do that more quickly than other students, and they can do it while they are engaged in other activities. That is, gifted readers don't need as much drill and practice; they need engagement, thought-provoking questions, and imaginative projects. Such activities as writing, extended laboratory projects, building and demonstration projects, and creative and artistic responses will allow gifted readers to work through the material, learn it, and respond to it.

Activities for Independent Readers

A number of activities that are more student-directed can be helpful to independent readers. Those readers who are more self-directing can develop projects, laboratory demonstrations, learning centers, or LAPs for use by other students in the class. They can undertake research topics requiring wider reading and the integration of information from multiple sources. They often can translate visual material into text, or the reverse. The creative teacher can identify activities in each teaching unit which independent readers can choose to complete.

For independent readers who are less self-directing, teacher direction remains important. Teacher-directed activities, like study guides, can be altered to emphasize higher levels of comprehension, comparison and contrast of various materials, and written responses at the evaluation level. In each of these activities, teachers can develop parallel activities, so that all levels of readers are doing the same type of activity, such as a study guide, but the guides are on different levels. That way, independent readers are not forced to do the same thing as frustration and instructional readers—a sure cause of boredom and resentment; instead, each level will be working with challenging material that is suitable for their reading level.

Teachers need to continue their watchful guidance of independent readers. They need the same nurturing and support as other readers. They have the same attitude concerns as other readers. They need to be challenged and encouraged, the same as other readers. Careful planning enables teachers to provide appropriate activities for independent readers.

TEACHING FRUSTRATION LEVEL READERS

The frustration level readers are those for whom the textbook is clearly too difficult. Even if they are able to say the words, they are unable to gain meaning. The procedures of the Directed Reading Activity (DRA) are inadequate in helping frustration level readers.

The content area teacher can identify frustration level readers at the beginning of the school year by administering a cloze test using the content area textbook (see Chapter 8). The cloze test, however, does not indicate the reading level of the student. It merely shows that the student

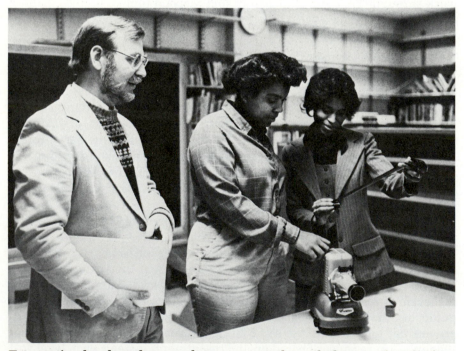

Frustration level readers can learn content through the use of media in addition to reading. Here, some Middlewood teachers preview materials in the school media center.

cannot read the textbook well enough to gain information from it for study of the content area.

Teachers may have access to standardized reading test scores that provide some indication of reading level. Some students, however, do not perform as well as they can on such tests because they are not motivated by a standardized test, they may work too slowly to achieve within the time limits of the test, or they may not understand the directions if English is not their native language.

If the frustration level readers are included in a special reading program, the specialist can probably provide information on the reading level of each student; or if the students are mainstreamed from a learning disabilities or special education room, their reading levels should be included on the IEP. On the other hand, without input from a specialist, how can a content teacher know at what level other materials should be given to those students who cannot read the textbook? Probably the easiest solution is to create a cloze test for the less difficult alternative materials. In this manner, the content teacher has some estimate of reading level for those students who cannot comprehend information from the textbook.

Other characteristics of frustration level readers are important. Do they have prior knowledge or experience related to the content area? If so, they have an advantage because they can draw on a strong conceptual background in relating new material to what is already known. Many vocational students may have had "hands-on" experience in wiring circuits or welding. This background experience will help them read the vocational instructional materials. Unfortunately, poor readers often do not have a strong knowledge base because their limited reading skills have hindered their learning. Usually they have gained what knowledge they have through listening, television, or firsthand experiences.

The interest and motivation levels of these students are also important. Unfortunately, most of them have experienced frustration in learning when instruction has not been adapted to their level. They have been forced to try to read what they cannot understand, and they have been ridiculed or harassed when they have failed to complete assignments correctly. A few frustration level readers feel good about themselves because of their achievements in sports, hobbies, scouts, and the like. For others, strong family support maintains their motivation and interest even though they meet frequent failure and frustration.

Many frustration level readers, however, do not feel good about themselves as learners. By the time the content area teacher has them in class, they have already determined how they will meet frustration. A few, of course, who do have healthy self-concepts in spite of frustration, attempt to do the assigned work, seeking help from friends, parents, and the teacher. Many students, however, have given up and decided that they cannot do the work; they may become disruptive out of sheer boredom and frustration, or they may withdraw.

The picture of the frustration level reader is by and large not a rosy one. S/he is not easy to teach, nor is s/he always responsive to a teacher's attempt to help. Teachers must constantly remind themselves that learning to read or learning from reading has not been easy for this student. It takes time to build a trusting relationship with a teacher.

The content teacher needs to find out what the frustration level readers can do. For example, Betsy is very interested in farming. In Betsy's case, a teacher's interest in her dairy cattle is important in establishing a good relationship. A teacher who does not take her efforts seriously, or who makes fun of her, would very likely produce "turn off" behavior in Betsy. On the other hand, if the content study could be related to Betsy's concerns, such as calculating in math class the cost of raising a dairy cow, Betsy's interest in the content area would be aroused. Her attitude toward the subject, teacher, and school in general could improve substantially. The secret is, of course, finding out what does interest Betsy and showing an interest in it and respect for her.

Instructional Strategies for Frustration Level Readers

Because using the content area textbook, even with the support of the Directed Reading Activity, is inappropriate for frustration level readers, the teacher must find some other means of presenting the content. It is important to make adaptations for frustration level readers rather than ignoring the problem. It does no good to blame the students for not doing their homework when they are incapable of reading the assigned material.

The content teacher does have some options for teaching frustration level readers (see Figure 13.1). S/he may use the textbook supplemented by study guides, or s/he may modify the textbook to change not only its reading level but also its content.

Let's take a closer look at these options.

ALTERNATIVES TO TEXTBOOKS

Unmodified Textbooks	**Modified Textbook**
Study Guides	Alternative reading materials
	Teacher rewritten version
	Morning letter technique
	Student rewritten version
	Language experience approach
	Tape recording

Figure 13.1

Alternative Reading Materials

An obvious alternative, although not necessarily an easy one, is to use other reading materials. The teacher may be able to locate textbooks or supplementary materials intended for use with younger children which cover the same content. The librarian or reading specialist may be able to help locate alternative reading materials. Many textbooks list additional materials at the end of a unit or chapter; some of these may be useful if written at a lower reading level. As long as the material is not too child-ish, it may be exactly what frustration level readers need. Greater depth of content and concepts may be attained through other media and class discussion.

Teachers can estimate the appropriateness of a lower level textbook in terms of reading level by having the frustration level readers take a cloze test on that material. If the student scores at the instructional or indepen-dent reading level, the lower level textbook can be used as the basic as-signed material to be supplemented with audio-visual materials and classroom activities.

Often, however, a lower level textbook is simply not available. In that case a unit approach, in which a variety of materials—including maga-zines, pamphlets, journals, fiction, newspapers, audio-visual materials, and perhaps textbooks—are used as sources, makes sense. While the unit approach is described elsewhere (see Chapter 10), it is important to note that frustration level readers can be given appropriate easy-to-read mate-rials without obviously identifying that they are reading something dif-ferent. Since all students are reading different materials, it is less obvious that the frustration level readers are using easier materials.

Teachers can collect and key alternative materials to the topics in the various units. Readability formulas (see Chapter 7) permit the teacher to estimate the difficulty level of the materials so that appropriate alterna-tive reading materials may be assigned to frustration level readers.

In addition to alternative reading materials, other strategies may be appropriate for frustration level readers. These strategies may be used to supplement the textbook or be used as part of a unit approach.

The Teacher-Rewritten Textbook Version

The teacher may decide to rewrite the textbook in addition to or instead of using alternative reading material. Since this is no easy task, the teacher should rewrite only crucial portions of the textbook for which no suitable alternative reading material exists.

To simplify the text, the teacher can substitute easier words for diffi-cult vocabulary, usually decreasing the length of the words, but s/he should keep in mind that students do need to learn some technical termi-nology. For example, it is hard to talk about photosynthesis without using the word. "Photosynthesis" is a long word, although not necessarily a difficult one, once the students learn the word parts. Therefore, the teacher can identify and teach the key vocabulary words that are also concept labels—words essential to teaching the concepts—before assigning the reading material so that students will not have difficulty reading these words. The teacher can then eliminate or replace other difficult words that are not essential to the content.

Also, the teacher can reduce sentence length where possible. S/he should replace complex sentences with simple sentences, but be sure to retain connectives with meaning. For example, a sentence might state, "Because John was sick, he left school." Simplifying this complex sentence into two simple sentences ("John was sick. He left school.") would do away with the notion of causality, and, in fact, short, choppy sentences are more difficult to understand (Pearson, 1974).

Indeed, reducing sentence length does not guarantee more readable material, so the teacher should modify only very long sentences containing several clauses. A sentence with a dependent clause between the subject and verb, as demonstrated by this sentence, should be rewritten. (The clause "as demonstrated by this sentence" interrupts the flow of thought between the subject and verb.) The passive voice, in which the subject is acted upon (as in this and the previous sentence), should also be avoided. (Restated in the active voice: "We should avoid the passive voice.")

When rewriting, the teacher should try to keep the sense of the whole paragraph or section in mind instead of rewriting sentence by sentence. Doing so will help him/her to restate the main ideas in very simple language.

The teacher can check rewritten versions for readability level by applying a readability formula such as the Fry Graph (see Chapter 7). Or, s/he can observe underachieving readers while they use a rewritten version to see if the new version has eliminated difficulties.

The Morning Letter Technique

A technique called the "morning letter" has been used for many years in the State College, Pennsylvania, Area School District. Because social studies and language arts are taught together as a block in the elementary grades, the teacher uses the morning letter both to present content and to teach reading skills. The technique involves writing on the chalkboard or chart a message to the students that introduces the content to be studied. The letter contains key vocabulary and concepts that the teacher wishes to introduce. Reading the morning letter is followed by reading skill instruction using the words in the letter as examples. The students each have their own morning letter booklets in which they record information; they usually also keep a daily journal pertaining to the content of the morning letters. The students read other sources of information about the content, such as library books or textbooks. They may incorporate information gleaned from these sources into their journals and research reports.

Figure 13.2 contains an example of the morning letter technique. The morning letter, which is for a social studies unit on Japan, conveys information about everyday life that the teacher wants her fifth-grade students to learn. She has used a cloze format to stimulate active comprehension. The students will comprehend the selection better if they must think about the omitted words. Note that the deletions are irregularly spaced, rather than at regular intervals such as every fifth word as in a cloze test. The deleted words are those that the students should be able to supply if they are comprehending the letter. The teacher has used some enrich-

MORNING LETTER FROM A SOCIAL STUDIES UNIT

_____, 19___

Dear _____,

Japanese homes are small and built close together. _____ in the city have tiled roofs; homes in the country have thatched _____.

The rooms in Japanese houses do _____ have much furniture. There are _____ chairs, couches, or beds. Square, flat cushions are _____ on the floor beside a low table for eating or drinking tea. At night thick comforters, or futons, are spread out on the _____ to make beds. During winter months an iron pot called a hibachi is _____ in the middle of the room in a pit to help keep the people _____.

In one corner of the main _____ is a raised platform where a flower arrangement or other artwork is displayed beneath a long hanging scroll picture.

Most Japanese homes _____ gardens, which are also works of art. These _____ are very quiet and peaceful areas. The house is often built around the _____ so that everyone inside can _____ it from all the windows. The garden might have flowers and _____ tiny cherry trees. Water might drop down _____ some rocks.

The kitchen is a small _____. It does have _____ electric stove, a sink, _____ a refrigerator.

These _____ homes are small and quite simple. They are _____ attractive though for these people in this island country.

Your teacher,
Mrs. Yendol

Figure 13.2
Prepared by Maureen Yendol, State College, Pa., Area School District. Reprinted by permission.

ment words, such as "futon" and "hibachi," but she has not deleted these words. Comprehension questions following the letter focus on the main idea, inferences, and vocabulary. These constitute the skill development aspects of the morning letter technique.

Teachers might use a morning letter as an introduction to new vocabulary and concepts for all students. For the frustration level readers, the morning letter might become the sole text (if it is placed on a ditto master) supplemented by other activities, such as learning centers and media presentations, while the better readers read the textbook or other more difficult reading materials. This technique has been used successfully in secondary content classes; the teacher uses the morning letter (or "editorial") to present content concepts and vocabulary before a reading assignment.

The Student-Rewritten Textbook Version

Teachers might also use student rewritten versions of the textbook with underachieving readers. Asking the average and better readers to summarize important selections from their reading material is an excellent way to enhance their reading comprehension (Anderson & Armbruster, 1982); it also helps teachers determine which students can restate main ideas in their own words. The students, individually or in groups, write their paraphrased versions on ditto masters, which are then duplicated for use with the poor readers. A teacher may want to retain these versions to use with next year's frustration level readers. While s/he has to spend time checking the student-rewritten versions, s/he saves time by having students do the rewriting. The greater reward is that the underachieving reader can read the summaries rather than the textbook to learn the content. The average and above-average students benefit from the writing experiences in paraphrasing the textbook.

The Language Experience Approach

The language experience approach (LEA) is often thought of in terms of beginning reading, but the principles and procedures also apply to content area reading (Askov & Lee, 1980). Briefly, LEA involves group discussion of some type of stimulus or group experience. Afterward, the students dictate the main ideas as you write them down on chart paper. Students are able to read the material written on the chart because it is written in their own words. If they forget a particular word, they can usually remember it by rereading the sentence.

In using LEA in content area studies, the most important consideration is finding an appropriate stimulus. Since the LEA is to replace the textbook for the frustration level readers, the stimulus should contain the essential content, concepts, and vocabulary. Sometimes a film, audiotape, demonstration, or guest speaker may provide the stimulus for group discussion. After discussion, the teacher asks the students to state the main ideas in their own words and then records these on a chart, which may later be transcribed on a ditto master. The dictated selection can act as a rewritten version of the textbook for the underachieving readers. They will be able to read it because they helped write it. The better readers may read the textbook version for greater depth and description.

Tape Recording

Another technique (which we would not endorse as the sole technique for presenting content) is tape recording textbook material. The frustration level readers during independent study time may listen to the material in the library or at a listening post in the corner of the classroom. Some suggestions are in order:

1. The teacher selects only the most essential portions of the textbook for taping. Usually s/he can omit some paragraphs within a section. The students can follow the teacher's (or volunteer's) oral reading in their textbooks.
2. The teacher directs their attention to graphic material, such as maps, graphs, and tables, that may help them understand the content.
3. Students should receive a study guide to accompany the tape (see Chapter 5) so they can respond to the material whether they read it or listen to it.

Younger students usually accept this technique without difficulty. Sometimes older students, especially at the secondary level, dislike having to study in such an overtly different way from their peers. Teachers who have used this technique with older students report that students often abuse the time at the listening post or in the library. They do not want to be singled out as being poor readers, and they resent the time it takes to listen to the material.

The elimination of the need to read when using this technique troubles us. For this reason, teachers should use oral reading only occasionally, and then in small doses. The teacher may read to the frustration level readers in class or use tape recordings.

Special Techniques

Some students have difficulty learning words in the usual methods followed in school. Most instruction is largely dependent on the visual and auditory learning modalities. Some students, however, need reinforcement through the tactile modality (the sense of touch). Unfortunately, the sand table which is typically found in the kindergarten room is usually not used when children are learning to read. Most modern reading instructional programs are heavily dependent on phonics in teaching word recognition skills. But some students seem to be unable to learn through the auditory modality (phonics). As a result, they fall behind in reading.

Like all students, when these students face the task of learning new vocabulary in content area reading, they need vocabulary instruction prior to reading. Some of them, however, may need to have tactile reinforcement of the words in order to remember them. It may be inadequate to present vocabulary through only the visual and auditory modalities. Some students may need to trace words written in crayon with their finger while they say the words, followed by writing the words with a pencil. The words may be written on index cards and kept in their own file of new and known words.

It is necessary to review content vocabulary frequently. The teacher should not assume that words, once learned, will be remembered if they are not reviewed. The important words should be presented in a different context. If a student does not recognize a word that was once learned, then s/he should go back to tracing the word while saying it aloud.

Frustration level readers also are often those students who benefit from manipulative materials. For example, in the vocabulary learning center described in Chapter 11, students manipulate cubes to form new words containing roots and affixes. Because they can manipulate the word parts physically, they gain a better grasp of word parts and how they affect meaning. Some students, most often frustration level readers, need physical involvement in learning.

Frustration level readers also benefit from frequent writing experiences in the content classroom. After reading assigned material, they should be asked to state in their own words what they have learned. Not only does this procedure help them identify the important ideas in assigned reading, but it also provides practice in using the new vocabulary. It is a good check on what each student is learning, providing the teacher with a technique by which to monitor instructional progress. Needless to say, the more opportunities that students have to express themselves in writing, the easier written expression becomes for the student. Increased facility in writing has positive effects on reading abilities as well. The structured approach for helping students get a content area writing activity started, which is described in detail in Chapter 6, is particularly effective with frustration level readers.

Frustration level readers may have vast experiences to draw on, but these experiences may be unrelated to school learning. Because of limited reading abilities, they may not have had access to concepts that are ordinarily gained through incidental reading. Therefore, the content area teacher must be especially careful not to assume a conceptual background that is not present.

As teachers, we usually function with a middle-class set of values and assumptions. Our frustration level students, however, may not be operating with the same frame of reference if they come from less advantaged homes. As teachers, then, we must be careful not to assume that we share a common set of background experiences with our students—unless the teacher has grown up in the community in which s/he teaches. Differences in values and experiences become particularly important in subject areas such as English and social studies, and especially in developing the higher levels of thinking on Barrett's taxonomy (see Appendix 2). Teachers are safer to provide conceptual background for new learning rather than to assume that frustration level readers already have that background.

SUMMARY

We have discussed various handicaps which may interfere with learning, and we have discussed the wide range of problems in reading and writing faced by exceptional students—labeled as independent or frustration level readers. For these groups, the usual grade-level curriculum materials are inappropriate. Content teachers will be wise to note their students with IEPs and work carefully with the counselor or special education resource teacher to identify the reading and writing levels and strengths of these students. Specific student learning problems and the implementation of the specific objectives given in IEPs provide the content teacher with direction in working with exceptional students. An individualized approach is not only a legal mandate, it is the only professionally appropriate way to work with exceptional students. Content teachers with such students in their classes will need to learn more about specific exceptionalities. The reference list at the end of this chapter is a modest beginning to such reading.

The independent reader may or may not be gifted, in terms of intellectual ability. Independent readers can read the text with little teacher assistance, but they need regular instruction and teacher support, just as other readers do. Appropriate activities for independent readers may differ depending on how self-directing those readers are. Student-directed and teacher-directed activities are available to provide appropriate learning experiences for independent readers. Writing opportunities are an important factor in the growth of these students.

Similarly, we have suggested techniques for modifying content area textbooks for frustration level readers so that they can learn the content material when grade-level texts are too difficult. These techniques do not replace the need to read but provide more realistic reading tasks. Writing is an important reinforcement for learning from reading for frustration level readers.

REFERENCES

Anderson, T. H. & Armbruster, B. B. (1982). Reader and text-studying strategies. In W. Otto & S. White (Eds.), *Reading expository material* (pp. 219–42). New York: Academic Press, Inc.

Askov, E. N. & Lee, J. W. (1980). The language experience approach in the content area classroom. *The Journal of Language Experience, 2*, 13–20.

Cartwright, G. P., Cartwright, C. A., & Ward, M. E. (1981). *Educating special learners.* Belmont, CA: Wadsworth, Inc.

Gallagher, J. J. (1975). *Teaching the gifted child* (2nd ed.). Boston: Allyn & Bacon, Inc.

Pearson, P. D. (1974). The effects of grammatical complexity on children's comprehension, recall and conception of certain semantic relations. *Reading Research Quarterly, 10*, 155–89.

SUGGESTIONS FOR FURTHER READING

Alley, G. & Deshler, D. (1979). *Teaching the learning disabled adolescent: Strategies and methods.* Denver: Love. Chapter 3.

Alvermann, D. E. (1987). Integrating oral and written instruction. In D. E. Alvermann et al. (Eds.), *Research within reach: Secondary school reading* (pp. 109–129). Newark, DE: International Reading Association.

Berger, A. & Robinson, H. A. (Eds.). (1982). *Secondary school reading: What research reveals for classroom practice.* Urbana, IL: National Council of Teachers of English.

Blankenship, C. & Lilly, M. S. (1981). *Mainstreaming children with learning and behavior problems: Techniques for the classroom teacher.* New York: Holt, Rinehart and Winston.

Cicchelli, T. & Ashby-Davis, C. (1986). *Teaching exceptional children and youth in the regular classroom.* Syracuse, NY: Syracuse University Press.

D'Zamko, M. E. (1985). *Helping exceptional students succeed in the regular classroom.* West Nyack, NY: Parker.

Ellis, A. W. (1984). *Reading, writing and dyslexia: A cognitive analysis.* Hillsdale, NJ: Lawrence Erlbaum Associates, Inc.

Gillespie-Silver, P. (1979). *Teaching reading to children with special needs.* Columbus, OH: Merrill Publishing Co.

Giordano, G. (1984). *Teaching writing to learning disabled students.* Rockville, MD: Aspen Systems Corporation.

Gulliford, R. (1985). *Teaching children with learning difficulties*. Philadelphia: NFER-Nelson.

Hume, C. (1981). *Reading retardation and multisensory teaching*. Boston: Routledge and Kegan Paul, Inc.

Kaluger, G. & Kolson, C. (1978). *Reading and learning disabilities* (2nd ed.). Columbus, OH: Merrill Publishing Co.

Kirk, S., Kliebhan, M., & Lerner, J. W. (1978). *Teaching reading to slow and disabled learners*. Boston: Houghton Mifflin Co.

Labuda, M. (1985). *Creative reading for gifted learners*. Newark, DE: International Reading Association.

Morsink, C. V. (1984). *Teaching special needs students in regular classrooms*. Boston: Little, Brown & Co., Inc.

Polette, N. (1982). *Three r's for the gifted: Reading, writing, and research*. Littleton, CO: Libraries Unlimited.

Reynolds, B., Kopelke, K., & Durden, W. G. (1984). *Writing instruction for verbally talented youth: The Johns Hopkins model*. Rockville, MD: Aspen Systems Corporation.

Ross, M., Brackett, D., & Maxon, A. (1982). *Hard of hearing children in regular schools*. Englewood Cliffs, NJ: Prentice-Hall.

Savage, J. F. & Mooney, J. F. (1979). *Teaching reading to children with special needs*. Boston: Allyn & Bacon, Inc.

Schwartz, L. L. (1984). *Exceptional students in the mainstream*. Belmont, CA: Wadsworth, Inc.

Scott, E. P. (1982). *Your visually impaired student: A guide for teachers*. Baltimore: University Park Press.

Semmel, M. I. & Agard, J. A. (1985). *Mainstreaming, learners, and their environment*. Cambridge, MA: Brookline Books.

Shea, T. M. & Bauer, A. M. (1987). *Teaching children and youth with behavior disorders*. 2nd ed. Englewood Cliffs, NJ: Prentice-Hall.

Stephens, T. M., Blackhurst, A. E., & Magliocca, L. A. (1982). *Teaching mainstreamed students*. New York: John Wiley & Sons, Inc.

Turnbull, A. P. & Schulz, J. B. (1979). *Mainstreaming handicapped students: A guide for the classroom teacher*. Boston: Allyn & Bacon, Inc.

Wilkins, G. & Miller, S. (1983). *Strategies for success, an effective guide for teachers of secondary-level slow learners*. New York: Teachers College Press.

Woodward, D. M. & Peters, D. J. (1983). *The learning disabled adolescent: Learning success in content areas*. Rockville, MD: Aspen Systems Corporation.

PART V

CONTENT AREA READING AND WRITING AND THE TOTAL SCHOOL PROGRAM

What are the components of a comprehensive reading and writing program?

How do reading and writing fit into the total school program?

Is it possible to integrate the teaching of reading and writing in every classroom?

What resources are available to content teachers as they try to include reading and writing in their lesson plans?

What is the most effective way to encourage professional growth among teachers?

We hope by now that we have convinced you of the importance of integrating reading and writing instruction in every content area classroom. We hope our ideas for doing so have sounded both possible and practical and that you will be able to implement many of them in your own classrooms.

We conclude this book with two critical considerations. First, we define what we consider a model schoolwide reading/writing program which should serve as a model for you. Then we discuss the concept of institutional change and present a workable model for those working to bring about change in any educational setting.

CHAPTER FOURTEEN

The Schoolwide Reading and Writing Program*

SCENARIO

The school year is about over. Students and teachers are beginning to think about that welcome summer break. We rejoin our friends Marge, John, Don, and Bev as they gather to plan for the end-of-year faculty picnic.

"How in the world did it get to be the end of May already?" asked Bev as she arrived at the planning meeting.

"Isn't it amazing how fast time seems to go once spring arrives? As usual, I'm beginning to think that I'll never cover all that I planned to," replied John.

Don appeared, almost buried beneath a stack of books and papers. "Who ever said we couldn't get it all covered? As you can see, I'm giving it a good try!"

"I'd say almost everyone on the staff is giving it a good try," said Marge as she joined the group around the conference table. "When you think of all the things we've talked about implementing this year . . . unit plans, improved vocabulary development, critical thinking activities, improving writing skills, I'm amazed at how much we've all accomplished. I confess that when I took on this job as reading specialist, I had serious doubts that anything would change very much. I was wrong."

"That's nice to hear, Marge, and I agree with you," replied Don. "We *have* done a lot toward getting reading and writing into our content area teaching. Even Janet, who is new to this whole ballgame, has been able to move toward that goal this year."

"Right on, Don," said John. "But let's not kid ourselves. We have a long way to go. Those of us sitting around this table have all made a concerted effort to try some of the ideas Marge has suggested. And we've had some success. But there are a lot of folks around here who remain highly resistant

*This chapter was written by Brenda S. Townsend of The Pennsylvania State University.

to anything that involves changing their basic commitment to teach only the content of their subject."

"Well put, John," responded Marge quickly. "I know too well that not everyone agrees that reading and writing are critical components of content teaching. There are still those who tell me that teaching reading is *my* job, not theirs. They fail to see the whole picture, what I've often referred to as the 'schoolwide reading/writing program.' But overall, I feel pretty positive about what has happened around here. We have a good base from which to build next year. For right now, though, how about if we work on integrating a good time into the curriculum? We have a picnic to plan for. Who wants to be in charge of grilling the hot dogs?"

OVERVIEW

A complete reading program should be designed to meet the varying needs of the students enrolled in the school, as well as to reflect the school district's philosophy. This chapter describes the major components of a comprehensive reading program that encompasses differing reading abilities in terms of students' skill development, habits, and attitudes.

A school reading program should provide instruction for all students and, depending on the students' present reading achievement, that instruction may be developmental, corrective, or remedial (Early, 1984). The *developmental* strand emphasizes ongoing efforts to help students refine and build the skills they already possess. *Corrective* reading refers to instruction that aids students in correcting specific skill weaknesses when their general reading ability is adequate. Students who have not acquired basic reading skills are in need of *remedial* assistance. Each of these strands, as Marge has helped the Middlewood staff understand, must be addressed as part of content area reading instruction.

Content teachers will have students whose reading skill development may require instruction based on these different classifications. These teachers may well feel that the task of teaching reading and writing in their content classes is enormous, even overwhelming. As Marge laments, they may protest, "My job is teaching content, not reading and writing. That's the reading teacher's problem." This notion is understandable, but reading and writing are *not* the sole responsibility of the reading teacher. The task is large and important, and it should not be minimized. As Bev, John, and Don have discovered since our initial encounter with them, when classroom teachers assume (and share) the responsibilities for helping students read and write better, their jobs become more, not less, manageable.

COMPONENTS OF A COMPLETE READING PROGRAM

Practicing teachers who have worked through unit planning, selection of alternative reading materials, and various other instructional techniques suggested in earlier chapters report that it has taken them as long as three years to convert a full year's course to a format which reflects careful integration of reading and writing with content. Teachers have a limited amount of time to spend in planning. New teachers like Janet who feel overwhelmed by the amount of planning described in this text are therefore advised to take things one step at a time. Implementing these teaching techniques becomes easier as teachers gain more practice with them. Practice also helps teachers identify which techniques fit their specific content area or particular students better. This is the basis for the professional judgments that have been discussed elsewhere in this book.

Teaching reading as part of content classes is only one component of a complete school reading program. The three major components that should be present at all levels of schooling, kindergarten through twelve, are: the developmental reading program (including corrective reading instruction), the content reading program, and the remedial reading program. The relative emphasis to be placed on each component will differ as grade levels increase. Figure 14.1 presents a graphic version of the changing emphasis on the three components at different grade levels. The figure is suggestive rather than prescriptive, intended to illustrate an approximation of the emphasis in effective school reading programs.

CHANGING EMPHASIS ON THE COMPONENTS OF THE READING PROGRAM

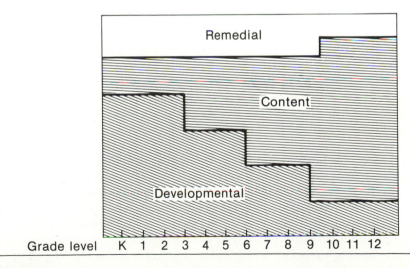

Grade level   K 1 2 3 4 5 6 7 8 9 10 11 12

Figure 14.1

The Developmental Reading Component

Becoming a mature reader is a continuous process through all grade levels. A broad reading program that serves to increase reading ability must recognize the sequential development of reading skills. *Developmental reading* involves teaching students how to read, that is, the basic processes of reading and their applications in students' developing lifestyles.

In the primary grades, developmental reading is easy to identify. It refers to the process of beginning reading, the need for students to be taught and to practice reading to become fluent readers. As students progress through the grades, developmental concerns shift to advancing students' word attack skills and their use of higher levels of comprehension, including critical reading skills. The need for instruction in working with expository writing, searching skills, and multiple sources becomes paramount. When students reach senior high school, developmental tasks may be more vocationally oriented or geared to higher level study skills. The emphasis on developing new reading skills gradually diminishes as students move to higher skill levels. However, the need for a developmental component in the total reading program never completely disappears as students continue to refine the skills they already possess. As content teachers discover that students with adequate overall reading ability exhibit difficulty in content reading skills, corrective reading instruction within the developmental program becomes an issue.

The Content Reading Component

General reading development is enhanced through practice; content reading can provide this practice through application of learned reading skills. This application reinforces the concept that reading is a process in which the content of the writer's message and the reader's reaction to that message are inseparable (Hill, 1979; Rosenblatt, 1976). In addition to the reinforcement of reading skills, content reading affords opportunities for challenging students to learn new reading skills specific to content subjects. These new skills reflect the increasing complexity of reading demands that are central to academic learning at successive instructional levels.

It is important to keep in mind that content reading is not limited to the middle and secondary school levels. Students begin reading materials in math, science, and social studies in the elementary grades. Teachers in the primary grades may not emphasize content reading, however, since reading materials at those levels are more often written in the narrative form, not the expository form typical of higher level content materials. Content reading therefore becomes the emphasis of the reading program beginning with the intermediate grades (4–8) and continues to be the major focus through the secondary school years. In essence, content reading is the *application* of developmental reading skills to the situations in which adults use reading—to gain information.

The Remedial Reading Component

Defining "remedial reading" is not a simple task. Different sources suggest different definitions. However, remedial students are most commonly defined as: 1) those students in grades four through eight who read two or more grade levels below grade placement, and those in grades nine through twelve who read three or more grade levels below grade placement as measured by a standardized reading achievement test (Spache, 1976).

These students are not necessarily exceptional, as defined by PL 94-142, although they may be. They may also be bilingual or bidialectal; however, not all exceptional, bilingual, or bidialectal students need remedial help in reading. Teachers, students, and society at large should avoid stereotyping students in this way. Teachers should instead consider which students need remedial reading help based solely on each individual's diagnosed needs in reading.

Schools should maintain an effective remedial component throughout the school reading program. This represents a philosophical position that the school, and indirectly the society supporting the school, owes its young people a continuing opportunity to master this most basic of skills, reading. As a country and as a profession, we have accepted the proposition that literacy is important, indeed fundamental, to a democratic society. Thus, we need to provide support for those students who do not attain the increasing reading levels of their peers and are classified as needing remedial help. Students who need remedial instruction should receive intensive reading assistance to supplement the regular classroom reading instruction.

THE ORGANIZATION OF THE SCHOOL READING PROGRAM

The organization of reading programs will vary in different situations. Several factors will help to establish a particular school's program. These factors include the characteristics of the student population and the availability of funds, facilities, materials, and personnel. The professional climate of the school—that is, administrative and faculty commitment—will also influence the operation and success of the program.

School administrators, particularly the *principal,* need to demonstrate instructional leadership. Wilhite (1984) has delineated three categories of the principal's role in the reading program based on a survey of principals' views of their roles. Some of the principal's duties are administrative and

Marge works closely with two remedial readers in the reading resource room, an important part of the schoolwide reading/writing program at Middlewood.

are mainly concerned with the selection, evaluation, and development of staff. Operational responsibilities include planning for facilities and financing, as well as implementing and evaluating programs. The principal should also be involved in public relations to help facilitate the communication between school and community. The principal can play a major role in shaping the reading program of a particular school by providing the innovative leadership that helps determine, but not dictate, the program direction.

Many school districts support an organized district-wide reading program, from kindergarten through grade twelve, that is usually managed by a *reading supervisor or coordinator*. This professional position requires not only teaching experience, but experience as a reading teacher or specialist. The reading supervisor, like the principal, has administrative duties that include overseeing the complete reading program, selecting and evaluating reading teachers, ordering materials, and organizing staff development programs on reading for the entire faculty.

Frequently, the reading supervisor is also the school district's director of the supplementary federally funded reading program. Chapter 1 of the Education Consolidation and Improvement Act of 1981 was designed to provide intensive remedial education for students from disadvantaged or poverty-level homes. It replaced Title I, a part of the federal educational programs of the 1960s included in the Elementary and Secondary Education Act (ESEA). This program was reauthorized in 1988 under the Hawkins-Stafford Elementary and Secondary School Improvement Amendments. Under this program, the federal government provides grants to the states, which set up their own system of eligibility and funding within the federal guidelines. In many parts of the country, a large portion of the remedial reading instruction provided in the schools is supported by this funding. In these programs, students receive supplemental instruction in reading skills after careful diagnosis. Parental involvement is required, although the types of programs for parents vary widely among states.

Chapter I teachers, that is, teachers supported by federal funds, are *reading specialists* or people hired specifically for reading instruction. In many states, reading specialist certification is a level beyond initial teacher certification requiring graduate work in reading in addition to several years of classroom teaching experience. As reading specialists, these teachers provide supportive reading instruction to small groups of students on the basis of diagnostic evaluation of their reading difficulties. Reading classes maintain a small teacher-pupil ratio (generally one to six in elementary schools, one to ten in secondary schools). In many cases, Chapter I teachers also serve as resources for content teachers, particularly at the middle and secondary levels.

RESOURCE PERSONS IN THE SCHOOLWIDE PROGRAM

The *resource teacher in reading* is an important part of the schoolwide reading program. The most important function of this teacher, for our purposes, is working with content teachers in developing the materials and plans described in this book. Like Marge at Middlewood Middle and Secondary School, the reading resource teacher is an excellent source for alternative reading materials, especially materials written at lower reading levels. This teacher is also a resource for teaching techniques—new ways to teach vocabulary, study skills, or critical reading—and is usually responsible for testing students' reading levels.

Content teachers should refer to the reading resource teacher any students who exhibit difficulty in reading content materials and who have not already undergone diagnostic testing in reading. They might also examine a student's permanent record files for the results of previous diagnostic testing. It is important for content teachers to seek out the reading resource teacher in their school to discuss what services are being provided to assist them in their work. Bev, John, Don, and Janet have all learned how best to utilize Marge's specialized training as they have encountered students with problems in reading and writing.

Other personnel within the school play lesser roles in the schoolwide reading program. The school *librarian* is an important resource for identifying and ordering materials for specific classes. S/he can instruct teachers in research processes and library procedures. Content teachers should use the librarian's expertise in developing reading lists, formulating lists of research topics, and building classroom libraries for specific units. These resources include periodicals and reference materials, such as maps, as well as books.

Another resource person is the *audiovisual specialist*. This person is an excellent source of media materials (for example, films, filmstrips, or slides) that are appropriate for particular units. Teachers who want to develop their own media—videotapes, audiotapes, slides, transparencies, and the like—may consult the AV specialist for assistance. The AV specialist is familiar with the district's resources in materials and equipment for building new AV materials as well as the availability of materials from other sources. In some states, the duties of the librarian and the audiovisual specialist may be combined to some extent in a position called *media specialist*.

A further resource person for content teachers is the *special education resource teacher*. This teacher, who is certified to deal with exceptional children, may teach a self-contained class of special students or operate a special education resource room. In the resource room, exceptional students who are mainstreamed in some subjects receive separate instruction for other subjects. The special education resource teacher is an excellent source for information on specific handicaps, for instructional materials designed specifically for exceptional children, for advice on implementing IEPs, and for general support in working with exceptional students. (You may recall Janet's concern in Chapter 13 when she discovered that a student was to be mainstreaming into one of her classes.) Marge urged her to consult with the school psychologist, Robert Diaz, as well as the students' resource room teacher for advice. The resource room specialist is also a key person for tapping into the vast array of specialists available for specific handicapping conditions, such as speech clinicians, and for the more general needs served by the school psychologist (Cartwright, Cartwright & Ward, 1981).

A final resource person for the content teacher is the *school counselor*. Counselors serve a wide variety of needs within schools, from running the schoolwide testing programs to scheduling students' classes to counseling individual students. Counselors are often involved in the IEP process, as well as in helping students and their parents make decisions about program and specific courses. Content teachers will find that counselors, in most instances, maintain the permanent records of students. Thus, when the content teacher needs information on past experiences and performance of a student, primary sources are the counselor and the permanent records. The counselor is also a source of information on a student's immediate problems, such as divorce or illness in the family, or on recurrent school problems, like truancy or disciplinary problems. A counselor can identify serious and continuing reading problems, often coupled with

The school psychologist can provide valuable information for both resource teachers and classroom teachers. Here, Middlewood's psychologist, Bob Diaz, meets with Bev and one of her math students to explain the results of a recent testing session.

other personal problems, when s/he goes over a student's records with the student.

The resources of a school with a schoolwide reading program, both people and materials, are many and varied. A program like the one described here provides all sorts of support mechanisms for content teachers who may seek them out. By and large, these resources will not come to the teacher; the teacher must go to them. As the teachers at Middlewood have discovered, they need to ask Marge for help; in order to develop a beneficial working relationship with resource people, content teachers should consider the following guidelines (Robinson & Good, 1987).

The teacher and the resource person should develop a cooperative relationship to help each other provide appropriate services to students. They should be candid about their concerns and discuss them openly. In addition to discussions, the teacher should invite the resource person to observe and participate in class activities to promote objective evaluation of teaching procedures or student behavior. The teacher should also keep the resource person informed of current classroom curriculum and student performance, especially for students who receive multiple services. These services should be coordinated to avoid giving conflicting, isolated, or disjointed instruction.

Unfortunately, not all schools have the complete reading program described here, nor do they all have professional employees like Marge who are willing to work cooperatively with content teachers. It becomes important for content teachers to seek the resources available in the teaching situation in which they find themselves. Then they must use the available resources to help themselves and the students they teach. The professional teacher is knowledgeable of available resources and is willing to use the expertise of others to fulfill obligations in a proficient manner.

WHAT ABOUT THE SCHOOLWIDE WRITING PROGRAM?

Conceptualizing writing as a curriculum component for kindergarten through grade twelve is just as critical as considering reading in this way. Throughout this text we have referred to the importance of providing a great deal of teacher-directed instruction in writing in order that students acquire the skills required for effective, clearly written communication. Writing instruction within the context of the content area classroom is not only desirable but essential, not only practical, but possible.

Just as reading demands change as students move upward in the grades, so do the demands of writing. In the early grades, most of what students read is in the narrative, or story, form. Gradually they begin to read more and more in the areas of social studies, science, and math where the reading becomes less narrative and more expository in form. Such a shift demands not only increased reading proficiency but a shift in the kinds of skills needed.

Likewise, during the early years, students generally do most of their writing in the narrative form, retelling stories of their own experiences or fantasizing experiences using their developing imaginations. Gradually they are expected to begin writing in a variety of forms. They may be asked to write persuasive essays, business letters, or investigative reports. These demand more precision and logic than most narrative writings. Students will not make the transition to such demanding assignments without careful, directed instruction at each grade level and in each content area classroom (Lee, 1987).

Thus, the early reading program helps students master the basics of decoding and bringing meaning to the printed page; the early writing program should help students acquire the confidence to express themselves on paper. But neither discipline can stop there. As already described in some detail in this chapter, the *schoolwide reading program* takes students from the basics through the specifics needed at each successive grade level. Likewise, the *schoolwide writing program* takes students from the basics of written expression through the specific competencies they will need if they are to acquire skill in written language. In Chapter 6 you got a firsthand look at how Don effectively used content area writing to make this transition from "learning to write" to "writing to learn."

EVALUATING THE SCHOOLWIDE READING/WRITING PROGRAM

The schoolwide reading/writing program should be evaluated periodically to determine if it is indeed effective in meeting the needs of the students. This evaluation should be conducted by representatives of the faculty from the different content areas as well as by resource personnel to provide as much pertinent data as possible.

A four-stage model can be used to evaluate reading programs (Burg et al., 1978). A *needs assessment* is the first stage of the model. In this stage, those conducting the assessment should identify the short- and long-term goals of the program. During the *program planning* stage, teachers use the goals identified in the first stage to design a new program or modify an existing one. They also develop an evaluation plan at this point to determine data collection procedures and desired outcomes. The *formative evaluation* stage is concerned with monitoring the progress of the ongoing program. Teachers examine this progress in terms of teacher behavior, student-teacher interaction, and student achievement. The last stage, *summative evaluation,* is conducted at the end of the program. This stage provides data on the success of the entire program. In addition to gathering information on student achievement, teacher behavior, and classroom and school characteristics, the program's administrators can gather opinions about the program from teachers, resource personnel, students, parents, and outside consultants.

The evaluation process will identify the major strengths and weaknesses of the program and indicate necessary classroom instructional changes. A school should maintain an evaluation system that provides for periodic appraisal to keep the program vital and meaningful.

SUMMARY

Content teachers need to understand the three components of the complete reading program—the developmental, content, and remedial components. The resources available within these components are important for content teachers to understand and use: the reading resource teacher, often a Chapter I teacher; the reading supervisor or coordinator; the principal; the librarian; the audiovisual specialist; the special education resource teacher; the school psychologist; and the counselor. The content teacher can receive support from many resource persons, but they must be sought out and used appropriately.

The schoolwide writing program should be visible and clearly defined so that teachers and students know how writing skills are involved throughout the curriculum. As students move upward through the grades, they will be expected to write at increasingly diverse and complex levels.

Evaluation is an important part of the schoolwide reading/writing program. Personnel from several areas of a school and different grade levels and subject areas should be involved in the process. Periodic evaluation will help determine the focus, structure, and direction of the reading/writing program.

REFERENCES

Burg, L. A., Kaufman, M., Korngold, B., & Kovner, A. (1978). *The complete reading supervisor*. Columbus, OH: Merrill Publishing Co.

Cartwright, G. P., Cartwright, C. C. & Ward, M. E. (1981). *Educating special learners*. Belmont, CA: Wadsworth, Inc.

Early, M. (1984). *Reading to learn in grades 5 to 12*. New York: Harcourt Brace Jovanovich.

Hill, W. R. (1979). *Secondary school reading: Process, program, procedure*. Boston: Allyn & Bacon, Inc.

Lee, J. W. (1987). Topic selection in writing: A precarious best practical balancing act. *The Reading Teacher, 41,* 180–184.

Robinson, R. & Good, T. L. (1987). *Becoming an effective reading teacher*. New York: Harper and Row Publishers, Inc.

Rosenblatt, L. (1976). *Literature as exploration* (3rd ed.). New York: Noble and Noble Publishers, Inc.

Spache, G. D. (1976). *Diagnosing and correcting reading disabilities*. Boston: Allyn & Bacon, Inc.

Wilhite, R. K. (1984). Principals' views of their role in the high school reading program. *Journal of Reading, 27,* 356–358.

SUGGESTIONS FOR FURTHER READING

Alvermann, D. E., Moore, D. W., & Conley, M. W. (Eds.). (1987). *Research within reach: Secondary school reading*. Newark, DE: International Reading Association.

Hill, W. R. (1979). *Secondary school reading: Process, program, procedure*. Boston: Allyn & Bacon, Inc.

CHAPTER FIFTEEN

Encouraging Teachers' Professional Growth

SCENARIO

We've covered a lot of territory since that first glimpse of the staff at Middlewood Middle and Secondary School. We've overheard their complaints about administrative edicts, and we've witnessed their frustrations with students unable to read assignments and their triumphs as they found that suggested strategies *can* make a difference in the classroom.

Let's take one last look at some of Middlewood's staff members as they gather for coffee prior to the final faculty meeting of the year. One of the items on the agenda is "New teaching ideas for next year." As we've come to expect, some teachers seem to have negative roles in staff exchanges. Despite positive changes in curriculum, despite successful experiences with new teaching ideas, despite effective support services, there are always those who will approach any hint of "change" with great suspicion and the defeatist attitude that insists "it won't work."

"This coffee better be good and strong, John. I don't look forward to this meeting," complained Bev. "Why doesn't this administration just leave the teaching to us instead of always coming up with suggestions for change?"

"I agree," grumbled Don, joining his colleague from the math department at the coffee urn. "I recall too vividly the year I came here and the big move was team teaching in our department. I got a notice two weeks before Labor Day that two of us were expected to handle all the science classes in seventh and eighth grade."

"I remember that innovation well, Don," laughed Bev. "Your 'partner' left the profession after that year!"

"Do you remember when they brought in SPI?" asked Bev. "What did that stand for? Self-Programmed Instruction?"

"No, I think it was Self-Paced Instruction, wasn't it?" replied Don.

"Yes, and that experiment didn't work out so well either," said Bev. "I really thought it was a good idea and tried a lot of the suggestions that university expert gave us. I still use a lot of the materials, in fact. But most teachers just ran off hundreds of dittoes and called it innovation. Somehow the initial enthusiasm wore off and the program fizzled."

"Good point, Bev. But you know, it seems to me that good ideas too often get lost around here," observed Don. "Look at all the suggestions Marge has made the past couple of years for helping our students improve their reading and writing skills in our classes. You have to admit that most of her ideas have been practical and have gotten us good results. Wouldn't it be too bad to lose all the momentum we've built up?"

They arrived in the library where the rest of the faculty were gathering for the meeting. "I guess you're right," conceded Bev. "When good ideas come along, we've got to be sure we don't lose them among all the other things that are going on. Maybe we can bring up that idea at the end of our meeting today. It would be a good way to end the year on a positive note and give all of us something to think about in terms of professional growth for next fall."

OVERVIEW

In this chapter we discuss change as a process, not as an isolated event. We examine change as it relates to education and the unique culture of schools. Change can be very threatening to staff. Therefore, we analyze the factors which can inhibit the change process, and we suggest methods of facilitating change. These methods take into consideration the forces which inhibit change as well as the forces which enable change. We also take a look at the functional roles of individuals who are involved in the change process.

The chapter concludes with two important models for initiating and assessing change. These are generic models which have been adapted for implementing content area reading and writing. They have proven to be effective in many school settings with many endeavors. Finally, we suggest some ways for teachers to change their own behavior, as well as that of their peers.

TEACHER REACTION TO CHANGE

Many teachers comprehend the term *change* in the same way some of their students understand the word *criticism*. To students, criticism connotes only the negative, fault-finding aspect of the concept; but as we know, criticism can be positive. It may result in personal development. To some teachers, the word "change" connotes trouble and frustration. It carries an implicit notion that something is lacking in their current practice. But just as criticism can be very positive, so can change. In one sense, education *is* change. Many staff developers view teachers who resist change as exhibiting the ultimate paradoxical behavior. Teachers want students to change (learn), but teachers themselves resist change (growth). One of the most difficult hurdles for someone who wishes to introduce change is to get teachers to believe that they are not being accused of doing something wrong. It is important to acknowledge that most teachers do a very good job; and the suggestions in this book are offered to help teachers move from very good to excellent. It is just as the old cliché says, "One either gets better or gets worse: there is no standing still."

Proposing that teachers include more reading and writing in their classrooms is a change process, but educational change has had a history of failure. Many teachers have had to endure one administrative edict after another in the name of change. They have had neither the appropriate amount of preparation nor the necessary amount of time to implement the innovations that they have been asked to implement.

Anyone who is genuinely interested in initiating change within a school will benefit by first considering the research. Because there is inherent potential for trauma with any change, it is useful to know some of the reasons why people feel uncomfortable when faced with change. Through his extensive study on this subject, Ronald Havelock (1973) identified the following as common causes for resisting change:

1. *Uncertainty* as to just what a change will bring. Even though the current situation may not be satisfactory to teachers, they may not care to risk the possibility of a poorer situation.
2. *Ignorance* of the need for or purpose of the change. Often changes are made with little or no explanation to teachers, sometimes with the presumption that this is none of their business.
3. *Pressure* of the work group. Each member of the work group often reacts so as not to offend the others, even though as an individual s/he does not feel as strongly as his/her actions would indicate. Every work group has certain ingrained policies, some expressed and others implied, that constitute a "code of behavior" and that help to govern the actions and reactions of its members. People's reactions to change are usually influenced by what they know or anticipate that the group wants, even to the point of sacrificing personal gain for continued approval of co-workers. According to Havelock's findings, older members, who are the most frequent and stubborn resistors, are often the most influential persons in the work group.
4. *Fear* of economic insecurity. A change may result in displacement of employees or a reduction in their earnings. The matter

may arise especially if teachers show an inability to master the new method, or at least to reach the level of proficiency that they had attained under the replaced method.

5. An *antagonistic attitude* toward the person introducing the change or what s/he represents. It may be a personal antagonism, or it may be an antagonism toward his/her function or toward management in general. The latter, an attitude that is often hostile, causes individuals and groups to resist almost any change, in fact almost everything but the pay check, that comes from the direction of management. This might be called "resistance on general principles." The underlying attitude is common.

6. *Origination or introduction by an "outsider."* Superintendents and/or principals are usually considered as external to the teachers' economic and social group; in fact they are frequently quite unpopular. If such persons introduce or are known to have originated a change, teachers are likely to feel resentful.

7. *No participation* in formulation of the new method or policy. It appears to teachers that changes are often adopted without their best interests in mind. They want an opportunity to express and protect these interests and to have a part in deciding what they must do and how.

8. *A tactless approach* on the part of the person introducing the change.

9. *Inopportune timing.* Resistance may have been received only because the change was introduced when feeling was running high between the work group and management or because the change was made with little or no advance notice.

Figure 15.1 shows another view of the forces which inhibit and enable change. Adapted from Otto (1973), this model illustrates the dynamics of pedagogical change. One very important factor is that change is a complex process, not a single event. It takes *time*, probably at least two years (Crofton et al., 1981). Because individuals perceive change to be an event, they expect quick implementation and fast results. When their expectations are not met, they often abandon the change or innovation. A few cases in point are team teaching, new math, and open education.

A second factor affecting the adoption of change is *energy*. Most teachers feel that they work very hard. When they are faced with change, many believe they will be expected to work even harder. Teachers need to believe that investing their energy will be worth something in the long run. Change requires hard work.

A third factor affecting change has to do with *productivity*. When teachers invest energy they are eager to realize benefits from the investment. Unfortunately, the benefits of an innovation are not always felt immediately. Often teacher and student productivity gets worse before getting better. On the other hand, a change or innovation could bring about a halo

DYNAMICS OF PEDAGOGICAL CHANGE

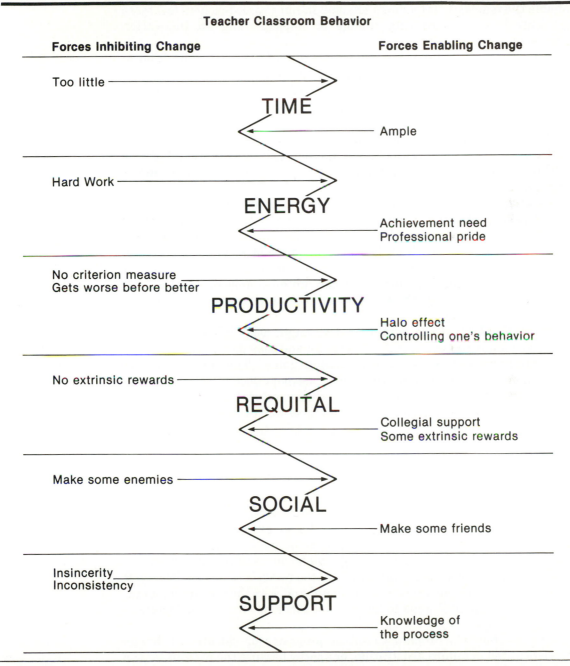

Teacher Classroom Behavior

Forces Inhibiting Change   **Forces Enabling Change**

Too little ——————————————►

TIME

◄——————————— Ample

Hard Work ——————————————►

ENERGY

◄——————————— Achievement need
Professional pride

No criterion measure ————————►
Gets worse before better

PRODUCTIVITY

◄——————————— Halo effect
Controlling one's behavior

No extrinsic rewards ——————————►

REQUITAL

◄——————————— Collegial support
Some extrinsic rewards

Make some enemies ——————————►

SOCIAL

◄——————————— Make some friends

Insincerity ————————————————►
Inconsistency

SUPPORT

◄——————————— Knowledge of
the process

Figure 15.1

Adapted from "Dynamics of Curriculum Change" by Wayne Otto and Lawrence Erickson, *Inservice Education to Improve Reading Instruction*, p. 3. Reprinted with permission of Wayne Otto and the International Reading Association.

effect wherein attention is focused on a teacher's efforts. The attention can enable the teacher to implement change. In some cases teachers feel more in control when instituting change or implementing an innovation themselves.

A fourth factor influencing change is *requital*. A potent inhibition to educational change is the fact that there are no extrinsic rewards. Some districts have recognized this and have offered incentives. For other teachers, the support and enthusiasm of their colleagues has enabled them to implement change.

There are *social* factors affecting change, as well. Each school has a culture. There are often "pro-change" factions and "anti-change" factions within a faculty. Peer pressure can be a potent inhibitor or enabler in the change process.

Finally, the amount of support a teacher gets to achieve change is critical. Constant support from administrators, consultants, or other teachers can be a powerful enabler when teachers attempt to implement change. The success of peer coaching is a good example of what can be accomplished when teachers are given support via feedback. Inconsistency or mere lip service from administrators can inhibit change dramatically. A pattern of insincerity with regard to supporting change can inhibit the process permanently.

Understandably, some administrators might ask, "What's the big issue? We simply tell our teachers to change and they do so." Wrong. Good teachers have learned to "play the change game." They may appear to implement the change, but when the classroom door closes, they only implement what they truly value. If the change process is not perceived as worthwhile, all the directives in the universe won't bring about changes in classroom practice.

THE POSITIVE ASPECTS OF CHANGE

Change can be a very positive experience when it is perceived as growth. Some prerequisite considerations about change are necessary, however, before it can be called "growth." In order to be successful, change should be both rational and responsible; it should be purposeful and systematic; and it should have a close relationship to the needs of students (Becker & Hahn, 1977). Without relevance, purpose, and a method of implementation, any change is doomed to failure. Let's look at some of the factors of positive change.

Change should be *rational*. Countless programs for educational change have resulted in failure, frustration, or apathy because the reasons for the programs were either unclear or unrealistic. Because a school district receives a grant, for example, is not sufficient cause for attempting to implement a program. A change is not warranted simply because an administrator champions a specific program. Even when the need for change is obvious to an individual or group, others who will be expected to make the change must be thoroughly acquainted with the rationale before they can be expected to "buy" into it. For example, it is not sufficient to say that as many as 50 percent of secondary students cannot comprehend their textbooks (Estes & Vaughn, 1978). That may not be true in a given setting, but rational change should come as a result of student needs as determined by school-specific research.

Change should be *responsible*. There should be some orientation prior to the implementation of a change program. Possible starting points for responsible change are gaps between research and practice, results of a school-specific needs assessment, or some otherwise clearly indicated student need. How well do students comprehend their texts? How much do teachers rely on texts to determine student achievement? Is student writing effective for a given subject? What are the collective perceptions of the faculty concerning student reading and writing skills?

Change should be *purposeful*. Without clear goals and specific outcomes, a program for change may lose momentum. If the purpose or purposes are not clear in the beginning, then a program could end up obtaining unanticipated or unintended results. Who will define a purpose for a reading and writing program in the school? How will the staff be included in determining a purpose for such an effort?

Change should be *systematic*. Change occurs over time and not without careful planning. It should be organized with consideration for group behaviors. Perhaps the best examples of dismal attempts to effect change within a school district are one-shot inservice programs. Changing human behavior is such a complex endeavor that it is foolish to think an isolated lecture or workshop will have any lasting effect on educational practice. If change is to result in growth, it must be implemented systematically over time.

Only when change is perceived as growth can it truly be helpful in developing new skills among teaching staff. Positive change is, in effect, staff development of the very best kind. Day (1984) defines staff development as a process designed to foster professional growth for individuals within a respectful, supportive, positive organizational climate which has as its ultimate aim better learning for students and continuous responsible self-renewal for educators. Not all change processes result in staff development, but successful change efforts can draw upon and be guided by research on staff development.

A MODEL FOR CHANGE

One model of staff development can be particularly useful in implementing a reading and writing program in a school (Wood, Thompson, & Russell, 1981). The five steps in this model are readiness, planning, training, implementation, and maintenance (RPTIM). Using the idea that staff development is done *with* someone and not *to* someone, the creators of RPTIM suggest that the group to be affected by the change also be included in directing that change. Therefore, keep in mind as you read about this model that an entire group works through these stages. This is a process where consensus is important and cooperation essential.

Readiness

Readiness is a crucial stage in the design of staff development programs. Readiness activities provide a time for those involved in the proposed change to get better acquainted while becoming familiar with the issues to be addressed. Task-oriented individuals sometimes have a problem with activities designed to build trust and create positive working relationships, but without these activities groups may work in a climate that is not conducive to professional growth. This stage should result in 1) a written set of goals (desired changes in professional behavior) that individuals involved in the change process should select and understand; 2) a broad description of the practices selected to achieve these goals; and 3) a very general five-year plan for implementing the desired change.

Middlewood teachers discuss the need for improving the teaching of reading and writing across the curriculum. The readiness stage is critical to the process of change.

Planning

During this stage, planners further define the goals into more specific program objectives, conduct a needs assessment, plan activities, and identify resources. They also project a plan of action including the activities, the time-lines, the people to be involved, and the costs involved for subsequent training and implementation. Rational planning for change would also include a review of the literature to determine what experts in the field can contribute to formulating the proposed change. In Figure 15.2, Marge has agreed to lead a team of four teachers to prepare a summary of current research on needs assessments.

Training

This stage of the model deals with changing the attitudes, skills, or content knowledge of the staff. Training may take the form of workshops, graduate courses, or group independent study. During training, the staff would engage in structured activities designed to accomplish predetermined goals. While training can occur throughout a school district, it has been determined that the school building is the most promising unit in which to achieve change (Goodlad, 1984). Learning teams within a building can act as support groups to carry out the change program.

A mini RPTIM exists within the training stage. Teams need to go through an orientation experience to achieve readiness. While the goals have been planned previously, specific outcomes should be clarified before learning teams embark on a change program. Training should take the characteristics of adult learners into account and should capitalize on experiential learning with choices for participants. At the conclusion of the training, the authors of the model suggest that participants make a

SAMPLE MANAGEMENT CHART FOR CHANGE

Goals & Objectives	Activities	Person(s) Involved	Person(s) Responsible	Timelines	Resources Needed
Develop a Needs Assessment to determine the current-status of content-specific reading skills	Summarize the current research	Marge Don Bev John	Marge	Rough Draft by 9/15; Pilot on 9/30; Final Draft on 10/15	• Relevant research findings • List of issues from staff • Release time for committee

Figure 15.2

commitment to use what has been learned. It is appropriate at this stage to identify the evaluation techniques that will be used to assess the change. The authors should consider both cognitive and affective measures, evaluating process as well as product outcomes.

When the training of staff is at issue, the question of using outside consultants usually arises. There are points to be made on both sides of this issue. Often the district or school has sufficient expertise to train staff. In cases where this is true, using "in-house" trainers may be advisable. Some resident experts do not always feel comfortable training colleagues with whom they work every day. Some trainers, while eager, do not have the credibility necessary to lead a training program. Good outside consultants often have the credibility but lack the intimacy with the staff members to be effective trainers. Outsiders may also be too expensive or too remote. Perhaps the best approach to training is to use a combination of both.

Implementation

Teachers everywhere can testify to the fact that most inservice programs designed to change teachers' behavior have resulted in fostering no change whatsoever in the classroom. The other steps in this model are useless unless implementation of new skills, attitudes, or behaviors occurs. It is important that training result in implementation as soon as possible. It is also important that follow-up assistance be readily available when teachers attempt to implement something new into their repertoire.

Peer coaching or colleague consultation, as described by Goldsberry (1982), is one method used to assist the implementation of a change. Teachers who go through training together are in the best position to confer about implementation of a new skill. Boyan and Copeland (1978) suggest that classroom observation and data collection are just as important as conferencing. These methods result in the encouragement and feedback for teachers which not only ensures implementation of the change but also paves the way for the final stage of the RPTIM model.

Maintenance

The final stage of the RPTIM model involves assessing and maintaining the skills acquired during training. Wood et al. (1981) refer to this stage as a continuous review. When the maintenance stage is reached, one cycle of RPTIM is complete. As in any systematic attempt to change, an evaluation of the program will yield information on which to build. Therefore, readiness and planning begin again and the RPTIM process may begin another cycle.

While RPTIM is a general framework for educational change, it can be used effectively with staff development in reading and writing. Many teachers are aware that reading from text is a major obstacle for their students. Even more teachers recognize that writing is arduous and re-pugnant for too large a portion of their students. In some districts the need may be present in the minds of faculty: it may only be a matter of bringing teachers together to discuss these issues. Building faculty consensus to deal with reading and writing, mobilizing admininstrative support, and identifying individuals to play special roles in this process is the first stage of readiness for focusing on these vital aspects of the curriculum.

CHANGE AGENTS

The individuals who play these special roles are involved in creating an awareness of new ideas; assessing the needs and concerns of students, parents, and teachers; and relating research results to such concerns. Becker and Hahn (1977) refer to these people as "change agents." In the case of reading and writing, these individuals may be classroom teachers, reading specialists, principals, or central office administrators. Ideally, all of those individuals will be involved in any decision-making process with regard to building a reading and writing program across the curricu-lum. Administrative support is essential but insufficient to ensure a last-ing change. It is crucial that teachers have a legitimate role in the plan-ning, implementation, and maintenance of any program. More than one good program conceived at the administrative level has encountered strong resistance because the people who were expected to implement the idea—teachers—had no say, and therefore no ownership in the program. Change is best done *with* teachers, not *to* them.

Research results from numerous studies (Goodlad, 1984) have indicat-ed that the individual school is the most effective unit with which to work in order to bring about change. Since change is a diffusion process, it is useful to examine the dynamics of a school prior to embarking on any new program. In their insightful text, *Workbook for Educational Change* (1977), James Becker and Carol Hahn suggest that there are two ways of examining school dynamics or organizational climates which may be use-ful in developing change. One way is to look at individuals in terms of the function they perform in the change process: Do they initiate ideas? Do they influence other people's opinions? Do they need to give their approval in order for the change to be considered? Are they first or last to adopt new ideas?

Another way to view individuals is by the formal positions they hold. According to Becker and Hahn, functional roles are informal roles. Three such roles are *inside advocate, opinion leader,* and *legitimizer.* These roles are situational in nature. Depending on the proposed change, a person may be an opinion leader in one instance and a legitimizer in another.

Rodgers and Shoemaker (1971) have reported on other functional roles. Let's examine these roles with reading and writing across the curriculum as our focus.

INDIVIDUAL ROLES IN THE CHANGE PROCESS

A legitimizer is someone in the social system who supports a change agent's efforts, while the inside advocate is a person from within the system who sees it as in his/her best interest for the system to adopt a program for reading and writing throughout the curriculum. The inside advocate then moves the idea through formal or informal channels. At Middlewood this person could be Don or Bev, but Marge is a more likely candidate. Unfortunately, many potential inside advocates are not aware that a problem exists throughout a district. To compound the problem, outside change agents do not know which people are potential advocates within a particular school staff. Identifying inside advocates, bringing them together, and linking them with outside change agents can be crucial to a successful reading and writing program.

A second functional role of great importance to change is that of an opinion leader. Jwaideh and Marker (1973) have described opinion leaders as the persons who are able to influence informally the attitudes or overt behaviors of other members of a social system. These leaders often provide information and advice about innovations to many other members. Marge has filled this role throughout this book. Opinion leadership is a type of informal leadership that is not necessarily related to a person's formal status in the system, although formal leaders may function also as opinion leaders.

Opinion leaders may hold a leadership role on the basis of their expertise or technical competence, their social accessibility, or their conformity to the norms of their system. Because of these characteristics, they often serve as models for the behavior of their followers with regard to innovations. The opinion leaders in a modern social system tend to be innovative, whereas the opinion leaders in a traditional social system often are non-innovative (Jwaideh & Marker, 1973).

It is important for change agents to realize that opinion leaders are accepted as "one of us" by members of their social system and that they follow the norms of that system. Opinion leaders are not likely to deviate much from tradition and do not take great risks in trying new things. In fact, people who first try innovations may be rejected by members of their social systems as deviates, and a change agent's close identification with that innovator could hinder his/her efforts to bring about change.

Self-report, reports by all members, and reports from key individuals about who turns to whom for ideas and opinions will help identify opinion leaders. At faculty meetings or principals' meetings and in the teachers' lounge or lunchroom, it will be obvious whose opinions seem to be respected and considered carefully by others.

It is important to consider individuals and their informal status in an organization before selecting a group to initiate a change program. Too often, new programs are doomed because an administrator is not aware of a staff member's status. Unfortunately, committee members are selected or not selected for the wrong reasons. Other staff perceive them to be "friends of the administration." One school superintendent selected a staff development committee by choosing his most resistant teachers. Through the use of RPTIM, they became a cohesive group of leaders that had a dramatic influence in creating a successful staff development model.

ASSESSING THE CHANGE PROCESS

Once a committee is formed, the planning complete, other teachers trained, and the program implemented, it becomes necessary to determine what impact a program is having in the classroom. It has been suggested that change has numerous dimensions. Teachers demonstrate a wide variation in the degree of their use of new techniques (Hall et al., 1979). Figure 15.3 offers various levels of use of a reading/writing program. When a program is in place, teachers can identify the level of their

LEVELS OF USE OF A READING/WRITING PROGRAM[1]

Typical Behaviors

Level of Use	Behavioral Indices of Level
VI RENEWAL	The user is seeking more effective alternatives to the established use of Reading/Writing in the Content Areas.
V INTEGRATION	The user is making deliberate efforts to coordinate with others in implementing the Reading/Writing Program.
IVB REFINEMENT	The user is making changes to increase outcomes.
IVA ROUTINE	The user is making few or no changes and has an established pattern of use.
III MECHANICAL USE	The user is using the Reading/Writing Program in a poorly coordinated manner and is making user-oriented changes.
II PREPARATION	The user is preparing to use new techniques in Reading/Writing.
I ORIENTATION	The user is seeking out information about the Reading/Writing Program.
0 NONUSE	No action is being taken with respect to Reading/Writing.

Figure 15.3

[1]For further information, see Hall, G. E., Wallace, R. C., and Dossett, W. F., "A Developmental Conceptualization of the Adoption Process Within Educational Institutions," Procedures for Adopting Educational Innovations Project, Research and Development Center for Teacher Education, University of Texas at Austin.

use of reading/writing activities on this chart. Analyzing a faculty's use of desired behaviors in this way can help evaluate the effectiveness of the change process.

Assessing change is vitally important for several reasons. Teachers need to know that the change has made a significant difference in their students. Administrators need to see demonstrable change in order to continue their interest and support. Boards of education need to see evidence of the positive effects of change so that they can justify the support of the district. In public schools, accountability is a priority.

There are numerous assessment models, including Hall's "Levels of Use" mentioned above. Assessors who state goals and objectives, select observable outcomes, and systematically measure those outcomes may customize these procedures to fit the local change process. They can sustain enthusiasm for change by regularly reporting the results of the assessment to the teacher participants, the administration, the school board, and the public. Don and Bev will be more willing to continue their work if they feel they are succeeding and if they feel that their colleagues know about their success.

Change is a fact of life in schools and in society in general. Yet, though we know this is true, we all find it uncomfortable at times. Those of us who are asked to encourage and direct change need to be sensitive to the needs of those who are asked to change.

SUMMARY

Changing professionals' behavior is a complex process. Significant factors in change include time, energy, productivity, requital, social pressures, and support. We have identified a number of causes for resisting change, including uncertainty about the nature of the change, ignorance of its purpose, pressure within the work group, fear of economic insecurity, antagonistic attitudes, introduction by outsiders, and lack of participation by the group to be changed. Principles underlying effective change include an emphasis on professional growth. Change should be rational, responsible, purposeful, and systematic. This chapter contains a five-part model of staff development. The five steps in this model are readiness, planning, training, implementation, and maintenance (RPTIM). Functional roles of the change process include the inside advocate, the opinion leader, and the legitimizer. The participants' assessment of the effectiveness of change processes is important to assure success.

REFERENCES

Becker, J. & Hahn, C. L. (1977). *Wingspread workbook for educational change* (rev. ed.). Boulder, CO: Social Science Education Consortium.

Boyan, N. J. & Copeland, W. D. (1978). *Instructional supervision training program*. Columbus, OH: Merrill Publishing Co.

Crofton, C. (1987). Teacher receptivity to systemwide change. In R. F. Waugh & K. F. Punck (Eds.), *Review of Educational Research, 57*(3), 237–254.

Day, B. D. (1984). Foreword. In R. S. Brandt & N. Olson (Eds.), *Staff development/organization development* (p. vii). Association for Supervision and Curriculum Development.

Estes, T. H. & Vaughn, J. L. (1978). *Reading and learning in the content classroom*. Boston: Allyn & Bacon, Inc.

Goldsberry, L. (1982). *Supervision of teaching: Colleagueship in supervision*. Alexandria, VA: Association for Supervision and Curriculum Development

Goodlad, J. (1984). *A place called school: Prospects for the future*. New York: McGraw-Hill Publishing Co.

Hall, G. et al. (1979). A concerns based approach to facilitating change. *Educational Horizon, 57*, 202–208.

Havelock, R. G. (1973). *The change agent's guide to innovation in education*. Englewood Cliffs, NJ: Educational Technology Publications.

Jwaideh, A. R. & Marker, G. W. (1973). A new approach towards changing social studies education. *Indiana Social Studies Quarterly, 26* (1), 5–29.

Otto, W. & Erickson, L. (1973). *Inservice education to improve reading instruction*. Newark, DE: International Reading Association.

Rodgers, E. M. & Shoemaker, F. F. (1971). *Communication of innovations: A cross cultural approach*. New York: Free Press.

Wood, F., Thompson, S., & Russell, F. (1981). Designing effective staff development programs. In B. Dillon-Peterson (Ed.), *Staff development/ organization development*. Alexandria, VA: Association for Supervision and Curriculum Development.

SUGGESTIONS FOR FURTHER READING

Beam, R. M. & Wilson, R. M. (1981). *Effecting change in school reading programs: The resource role*. Newark, DE: International Reading Association.

Shanker, J. L. (1982). *Guidelines for successful reading staff development*. Newark, DE: International Reading Association.

Siedow, M. D., Memory, D. M., & Bristow, P. S. (1985). *Inservice education for content area teachers*. Newark, DE: International Reading Association.

Staff Development/Organization Development. (1981). Alexandria, VA: Association for Supervision and Curriculum Development.

Principles of Learning*

LEARNING PROCESS

1. Students learn best by being actively involved. If they can do a task themselves, they will learn better than if they just read about it.
2. Learning is more effective if the students show "readiness" for what is to be learned.
3. Higher level skills develop slowly.
4. Interaction enhances many types of learning.
5. Learning is enhanced in a supportive, non-threatening atmosphere.
6. If a learner feels good about himself, he has less difficulty with learning. If he has low self-concept, he has more difficulty with learning.
7. One effective way to learn subject matter is to teach it.
8. Non-school subjects are markedly superior to others for "strengthening mental powers." General improvement as a result of study of any subject depends on instruction designed to build up generalizations about principles, concept formation, and improvements of techniques of study, thinking, and communication.
9. Learners must participate to learn effectively.

MOTIVATION

10. Pupils think when they encounter an obstacle, difficulty, puzzle, or challenge in a course of action which interests them. The process of thinking involves designing and testing plausible solutions for the problem as understood by the thinker.
11. The most effective effort is put forth by children when they attempt tasks which fall in the "range of challenge"—not too easy and not to hard—where success seems quite possible but not certain.
12. Disequilibrium, or a perceived discrepancy, is important to learning in that the learner naturally seeks to resolve the discrepancy and reach a new equilibrium.

*Prepared by Jim Levin of The Pennsylvania State University. Used with permission. For further information about learning principles, see G. Watson (1964), What psychology can we trust, in R. E. Ripple, *Readings in learning and human abilities* (pp. 26–37), New York: Harper & Row, Publishers; P. L. Hosford (1973), *An Instructional Theory: A beginning*, Englewood Cliffs, N.J.: Prentice-Hall; and R. M. W. Travers (1977), *Essentials of learning* (4th ed.), New York: Macmillan Publishing Company.

13. Children are more apt to throw themselves wholeheartedly into any project if they themselves have participated in the selection and planning of the enterprise.

REINFORCEMENT

14. Positive or reward reinforcement is more likely to result in learning than negative reinforcement. A teacher who compliments and encourages students is more likely to obtain higher achievement than one who tells them their work is poor or derides them for poor achievement.
15. Intrinsic reward provides more long-range benefit than extrinsic reward. Feelings of accomplishment hold more reward than obtaining a gold star every time something is done correctly. It also has the greatest transfer value to other life situations.
16. Sheer repetition without indications of improvement or any kind of reinforcement is a poor way to attempt to learn.
17. Threats and punishment have variable and uncertain effects upon learning; they may make the punished response more or less likely to recur; they set up avoidance tendencies which prevent further learning.
18. Opportunity for fresh, novel, stimulating experiences is a kind of reward which is quite effective in conditioning and learning.
19. Reinforcement is most effective when it occurs immediately following the appropriate behavior. The reinforcement must be clearly connected with the desired behavior in the mind of the learner.

TRANSFER

20. What is learned is most likely to be available for use if it is learned in a situation much like that in which it is to be used and immediately preceding the time when it is needed.
21. Students learn how to transfer knowledge to new situations only to the extent that they see possibilities for transfer and have opportunities to apply that knowledge. Insights about the transferability seldom occur automatically.
22. Learning is enhanced by a wide variety of experiences related to the idea being presented. In-depth learning is better than attempting to cover many topics in a short time.

RETENTION

23. Forgetting proceeds rapidly at first, then more and more slowly; recall shortly after learning reduces the amount forgotten.

24. Short-term practice sessions are more effective than long-term sessions. Similarly, reading or listening in several short bursts is more effective than attempting to keep one's mind on the subject for long sessions.
25. Learning is increased when it is provided in a rich and varied environment. Bare rooms are not conducive to stimulating learning.
26. The greater the number of senses involved in a learning experience, the more proficient the learning.
27. Improvement of memory depends on improvement of retrieval, which depends on organization.
28. Meaningful material is most easily learned and best retained. If, along with the instruction, a student is aware of the value to be gained by learning the information being presented, the learning process will be easier and the retention will be longer.
29. Mere exposure to content is not sufficient for learning and retention.

MEANING

30. There must be an integration of experience, language, and thought for effective learning.
31. Learning from reading is increased if time is spent on recalling what has been read rather than on re-reading.
32. Generally, learning proceeds most easily if information is presented in order from: simple to complex; familiar to strange; tangible to symbolic; and concrete to abstract.

TEACHING AND TEACHERS

33. Teachers are learners while teaching.
34. Good instructional process exemplifies and controls standards of conduct toward a climate that is warm, rational, and receptive to the efforts of all learners.
35. The good teacher's role is not so much that of explaining content to learners as helping them find the meaning of content.
36. The good teacher will see the implications of much that is known about the growth and development of his/her learners.
37. Teachers can promote analysis, discovery, and probing through questions and by pointing out facts that seem contradictory.

INDIVIDUAL DIFFERENCES

38. Individual differences in age, socioeconomic background, IQ, temperament, human relationship skills, and physical abilities all demand instructional adaptations.

39. Pupils vary not only in their present performance but in their rate of growth and the "ceiling" which represents their potential level of achievement. Some "late bloomers" may eventually surpass pupils who seem far ahead of them in grade school.

GROUP RELATIONS

40. Pupils learn much more from one another; those who have been together for years learn new material more easily from one of their own group than they do from strangers.
41. When groups act for a common goal there is better cooperation and more friendliness than when individuals in the group are engaged in competitive rivalry with one another.
42. Leadership qualities vary with the demands of the particular situation. A good leader for a football team may or may not be a good leader for a discussion group, a research project, or an overnight hike; leadership is not a general trait.

Barrett's Taxonomy of Reading Comprehension*

1.0 **Literal Recognition or Recall.** Literal comprehension requires the recognition or recall of ideas, information, and happenings that are explicitly stated in the materials read. *Recognition Tasks,* which frequently take the form of purposes for reading, require the student to locate or identify explicit statements in the reading selection itself or in exercises that use the explicit content of the reading selection. *Recall tasks* demand the student to produce from memory explicit statements from a selection; such tasks are often in the form of questions teachers pose to students after a reading is completed. Two additional comments seem warranted with regard to literal comprehension tasks. First, although literal comprehension tasks can be overused, their importance cannot be denied, since a student's ability to deal with such tasks is fundamental to his ability to deal with other types of comprehension tasks. Second, all literal comprehension tasks are not necessarily of equal difficulty. For example, the recognition or recall of a single fact or incident may be somewhat easier than the recognition or recall of a number of facts or incidents, while a more difficult task than either of these two may be the recognition or recall of a number of events or incidents and the sequence of their occurrence. Also related to this concern is the hypothesis that a recall task is usually more difficult than a recognition task, when the two tasks deal with the same content and are of the same nature. Some examples[1] of literal comprehension tasks are:

1.1 Recognition or Recall of Details. The student is required to locate or identify or to call up from memory such facts as the names of characters, the time a story took place, the setting of

---

[1]Although the examples in each of the categories are logically ordered from easy to difficult, it is recognized that such a finite hierarchy has not been validated. Therefore, the user of the Taxonomy should view the examples as some of the tasks that might be used to help students produce comprehension products that relate to the type of comprehension described in each of the four major categories of the Taxonomy.

a story, or an incident described in a story, when such facts are explicitly stated in the selection.

1.2 <u>Recognition or Recall of Main Ideas.</u> The student is asked to locate or identify or to produce from memory an explicit statement in or from a selection which is the main idea of a paragraph or a larger portion of the selection.

1.3 <u>Recognition or Recall of Sequence.</u> The student is required to locate or identify or to call up from memory the order of incidents or actions explicitly stated in the selection.

1.4 <u>Recognition or Recall of Comparisons.</u> The student is requested to locate or identify or to produce from memory likenesses and differences among characters, times in history, or places that are explicitly compared by an author.

1.5 <u>Recognition or Recall of Cause and Effect Relationships.</u> The student in this instance may be required to locate or identify or to produce from memory reasons for certain incidents, events, or characters' actions explicitly stated in the selection.

1.6 <u>Recognition or Recall of Character Traits.</u> The student is requested to identify or locate or to call up from memory statements about a character which help to point up the type of person he was when such statements were made by the author of the selection.

2.0 **Inference.** Inferential comprehension is demonstrated by the student when he uses a synthesis of the literal content of a selection, his personal knowledge, his intuition and his imagination as a basis for conjectures or hypotheses. Conjectures or hypotheses derived in this manner may be along convergent or divergent lines, depending on the nature of the task and the reading materials involved. For example, inferential tasks related to narrative selections may permit more divergent or creative conjectures because of the open-ended possibilities provided by such writing. On the other hand, expository selections, because of their content, may call for convergent hypotheses more often than not. In either instance, students may or may not be called upon to indicate the rationale underlying their hypotheses or conjectures, although such a requirement would seem to be more appropriate for convergent rather than divergent hypotheses. Generally, then, inferential comprehension is elicited by purposes for reading, and by teachers' questions which demand thinking and imagination which are stimulated by, but go beyond, the printed page. Examples of inferential tasks related to reading are:

2.1 <u>Inferring Supporting Details.</u> In this instance, the student is asked to conjecture about additional facts the author might have included in the selection which would have made it more informative, interesting, or appealing.

2.2 <u>Inferring the Main Idea</u>. The student is required to provide the main idea, general significance, theme, or moral which is not explicitly stated in the selection.

2.3 <u>Inferring Sequence</u>. The student, in this case, may be requested to conjecture as to what action or incident might have taken place between two explicitly stated actions or incidents; he may be asked to hypothesize about what would happen next; or he may be asked to hypothesize about the beginning of a story if the author had not started where he did.

2.4 <u>Inferring Comparisons</u>. The student is required to infer likenesses and differences in characters, times, or places. Such inferential comparisons revolve around ideas such as: "here and there," "then and now," "he and he," "he and she," and "she and she."

2.5 <u>Inferring Cause and Effect Relationships</u>. The student is required to hypothesize about the motives of characters and their interactions with others and with time and place. He may also be required to conjecture as to what caused the author to include certain ideas, words, characterizations, and actions in this writing.

2.6 <u>Inferring Character Traits</u>. In this case, the student may be asked to hypothesize about the nature of characters on the basis of explicit clues presented in the selection.

2.7 <u>Predicting Outcomes</u>. The student is requested to read an initial portion of a selection, and on the basis of this reading, to conjecture about the outcome of the selection.

2.8 <u>Inferring about Figurative Language</u>. The student, in this instance, is asked to infer literal meanings from the author's figurative use of language.

3.0 **Evaluation.** Evaluation is demonstrated by a student when he makes judgments about the content of a reading selection by comparing it with external criteria, e.g., information provided by the teacher on the subject, authorities on the subject, or by accredited written sources on the subject; or with internal criteria, e.g., the reader's experiences, knowledge, or values related to the subject under consideration. In essence, evaluation requires students to make judgments about the content of their reading—judgments that have to do with its accuracy, acceptability, worth, desirability, completeness, suitability, timeliness, quality, truthfulness, or probability of occurrence. Examples of evaluation tasks related to reading are:

3.1 <u>Judgments of Reality or Fantasy</u>. The student is requested to determine whether incidents, events, or characters in a selection could have existed or occurred in real life on the basis of his experience.

3.2 <u>Judgments of Fact or Opinion.</u> In this case, the student is asked to decide whether the author is presenting information which can be supported with objective data or whether the author is attempting to sway the reader's thinking through the use of subjective content that has overtones of propaganda.

3.3 <u>Judgments of Adequacy or Validity.</u> Tasks of this type call for the reader to judge whether the author's treatment of a subject is accurate and complete when compared to other sources on the subject. In this instance, then, the reader is called upon to compare written sources of information with an eye toward their agreements or disagreements, their completeness or incompleteness, and their thoroughness or superficiality in dealing with a subject.

3.4 <u>Judgments of Appropriateness.</u> Evaluation tasks of this type require the student to determine whether certain selections or parts of selections are relevant and can contribute to resolving an issue or a problem. For example, a student may be requested to judge the part of a selection which most appropriately describes a character. Or he may be called upon to determine which references will make significant contributions to a report he is preparing.

3.5 <u>Judgments of Worth, Desirability, or Acceptability.</u> In this instance, the student may be requested to pass judgments on the suitability of a character's action in a particular incident or episode. Was the character right or wrong, good or bad, or somewhere in between? Tasks of this nature call for opinions based on the values the reader has acquired through his personal experiences.

4.0 **Appreciation.** Appreciation has to do with students' awareness of the literary techniques, forms, styles, and structures employed by authors to stimulate emotional responses in their readers. Obviously, tasks which fall into this category will require varying degrees of inference and evaluation, but their primary focus must be on heightening students' sensitivity to the ways authors achieve an emotional as well as an intellectual impact on their readers. More specifically, appreciation involves cognizance of and visceral response to: (a) the artistry involved in developing stimulating plots, themes, settings, incidents, and characters, and (b) the artistry involved in selecting and using stimulating language, in general. Examples of tasks that involve appreciation are:

4.1 <u>Emotional Response to Plot or Theme.</u> Tasks of this type are based on the assumption that the plot or the theme of a given selection has stimulated and sustained a feeling of fascination, excitement, curiosity, boredom, sentimentality, tenderness, love, fear, hate, happiness, cheerfulness, or sadness. Provided this assumption is met, the students may be requested to determine what the author did in the process of developing the plot or theme that elicited a given emotional response.

4.2 <u>Identification with Characters and Incidents.</u> Some appreciation tasks should require students to become aware of the literary techniques and devices which prompt them to sympathize or empathize with a particular character, or to reject him/her, for that matter. Other tasks should require students to consider the placement, nature, and structure of events or incidents which cause them to project themselves into the action.

4.3 <u>Reactions to the Author's Use of Language.</u> In this instance, the student is required to recognize and respond to the author's craftsmanship as reflected in his/her selection of and use of words. Such tasks may deal with the connotations and denotations of selected words and the influence they have on a reader's feelings. In addition, students should at times note figures of speech, e.g., similes and metaphors, and the effect their use has on the reader.

4.4 <u>Imagery.</u> Tasks of this nature require the reader to recognize and react to the author's artistic ability to "paint word pictures." In other words, students should become sensitive to the techniques an author uses in order to enable them to see, smell, taste, hear, or feel things through reading.

Process and Behavior Terms to Use with
Instructional Objectives

Level	Process for GO	Behavior for SLO
Affective Domain		
Receiving	Listens attentively Shows awareness of the importance of learning Shows sensitivity to social problems Accepts differences of race and culture Attends closely to the classroom activities	Asks, chooses, describes, follows, gives, holds, identifies, locates, names, points to, selects, sits erect, replies, uses
Responding	Completes assigned homework Obeys school rules Participates in class discussion Completes laboratory work Volunteers for special tasks Shows interest in subject Enjoys helping others	Answers, assists, complies, conforms, discusses, greets, helps, labels, performs, practices, presents, reads, recites, reports, selects, tells, writes
Valuing	Demonstrates belief in the democratic process Appreciates good literature (art, music) Appreciates the role of science (or other subjects) in everyday life Shows concern for the welfare of others Demonstrates problem-solving attitude Demonstrates commitment to social improvement	Completes, describes, differentiates, explains, follows, forms, initiates, invites, joins, justifies, proposes, reads, reports, selects, shares, studies, works
Organization	Recognizes the need for balance between freedom and responsibility in a democracy Recognizes the role of systematic planning in solving problems Accepts responsibility for own behavior Understands and accepts own strengths and limitations Formulates a life plan in harmony with his abilities, interests, and beliefs	Adheres, alters, arranges, combines, compares, completes, defends, explains, generalizes, identifies, integrates, modifies, orders, organizes, prepares, relates, synthesizes

From *Measurement and Evaluation in Teaching* by Norman E. Gronlund. Copyright © 1985 by Norman E. Gronlund. Reprinted with permission of Macmillan Publishing Company.

| Characterization by a Value or Value Complex | Displays safety consciousness
Demonstrates self-reliance in working
    independently
Practices cooperation in group activities
Uses objective approach in problem solving
Demonstrates industry and self-discipline
Maintains good health habits | Acts, discriminates, displays, influences, listens, modifies, performs, practices, proposes, qualifies, questions, revises, serves, solves, uses, verifies |

Psychomotor Domain

Perception	Recognizes malfunction by sound of machine Relates taste of food to need for seasoning Relates music to a particular dance step	Chooses, describes, detects, differentiates, distinguishes, identifies, isolates, relates, selects, separates

Set	Knows sequence of steps in varnishing
	    wood
	Demonstrates proper bodily stance for
	    batting a ball
	Shows desire to type efficiently
		Begins, displays, explains, moves, proceeds, reacts, responds, shows, starts, volunteers

Guided Response	Performs a golf swing as demonstrated Applies first aid bandage as demonstrated Determines best sequence for preparing a meal	Assembles, builds, calibrates, contracts, dismantles, displays, disects, fastens, fixes, grinds, heats, manipulates, measures, mends, mixes, organizes, sketches
Mechanism	Writes smoothly and legibly Sets up laboratory equipment Operates a slide projector Demonstrates a simple dance step	(Same list as for Guided Response)
Complex Overt Response	Operates a power saw skillfully Demonstrates correct form in swimming Demonstrates skill in driving an automobile Performs skillfully on the violin Repairs electronic equipment quickly and accurately	(Same list as for Guided Response)

Adaptation	Adjusts tennis play to counteract opponent's
	    style
	Modifies swimming strokes to fit the
	    roughness of the water
		Adapts, alters, changes, rearranges, reorganizes, revises, varies

Origination	Creates a dance step Creates a musical composition Designs a new dress style	Arranges, combines, composes, constructs, creates, designs, orginates

Cognitive Domain

| Knowledge | Knows common terms
Knows specific facts
Knows methods and procedures
Knows basic concepts
Knows principles | Defines, describes, identifies, labels, lists, matches, names, outlines, reproduces, selects, states |

Comprehension	Understands facts and principles Interprets verbal material Interprets charts and graphs Translates verbal material to mathematical formulas Estimates consequences implied in data Justifies methods and procedures	Converts, defends, distinguishes, explains, extends, generalizes, gives examples, infers, paraphrases, predicts, rewrites, summarizes
Application	Applies principles to new situations Applies theories to practical situations Solves mathematical problems Constructs charts and graphs Demonstrates correct usage of a procedure	Changes, computes, demonstrates, discovers, manipulates, modifies, operates, predicts, prepares, produces, relates, shows, solves, uses
Analysis	Recognizes unstated assumptions Recognizes logical fallacies in reasoning Distinguishes between facts and inferences Evaluates the relevancy of data Analyzes the organizational structure of a work (art, music, writing)	Breaks down, diagrams, differentiates, discriminates, distinguishes, identifies, illustrates, infers, outlines, points out, relates, selects, separates, subdivides
Synthesis	Writes a well-organized theme Gives a well-organized speech Writes a creative short story (or poem) Proposes a plan for an experiment Integrates learning from different areas into a plan for solving a problem Formulates a new scheme for classifying objects (or events, or ideas)	Categorizes, combines, compiles, creates, devises, designs, explains, generates, modifies, organizes, plans, rearranges, reconstructs, relates, reorganizes, revises, rewrites, summarizes, tells, writes
Evaluation	Judges the consistency of written material Judges the adequacy with which conclusions are supported by data Judges the value of a work (art, music, writing) by use of internal criteria Judges the value of a work (art, music, writing) by use of external standards	Appraises, compares, concludes, contrasts, criticizes, describes, discriminates, explains, justifies, interprets, relates, summarizes, supports

Evaluation Procedures Chart*

	Cognitive Domain						Affective Domain	Psychomotor Domain			
	K	C	Ap.	An.	S	E		Per.A.	Phy.A.	S.M.	N.D.C.
Objective-simple forms											
short answer	X	X	X								
alternative response	X	X	X								
matching	X	X	X								
Objective-complex forms											
multiple choice	X	X	X	X							
interpretive exercise			X	X							
Subjective-essay											
restricted response		X	X	X							
extended response				X	X	X					
Observational											
anecdotal record							X	X	X	X	X
rating scale		X	X	X	X		X	X	X	X	X
checklist		X	X	X	X		X	X	X	X	X
peer appraisal				X				X	X	X	X
Self-report											
interview							X				
questionnaire							X				
Work-sample tests											
physical measurement								X	X	X	X
time period								X	X	X	X
comparative standards								X	X	X	X

*In isolated instances teachers may be able to justify using evaluation items in categories other than those checked.

That's NEWS To Me*

THIS CENTER IS DESIGNED TO GIVE YOU EXPERIENCE WITH:

1. different kinds of newspapers
2. major sections in a newspaper

HOW TO WORK THROUGH THIS CENTER . . .

1. Listen to the tape on different kinds of newspapers. It will give you some directions also.
2. You will notice that the center is divided into sections which are color-coded. The sections are some of the different kinds of articles you can find in the paper. Here is the color-coding system:

NEWS	red	choose 1 red activity
EDITORIALS	green	choose 1 green activity
FEATURES	yellow	choose 1 yellow activity
SPORTS	blue	choose 1 blue or 1 light blue activity
ENTERTAINMENT	light blue	
CLASSIFIED	purple	choose 1 purple, brown, or orange activity
PICTURES	orange	
ADS	brown	

Altogether you will do five activities—one News, one Editorial, one Feature, one from Sports or Entertainment, and one from Classifieds, Ads, or Pictures.

*This learning center was created by Andrea Lee, OHM, Marygrove College, Detroit, and Gillian Craig. Reprinted by permission.

Turn Page . . .

EVERY activity which you choose MUST be completed on your own paper. You may write one-word answers except where the directions tell you to do something else. Your paper should look like this:

NAME
ACTIVITY COLOR; NUMBER & LETTER:
1. 2. 3.   ANSWERS & 4.   CORRECTIONS 5.
draw a line to separate activities
ACTIVITY COLOR; NUMBER & LETTER:
1. 2. 3.   ANSWERS & 4.   CORRECTIONS 5.

1. DO NOT write on Activity Cards   3. Extra activities = EXTRA CREDIT

2. Put your finished paper in the correct place

PLEASE PUT ALL MATERIALS BACK IN THE CORRECT PLACES . . .

When you have finished everything (at least 5 activities), list five ways you can use the newspaper which did not occur to you before. If you can think of ways not shown in this center, better yet!

1. _____   4. _____

2. _____   5. _____

3. _____

Finally, describe in a few sentences where you can see reading skills on the LITERAL, INFERENTIAL, EVALUATIVE and APPRECIATIVE levels being developed here. (Refer to Barrett's Taxonomy if necessary.) How could you apply this in your classroom?

(Use the back of this sheet.)

3. When the tape tells you, take a ticket from the pocket marked TICKETS—your ticket will tell you what color activity to do first, second, etc. This is planned so no section of the center will get too crowded.
4. Choose your activities from the box marked "Reading the Paper." You will notice that each article has a color, a number and a letter.
   —The color tells you what kind of article it is.
   —The number will help you locate the activity or task card and the key.
   —The letter (A or B) tells you the difficulty level.
     A = easier; can be accomplished quickly
     B = harder; will take a longer time.

So YELLOW 4A — Would tell you it is a Feature article; that you can find the activity card under yellow-4 in the activity box, or the key under yellow-4 in the key cards; and that it is an easy activity which you can finish in a fairly short time.

TO MEET THE OBJECTIVES OF THIS CENTER, YOU MUST:

1. Listen to and follow instructions on tape.
2. Read and follow instructions on the center display.
3. Complete 5 activities according to the color-coding system on the first page of this booklet:

EVALUATION — Take the key and score your own—where answers are given; your teacher will score the rest. Correct your own mistakes.

TO BE ELIGIBLE FOR
O   OUTSTANDING = at least 3 "B" level activities chosen/completed.
S   SATISFACTORY = at least 2 "B" level activities chosen/completed.
A   ACCEPTABLE = all "A" level activities chosen/completed.
R   RECYCLE = activities not finished; incorrect format; mistakes.

DOING HISTORY
A Learning Activity Packet*

TEACHER'S INTRODUCTION

This Learning Activity Packet is designed for average to above average eleventh- or twelfth-grade American history students and is to be used in conjunction with a study of urban growth and city development in the post-Civil War period. The packet specifically examines the issue of governmental corruption via political machines through the use of primary source material.

The student will need a dictionary and pencil for the daily activities. Separate paper and pen are suggested for writing the final evaluation.

The packet can be completed during five class periods in daily increments which if not completed in class must be taken home and finished. The final evaluation is a take-home assignment to be done after the fifth day's work is completed. Some students may be able to work ahead of the schedule.

At two points in the packet the teacher will initial the student's progress.

The pretest is designed to guide the student's anticipation of concepts contained in the packet. It is assumed that most of the terms will be familiar to the student from text readings or classroom discussion of the subject matter. Students who score below 70 percent on the pretest should review their comprehension of the terms and events included on the test before beginning work on the LAP.

READABILITY SCORES

Readability of this LAP was measured by the McLaughlin SMOG formula. This method of evaluation was selected because it is geared for material to be read without instructional guidance. While the first seven exercises should aid the student in reading the primary source material, the main LAP content material must be read and understood on an independent reading level.

*Prepared by Donna Miller, Signal Mountain, Tennessee.

Material	Total polysyllabic words in thirty (total) sentences	nearest Sq. Root	+3 =	Grade Level
Instructional/Explanatory Dialogue	53	7		10
Geo. W. Plunkitt Reading	33	6		9
L. Steffens Reading	67	8		11

OBJECTIVES

Given instruction and practice in interpreting primary source material, the student will read and assess two documents included in the packet and write an evaluation which expresses and supports the student's opinion of the "boss system."

The student will:

Recognize the difference between fact and opinion.

Identify words, phrases, and sentences that attempt to influence the reader.

Define different points of view as presented by different authors.

Evaluate an issue's morality, showing support and justification for the student's opinion.

STUDENT'S INTRODUCTION

This is a Learning Activity Packet (LAP). Its purpose is to let you *do* something about American history, not just memorize it.

There are exercises in the Packet that you will do in class each day for a week. At the end of the week, using all of the hints and clues you have learned in the Packet, you will be asked to write a short essay interpreting a situation that existed about the time your grandparents' parents were your age.

The wonderful thing about interpreting history is that there is no "right" or "wrong" answer. As long as you prove that you have used your mind and can support your opinion, your essay will be a good one! The exercises in this packet will teach you how to evaluate a historical reading source so that you can "do" some history yourself, that is, form an opinion of your own.

You will do the exercises in order. You may work ahead—that is, if you finish "day 1" today and still have time left, you may start "day 2." If you don't complete a day's work you will have to take the packet home and finish it so that you will stay on schedule. The final essay will be a take-home assignment.

Good Luck! You can do it! You can "do" history!

PRETEST

This "Pretest" is to be taken before you start your LAP. Not to worry, you will not be graded on it! The purpose of the pretest is to "jog" your memory about some of the terms you have learned in history that will be used in this packet. If you miss more than three, you need to review and make sure that you know them before doing the packet.

Match the terms on the left with the definitions on the right.

Muckraking

1. _____ a document written by someone directly involved, or observing, an event

Polls

2. _____ a type of unofficial governing organization

Imperialism

3. _____ common in cities with weak official government

Tenements

4. _____ an expansionist movement in which a country acquires colonies and dependencies

Primary source

5. _____ Democratic party's unofficial political machine in N. Y. City in 1870s

Ward boss

6. _____ a type of journalism of the early 1900s that exposed corruption

Tammany Hall

7. _____ acquiring money or position by dishonest or questionable means

Boss system

8. _____ at first multiple-family rented buildings, eventually used for slum buildings

Graft

9. _____ section of a large city, divided for governing purposes, like a district voting place

Ward

10. _____ person elected by residents of a city area to represent them in local government affairs.

Check your answers in the back at the bottom of the Answer Key.

DAY ONE

FACT OR OPINION?

Exercise 1

Write five sentences telling me about your favorite musical performing group. (There are no right or wrong answers here. I just want to know five things about the group.)

EXAMPLE: There are five people in this group. They play really hot music!

1.

2.

3.

4.

5.

Now go back and look at your sentences. Some probably tell real facts about your favorite group; other sentences may give *your* opinion of the group. Go back and put an "F" (fact) or "O" (opinion) by each sentence you wrote.

HINT: The first example was fact; the second was a personal opinion.

DAY ONE

FACT OR OPINION?

<u>Exercise 2</u>

Here is a review for a record or tape that appeared in the newspaper. As you read it, watch for facts and opinions. Can you tell the difference?

Soundtrack. "Lethal Weapon." (Warner Bros. 25561–1).[1]
    Exciting, atmospheric soundtrack to Mel Gibson/Danny Glover film incorporates all the right elements—sleaze, suspense, furtiveness, danger, explosive action, and death. All music save the title cut, a fine pop rocker by Honeymoon Suite, was written by Michael Kamen and Eric Clapton in a jazzy vein. Particular draws throughout are the evocative solos of guitarist Clapton and saxophonist David Sanborn. Music may fit the movie almost too well to have much commercial attraction for any but genuine soundtrack enthusiasts, however.

What are the *real facts* that you find in the review? Write them below.

_____

_____

_____

Now check the answer key in the back of the packet. Did you find all the facts? Did you think some things were facts that really weren't? Tricky, isn't it?

DAY ONE

FACT OR OPINION?

<u>Exercise 3</u>

One way to tell the difference between fact and opinion is to pretend that the author has written either "I know that" or "I feel that" in front of each phrase or sentence.

[1]Review of "Lethal Weapon" by Nikki C. Hasden, *The Chattanooga Times*, Friday, April 10, 1987. Reprinted by permission.

DAY ONE

Go back to the review. Underline <u>once</u> each word, phrase, or sentence that could have "I know that" written in front of it. Put <u>double</u> underlines under those that could have "I feel (or think) that . . ."

Now check the answer key. Are you getting the hang of it?

DAY TWO

DESCRIPTION

<u>Exercise 4</u>

Writers often use descriptive words to convey their opinions or to make their writing more interesting. Compare these statements:

He has blue eyes.
He has deep blue eyes that sparkle.

The fact is that the eyes are blue. By adding the descriptive words "deep" and "that sparkle" the author tells us how he feels about the eyes and makes them more interesting.

Tell me ten facts about yourself or your family on the first line of each number below. On the second line retell the fact using descriptive words that express your opinion.

EXAMPLE: I have a younger sister.
My little sister is a spoiled brat.

1. _____
   _____
2. _____
   _____
3. _____
   _____
4. _____
   _____
5. _____
   _____
6. _____
   _____
7. _____
   _____
8. _____
   _____

DAY TWO

9. _____

   _____

10. _____

    _____

DAY TWO

DESCRIPTION

Exercise 5

Authors usually want their readers to agree with what they are saying; they want us to like or dislike the subject as they do. We do the same thing: when we write or talk, we use certain words and phrases to express our opinion of the subject.

The passages on the next two pages express definite opinions from their authors. Read them, and as you read, underline words or phrases that express a positive or negative opinion. Use a dictionary if you are not sure of meanings.

HINT: All of the descriptive words and phrases are not negative or positive; some of them are neutral and some of them depend on *your* interpretation. For example, you may think that the word "wacky" is sort of neat, a good way to be, but your grandfather might find it to be rather undesirable. If a word in the passages affects your feelings, go ahead and underline it.

'Clockwise' Ticks with Stale Slapstick and a Single Joke that Tires the Mind[2]

By Randy Arnold
The Chattanooga Times

When it comes to wacky, madcap comedy, no one does better than England's Monty Python. John Cleese has been a standout for the troupe for years, but he could have used some Python-like material in his latest film, *Clockwise*.

What *Clockwise* misses is the broad eccentricity that made Monty Python so popular. This film dwells too much on one joke, a gag which deals

[2]From review of "Clockwise" by Randy Arnold, *The Chattanooga Times*, Friday April 10, 1987. Reprinted by permission.

DAY TWO

on the direction left and the comment right. The first time it's obvious, after that it's tiresome. . . .

Clockwise is a perfect example of how comic actors aren't funny unless they have funny material. Its slapstick of falling in mud, ripping off fenders from cars and having sleeves fall off jackets are basically rehashed gags. Cleese, because he has nothing really funny to work with, just walks through the part and with all the attention being focused on him, nobody else has the opportunity to shine in the other scenes, though Penelope Wilton tries as Stimpson's former girlfriend who meets up with him after 20 years.

A one-joke script, padded with stale slapstick, doesn't bring out the talent of Cleese or laughs from the audience. What Cleese, or anybody else connected with *Clockwise*, should have done was to have turned the film over to Monty Python. Then, perhaps, you might have been able to get your money's worth. *Clockwise*, like time itself, slowly ticks away. . . .

The Enigmatic Prince Explores Diverse Styles and a Wealth of Feelings[3]

by Nikki C. Hasden
The Chattanooga Times
Prince. "Sign of the Times." (Paisley Park, 25577, 2-record set).

Will the real Prince please stand up? That may be the request of the decade, for this pop-funk mastermind has a multifaceted personality that continues to be an enigma. However, certain aspects of his music remain constant—his strong commitment to experimentation, his knack for coming up with extraordinary arrangements often carried out singlehandedly, and the tendency to place all of his energies and mysteriousness into his music and performances.

The direction Prince takes on this new album, his third release in under two years, makes it one of the most diverse and visionary projects he has even done, as well as one of the most commercial.

Many are saying he has finally exorcised some of his most radical music inclinations, so that much of this album returns to the brilliant funk synthesis of 1982's masterpiece, *1999*. Certainly those craving potent funk should find it here in plenty, from *Housequake* (in declamatory, assertive James Brown style) to *Beautiful Night* (recorded live with the Revolution) and *U Got the Look* (with Sheena Easton) both offering typical Minneapolis rhythms. A couple of similar numbers have jazzy or bluesy overtones, such as *Hot Thing*, with Eric Leeds' saxophones. . . .

[3]From review of "Prince—Sign of the Times" by Nikki C. Hasden, *The Chattanooga Times*, Friday, April 10, 1987. Reprinted by permission.

DAY TWO

How did the authors of the two reviews make you feel? Try to forget what you already think about John Cleese and Prince. Based just on what the authors say, would you want to go see the movie *Clockwise*? Write one or two sentences explaining your answer.

_____
_____
_____
_____

Would you like to buy Prince's new album? Why or why not? Write one or two sentences explaining your answer.

DAY TWO

POINT OF VIEW

Exercise 6

The two selections you have just read were written by reviewers, people who are paid to observe, form an opinion, and write about it. Much that we read, however, is written by people who form an opinion first, then observe, and then write about it.

The following paragraph has blanks in it. Read it at first pretending that you tan beautifully, look great in a bathing suit, love warm weather, and swim well. Fill in each top blank with an appropriate word.

Next read the paragraph again and pretend that you sunburn easily, hate hot weather, are afraid of water, and break out in hives if you eat seafood. Fill in the bottom blanks.

I just got back from a _____ trip to the beach and I had a
_____
_____ time. The weather was _____, the sun shone
_____   _____
_____ of the time and the wind was _____. We stayed at a
_____   _____
_____ motel very _____ the water. I spent _____
_____   _____   _____
time lying on the _____ sand and it felt just _____. One day
_____   _____

DAY TWO

I got on my float and went out _____. It made me feel _____.
_____

We had _____ seafood to eat, and that was the _____ part of
_____   _____

the trip. After five days at the beach I look _____. I _____ to
_____   _____

go again soon.

The paragraph is entirely different the second time, isn't it?
Yet each paragraph would be true and correct for the person you pre-
tended to be when you wrote it.

**Before you go any further, have your teacher check your progress and
initial here.**

Teacher's initial _____

DAY THREE

REVIEW

It is important to recognize where an author is coming from when you
read. So far you have learned three different kinds of clues to help you
identify an author's point of view. What are they? (Yes, you may look back
if you need to.)

1.
2.
3.

Your next challenge is to keep all of these clues in mind as your read, to
be a dectective asking questions and looking for the author's real meaning. Then you will be able to figure out why the author wrote what he or
she wrote, and more importantly, whether you agree or disagree with it.
There *is* a way to make this work!
To help you get in the habit of asking questions as you read, try the
following notation system:

DAY THREE

	Put this notation in the margin:
If an idea:	
Is a fact	F
Is a fact but the author has exaggerated a bit	F+
Is an opinion	O
Makes you think "I agree"	yes
Makes you think "I disagree"	no
Is a new thought *or* a new way of seeing or understanding something	!
Confuses you or leaves something unclear (makes you think "I don't understand")	?

DAY THREE

NOTATION

Exercise 7

Here is a short selection to let you practice the notation system. As you read, place notations in the margin beside the ideas that raise questions in your mind.

This selection will also give you some practice interpreting historical documents. It is taken from a political speech made in 1898 urging the United States government to adapt an imperialistic policy of expansion.

As you make your notations, think about the clues and the author's real intention.

It is a noble land that God has given us; a land that can feed and clothe the world; a land whose coastlines would inclose half the countries of Europe; a land set like a sentinel between the two imperial oceans of the globe, a greater England with a nobler destiny....

Therefore, in this campaign, the question is larger than a party question. It is an American question. It is a world question. Shall the American people continue their march toward the commercial supremacy of the world? Shall free institutions broaden their blessed reign as the children of liberty wax in strength, until the empire of our principles is established over the hearts of all mankind?...

DAY THREE

The Opposition tells us that we ought not govern a people without their consent. I answer, The rule of liberty that all just government derives its authority from the consent of the governed, applies only to those who are capable of self-government. We govern the Indians without their consent, we govern our territories without their consent, we govern our children without their consent. How do they know that our government would be without their consent? Would not the people of the Philippines prefer the just, humane, civilizing government of this Republic to the savage, bloody rule of pillage and extortion from which we have rescued them?[4]

Now look back at your notations. What do they tell you about the speech? What do they tell you about your feelings? Notations can help you decide what you think about a reading selection; they can show you whether you agree or disagree with the author.

This will be very important in the next part of the packet. Before you start on the final section, have your teacher check off your notation practice.

Have your teacher check your progress and initial here. _____

DAYS FOUR AND FIVE

"DOING" HISTORY

Exercise 8

Now you have a chance to practice all of the tricks you have learned as you read the following two primary source documents about big city government in America around 1900. When you finish reading you will be asked to make a decision: was the Tammany Hall system in New York City right or wrong? You will have to explain your decision and tell why you feel the way you do.

Instructions:

1. Read the beginning paragraph about each author so you will understand his personal situation.

---

[4]"Albert J. Beveridge: The March of the Flag 1898," first published in the *Indianapolis Journal* for September 17, 1898.

2. Use the notation system as you read. (The more notations you make, the more thinking you are doing and the easier it will be to decide what you think.)
3. Watch for all the clues that you have learned. Remember, *how* something is said tells you a lot about the author's purpose.
4. There may be references to people or events with which you are unfamiliar . . . Just note them with a "?" and keep going! They won't really matter too much in your final analysis.

Good Luck . . . You are ready to "do" some history!

Reading Number 1: About the Author

George Washington Plunkitt was ward boss of the Fifteenth Assembly District in New York City and one of the powers of Tammany Hall when Tammany was supreme. His ideas and speeches were recorded by William Riorden, a newspaper writer who often interviewed Plunkitt. Plunkitt was a millionaire at the time of these interviews, having made a fortune in contracting, real estate, transportation, and every other business out of which he could make money.

Primary Source

How to Make Money in Politics[5]

**George Washington Plunkitt
Talks About Honest Graft**

Honest Graft and Dishonest Graft

Everybody is talkin' these days about Tammany men growin' rich on graft, but nobody thinks of drawin' the distinction between honest graft and dishonest graft. There's all the difference in the world between the two. Yes, many of our men have grown rich in politics. I have myself. I've made a big fortune out of the game, and I'm gettin' richer every day, but I've not gone in for dishonest graft—blackmailin' gamblers, saloon-keepers, disorderly people, etc.—and neither has any of the men who have made big fortunes in politics.

"There's an honest graft, and I'm an example of how it works. I might sum up the whole thing by sayin': 'I seen my opportunities and I took 'em.'

"Just let me explain by examples. My party's in power in the city, and it's goin' to undertake a lot of public improvements. Well, I'm tipped off, say, that they're going to lay out a new park at a certain place.

[5]William L. Riordan (ed.) *Plunkitt of Tammany Hall.* New York: McClure, Phillips & Co., 1905, pp. 3–10, 46–61.

DAYS FOUR AND FIVE

"I see my opportunity and I take it. I go to that place and I buy up all the land I can in the neighborhood. Then the board of this or that makes its plan public, and there is a rush to get my land, which nobody cared particular for before.

"Ain't it perfectly honest to charge a good price and make a profit on my investment and foresight? Of course, it is. Well, that's honest graft.

"Or, supposin' it's a new bridge they're goin' to build. I get tipped off and I buy as much property as I can that has to be taken for approaches. I sell at my own price later on and drop some more money in the bank.

"Wouldn't you? It's just like lookin' ahead in Wall Street or in the coffee or cotton market. It's honest graft, and I'm lookin' for it every day in the year. I will tell you frankly that I've got a good lot of it, too.

"I'll tell you of one case. They were goin' to fix up a big park, no matter where. I got on to it, and went lookin' about for land in that neighborhood.

"I could get nothin' at a bargain but a big piece of swamp, but I took it fast enough and held on to it. What turned out was just what I counted on. They couldn't make the park complete with Plunkitt's swamp, and they had to pay a good price for it. Anything dishonest in that?

"Up in the watershed I made some money, too. I bought up several bits of land there some years ago and made a pretty good guess that they would be bought up for water purposes later by the city.

"Somehow, I always guessed about right, and shouldn't I enjoy the profit of my foresight? It was rather amusin' when the condemnation commissioners came along and found piece after piece of the land in the name of George Plunkitt of the Fifteenth Assembly District, New York City. They wondered how I knew just what to buy. The answer is—I seen my opportunity and I took it. I haven't confined myself to land; anything that pays is in my line.

"For instance, the city is repavin' a street and has several hundred thousand old granite blocks to sell. I am on hand to buy, and I know just what they are worth.

"How? Never mind that. I had a sort of monopoly of this business for a while, but once a newspaper tried to do me. It got some outside men to come over from Brooklyn and New Jersey to bid against me.

"Was I done? Not much. I went to each of the men and said: 'How many of these 250,000 stones do you want? One said 20,000, and another wanted 15,000, and another wanted 10,000. I said: 'All right, let me bid for the lot, and I'll give each of you all you want for nothin'.

"They agreed, of course. Then the auctioneer yelled: "How much am I bid for these 250,000 fine pavin' stones?"

" 'Two dollars and fifty cents,' says I.

" 'Two dollars and fifty cents!' screamed the auctioneer. 'Oh, that's a joke! Give me a real bid.'

"He found the bid was real enough. My rivals stood silent. I got the lot for $2.50 and gave them their share. That's how the attempt to do Plunkitt ended, and that's how all such attempts end.

"I've told you how I got rich by honest graft. Now, let me tell you that most politicians who are accused of robbin' the city get rich the same way.

"They didn't steal a dollar from the city treasury. They just seen their opportunities and took them. That is why, when a reform administration comes in and spends a half million dollars in tryin' to find the public robberies they talked about in the campaign, they don't find them.

"The books are always all right. The money in the city treasury is all right. Everything is all right. All they can show is that the Tammany heads of departments looked after their friends, within the law, and gave them what opportunities they could to make honest graft. Now, let me tell you that's never goin' to hurt Tammany with the people. Every good man looks after his friends, and any man who doesn't isn't likely to be popular. If I have a good thing to hand out in private life, I give it to a friend. Why shouldn't I do the same in public life?

"Another kind of honest graft. Tammany has raised a good many salaries. There was an awful howl by the reformers, but don't you know that Tammany gains ten votes for every one it lost by salary raisin'?

"The Wall Street banker thinks it shameful to raise a department clerk's salary from $1500 to $1800 a year, but every man who draws a salary himself says: 'That's all right. I wish it was me.' And he feels very much like votin' the Tammany ticket on election day, just out of sympathy.

"Tammany was beat in 1901 because the people were deceived into believin' that it worked dishonest graft. They didn't draw a distinction between dishonest and honest graft, but they saw that some Tammany men grew rich, and supposed they had been robbin' the city treasury or levyin' blackmail on disorderly houses, or workin' in with the gamblers and lawbreakers.

"As a matter of policy, if nothing else, why should the Tammany leaders go into such dirty business, when there is so much honest graft lyin' around when they are in power? Did you ever consider that?

"Now, in conclusion, I want to say that I don't own a dishonest dollar. If my worst enemy was given the job of writin' my epitaph when I'm gone, he couldn't do more than write: " 'George W. Plunkitt. He Seen His Opportunities, and He Took 'Em.' "

To Hold Your District—Study Human Nature and Act Accordin'

"There's only one way to hold a district; you must study human nature and act accordin'. You can't study human nature in books. Books is a hindrance more than anything else. If you have been to college, so much

DAYS FOUR AND FIVE

the worse for you. You'll have to unlearn all you learned before you can get right down to human nature, and unlearnin' takes a lot of time. Some men can never forget what they learned at college. Such men may get to be district leaders by a fluke, but they never last.

"To learn real human nature you have to go among the people, see them and be seen. I know every man, woman, and child in the Fifteenth District, except them that's been born this summer—and I know some of them, too. I know what they like and what they don't like, what they are strong at and what they are weak in, and I reach them by approachin' at the right side.

"For instance, here's how I gather in the young men. I hear of a young feller that's proud of his voice, thinks that he can sing fine. I ask him to come around to Washington Hall and join our Glee Club. He comes and sings, and he's a follower of Plunkitt for life. Another young feller gains a reputation as a base-ball player in a vacant lot. I bring him into our base-ball club. That fixes him. You'll find him workin' for my ticket at the polls next election day. Then there's the feller that likes rowin' on the river, the young feller that makes a name as a waltzer on his block, the young feller that's handy with his dukes—I rope them all in by givin' them opportunities to show themselves off. I don't trouble them with political arguments. I just study human nature and act accordin'.

"But you may say this game won't work with the high-toned fellers, the fellers that go through college and then join the Citizens' Union. Of course it wouldn't work. I have a special treatment for them. I ain't like the patent medicine man that gives the same medicine for all diseases. The Citizens' Union kind of a young man! I love him! He's the daintiest morsel of the lot, and he don't often escape me.

"Before telling you how I catch him, let me mention that before the election last year, the Citizens' Union said they had four hundred or five hundred enrolled voters in my district. They had a lovely headquarters, too, beautiful roll-top desks and the cutest rugs in the world. If I was accused of havin' contributed to fix up the nest for them, I wouldn't deny it under oath. What do I mean by that? Never mind. You can guess from the sequel, if you're sharp.

"Well, election day came. The Citizens' Union's candidate for Senator, who ran against me, just polled five votes in the district, while I polled something more than 14,000 votes. What became of the 400 or 500 Citizens' Union enrolled voters in my district? Some people guessed that many of them were good Plunkitt men all along and worked with the Cits just to bring them into the Plunkitt camp by election day. You can guess that way, too, if you want to. I never contradict stories about me, especially in hot weather. I just call your attention to the fact that on last election day 395 Citizens' Union enrolled voters in my district were missin' -and unaccounted for.

DAYS FOUR AND FIVE

"I tell you frankly, though, how I have captured some of the Citizens' Union's young men. I have a plan that never fails. I watch the City Record to see when there's civil service examinations for good things. Then I take my young Cit in hand, tell him all about the good thing and get him worked up till he goes and takes an examination. I don't bother about him any more. It's a cinch that he comes back to me in a few days and asks to join Tammany Hall. Come over to Washington Hall some night and I'll show you a list of names on our rolls marked 'C.S.' which means, 'bucked up against civil service.'

"As to the older voters, I reach them, too. No, I don't send them campaign literature. That's rot. People can get all the political stuff they want to read—and a good deal more, too—in the papers. Who reads speeches, nowadays, anyhow? It's bad enough to listen to them. You ain't goin' to gain any votes by stuffin' the letter boxes with campaign documents. Like as not you'll lose votes, for there's nothin' a man hates more than to hear the letter-carrier ring his bell and go to the letter-box expectin' to find a letter he was lookin' for, and find only a lot of printed politics. I met a man this very mornin' who told me he voted the Democratic State ticket last year just because the Republicans kept crammin' his letter-box with campaign documents.

"What tells in holdin' your grip on your district is to go right down among the poor families and help them in the different ways they need help. I've got a regular system for this. If there's a fire in Ninth, Tenth, or Eleventh Avenue, for example, any hour of the day or night, I'm usually there with some of my election district captains as soon as the fire-engines. If a family is burned out I don't ask whether they are Republicans or Democrats, and I don't refer them to the Charity Organization Society, which would investigate their case in a month or two and decide they were worthy of help about the time they are dead from starvation. I just get quarters for them, buy clothes for them if their clothes were burned up, and fix them up till they get things runnin' again. It's philanthropy, but it's politics, too—mighty good politics. Who can tell how many votes one of these fires bring me? The poor are the most grateful people in the world, and let me tell you, they have more friends in their neighborhoods than the rich have in theirs.

"If there's a family in my district in want I know it before the charitable societies do, and me and my men are first on the ground. I have a special corps to look up such cases. The consequence is that the poor look up to George W. Plunkitt as a father, come to him in trouble—and don't forget him on election day.

"Another thing, I can always get a job for a deservin' man. I make it a point to keep on the track of jobs, and it seldom happens that I don't have a few up my sleeve ready for use. I know every big employer in the district and in the whole city, for that matter, and they ain't in the habit of sayin' no to me when I ask them for a job.

DAYS FOUR AND FIVE

"And the children—the little roses of the district! Do I forget them? Oh, no! They know me, every one of them, and they know that a sight of Uncle George and candy means the same thing. Some of them are the best kind of vote-getters. I'll tell you a case. Last year a little Eleventh Avenue rosebud whose father is a Republican, caught hold of his whiskers on election day and said she wouldn't let go till he'd promise to vote for me. And she didn't.

On "The Shame of the Cities"

"I've been readin' a book by Lincoln Steffens on 'The Shame of the Cities.' Steffens means well but, like all reformers, he don't know how to make distinctions. He can't see no difference between honest graft and dishonest graft and, consequent, he gets things all mixed up. There's the biggest kind of a difference between political looters and politcians who make a fortune out of politics by keepin' their eyes wide open. The looter goes in for himself alone without considerin' his organization or his city. The politician looks after his own interests, the organization's interests, and the city's interest all at the same time. See the distinction? For instance, I ain't no looter. The looter hogs it. I never hogged. I made my pile in politics, but, at the same time, I served the organization and got more big improvements for New York City than any other livin' man. And I never monkeyed with the penal code.

"The difference between a looter and a practical politician is the difference between the Philadelphia Republican gang and Tammany Hall. Steffens seems to think they're both about the same; but he's all wrong. The Philadelphia crowd runs up against the penal code. Tammany don't. The Philadelphians ain't satisfied with robbin' the bank of all its gold and paper money. They stay to pick up the nickels and pennies and the cop comes and nabs them. Tammany ain't no such fool. Why, I remember, about fifteen or twenty years ago, a Republican superintendent of the Philadelphia almshouse stole the zinc roof off the buildin' and sold it for junk. That was carryin' things to excess. There's a limit to everything, and the Philadelphia Republicans go beyond the limit. It seems like they can't be cool and moderate like real politicians. It ain't fair, therefore, to class Tammany men with the Philadelphia gang. Any man who undertakes to write political books should never for a moment lose sight of the distinction between honest graft and dishonest graft, which I explained in full in another talk. If he puts all kinds of graft on the same level, he'll make the fatal mistake that Steffens made and spoil his book.

"A big city like New York or Philadelphia or Chicago might be compared to a sort of Garden of Eden, from a political point of view. It's an orchard full of beautiful apple-trees. One of them has got a big sign on it, marked: 'Penal Code Tree—Poison.' The other trees have lots of apples on them for all. Yet, the fools go to the Penal Code Tree. Why? For the reason, I guess, that a cranky child refuses to eat good food and chews up a box of matches with relish. I never had any temptation to touch the Penal Code Tree. The other apples are good enough for me, and O Lord! how many of them there are in a big city!

"Steffens made one good point in his book. He said he found that Philadelphia, ruled almost entirely by Americans, was more corrupt than New York, where the Irish do almost all the governin'. I could have told him that before he did any investigatin' if he had come to me. The Irish was born to rule, and they're the honest people in the world. Show me the Irishman who would steal a roof off an almshouse! He don't exist. Of course, if an Irishman had the political pull and the roof was much worn, he might get the city authorities to put on a new one and get the contract for it himself, and buy the old roof at a bargain—but that's honest graft. It's goin' about the thing like a gentleman—and there's more money in it than in tearin' down an old roof and cartin' it to the junkman's—more money and no penal code.

"One reason why the Irishman is more honest in politics than many Sons of the Revolution is that he is grateful to the country and the city that gave him protection and prosperity when he was driven by oppression from the Emerald Isle. Say, that sentence is fine, ain't it? I'm goin' to get some literary feller to work it over into poetry for next St. Patrick's Day dinner.

"Yes, the Irishman is grateful. His one thought is to serve the city which gave him a home. He has this thought even before he lands in New York, for his friends here often have a good place in one of the city departments picked out for him while he is still in the old country. Is it any wonder that he has a tender spot in his heart for old New York when he is on its salary list the mornin' after he lands?

"Now, a few words on the general subject of the so-called shame of cities. I don't believe that the government of our cities is any worse, in proportion to opportunities, than it was fifty years ago. I'll explain what I mean by 'in proportion to opportunities.' A half a century ago, our cities were small and poor. There wasn't many temptations lyin' around for politicians. There was hardly anything to steal, and hardly any opportunities for even honest graft. A city could count its money every night before goin' to bed, and if three cents was missin', all the fire-bells would be rung. What credit was there in bein' honest under them circumstances? It makes me tired to hear of old codgers back in the thirties or forties boastin' that they retired from politics without a dollar except what they earned in their profession or business. If they lived to-day, with all the existin' opportunities, they would be just the same as twentieth century politicians. There ain't any more honest people in the world just now than the convicts in Sing Sing. Not one of them steals anything. Why? Because they can't. See the application?

"Understand, I ain't defendin' politicans of to-day who steal. The politician who steals is worse than a thief. He is a fool. With the grand opportunities all around for the man with a political pull, there's no excuse for stealin' a cent. The point I want to make is that if there is some stealin' in politics, it don't mean that the politicians of 1905 are, as a class, worse than them of 1835. It just means that the old-timers had nothin' to steal, while the politicians now are surrounded by all kinds of temptations and some of them naturally—the fool ones—buck up against the penal code."

Reading Number 2: About the Author

Lincoln Steffens was one of the most perceptive and eloquent American journalists of all time. After learning his craft on New York City newspapers, he became managing editor of *McClure's Magazine*. There he drifted into a project that helped to launch a sensationally successful style in American journalism—muckraking, the writing of detailed and careful studies of the corruption of city governments and corporations. The magazine printed one article on each of eight cities between October 1902 and November 1903, collected in 1904 as a book, *The Shame of the Cities*. Below is a portion of Steffens' article on New York City.

Primary Source

New York: Good Government to the Test[6]

Just about the time this article will appear, Greater New York will be holding a local election on what has come to be a national question—good government. . . .

Do we Americans really want good government? Do we know it when we see it? Are we capable of that sustained good citizenship which alone can make democracy a success? Or, to save our pride, one other: Is the New York way the right road to permanent reform?

For New York has good government, or, to be more precise, it has a good administration. It is not a question there of turning the rascals out and putting the honest men into their places. The honest men are in, and this election is to decide whether they are to be kept in, which is a very different matter. Any people is capable of rising in wrath to overthrow bad rulers. Philadelphia has done that in its day. New York has done it several times. With fresh and present outrages to avenge, particular villains to punish, and the mob sense of common anger to excite, it is an emotional gratification to go out with the crowd and "smash something." This is

[6]Lincoln Steffens, *The Shame of the Cities*. New York: McClure, Phillips & Co., 1904.

nothing but revolt, and even monarchies have uprisings to the credit of their subjects. But revolt is not reform, and one revolutionary administration is not good government. That we free Americans are capable of such assertions of our sovereign power, we have proven; our lynchers are demonstrating it every day. That we can go forth singly also, and, without passion, with nothing but mild approval and dull duty to impel us, vote intelligently to sustain a fairly good municipal government, remains to be shown. And that is what New York has the chance to show; New York, the leading exponent of the great American anti-bad government movement for good government. . . .

Tammany is bad government; not inefficient, but dishonest; not a party, not a delusion and a snare, hardly known by its party name—Democracy; having little standing in the national councils of the party and caring little for influence outside of the city. Tammany is Tammany, the embodiment of corruption. All the world knows and all the world may know what it is and what it is after. For hypocrisy is not a Tammany vice. Tammany is for Tammany, and the Tammany men say so. Other rings proclaim lies and make pretensions; other rogues talk about the tariff and imperialism. Tammany is honestly dishonest. Time and time again, in private and in public, the leaders, big and little, have said they are out for themselves and their own; not for the public, but for "me and my friends"; not for New York, but for Tammany. Richard Croker said under oath once that he worked for his own pockets all the time, and Tom Grady, the Tammany orator, has brought his crowds to their feet cheering sentiments as primitive, stated with candor as brutal.

The man from Mars would say that such an organization, so self-confessed, could not be very dangerous to an intelligent people. Foreigners marvel at it and at us, and even Americans—Pennsylvanians, for example—cannot understand why we New Yorkers regard Tammany as so formidable. I think I can explain it. Tammany is corruption with consent; it is bad government founded on the suffrages of the people. The Philadelphia machine is more powerful. It rules Philadelphia by fraud and force and does not require the votes of the people. The Phildelphians do not vote for their machine; their machine votes for them. Tammany used to stuff the ballot boxes and intimidate voters; to-day there is practically none of that. Tammany rules, when it rules, by right of the votes of the people of New York.

Tammany corruption is democratic corruption. . . .

Tammany's democratic corruption rests upon the corruption of the people, the plain people, and there lies its great significance; its grafting system is one in which more individuals share than any I have studied. The people themselves get very little; they come cheap, but they are interested. Divided into districts, the organization subdivides them into precincts or neighborhoods, and their sovereign power, in the form of votes, is

DAYS FOUR AND FIVE

bought up by kindness and petty privileges. They are forced to a surrender, when necessary, by intimidation, but the leader and his captains have their hold because they take care of their own. They speak pleasant words, smile friendly smiles, notice the baby, give picnics up the River or the Sound, or a slap on the back; find jobs, most of them at the city's expense, but they have also newsstands, peddling privileges, railroad and other business places to dispense; they permit violations of the law, and, if a man has broken the law without permission, see him through the court. Though a blow in the face is as readily given as a shake of the hand, Tammany kindness is real kindness, and will go far, remember long, and take infinite trouble for a friend.

The power that is gathered up thus cheaply, like garbage, in the districts is concentrated in the district leader, who in turn passes it on through a general committee to the boss. This is a form of living government, extra-legal, but very actual, and, though the beginnings of it are purely democratic, it develops at each stage into an autocracy. In Philadelphia the boss appoints a district leader and gives him power. Tammany has done that in two or three notable instances, but never without causing a bitter fight which lasts often for years. In Philadelphia the State boss designates the city boss. In New York, Croker has failed signally to maintain vice-bosses whom he appointed. The boss of Tammany Hall is a growth, and just as Croker grew, so has Charles F. Murphy grown up to Croker's place. Again, whereas in Philadelphia the boss and his ring handle and keep almost all of the graft, leaving little to the district leaders, in New York the district leaders share handsomely in the spoils.

There is more to share in New York. It is impossible to estimate the amount of it, not only for me, but for anybody. No Tammany man knows it all. Police friends of mine say that the Tammany leaders never knew how rich police corruption was till the Lexow committee exposed it, and that the politicians who had been content with small presents, contributions, and influence, "did not butt in" for their share till they saw by the testimony of frightened police grafters that the department was worth from four to five millions a year. The items are so incredible that I hesitate to print them. Devery told a friend once that in one year the police graft was "something over $3,000,000." Afterward the syndicate which divided the graft under Devery took in for thirty-six months $400,000 a month from gambling and poolrooms alone. Saloon bribers, disorderly house blackmail, policy, etc., etc., bring this total up to amazing proportions.

Yet this was but one department, and a department that was overlooked by Tammany for years. The annual budget of the city is about $100,000,000, and though the power that comes of the expenditure of that amount is enormous and the opportunities for rake-offs infinite, this sum is not one-half of the resources of Tammany when it is in power. Her resources are the resources of the city as a business, as a political, as a social power. If Tammany could be incorporated, and all its earnings, both legitimate and illegitimate, gathered up and paid over in dividends, the stockholders would get more than the New York Central bond and stock-holders, more than the Standard Oil stockholders, and the controlling clique would wield a power equal to that of the United States Steel Company. Tammany, when in control of New York, takes out of the city unbelievable millions of dollars a year.

No wonder the leaders are all rich; no wonder so many more Tammany men are rich than are the leaders in any other town; no wonder Tammany is liberal in its division of the graft. Croker took the best and the safest of it, and he accepted shares in others. He was "in on the Wall Street end," and the Tammany clique of financiers have knocked down and bought up at low prices Manhattan Railway stock by threats of the city's power over the road; they have been let in on Metropolitan deals and on the Third Avenue Railroad grab; the Ice trust is a Tammany trust; they have banks and trust companies, and through the New York Realty Company are forcing alliances with such financial groups as that of the Standard Oil Company. Croker shared in these deals and businesses. He sold judgeships, taking his pay in the form of contributions to the Tammany campaign fund, of which he was treasurer, and he had the judges take from the regular real estate exchange all the enormous real estate business that passed through the courts, and give it to an exchange connected with the real estate business of his firm, Peter F. Meyer & Co. This alone would maintain a ducal estate in England. But his real estate business was greater than that. It had extraordinary legal facilities, the free advertising of abuse, the prestige of political privilege, all of which brought in trade; and it had advance information and followed, with profitable deals, great public improvements.

Though Croker said he worked for his own pockets all the time, and did take the best of the graft, he was not "hoggish." Some of the richest graft in the city is in the Department of Buildings: $100,000,000 a year goes into building operations in New York. All of this, from outhouses to sky-scrapers, is subject to very precise laws and regulations, most of them wise, some impossible. The Building Department has the enforcement of these; it passes upon all construction, private and public, at all stages, from plan-making to actual completion; and can cause not only "unavoid-able delay," but can wink at most profitable violations. Architects and builders had to stand in with the department. They called on the right man and they settled on a scale which was not fixed, but which generally was on the basis of the department's estimate of a fair half of the value of the saving in time or bad material. This brought in at least a banker's percentage on one hundred millions a year. Croker, so far as I can make out, took none of this! it was let out to other leaders and was their own graft. . . .

It is impossible to follow all New York graft from its source to its final destination. It is impossible to follow here the course of that which is well known to New Yorkers. There are public works for Tammany contractors. There are private works for Tammany contractors, and corporations and individuals find it expedient to let it go to Tammany contractors. Tammany has a very good system of grafting on public works; I mean that it is "good" from the criminal point of view—and so it has for the furnishing of supplies. Low bids and short deliveries, generally speaking (and that is the only way I can speak here), is the method. But the Tammany system, as a whole, is weak.

Tammany men as grafters have a confidence in their methods and system, which, in the light of such perfection as that of Philadelphia, is amusing, and the average New Yorker takes in "the organization" a queer sort of pride, which is ignorant and provincial. Tammany is 'way behind the times. It is growing; it has improved. In Tweed's day the politicians stole from the city treasury, divided the money on the steps of the City Hall, and, not only the leaders, big and little, but heelers and outsiders; not only Tweed, but ward carpenters robbed the city; not only politicians, but newspapers and citizens were "in on the divvy." New York, not Tammany alone, was corrupt. When the exposure came, and Tweed asked his famous question, "What are you going to do about it?" the ring mayor, A. Oakey Hall, asked another as significant. It was reported that suit was to be brought against the ring to recover stolen funds. "Who is going to sue?" said Mayor Hall, who could not think of anybody of importance sufficiently without sin to throw the first stone. Stealing was stopped and grafting was made more businesslike, but still it was too general, and the boodling for the Broadway street railway franchise prompted a still closer grip on the business. The organization since then has been gradually concentrating the control of graft. . . .

Tammany leaders are usually the natural leaders of the people in these districts, and they are originally good-natured, kindly men. No one has a more sincere liking than I for some of those common but generous fellows; their charity is real, at first. But they sell out their own people. They do give them coal and help them in their private troubles, but, as they grow rich and powerful, the kindness goes out of the charity and they not only collect at their saloons or in rents—cash for their "goodness"; they not only ruin fathers and sons and cause the troubles they relieve; they sacrifice the children in the schools; let the Health Department neglect the tenements, and, worst of all, plant vice in the neighborhood and in the homes of the poor. . . .

Philadelphia had a bad ring mayor, a man who promoted the graft and caused scandal after scandal. The leaders there, the wisest political grafters in this country, learned a great lesson from that. As one of them said to me:

"The American people don't mind grafting, but they hate scandals. They don't kick so much on a jiggered public contract for a boulevard, but they want the boulevard and no fuss and no dust. We want to give them that. We want to give them what they really want, a quiet Sabbath, safe streets, orderly nights, and homes secure. They let us have the police graft. But this mayor was a hog. You see, he had but one term and he could get his share only on what was made in his term. He not only took a hog's share off what was coming, but he wanted everything to come in his term. So I'm down on grafting mayors and grafting office holders. I tell you it's good politics to have honest men in office. I mean men that are personally honest."

So they got John Weaver for mayor, and honest John Weaver is checking corruption, restoring order, and doing a great many good things, which it is "good politics" to do. For he is satisfying the people, soothing their ruffled pride, and reconciling them to machine rule. I have letters from friends of mine there, honest men, who wish me to bear witness to the goodness of Mayor Weaver. I do. And I believe that if the Philadelphia machine leaders are as careful with Mayor Weaver as they have been and let him continue to give to the end as good government as he has given so far, the "Philadelphia plan" of graft will last and Philadelphia will never again be a free American city.

Philadelphia and New York began about the same time, some thirty years ago, to reform their city governments. Philadelphia got "good government"—what the Philadelphians call good—from a corrupt ring and quit, satisfied to be a scandal to the nation and a disgrace to democracy. New York has gone on fighting, advancing and retreating, for thirty years, till now it has achieved the beginnings, under Mayor Low, of a government for the people. Do the New Yorkers know it? Do they care? They are Americans, mixed and typical; do we Americans really want good government? Or, as I said at starting, have they worked for thirty years along the wrong road—crowded with unhappy American cities—the road to Philadelphia and despair?

Post Scriptum: Mayor Low was nominated on the Fusion ticket. Tammany nominated George B. McClellan. The local corporations contributed heavily to the Tammany campaign fund and the people of New York elected the Tammany ticket by a decisive majority of 62,696. The vote was: McClellan, 314,782; Low, 252,086.

DAYS FOUR AND FIVE

"DOING" HISTORY

Exercise 9

Now that you have read what two different authors have to say about "machine politics," you have probably formed some opinions of your own. Before you attempt to make a final judgment, however, let's review what Steffens and Plunkitt thought and felt about Tammany.

A great way to focus on a topic is the Cinquain. Cinquain is pronounced "sin-kān" but you don't have to be able to say it. You do have to be able to do it!

Instructions:

1. Cinquain is a five-line poetry form with these features: The first line is a one-word title, usually a noun.
2. The second line is a two-word description of the topic, usually two adjectives.
3. The third line is three words expressing action of the topic, usually three "-ing" words.
4. The fourth line is a four-word phrase describing the topic that usually shows feeling for the topic.
5. The fifth line is a one word synonym that restates the essence of the topic.

EXAMPLE: (remember the political speech?)

Imperialism
Noble Blessed
Rescuing Civilizing Ruling
America's True Grand Destiny
Expansion

You probably noticed that the example cinquain is written from the same point of view that the author of the speech projected, not from the point of view of, say, people of the Phillipines. Your job is to write two cinquains using "Tammany" as your title (and first line). Write one conquain as if you were Plunkitt and the other as if you were Steffens.

DAYS FOUR AND FIVE

Plunkitt: **Tammany**

———————   ———————

———————   ———————   ———————

———————   ———————   ———————   ———————

———————

Steffens: **Tammany**

———————   ———————

———————   ———————   ———————

———————   ———————   ———————   ———————

———————

There! That should help you sum up what each author was trying to say. Now you have to decide what you think about Tammany. For an overnight assignment, write a two-page essay that gives your opinion of the boss system as represented by Tammany Hall. Explain *why* and *how* you have reached your conclusions and describe exactly how the two authors influenced your evaluation.

When you have finished your essay, please fill out the Student Evaluation form at the end of the packet and turn it in to your teacher along with your essay.

ANSWER KEY

Exercise 2

Facts from review:
  The album is a soundtrack from a film.
  It is from the movie *Lethal Weapon*.
  The title song is by Honeymoon Suite.
  The rest of the music was by Michael Kamen and Eric Clapton.
  Clapton played the guitar.
  David Sanborn played the saxophone.

Exercise 3

Exciting, atmospheric soundtrack to Mel Gibson/Danny Glover film incorporates all the right elements—sleaze, suspense, furtiveness, danger, explosive action and death. All music save the title cut, a fine pop rocker by Honeymoon Suite was written by Michael Kamen and Eric Clapton in a jazzy vein. Particular draws throughout are the evocative solos of guitarist Clapton and saxophonist David Sanborn. Music may fit the movie almost too well to have much commercial attraction for any but genuine soundtrack enthusiasts, however.

Exercise 6

  1. Fact or Opinion
  2. Descriptive Words
  3. Point of View

Pretest Answers

  1. primary source
  2. boss system
  3. imperialism
  4. Tammany Hall
  5. muckrakers
  6. graft
  7. tenements
  8. ward
  9. poll
  10. ward boss

TEACHER SUGGESTIONS FOR STUDENT EVALUATION

The main goal of this LAP has been to encourage students to read and think independently and to form opinions of their own. Evaluation of such criteria must of necessity be more objective than subjective; however, some guidelines can be drawn.

Students in the age range for which this packet was designed should have little difficulty with the "Fact or Opinion" exercises, two of which are self-grading with the use of the answer key. The exercises dealing with descriptive terminology are more arbitrary in nature and depend to an extent on the student's own perceptions of desirability. The student's work in this area should be judged on the degree to which he participates in the work (i.e., how many concepts does he underline?) rather than in his actual opinions. The answers that the student supplies in Exercise 5 should be judged for their demonstration of logical analysis and cited support rather than on the student's personal opinion. Exercise 6 should reflect an imaginative and perceptive approach to opposite points of view and the notation practice in Exercise 7 should reflect at least one of each of the notation symbols.

It is important that the two cinquains be thoughtfully appraised, for their content (or lack of same!) will reflect the student's ability to define and then contrast two different opinions. The student's final essay must demonstrate a clear and logical opinion of the boss system as represented by Tammany Hall and should include justification for his/her position.

STUDENT EVALUATION FORM

This evaluation will give your teacher some idea of how well the Learning Activity Packet (LAP) works. Answer the questions honestly but do NOT put your name on this form.

1. Did you like working on your own the way you did in this LAP?
2. Overall, did you find the exercises too easy, too hard, or in between?
3. What did you like best about this LAP?
4. What did you like least about this LAP?
5. Did you learn anything that you can use again with other assignments or in other classes? If so, what was it?
6. Has this LAP made you feel any differently about studying American history? Better? Worse? (Be honest.)

Answer Below. You may also write on the back of this form.

A

Abbott, M. K., 253
Alexander, C. F., 279
Alexander, J. C., 200
Allen, W. H., 161
Alvermann, D., 8, 16, 17, 18, 59, 202
Anderson, T. H., 103, 109, 312
Applebee, A. N., 6, 11, 16, 39
Armbruster, B. B., 103, 109, 312
Askov, E. N., 99, 253, 312
Ausdubel, D., 85, 93
Auten, A., 11, 39

B

Bader, L., 219
Baker, L., 57
Baldwin, R. S., 149
Baratz, J. C., 279
Barrett, T. C., 31–33, 42, 49–50, 104, 140, 153, 305, 315
Becker, J., 338, 343, 344
Bennett, W., 285
Berman, S. L., 74
Bloom, B. S., 7, 9, 29, 32, 42, 49, 83, 104, 153, 305
Borich, G., 187, 199, 203, 223, 230
Bormuth, J. R., 186
Boyan, N. J., 342
Briggs, L. J., 7
Britton, J., 38

Brophy, J. E., 200
Brown, A. L., 57
Bryan, M., 231
Burg, L. A., 331
Burmeister, L. E., 33, 173
Byrne, M. A., 148, 151

C

Calfee, R., 55
Carlsen, G. R., 201, 202
Carrell, P. L., 287
Cartwright, C., 296, 328
Cartwright, G. P., 296, 328
Caruso, S., 221, 229
Chall, J., 144, 148, 149
Christenson, J., 142, 202
Coble, C. R., 70, 84
Collins, J., 128, 191
Cooper, C., 190
Copeland, W. D., 342
Corcoran, L. L., 146
Corno, L., 200
Craig, G., 266
Crofton, C., 336

D

Dale, E., 144, 148, 149, 159
Danielson, K. E., 58
Day, B. D., 339
Dewey, J., 55
Dolciani, M. P., 74
Donlan, D., 142, 173, 181
Dossett, W. F., 346
Drum, P., 55

Dupuis, M., 186, 283
Durkin, D., 16, 54–55

E

Eanet, M., 108
Early, M., 322
Englemann, S., 280, 281
English, R., 139
Erickson, L., 337
Eskey, D. E., 287
Estes, T. H., 108, 171, 231, 268, 339

F

Fader, D., 202, 204
Farr, R., 139
Fernandez, L., 257
Fichter, G. S., 70, 84
Filler, R. C., 200
Findley, W., 231
Fitzgerald, G. G., 149
Fitzpatrick, J. P., 285, 286
Flavell, J. H., 55
Fleck, H., 257
Flood, J., 17
Foster, S. G., 231
Francis, N., 25
Freilich, J., 74
Fry, E., 145, 147, 148, 149, 150, 151, 153, 165
Fulwiler, T., 57

G

Gagne, R., 7, 91, 93, 226

Gallo, D. R., 202
Garner, R., 60
Gaskins, I., 193
Gaughan, E. D., 146
Gibbons, D. D., 256
Girdon, M. B., 253
Gladney, M. R., 281
Goldsberry, L., 342, 343
Good, T. L., 200, 329
Goodlad, J., 341
Grabe, W., 287
Grant, C. A., 231
Graser, E., 189, 190
Graves, D. H., 193
Gray, W. S., 29
Gronlund, N. E., 169–70, 225, 230

H

Hafner, L. E., 82, 93
Hahn, C. L., 338, 343, 344
Hall, E., 277
Hall, G. E., 345, 346
Hanf, M. B., 87
Harrow, A. J., 9, 10
Hater, M. A., 148, 151
Havelock, R., 335
Hayes, D. A., 59
Heimlich, J. E., 87
Henry, G. H., 83–84, 86, 88, 91, 93
Herber, H., 29, 49–50, 71, 72, 85, 89, 93, 104
Hill, W. R., 324
Hodgkinson, H., 274
Holdzkom, D., 189
Holloway, K. F. C., 281
Huey, E. B., 29

J

Jacobson, L. F., 200
Jensen, A., 280, 281
Johnson, D., 56

Johnson, D. D., 87
Jongsma, E., 183
Joos, M., 27
Jwaideh, A. R., 344

K

Kamm, K., 99
Kane, R., 73, 148, 151
Kaufman, R. K., 149
Kemp, R. D. M., 224, 228
Kingsbury, C., 81
Kintsch, W., 8
Klare, G. R., 145
Klumb, R., 99
Krathwohl, D. R., 8–9, 32
Kubiszyn, T., 187, 199, 203, 223, 230
Kuykendall, C., 154

L

Laberge, D., 10
Labov, W., 279, 280, 281
Ladd, N. E., 146
Laosa, L. M., 285
Lapp, D., 6, 17
Lee, A., 266
Lee, J. W., 115, 117, 119, 123, 187, 191, 193, 253, 312, 330
Lehr, R., 11, 39
Likert, R., 204

M

McCracken, R. A., 115
McLaughlin, G. H., 149
McNeil, J. D., 71, 72, 198
Manzo, A. V., 108
Marker, G. W., 344
Marshall, N., 149
Martin, S., 222
Masia, B. B., 9
Morrison, B., 99

Murray, D., 189
Musselman, N. C., 92, 93
Myers, J. W., 38

N

Neuhard, R., 219
Nolan, J., 298

O

Odell, L., 190
Okey, J. R., 226
Olson, D. W., 146
Orlich, D. C., 222, 239
Osgood, C. E., 204
Otto, W., 8, 336, 337

P

Paris, S. G., 100, 101
Parkey, N., 253
Patrick, J. J., 147
Pearce, D. L., 219
Pearson, P. D., 56, 310
Petkosh, D., 205, 207
Piaget, J., 91
Pittleman, S. D., 87
Prewitt Diaz, J. O., 283, 285, 286
Purves, A., 17

R

Raygor, A. L., 149, 152, 165
Reed, A. J. S., 205
Reiter, I., 145
Remy, R. C., 147
Rice, D. R., 70, 84
Robinson, R., 329
Robinson, R. P., 108
Rodgers, E. M., 344
Rosenblatt, L., 8, 322
Rosenthal, R., 200

Rothkopf, E., 52–53
Russell, F., 339

S

Salem, J., 146
Samuels, S., 10
Schallert, D., 53
Schumacher, G. M., 145
Sealy, R. G., 235
Searles, J. E., 276
Shepherd, D. L., 173
Shipman, D. A., 205
Shoemaker, F. F., 344
Showers, D., 187
Shuy, R., 279, 281
Singer, H., 142, 145, 173, 181
Smith, F., 28, 29, 183
Smith, R. J., 106
Smith, R. L., 180, 185
Snow, E. R., 200

Snyder, S. L., 82, 243
Solorzano, L., 249
Spache, G., 108, 325
Stauffer, R. G., 29, 244, 251, 253
Swoope, K., 222

T

Teachner, R., 275
Thompson, S., 339
Thorndike, E. L., 55
Townsend, B. S., 321
Trost, M. A., 190
Tulley, M. A., 139

V

Valdivieso, R., 275, 285
Van Allen, R., 253
Van Dijk, T., 8

Van Horn, B., 294
Vaughn, J. L., 108, 149, 171, 231, 268, 339

W

Wallace, R. C., 346
Ward, M. E., 296, 328
Warncke, E. W., 205
Webster, V., 70, 84
Weirauch, D. C., 75
White, S., 8, 99
Wilhite, R. K., 325
Williams, F., 280
Wilson, R. M., 253
Winkley, C., 80
Wood, F., 339, 342

Y

Yendol, M., 311

SUBJECT INDEX

A

Abstraction, and readability, 147
Accent patterns, 79
Activation questions, 59
Active learning, 140–41
Acuity, 10, 11
Adjunct questioning, 52–53
Administrators, 338, 343
Adolescents, interests of, 142–43, 201–2; *see also* Students, interests of
Advance organizers, 53, 85
Affective domain, 8–9, 28, 32, 52
Affixes, 74, 75–76
Analogies, 91–92
Analysis, as level in cognitive hierarchy, 6, 7, 32, 305
Analytic scale scoring, 190
Ann Arbor case, 275
Application, as level in cognitive hierarchy, 7, 32
Appreciation, as level of comprehension, 32–33
Appreciation level questions, 51, 52, 247
Art, language experience approach in, 255
Assessment, 35–37, 168–94
Assigned topics, writing on, 116, 117
Attitudes, students', 8–9, 198–201, 202–5
Audiences, for writing, 119–20, 131
Audio-visual materials, 159; *see also* Media

Audio-visual specialists, 328
Auditory modality, 314
Automaticity, 10, 71

B

Basic reading skills, 199
Beginnings, of essay-type answers, 117, 118, 121
Behavior problems, in grouping, 232
Bibliographies, of teaching materials, 163
Bilingual education, 285
Bilingual Education Act (Title VII), 285
Black dialect, 279–81, 288
Blacks,
    and Ann Arbor case, 275
    dialect use of, 279–81
    growth of middle class, 275
    and standard English, 281
Blind students, 142, 297, 302
Book lists, 202
Books for You, 202
Books, of interest to adolescents, 201–2
Brain-damaged children, 297, 301
Brainstorming, 119, 120

C

Career-based reading, 30
Casual register, of language, 27, 28, 289

Categorizing, in concept development, 88, 105

Central Americans, 283, 284

Change
assessment of, 345
process of, 334–47
qualities of, 338–39
RPTIM model of, 339–43, 346
teachers' reaction to, 334–38

Change agents, 343–44

Chapter I teachers, 327

Cheerleaders, teachers as, 123

Chicanos, 283

Choice, and motivation, 209

Cinquains, 268–69

Classroom climate, 200

Cloze tests, 72–73, 74, 75, 183–86, 233, 303, 306–9, 311
sample of, 184–85

Coaches, teachers as, 100–1

Cognitive development, hierarchy of, 7, 28

Cognitive maps, 85

Cognitive theory, and comprehension, 49–53, 59

Communication, language as, 25

Community attitudes, to teaching materials, 140, 143, 163–64

Composing stage, of writing model, 40, 115, 122–24

Comprehension
in cognitive hierarchy, 7, 32
definition of, 7, 12
of independent level readers, 305
levels of, 31–33
measuring, 48–49
product vs. process approach, 48–49, 54–55, 59
and reading centers, 267
schema approach to, 53–54
self-monitoring of, 65–66
strategies to aid, 57, 60
taxonomy approach to, 31–33, 42, 49–53, 247, 252, 305, 315

teaching of, 15–16, 54–55, 248
vocabulary in, 63–95
and writing skills, 16, 57–58

Computers, 267, 302, 303

Concept development, 82–94
exercises for, 88–94

Conditional knowledge, 100

Conferencing stage, of writing model, 41, 115, 124–25

ConStruct technique, 108

Consultants, use of for training, 342

Consultative register, of language, 27, 28, 289

Content, grading of in writing, 191

Content area skills, assessment of, 171–82, 186

Content outlines, of instructional units, 222, 225

Content reading, demands of, 6, 56, 168–69

Content reading programs, 323, 324–25

Context clues, 71–74

Contracts, in student-directed activities, 261

Convergent comprehension, 32, 50–51

Coordination, in reading, 10–11

Corrective reading programs, 322, 323, 324

Criterion-referenced group reading inventories, 171–83, 186, 188, 233, 237
sample, 174–80

Criterion-referenced tests (CRT), 170–71

Criterion-referenced writing assessments, 188

Critical thinking, 104, 247, 251

Cuban-Americans, 283, 284

Culture
components, of, 276–78
differences in, 273–92

Curriculum, 220–21, 222

D

Dale-Chall formula, 148, 149
Decoding, 15, 19, 28, 64–65
Definitions, word, 71
Density, of text, 146–47, 153
Departmentalization, secondary
    school, 231
Derivational affixes, 75–76
Developmental reading program,
    322, 323, 324
Diagnostic grids, 237
Dialects, 26–27
    black, 279–81, 288
    differences in, 274, 288, 289
    rural white, 283
Dialogue journals, 58
Dictionaries, use of, 80
Directed reading activity (DRA),
    223, 234, 244–51, 260, 269–70,
    306, 308
Directed reading/thinking
    activity (DRTA), 251–53, 260
Divergent comprehension, 32,
    50–51
Domains of learning, 7–11, 28–
    32, 52, 226
DRA *see* Directed reading
    activity
DRTA *see* Directed reading/
    thinking activity

E

Editing checklists, 128–29
Editing stage, of writing model,
    41–42, 115, 126–31
Educable mentally retarded
    (EMR) students, 297, 300–1
Education, cultural attitude to,
    278, 285
*Educational Testing and
    Measurement*, 224, 230
Education Consolidation and
    Improvement Act, 326
Elementary and Secondary
    Education Act, 327

Elementary schools
    content reading in, 324
    grouping in, 230–31, 239
    special education classes in, 295
    writing in, 11, 324, 330
Emotionally disturbed students,
    297, 303
EMR *see* Educable mentally
    retarded
Energy, for change, 336
English, language experience
    approach in, 254
Enrichment activities, 59, 250–51
Essay-type responses
    beginnings of, 117, 118, 121
    writing of, 11, 115–32
Evaluation
    definition of, 169–70
    in instructional units, 230
    of LAPs, 263–64
    as level of comprehension, 31–
        32, 305
    of reading/writing programs,
        331
    see also Tests
Evaluation level questions, 51,
    52, 104, 247, 252
Exceptional students, 293–317,
    325, 328
    definition of, 296–98
Excluding, in concept
    development, 89
Expectancy, as part of reading
    schemata, 8
Experiences, grouping by, 238
Explicit text, 56
Expository writing, 19, 324, 330
Expressive writing, 14–15, 37
Extended family, and Puerto
    Rican culture, 286
Extrinsic motivation, 208, 211

F

Familiar words, pretesting, 69
Federally funded reading
    programs, 326–27

Fluency, in reading, 28, 29
Focus correction, 128, 191–92
Foreign languages, language experience approach in, 255
Foreign words, 80
Formal register, of language, 27, 28, 288
Formative evaluation stage, of reading/writing programs, 331
Frozen register, of language, 27
Frustration level readers, 34, 37, 64, 65, 78, 142, 233, 235, 306–15
    and language experience approach, 256, 260
Fry Graph, 145, 147, 148–49, 150, 151, 153, 165, 310
Functional reading, 29–30

G

General impression marking, 190
General objectives (GO), of curricula, 223
    sample, 227
Gifted students, 141–142, 144, 208, 296, 300, 303, 304–5
Globes, 102
Glossaries, use of, 80–81
Goals
    of content instruction, 36–37
    educational, 220–21
Grading, traditional, 190–91
Graphic materials, 102, 313; see also Media
Grouping, 210, 230–39, 244
Group reading inventories (GRI), 171–83, 233
    sample, 174–80

H

Handicapped children, 293–317
    definition of, 296–98
    tolerance of, 299–300

Hands-on experiences, 83, 209, 307
Hawkins-Stafford Elementary and Secondary School Improvement Amendment, 327
Hearing-impaired students, 297, 301–2
Hispanic-Americans, 275, 283–88
Holistic scoring, of writing, 190
Home economics, language experience approach in, 255
Homogeneous grouping, 231, 240
Horizontal articulation, of curriculum, 221
Human realm, of behavior, 276–77

I

IEP see Individualized educational programs
Immigrants, influence of schools on, 285
Implementation, as stage of change, 342
Implicit text, 56
Implying, in concept development, 91–92
Independent learning, 99
Independent level readers, 34–35, 142, 208, 233, 235–36, 303–6, 315
Independent study techniques, 107–9
Individual differences, in classroom, 13–14
Individualized educational programs (IEP), 295–96, 300, 301, 302, 303, 307, 315, 328
Individual reading inventories (IRI), 171–72
Industrial arts, language experience approach in, 255
Inference, as level of comprehension, 31, 305
Inferential level questions, 51, 52, 104, 247, 252

Infixes, 74
Inflectional affixes, 75–76
Informal reading inventories
  (IRI), 78–79, 303
Informal testing
  of reading skills, 171–87
  of writing skills, 187–93
Information, location of, 98–99
Informed Strategies for
  Learning, 100–1
Innovation *see* Change
Inside advocates, in change
  process, 344, 346
Instructional games, 268–69
Instructional level readers, 33–
  34, 64, 65, 233, 260
Instructional units, 218–30
  activities for, 226–27, 228
  components of, 221–30
  definition of, 218–19
  evaluation in, 230
  and frustration level readers,
    309
  materials for, 227, 229–30
  planning for, 219–20
  student grouping in, 230–39
Intelligence, and reading
  activities, 200
Interests, students', 142–43, 201–
  2, 202–5, 209–10, 237–38
Intimate register, of language,
  27
Intonation patterns, 79
Intrinsic motivation, 208, 209–11

J

Jargon, 27, 30
Joining, in concept development,
  88
Journals, use of, 57–58, 59

K

Knowledge, as level in cognitive
  hierarchy, 7, 32

L

Language,
  and culture, 277
  differences in, 26–27, 273–92
  grouping by, 238
  as learning tool, 14–15
  nature of, 25–26
  registers of, 27–28, 274, 282,
    288–89
  social styles of, 27–28
Language development, and
  learning centers, 265–66
Language experience approach,
  253–56, 260, 270, 289, 290,
  312–13
Language functions,
  interdependence of, 37–38
Language process, reading as a,
  65–67
LAP *see* Learning activity
  packages
Lau decision, 275
LD *see* Learning disabled
Learning activity packages, 262–
  65, 305
Learning centers, 78, 263, 265–
  69, 312
Learning disabled students, 297,
  301
Learning logs, 57–58, 59
Least restrictive environment
  (LRE), for special education
  students, 295–96
Legitimizers, in change process,
  344, 346
Letter, morning, 310–12
Letter form, for writing
  assignments, 120, 131
Librarian, role of, 327–28
Limited English proficiency
  (LEP) students, 238
Listening, as learning tool, 37
Listening centers, 268
Listening vocabularies, 65, 68
Literal level questions, 51, 52,
  104, 247, 252

Literal recognition, as level of comprehension, 31
Literature, and use of DRTAs, 251–53
LRE *see* Least restrictive environment

M

Mainstreaming, 296
Maintenance, as stage of change, 342–43
Maps, 102
Marielitos, 284
Material dimension, of human behavior, 276
Materials, teaching, 138–66; *see also* Media; Textbooks
Mathematical symbols, cloze procedures for, 73, 74
Mathematics
language experience approach in, 255
readability of, 150–51, 153
Measurement and Evaluation in Teaching, 169–70, 223, 230
Measurement, of ability, 170
Mechanics, grading of in writing, 191
Media
effectiveness of different, 159–63
and frustration level readers, 309, 312
for instructional units, 227, 229–30
selection of, 162–63
Media specialists, 328
Memorization, 59–60, 99
Metacognition, and comprehension, 4, 17–20, 54–55, 56–57, 59, 100–1
Mexican-Americans, 283, 285
Migrant education program, 284
Migration, educational problems of, 284, 285–87

Minority groups, 143, 273–92
Morning letter techique, 310–12
Motivation
of frustration level readers, 307
of gifted students, 304
to read, 4, 8–9, 12, 201, 205, 208–11, 260
Multiple-meaning words, 69
Music, language experience approach in, 255

N

Narrative writing, 13, 19, 116, 188, 324, 330
National Assessment of Educational Progress (NAEP), 6, 16, 114
Needs assessment stage, of reading/writing program, 331
New words, use of, 68, 78
Nicaraguans, 284
Non-English speaking students, 273–92
Norm-referenced tests (NRT), 170–71, 186
Notes, students', 108–9
Nuclear family patterns, 286

O

Open-ended assessments, of student attitudes, 203–4
Open-ended study guides, 106–7
Opening statements, in essays, 117, 118, 121
Opinion leaders, in change process, 344–45, 346
Oral language, 14–15, 25
and cultural transmission, 277–78
Outlining, 249–50

P

Paired choice assessments, of student attitudes, 204

Paraphrasing, 103
Parents, involving, 199–200, 285, 289–90
Partial outlines, in DRAs, 249–50
Peer coaching, in the change process, 342
Peer evaluation, of writing, 193
Peer pressure, 200–1
Phonics, 26, 78–79, 314
Physically handicapped students, 297–98, 303
Physical problems, in reading, 10–11
PL 94-142, 294, 295, 296, 298, 300, 304, 325
Planning
    in instructional units, 219–20
    as stage of change, 341
Positive reinforcement, 12
PQRST technique, 108
Prediction, in reading, 29
Prefixes, 74
Prequestions, 246, 247
Prewriting stage, of writing model, 40, 115, 118–22
Primary trait marking, 190
Principal, role in reading program, 325–26
Procedural knowledge, 100
Process approach
    to comprehension, 48–49, 54–55, 59
    to writing, 39–42, 115–32, 189, 191, 192–93
Product approach
    to comprehension, 48–49, 54–55, 59
    to writing, 39
Productivity, of change, 336, 338
Program planning stage, of reading/writing program, 331
Program series text analysis outline, sample of, 155–59
Pronunciation, 78–80
Psychomotor domain, of reading, 10–11, 28

Publication stage, of writing model, 41, 115–16, 131
Puerto Rican-Americans, 283, 284, 285–88
    attitude to school, 285
    migration of, 286

Q

Questions
    as comprehension aid, 49–53
    formulating in independent study, 109
    framing of, 116–17
    levels of, 49–53, 247, 252
    timing of, 52–53

R

Raygor Readability Estimate, 149, 152, 165
Readability, of textbooks, 142, 144–54
Readability formulas, 147–54, 256, 309
Readiness, as stage of change, 340
Reading
    cultural value of, 278
    definitions of, 28–31
    and exceptional children, 300–3
    grouping for, 230–31
    interaction with writing, 4, 17, 37–38
    as learning tool, 37
    motivation to, 4, 8–9, 12, 201, 205, 208–11, 260
    purpose of, 29–31, 57
    questionnaire on, 206–7
    second-language, 287, 288
    silent, 246, 252
    stages of, 28–29
    student attitudes to, 198–201

Reading aids, in textbooks, 145

Reading assessment, in early grades, 187–88

Reading assignments, completion of, 244–60

Reading centers, 265–67

Reading comprehension *see* Comprehension

Reading coordinators, 326

Reading levels
  assessment of, 35–37, 171–86
  of frustration level readers, 306–7
  grouping by, 233–36, 239
  of independent readers, 304
  and motivation, 209
  range of, 33–35, 142, 162–63

Reading proficiency statistics, 6

Reading program, school-wide, 321–32

Reading rates, 252

Reading resource teachers, 327

Reading skills, 6, 248–50

Reading supervisors, 326

Reading topics, adolescent, 201–2

Reading vocabularies, 65, 68

REAP technique, 108

Receptive language, 14–15, 37

Recreational reading, 30–31

Refocused semantic maps, 87

Registers, of language, 27–28, 274, 282, 288–89

Remedial reading programs, 322, 323

Remedial students, 253–54

Retention of learning, 13, 14

Revision stage, of writing model, 115, 122–23, 124–26

Rewards, of change, 338

Rewriting, of teaching materials, 256–59, 260, 270, 309–10, 312
  sample, 257–59

Roots, of words, 74

RPTIM model of change, 339–43, 346

Rural white culture, 282–83

S

Scale scoring, 190

Scanning, 252

Schema theory, 7–8, 13, 29, 53–54, 59

School boards, and textbook adoption, 140

School counselors, 328–29

School districts, educational goals of, 220–21

Schools, role of in immigrant life, 285

Science, language experience approach in, 254–55

Scope and sequence charts, of study skills, 101

Secondary schools, special education classes in, 295

Second-language reading, 287, 288

SEER technique, 147–48, 153

Selecting, in concept development, 90

Self-concept, 199, 307

Self-direction, 209, 261, 305

Self-evaluation, of writing, 193

Self-monitoring, as aid to comprehension, 55, 58, 59, 65–66

Self-questioning, in comprehension, 55

Self-selected topics, 30–31, 116, 117

Semantic differentials, in student attitude assessment, 204

Semantic maps, 87

Semantics, 26

Sentence length, 145, 147, 148, 310; *see also* Readability

Sentence structures, 145, 310

Sequential learning, 12–13

Severely and profoundly mentally retarded students (SPMR), 297, 301

Sex, influence on reading attitude, 200

Shopping list of ideas, in writing, 120

Silent reading, 246, 252

Singer Eyeball Estimate of Readability (SEER) formula, 147–48, 153

Skills
assessment of content-area, 171–82, 186
grouping by, 237

Skimming, 251, 252

Sloppy copy worksheets, 119

SMOG formula, 149–50

Socially and emotionally disturbed students, 297, 303

Social studies, language experience approach in, 254

Socioeconomic levels, and reading attitudes, 200

Sound patterns, 25–26, 78–80

South Americans, 283, 284

Spanish language students, 275, 283–88

Spatial dimension, of human behavior, 276

Speaking, as learning tool, 37

Speaking centers, 268

Speaking vocabularies, 68

Special education, 295; *see also* Exceptional students

Special education resource teachers, 328

Specific learning outcomes (SLO), of curriculum, 223
sample, 227

Speech and language impaired students, 297, 302

SPMR *see* Severely and profoundly mentally retarded

SQ3R technique, 108–9, 246

Staff development model (RPTIM), 339–43, 346

Standard English, 26–27, 279–81, 283, 288, 289

Standardized reading tests, 170–71, 307

Street language, 28

Structural analysis, 74–78

Structured overviews, 85–86

Structure of texts, in reading, 8

Student-directed activities, 244, 260–69, 270

Student evaluation forms, 264

Students
ability levels of, 33–35
attitudes of, 8, 198–208
interests of, 142–43, 201–2, 202–5, 209–10, 237–38

Study guides, 103–7, 107–8, 110, 235, 237, 305, 308, 313

Studying, as reading skill, 252

Study Skills in the Content Area, 99

Study skills, teaching of, 98–111

Suffixes, 74

Summated items, in assessment of student attitudes, 204

Summative evaluation stage, of reading/writing program, 331

Syllables
pronunciation of, 79, 80
and readability formulas, 148, 149

Symbols, as part of language, 25

Synonyms, 71, 90, 186

Syntax, 26

Synthesis, as level in cognitive hierarchy, 6, 7, 32, 305

System, of languages, 25

T

Tape recording, 313

Task analysis, 222

Taxonomy model, of comprehension, 31–33, 42, 49–53, 247, 252, 305, 315

Taxonomy of Educational Objectives, 104

Taxonomy of Reading Comprehension, 31, 32, 42, 104
Teacher-directed activities, for independent readers, 305
Teacher evaluation forms, 264
Teachers
    and change, 334–38
    as cheerleaders, 123
    and classroom climate, 200
    as coach, 100–1
    and exceptional students, 298–300
    and language differences, 288
    professional growth of, 333–47
    and resource persons, 329
    as role models, 122, 278
    traditional role of, 15
    workload of, 191, 192, 194
Teaching Strategies, 239
Tests
    definition of, 170
    formal, 170–71
    informal, 171
    in instructional units, 230
    teacher-made, 171–87
    see also Evaluation
Textbooks
    adoption of, 139–40, 154–159
    content, 19
    evaluating, 137–66
    and frustration level readers, 308–10, 312
    for gifted students, 304–5
    interest level of, 142–43
    problems of reading, 5–6, 19
    questions and answers, 105–6
    reading level of, 36
    and study skills, 101
    taping of, 313
    and unit plans, 220
Thinking
    critical, 104, 247, 251, 252
    processes of, 277
Title VII, 285
TMR *see* Trainable mentally retarded

Tolerance, for handicapped students, 299–300
Tracking, 231, 240
Trainable mentally retarded (TMR) students, 297, 301
Training, as stage of change, 341–42
Transfer, of learning, 4, 13, 17, 36, 78, 79

U

Underachieving readers, 104–5; *see also* Frustration level readers
Underlining, 103
Unit plans, 218–30; *see also* Instructional units

V

Values, teacher/student, 315
Vertical articulation, of curriculum, 221
Visual discrimination, 10–11
Visual materials, 256; *see also* Audio-visual materials; Media
Visual problems, 10–11
Vocabulary
    and concept development, 88–94
    development of, 63–95, 246
    manipulation of, 64–65, 70–82, 314
    pretesting of, 68–69
    and readability, 145–48
    retention of, 67, 314
    skills, 36
    see also Word attack skills; Words

W

Warncke Attitude and Interest in Reading Inventory (WAIRI), 205

Within-class grouping, 232, 244;
see also Grouping
Word attack skills, 64–65, 70–82,
250
Word-for-word reading, 70–71
Word processors, in writing
centers, 267
Words
families of, 76–77
length of, 145, 147, 148
meanings of, 26
parts of, 74–78
see also Vocabulary; Word
attack skills
*Workbook for Educational
Change,* 343
Writing
assessment of, 187–93
attitudes to, 199
and comprehension, 16, 57–58
as enrichment activity, 250–51
evaluation of, 188–93
and exceptional children, 300–3
extent of in content classes,
11–12

and foreign language students,
290
and frustration level readers, 314
functions of, 38–39
grouping by, 237
interaction with reading, 4, 17,
37–38
and language experience
approach, 253
as learning tool, 11–12, 37, 38
process approach to, 39–42,
115–32
product approach to, 39
teaching of, 11–12, 39–42,
115–32
vocabularies, 68
Writing Across the Curriculum,
38
Writing centers, 267
Writing programs, schoolwide,
330

Y

Your Reading, 142